Pearl Harbor
MYTH

OTHER BOOKS IN POTOMAC'S
MILITARY CONTROVERSIES SERIES

Gettysburg: The Meade-Sickles Controversy
by Richard A. Sauers

"Friends in Peace and War":
The Russian Navy's Landmark Visit to Civil War San Francisco
by C. Douglas Kroll

Forgotten Raiders of '42:
The Fate of the Marines Left Behind on Makin
by Tripp Wiles

ALSO BY GEORGE VICTOR

Hitler: The Pathology of Evil

THE

Pearl Harbor
MYTH
Rethinking
the
Unthinkable

GEORGE VICTOR

Potomac Books
Washington, DC

Library of Congress Cataloging-in-Publication Data
Victor, George.
  The Pearl Harbor myth : rethinking the unthinkable / George Victor.
  1st ed.
    p. cm. — (Potomac's military controversies)
  Includes bibliographical references and index.
  ISBN 1-59797-042-5 (alk. paper)
  1. Pearl Harbor (Hawaii), Attack on, 1941. 2. World War, 1939-
1945—Diplomatic history. 3. World War, 1939-1945—United States.
4. United States—Foreign relations—1933-1945. I. Title.
  D767.92.V53 2006
  940.54'26693—dc22
                                    2006024130

ISBN 10: 1-59797-042-5
ISBN 13: 978-1-59797-042-6

(alk. paper)

Printed in the United States of America on acid-free paper that meets
the American National Standards Institute Z39-48 Standard.

Potomac Books, Inc.
22841 Quicksilver Drive
Dulles, Virginia 20166

First Edition

10 9 8 7 6 5 4 3 2 1

CONTENTS

Preface   vii

1.	Birth of a Myth	1
2.	Establishing the Myth	17
3.	Warnings of the Pearl Harbor Attack	29
4.	Challenges to the Myth	53
5.	Secrecy and Cover-Up	61
6.	The Accused	81
7.	Background to War Between Japan and the United States	113
8.	Japan's Moves to Dominate East Asia	125
9.	Roosevelt's Tentative Moves against Germany	133
10.	Secret Alliance and Undeclared War	165
11.	Countdown in Washington: The July Turning Point	187
12.	Countdown in Tokyo	217
13.	Countdown in Washington: The November Turning Point	239
14.	Awaiting the Blow	263

Afterword: History and the Unthinkable   293
Notes   305
References   329
Index   345
About the Author   355

PREFACE

Twelve days before the attack on Pearl Harbor, President Franklin Roosevelt surprised his advisers by saying that war with Japan was about to begin. Secretary of War Henry Stimson noted in his diary:

> the question was what we should do. The question was how we should maneuver them into the position of firing the first shot without allowing too much danger to ourselves.[1]

Stimson's apparent meaning was unacceptable to generations of scholars. Most ignored his diary note. Others explained it away, saying he wrote it in haste, inadvertently making a poor choice of words. Lacking information about how he wrote it, they were expressing their belief: Stimson simply could not have meant what his words seemed to say. But according to Stimson, that was what he meant (chapter 13).

Japan had completed her preparation to attack Pearl Harbor, but her decision to carry it out awaited the outcome of a final offer to negotiate differences with the United States. After meeting with his advisers, Roosevelt decided to reject her final offer, in the expectation that Japan would then attack the United States.

Stimson's words suggest a picture of Roosevelt and his advisers as Machiavellians. By long tradition, our presidents are not seen as conspirators, manipulating our nation into war. The tradition is strong despite the fact that, like other nations, the United States entered most of her wars by manipulation.

Charles Beard had achieved recognition as a leading historian before writing *President Roosevelt and the Coming of the War*. His book was dismissed contemptuously as "history through a beard," and he was labeled a "conspiracy theorist" and a "revisionist." ("Revisionist" used to be a neutral-to-positive term for attempts to improve on prior accounts—an essential part of historical work. After World War II, especially as a reaction to Holocaust denial, it became a dismissive term.) A historian blasted Beard's "picture of President Roosevelt engaged in a colossal and profoundly immoral plot to deceive the American people into participating in the war . . ." Gordon Prange, long considered the leading authority on Pearl Harbor, rejected data and analyses about Roosevelt following such a plan because to accept them meant Roosevelt was "a traitor" (which is what some writers who presented the material called him). According to Prange, such a conspiracy was impossible because, "Somewhere along the line someone would have recalled his solemn oath to defend the United States . . . and have blown the whistle." Another reason was that "nothing in [Roosevelt's] history suggests that this man could plot to sink American ships and kill thousands of American soldiers and sailors."[2]

History has recorded many, many rulers' manipulations of their people into war without their subordinates blowing the whistle. Presidents James Polk, Abraham Lincoln, William McKinley, and Woodrow Wilson did it before Roosevelt; and others have done it after him. Another historian wrote:

> The main point . . . is that anybody who thinks that George Marshal, upright, honorable and incorruptible, could have been persuaded even by a President to mislead his subordinate commanders, by the devious suppression and distortion of vital information, in order to precipitate a war with Japan . . . is living in a dream world.[3]

In my view, General Marshall was indeed an outstanding chief of staff, upright, honorable, and incorruptible—as much so as his position permitted. Testifying to various tribunals investigating the Pearl Harbor disaster, other military officers vigorously denied that they had withheld vital information from field commanders. The denials were false. Marshall was an exception; he testified to a congressional committee that withholding vital information from commanders was routine practice. World War II documents show not only withholding of information from field commanders, but also distortion of it to mislead them.

That such manipulation of subordinates was commonplace is unacceptable to many. Some friends who helped with this book were troubled by my Machiavellian presentation of Roosevelt's leadership and my avoidance of judging him for it.

The book *The Pathology of Politics* by the philosopher of history, Carl Friedrich, helped me avoid moral judgments. His survey of government practices across the world was an effective reminder of something I should already have known: rulers ordinarily operate by conspiracy. We accept that foreign rulers do it, but deny it in our own. On matters considered patriotically sacred, denial is often so strong that a historical account — no matter how well supported by data — can be dismissed effectively by labeling it "a conspiracy theory."

Friedrich did not advocate Machiavellian action by rulers, but only Machiavellian writing of history — providing accounts of political events in terms of cause and effect, without moralizing. In his view, beginning with Thucydides, the best political histories were Machiavellian.

More important in deciding to avoid judgment was my strong impression that for six decades the history of Pearl Harbor has been distorted by defenders and attackers of Roosevelt. I found the best histories of how the United States entered World War II to be those most free of moral judgment (e.g., accounts by Raymond Dawson, Robert Divine, John Haight, James Leutze, Arnold Offner, and David Reynolds). Unfortunately the best-known books on what follows were written by defenders and attackers of Roosevelt.

In thinking about Roosevelt's place in history, Otto von Bismarck often came to mind. Bismarck achieved an extraordinary record of political successes. As chancellor of Prussia, he fostered creation of the German nation, and led it in limited wars that improved its position. He came from Prussia's upper class and remained devoted to their interests. Nonetheless he fathered Prussia's and then Germany's welfare systems — both rather advanced. An admiring biographer described him as "ruthless," and commented:

> He has often been accused of despising humanity; he did so no more and no less than every great statesman or general prepared to use human forces and sacrifice human lives for the attainment of great ends.[4]

Bismarck's political challenges were limited compared to one that Roosevelt confronted — the menace of an Attila bent on conquering and destroying much of the world.

Presidents who succeeded Roosevelt also ordered sacrifices, but toward smaller and sometimes meaner ends. Here Roosevelt's manipulations and the sacrifices he ordered are compared to those of Polk, Lincoln, McKinley, and Wilson, all of whom were implementing ends considered noble in the light of traditional values.

I am not the first admirer of Roosevelt to present him in Machiavellian terms. James MacGregor Burns, who served in his administration, called the first volume of his biography *Roosevelt: the Lion and the Fox*. He explained:

> A prince, wrote Machiavelli, must imitate the fox and the lion
> . . . a prudent ruler ought not to keep faith when by so doing it
> would be against his interest, and when the reasons which
> made him bind himself no longer exist. If men were all good,
> this precept would not be a good one.[5]

Burns added, "It was not strange that [Roosevelt] should follow Machiavelli's advice . . . for this had long been the first lesson for politicians."

A deception that Roosevelt worked hard at while president was to keep people ignorant of how severely polio had ravaged him. He considered that secret necessary to maintain his position as national leader, and with the help of family and aides he simulated being able to get to his feet and to walk. Many moralists forgave him that deception, but not those that follow.

A time when people are all good is only a dream, although we hope for civilization to advance enough for rulers and their people not to be well served by deception and manipulation. For now a realistic expectation is that rulers will continue to operate that way, and that "government conspiracy" will continue substantially to mean customary government operations. In my view, denying that and putting a patriotic gloss on actions by our own leaders is an obstacle to the advance of civilization.

Governments ordinarily cover up their conspiracies. When threatened with exposure of secret operations, they intensify their cover-ups. Across the world, administrations under attack have commonly resorted to "disappearances" — to imprisonment, torture, and killing. In the Pearl Harbor cover-up, at least that did not happen.

This book features data and conclusions from official military histories of the United States and other nations. Compared to histories by civilians, military ones are freer of moral judgment. And more importantly, U.S. Army and Navy historians had access to secret records. I have also relied on memoirs by people who worked closely with Roosevelt — speechwriters Samuel Rosenman and Robert Sherwood, and, his closest confidant on foreign policy in 1940 and 1941, Harry Hopkins.

Soviet secret agent Ishkak Akhmerov, who "controlled" Soviet espionage agents in the United States, said Hopkins was an agent in

1941—the year during which Hopkins's activities and statements figure in this book. According to Akhmerov, Hopkins was an "unconscious" (unwitting) agent. Information bearing on such allegations about Hopkins is too vague for evaluation. Whatever the truth may be, I found no evidence that Hopkins did anything for the Soviet Union in 1941, except what Roosevelt told him to do. (The only concrete allegation of an unauthorized act by Hopkins that may have benefited the Soviet Union is that he was the source of an item of information that someone else passed to her in 1944.) There are speculations that Hopkins influenced U.S. policy toward the Soviet Union in 1941, but no evidence of it. The published conclusion that Soviet Premier Joseph "Stalin instilled in Hopkins complete faith" when they met in 1941, and consequently Hopkins influenced Roosevelt's decision to support the Soviet Union, rests on no data.[6] On the contrary, after meeting Stalin, Hopkins reported to Roosevelt a statement Stalin gave him intended to influence Roosevelt, but advised Roosevelt not to believe it (chapter 11). Robert Sherwood and others who knew Hopkins and Roosevelt well emphasized that Hopkins was wholly devoted to implementing Roosevelt's policies and wishes.

Military ranks changed during the period covered. I have simplified ranks to avoid confusion from the changes and to minimize errors. Lieutenant Commanders and Commanders are both called "Commander." Lieutenant Colonels and Colonels are both called "Colonel." And Admirals and Generals of all ranks are called "Admiral" or "General."

In China, Japan, and Korea, family names come first. American writers have followed this usage for the Chinese, but put family names last for Japanese and Koreans. Here family names are put first for all of them. The name of Japan's prime minister during most of the events described here will be spelled "Konoe Fuminaro." In most books his family name is spelled "Konoye," fostering mispronunciation of what should sound like "Koh-noh-eh."

In dispatches sent by radio, punctuation marks were indicated by words: a period by "period," "stop" (or "X"), and a comma by "comma." For clarity in quoting the dispatches, punctuation marks are substituted.

Some original sources are available in only one place (e.g., Stimson's diary and his other papers, at Yale University). For these, I cite secondary sources when possible.

I received much valuable help, and am especially grateful to the late Edward Beach, Daryl Borquist, Morton Davis, Tore Kapstad (my son-in-law), the late Edward Kimmel and Thomas Kimmel (Husband Kimmel's son and grandson), Joseph Nevins, William O'Neill, Jerry

Piven, David Richardson (no relation to James Richardson), Irwin Schulman, the late Joseph Schulman, Donald Showers, John Taylor, Nik ten Velde (with translations of Dutch), Elizabeth and Marian Victor (my daughter and wife), and the staff of the West Orange library. Among those who helped, Davis O'Neill, Joseph Schulman, and Admiral Showers disagreed strongly with some of my interpretations. Admiral Richardson was extraordinarily patient in helping with naval matters, which were new to me.

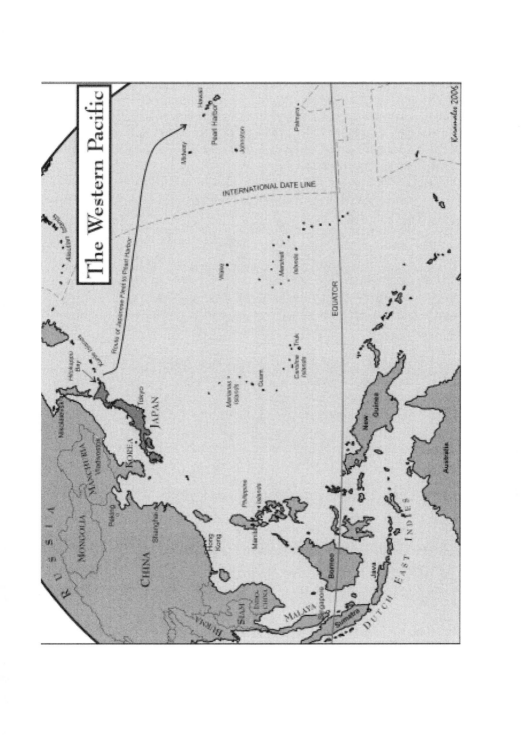

The Western Pacific

CHAPTER 1
BIRTH OF A MYTH

Early on a Sunday morning in Hawaii, carrier-based Japanese planes struck, catching U.S. Army and Navy forces unprepared. Army antiaircraft guns were not manned. Planes were destroyed before they could take off. Trapped in Pearl Harbor, much of the Pacific Fleet, including most of its battleships, was destroyed. The port was left a wreck, clogged with sunken warships. "Japan's devastating air strike . . . aroused the people of the United States as no other event in their history ever had."[1] What many called the worst military disaster in the nation's history left U.S. citizens stunned and angry. In addition, on that same December 7, 1941, Japan struck other U.S. and British territories, winning victories everywhere. Americans could not understand how the Japanese, whom they considered far weaker, could inflict such defeats on the powerful United States—a question that still provokes angry controversy.

As history has shown, "National disasters and their attendant shock need scapegoats,"[2] and this was no exception. The nation suffered a crisis of trust in its leaders, and many people feared a Japanese invasion of the West Coast. Desperate to regain confidence, Americans grasped at wild ideas and sought people to blame. Political enemies of President Franklin Roosevelt accused him of responsibility for the disaster, and even his friends were dismayed.

Although he was among the most beloved of presidents, Roosevelt was also hated. His welfare programs had upset conservatives, some of whom saw the programs—and him—as Communist. Among his passionate enemies was a powerful newspaper, the *Chicago Tribune*, to whom his welfare measures had stamped him a traitor. And those opposed to involvement in a European war[3] suggested that his efforts to intervene in the European conflict came from the failure of his domestic programs—that intervention was a desperate

1

effort to pull the United States out of the Great Depression.

The noninterventionist movement seemingly became powerful during the summer of 1940, with the founding of the Committee to Defend America First (better known by the selfish-sounding name of the America First Committee). It won much publicity and appeared more influential than it was. Its members held a variety of beliefs, but agreed that U.S. interests were insufficiently threatened by Germany to justify war. At one extreme were pacifists; at the other were Nazis, Nazi sympathizers, and non-Nazi admirers of Germany. Among the admirers was the aviation hero Charles Lindbergh, who quickly became the committee's chief spokesman. In this capacity he declared that the only people who wanted the United States to enter Europe's war were the Roosevelt administration, the British, and the Jews. Lindbergh's anti-Jewish statements made him an embarrassment to the committee, which restricted his speeches on its behalf. The committee dropped another officer, Henry Ford, for making even stronger anti-Semitic statements.

During 1941 rumors arose about a secret alliance that Roosevelt was making with Great Britain, and these spurred a move to impeach him. (The move came to nothing, but probably sensitized him to risks in exposure of secret operations.) In August, when his secret meeting with British Prime Minister Winston Churchill was made public, the *Chicago Tribune* wrote, "He comes of a stock that has never fought for this country and now he betrays it."[4]

Fortunately for Roosevelt, his enemies did not know on December 7 that the government had received warnings of Japan's coming attack.

> **What form would [public] anger have taken if the American people had known the most closely guarded secret and realized that [intelligence officers] had been reading the most confidential Japanese ciphers even before the attack, and that the Japanese war plans were no secret to American intelligence?**[5]

A few dozen people in the government knew about the code breaking and other intelligence, and the warnings they had produced. During investigations of the Pearl Harbor disaster in 1944, the question, did Roosevelt know? became hotly controversial—and remains so.

As soon as news of the disaster came in, people demanded an explanation. Within days, newspapers across the nation charged officials in Washington with responsibility for it, and on December 19, 1941 the House Naval Affairs Committee called for an investigation. While suppressing knowledge of the warnings of Japan's attack, the administration took the position that there had been no such warnings, and this became its main defense against spreading accusations. The administration hastily threw together an explanation of the disaster — an explanation that could be sustained only by keeping a lid on events leading to the attack. For the duration of World War II the administration managed to keep crucial information hidden. During 1942 the administration's account solidified into an official history, seized on by people desperate for a way to carry on and eager for vengeance against Japan.

War plans drawn up at Roosevelt's direction had given priority to defeating Germany. As a result, U.S. outposts in the Pacific had been only partly defended. The plans specifically anticipated a series of defeats if war with Japan broke out. To military and civilian leaders familiar with the plans, the losses on December 7 were no surprise, but the severity of the destruction at Pearl Harbor was.

Ignorant of those plans, the public was dumbfounded by the severity of U.S. losses. To many, their nation was a leading military power; to some, the strongest in the world. And a popular stereotype pictured the Japanese as a puny, backward race, incapable of competing militarily with any Western power. Americans thought the Japanese lacked inventiveness and initiative because their education fostered rote learning and passivity. Their society seemed feudal, lacking science and technology, struggling to achieve industrialization with manufacturing assets limited to cheap labor and imitation of western methods and machines. An extreme piece of propaganda pictured Japanese soldiers as naked, childish pygmies, going into battle wearing diapers! More common were cartoons picturing Japanese pilots as so short that they could hardly see out of their fighter planes' cockpits and so nearsighted that, despite their thick eyeglasses, they could hardly see beyond their own planes or fly straight. Japanese troops were said to be handicapped by an inability to see in the dark. And their planes were purported to be cheap versions of obsolete western models, made from bamboo, metal scrap, and plastics, because the Japanese were incapable of producing modern military equipment.[6]

The opposite was closer to the truth. Japanese sonar equipment and torpedoes were better than U.S. ones. Her battleships were much faster and carried heavier guns. Her aircraft carriers were also faster, and she had more of them. And her new navy fighter plane — the Mitsubishi *Zero* — had superior range, speed, maneuverability, and firepower (its shortcoming was a lack of armor). According to a U.S. naval historian, the then available U.S. fighter plane *Wildcat* was no match for a *Zero*. And Japan's new army fighter — the Nakajima *Oscar* — also was superior.[7]

Not all U.S. military leaders shared the stereotype, but it influenced some of them. While others warned civilian officials that Japan's forces were powerful, advisers to Roosevelt, including Army Chief of Staff George Marshall, expected that even a surprise attack on Pearl Harbor could be fought off with minimal loss. Cabinet members assured the nation that Japan posed no serious military threat; Navy Secretary Frank Knox declared that Pearl Harbor was "beyond the effective striking power of her Fleet." Some Navy officers said they could destroy the Japanese navy any morning before breakfast.[8] These misperceptions led the administration gravely to underestimate Pearl Harbor's vulnerability.

Great Britain, the U.S. partner in planning for war in the Pacific, had similarly relied on racist judgments of Japanese military power. Air Marshal Robert Brooke-Popham said in autumn 1941:

> I had a good close-up [view] of various sub-human specimens in dirty grey uniforms, which I was informed were Japanese soldiers. If these represent the average of the Japanese army . . . I cannot believe they would form an intelligent fighting force.[9]

Popham's officers in Malaya shared his impression. On December 7, expecting a Japanese invasion shortly, one said, "Don't you think [our troops] are worthy of some better enemy than the Japanese?"[10] Another said, "I do hope . . . we are not getting too strong in Malaya, because if so the Japanese may never attempt a landing."[11]

As a result of this misconception, "A bitter and humiliating price was paid . . . [T]he full extent was not appreciated until February–March 1942, with the surrender of Malaya."[12] In that British territory, "more than 100,000 men surrendered to the Japanese army of 30,000. The speed and flexibility of the attackers led General [Arthur] Percival to believe he was actually outnumbered."[13] British General Henry Pownall wrote, "I fear that we were frankly outgeneralled, outwitted and outfought. From the beginning to the end of the campaign we have been overmatched by better soldiers. A very painful admission, but it is an inescapable fact."[14] Pownall was more candid than American leaders, who stressed Japanese "sneakiness" and "treachery" to explain the Pearl Harbor disaster.

After catastrophes, the beliefs people have relied on are shaken and events make no sense. The world seems strange — shifting crazily and dangerously — and people cast about for ways to regain a sense of order by which to carry on. From loss of trust in their leaders, people may move to suspecting them of having betrayed the nation. Often they focus their suspicions on a minority group that has been a scapegoat in the past. And they question their own acts: Why is this happening to us? What have we done to deserve it? Vague suspicions sometimes turn to ideas of a secret plot carried out by a mysterious group operating in their midst. The more unexpected and incomprehensible the catastrophe, the more severe the stress. Most severe is a series of unexpected disasters, and this is how the United States experienced the defeats that began on December 7, 1941.

A nation often pulls itself out of such a crisis by creating a myth — a melodramatic account, mixing fact and fantasy — which becomes a sacred part of its history. Twenty-seven years prior to the Pearl Harbor attack, Germany declared war with high enthusiasm. Her confidence became overweening as she won sweeping victories on the Western Front and even greater ones on the Eastern Front, where Russia surrendered, ceding enormous territory to Germany. Public confidence remained high despite the stalemate that developed in France and despite the U.S. entry into the war.

Patriotic German propaganda was supported by the fact that in 1918 the battle lines were still in France — Germany had not been invaded. This helped Germans to believe in their own invincibility and to disregard crucial facts. Their nation had lost more soldiers than other participants in the war and was industrially exhausted. And her allies — Bulgaria, Turkey, and Austria-Hungary — had surrendered. Yet, right up to the end, as Germany stood alone against a growing alliance, many Germans believed not only that they were winning, but also that victory was at hand.

As a result of this wishful thinking, Germans experienced their surrender as an incomprehensible catastrophe. Other traumas followed — socialist and rightist coups, civil war, the crushing terms imposed on Germany by the victors, and a devastating economic collapse. The series of disasters gave birth to the myth of "the stab in the back": Germany had not been defeated in battle. Instead, her noble soldiers, on the verge of victory, had been betrayed by their government leaders. A more extreme idea, held by a small minority, was that the leaders responsible for the surrender were not true Germans. They were Jews, aided by German Christians serving as the Jews' dupes — agents of an international Jewish conspiracy bent on destroying Germany. While this Jewish conspiracy myth was not widely believed, most Germans suspected that it contained an element of truth.

The German myth of the stab in the back shared features with the myth that began to unfold in the United States after December 7, 1941. In California, people of Japanese descent became scapegoats during the early 1900s, as dread of a "Yellow Peril" and animosity toward "Japs" and "Chinks" took hold, and then spread across the nation. After Pearl Harbor, European Americans suspected that people of Japanese descent had engaged in espionage and sabotage, aiding the fleet attacking Hawaii. When Roosevelt proceeded to put Japanese Americans into concentration camps on suspicion that they might aid Japan in the war, Americans of European descent felt safer.

Suspicious of their leaders, searching for scapegoats, they focused on a crucial question: why had the Japanese caught U.S. forces in Hawaii off guard? A small group of people thought the commandants there—Gen. Walter Short and Adm. Husband Kimmel—had betrayed the nation. And most dangerous—when unity was needed for the war—was a small group's suspicion that Roosevelt had engineered the attack on Pearl Harbor to help the United States enter the war and save Great Britain from defeat by Germany.

U.S. Nazis and a minority of conservatives had long suspected Roosevelt of being a Jew, claiming his "real name" was Rosenfeld. A book widely circulated among conservatives in 1936 declared that he had "achieved more of the revolutionary Socialist program in a few months than all of the American Reds have in years."[15] It accused him of being part of a Jewish-Communist conspiracy to undermine the Constitution, seize absolute power, and destroy the nation.

These beliefs and suspicions possessed more than a kernel of truth. When France fell in 1940, leaving Britain standing alone against Germany, Roosevelt's greatest worry had been that Britain would fall too, and that victory in Europe would enable Adolf Hitler to mobilize that continent's vast resources for conquest of the Americas. Roosevelt had been exceptional in his realistic perception of Hitler's menace. Well before Hitler's first conquest, Roosevelt had begun to prepare the United States for war with Germany, arousing the suspicion and enmity of noninterventionists.

Suspicion of Roosevelt also had roots in World War I. In 1917 the United States had been led by President Woodrow Wilson into a crusade to end oppression—"the war to end war." The cynical carving up of enemy territory by the European victors, combined with postwar revelations of profiteering by U.S. arms makers, had caused bitter disillusionment and a resolve not to be drawn into another European war. In deference to the wave of noninterventionist sentiment, Roosevelt had presented himself as a peacemaker, disguising his hesitant measures to prepare for war. But the measures, which had been only partly hidden, had fed suspicion of his intent.

Since the summer of 1940 Great Britain had been hanging by a thread, saved temporarily by Hitler's decision to invade the Soviet Union instead of England. But Roosevelt's military advisers predicted an early Soviet collapse to be followed by a successful German invasion of England. Therefore, as the possibility of war with Japan loomed in 1941, Roosevelt's main concern — as noninterventionists suspected — was how to get his unwilling nation into the war against Germany. He and his cabinet discussed the possibility that, if Japan attacked U.S. territory, Congress would declare war not only on Japan but also on her ally, Germany.

By the end of November 1941, relations with Japan had reached a crucial point. The United States then rejected Japan's final proposal for negotiation, and instead made a counterproposal which some historians later called an ultimatum. It precipitated the Japanese attack, and Roosevelt's political enemies inferred that it had been intended to.

For thirty years Japan and the United States had considered war with each other to be a possibility and had planned for it. Japanese plans had centered on destroying the U.S. Fleet at the outset, specifically when the fleet visited Hawaii. U.S. plans had centered on keeping the fleet safe, and Hawaii had been fortified for that purpose. The planning and the administration's expectation since November that Japan was about to attack were hardly known by the public, but some in the government did know. That knowledge, and documents supporting it, posed a threat to the administration.

The administration's first public response to the Pearl Harbor attack was a statement to the press by Secretary of State Cordell Hull on December 7, which began, "Japan has made a treacherous and utterly unprovoked attack on the United States."[16] (He did not say the attack came as a surprise.) That afternoon Roosevelt met with his cabinet and planned his speech to Congress — his request for a declaration of war. Then he called in congressional leaders, both Democrats and Republicans. They listened respectfully to his account of the disaster until Senator Tom Connally interrupted. A Democrat and strong supporter of the president, Connally "sprang to his feet, banged the desk with his fist," and shouted at Roosevelt:

> **How did it happen that our warships were caught like tame ducks in Pearl Harbor? How did they catch us with our pants down? Where were our patrols?**[17]

Roosevelt answered weakly, "I don't know, Tom. I just don't know," and fell silent, obviously upset.

By Connally's own account, he was unable to control his anger. After directing some of it at Roosevelt, he vented the rest on Knox.[18] Others then joined in belaboring Frank Knox.

After the meeting the Democrats closed ranks behind Roosevelt.

However, he may not have realized this, as he turned again to the speech he would give the next day. During the night he was evidently much troubled, and consulted with Undersecretary Sumner Welles, his closest adviser in the State Department, as he worked further on his speech. According to an insider, Roosevelt stayed up until morning, which was unusual for him.[19] What troubled him probably was the danger to administration credibility posed by Connally's angry question. In any case, he decided to defend the administration by taking a risky position — a position contradicted by government records and known by members of the State Department and by military intelligence officers to be false.

The formal requirements of the speech were simply to report that hostilities had occurred and ask Congress for a declaration of war against Japan. In addition Roosevelt needed to justify and to rally the nation for a war which some noninterventionists were still calling unnecessary and that promised to be a long, hard one. And this required heading off criticism over the defeats and providing an explanation for them that would be accepted by the public and heal the nation. In view of Connally's outburst, Roosevelt may have feared his administration would be unable to prevent grave division in the nation. Providing a factual explanation of the defeats ran counter to Roosevelt's and the nation's political needs. To say the defeats resulted from a war strategy that gave priority to action in the Atlantic and the defeat of Germany while leaving Pacific outposts inadequately defended was politically self-destructive. (Winston Churchill had also kept secret the war strategy adopted in August 1940 by which British Pacific territories were defended only weakly. As a result, Japan's easy overrunning of Singapore — "the Gibraltar of the Far East" and "a symbol . . . of imperial might and invincibility . . . an impregnable fortress against which no enemy could prevail" — shocked Britain much as the Pearl Harbor disaster shocked the United States.[20]) It was similarly counterproductive for Roosevelt to say that he and his advisers had overestimated U.S. military strength and underestimated that of the Japanese. This information would come out later, but to say so on December 8 would provide Roosevelt's enemies with ammunition and confound the nation, splitting it further when unity was badly needed. It was suicidal. In such circumstances, for a ruler to give a factual account is rare indeed.

Wars ordinarily are preceded by strategic decisions based on secret intelligence about enemy intentions and capabilities, and U.S. decisions preceding Japan's attack were no exception. War announcements customarily omit secret strategies and intelligence, and rulers on both sides claim to have been acting openly in good faith. Trickiness (the root meaning of "treachery") is imputed to the enemy, while the conduct of one's own nation is characterized as innocent and just, lacking subtlety and deception, even to the extent of naïveté. Both sides commonly hide their own intentions, claiming to have been forced into war by an evil enemy.

Roosevelt's speech to Congress was a typical call to war in that, in explaining the defeats, countering accusations against the administration, and rallying the nation, it gave a misleading account of events which led the United States to enter World War II. Roosevelt was a charismatic orator. People who have not heard him speak may imagine the vibrancy of his voice and his ring of righteousness:

> Yesterday, December 7, 1941—a date which will live in infamy—the United States of America was suddenly and deliberately attacked by naval and air forces of the Empire of Japan. The United States was at peace with that Nation and, at the solicitation of Japan, was still in conversation with its Government and its Emperor looking toward the maintenance of peace in the Pacific . . . It will be recorded that the distance of Hawaii from Japan makes it obvious that the attack was deliberately planned many days or even weeks ago. During the intervening time the Japanese Government has deliberately sought to deceive the United States by false statements and expressions of hope for continued peace . . . . [A]lways will our whole Nation remember the character of the onslaught against us.[21]

By saying "the Japanese Government . . . sought to deceive the United States," Roosevelt suggested — but did not say — that the administration had been caught by surprise.

His speech was effective; with only one nay, Congress declared war on Japan. Roosevelt had considered also asking for a war declaration against Germany, but had put it off. He thought that the public and Congress were more willing to fight Japan than Germany. While holding back, Roosevelt probably failed to realize that Japan's attacks had killed the noninterventionist movement. But on December 11, Hitler solved Roosevelt's problem by declaring war on the United States.

Roosevelt's prophecy was borne out; December 7, 1941, has lived in infamy ever since. Nowhere in this speech or the next one did Roosevelt use the phrase "sneak attack" or suggest that deceptiveness was a Japanese trait. Nonetheless the idea of the sneak attack became the basis on which Americans came to terms with the defeats. It provided a simple explanation and fitted the prevailing stereotype of the Japanese. Much was made of the fact that Japan had attacked before declaring war, as if that were deviant and evil. But, "Contrary to popular myth, it has been normal practice for centuries for fighting to start before an actual declaration of war."[22] And months before, Roosevelt had secretly ordered naval combat in the Atlantic without a war declaration.

On December 9 Roosevelt repeated key parts of his congressional speech in a radio address to the nation:

> The sudden criminal attacks . . . provide the climax of international immorality . . . . The Japanese have treacherously violated the long-standing peace between us . . . . I can say with utmost confidence that no Americans today or a thousand years hence, need feel anything but pride in our patience and our efforts through all the years toward achieving a peace in the Pacific which would be fair and honorable to every nation, large or small. And no honest person, today or a thousand years hence, will be able to suppress a sense of indignation and horror at the treachery committed by the military dictators of Japan, under the very shadow of the flag of peace borne by their special envoys in our midst. We may acknowledge that our enemies have performed a brilliant feat of deception, perfectly timed and executed with great skill.[23]

In saying the Japanese had "performed a brilliant feat of deception," he virtually stated that the administration had been caught by surprise. In another speech to Congress on December 15, he went further: "We did not know then, as we know now, that they had ordered and were even then carrying out their plan for a treacherous attack upon us."[24]

Perhaps until then Roosevelt had been wrestling with the question of what position to take in defending his administration. After his second speech to Congress, he and his advisers insisted they had received no warnings of Japan's coming attack. In investigations that followed, ranking military officers testified that not a single warning of the attack on Pearl Harbor had been received. By the time a congressional committee published twenty warnings in 1946, a great war had been fought successfully with the slogan "Remember Pearl Harbor!" By then the administration's account was established history, and it remained established history. It was even declared by a federal court of appeals to be "the law of the land."[25]

That Japan had taken pains to surprise the United States at Pearl Harbor was true. As will be seen, however, her efforts at secrecy had failed, and Washington had received about 230 indications that Japan would attack. This dramatic number does not tell who knew what or when. Most of the warnings were in code, and only a fraction were decoded before the attack. The questions then became: which of the warnings were decoded in time and how clear were they and uncoded warnings?

In addition, despite Roosevelt's claim that Japan had deceived the United States with false talk of peace, her foreign officers had repeatedly told U.S. officials that failure of diplomatic talks between the two nations would lead to war. Early in September 1941 the Japanese government had made a fateful decision to make war on the United States unless a compromise could be negotiated. Three weeks later Ambassador Nomura Kichisaburo had given Hull a note including:

> Eager as we are for peace, we will not bow under the pressure of another country, nor do we want peace at any price. It is a characteristic trait of our people to repel, rather than submit to, external pressure.[26]

On November 18, Nomura's associate, Kurusu Saburo, had told Hull that economic sanctions imposed by the United States had aroused a sense that Japan must go to war with America while she still could. On November 26, Foreign Minister Togo Shigenoro had hinted the same to U.S. Ambassador Joseph Grew. And on December 1 and 2, Kurusu had warned Hull that Japan would go to war with the United States.[27]

That Nomura's and Kurusu's statements were not empty threats was known in Washington from intercepted cables between Togo and Nomura.[28] Having received these warnings and independent intelligence of Japan's preparations to attack, the United States rejected Japan's final proposal for negotiation on November 26, responding with a note expected to bring on a quick attack. Hull later said,

> I and other high officers of our Government knew that the Japanese military were poised for attack. We knew that the Japanese . . . had set a time limit for acceptance by our Government of their . . . proposal of November 20.[29]

And he testified,

> Before and after presenting that proposal Ambassador Nomura and Mr. Kurusu talked emphatically about the urgency of the situation and intimated vigorously that this was Japan's last word and if an agreement along these lines was not quickly concluded ensuing developments might be most unfortunate.[30]

To put Roosevelt's insistence on Japanese deceit in another perspective, it is worth noting that two years earlier Germany had invaded Poland without warning or a declaration of war. The attack came while Germany was pretending to negotiate her differences with Poland. The next year Germany invaded Denmark, Norway, Holland, Belgium, Luxembourg, and France — all without warning. And early on a Sunday morning in June 1941, she invaded the Soviet Union, with whom she had a nonaggression pact still in force. But the stereotype of Germans did not include treachery, and Americans did not consider those attacks as sneaky as they considered Japan's attacks on the United States.

Despite the realities of warfare and despite U.S. leaders' anticipation of Japan's attack, the idea of the sneak attack served two important functions. It helped Americans overcome their fear and despair by reaffirming their belief that the United States was more powerful than Japan and had been defeated because she was taken by surprise. The "sneak attack" became the administration's bulwark against accusations of treason; the keystone was the claim that no intelligence had revealed Japan's intention to attack Pearl Harbor.

Roosevelt noted in his December 8 speech to Congress that Pearl Harbor was only one of five U.S. territories attacked by Japan. The commanders in Hawaii had not expected to be attacked, while commanders in the other territories were expecting the attacks that fell on them. Nonetheless, Japanese forces overwhelmed defenders everywhere. Although the United States had a much larger population and a far greater military-industrial potential, Japan deployed far greater military power in the Pacific at the time. Unpreparedness increased U.S. losses at Pearl Harbor, but Japan's military power and efficiency were the main reasons for her successes.

For Roosevelt to say so, however, offered no relief to his bewildered nation or his besieged administration. With people still clinging to stereotypes of Japanese inferiority, such a truth was likely to increase their fear. Rather, like Germans after the defeat of 1918, many people preferred to hear that the United States had suffered defeats despite her superiority — that she had been betrayed. Rumors to this effect were already beginning to circulate and, after his speech, Roosevelt countered accusations by building on these rumors.

According to one rumor, the army and navy in Hawaii had been lax, with much partying and dereliction of duty and weekends marked by drunkenness and hangovers, which rendered military personnel unfit for duty on December 7. According to another, General Short and Admiral Kimmel had been on poor terms and had failed to cooperate with each other in defending Pearl Harbor.

Investigations from 1941 to 1946 established that laxity and drinking had been no more of a problem in Hawaii than elsewhere and that "on the morning of Sunday, December 7, 1941, Army posts and Naval vessels and stations were adequately manned . . . by men fit for duty."[31] The first investigation of the Pearl Harbor disaster, done by the Roberts Commission, concluded erroneously that Short and Kimmel had failed to cooperate. Perhaps relying on the Roberts Commission's report, in 1944 Vice President Harry Truman wrote that Short and Kimmel had not even been "on speaking terms" and that their lack of cooperation had been a "root cause" of the defeat.[32] And in 1958 Representative Clarence Cannon declared in the House:

> The catastrophic defeat . . . need not have happened . . . . [A]t the time of the attack the Naval Commander, Admiral Kimmel and the Army Commander General Short were not even on speaking terms. And . . . although both had been repeatedly alerted "over a period of weeks prior to the attack" they did not confer on the matter at any time. At one of the most critical periods in the defense of the nation, there was not the slightest cooperation between the Army and the Navy . . . It was not the Japanese superiority winning the victory. It was our own lack of cooperation between Army and Navy throwing victory away.[33]

A striking feature of Cannon's statement is its similarity to the German stab-in-the-back myth. His words reflected rumors and ignored findings that were long available by then, including the conclusion of the Naval Court of Inquiry on Pearl Harbor:

> the relations between . . . Kimmel and . . . Short . . . were friendly, cordial and cooperative . . . . there was no lack of interest, no lack of appreciation of responsibility, and no failure to cooperate.[34]

Investigations that followed that of the Roberts Commission established that Kimmel and Short had been friends and had cooperated rather well (and far better than the commanders in the Philippines). Nonetheless belief in the rumors persists into this century.

After December 7, opponents of Roosevelt raised in public the question Connally had asked in private. Government leaders said they had ordered Short and Kimmel to go on the alert against an attack. These orders were introduced as evidence at the tribunals investigating the disaster, but they specified Japan's expected targets as the

Philippines and Samoa, Guam, Wake, Midway, and territories not belonging to the United States. Pearl Harbor was omitted as a possible target. To explain why military intelligence had apparently failed to obtain advance warning of the Pearl Harbor attack, the chiefs of army and navy intelligence testified that they had lacked adequate intelligence operations because Congress had hardly funded them. In brief, the administration defended itself for not having sent adequate warnings to Short and Kimmel to prepare for an air attack by claiming it had had no way of knowing the attack on Pearl Harbor was coming. Nonetheless, it took the position that warnings it sent them were sufficient for Kimmel and Short to have gone on full alert for the attack — a position examined in chapter 6.

Book after book accepted the claim that lack of funds and staff had prevented military intelligence from discovering plans for the Pearl Harbor attack; the claim became an enduring part of the myth. Military intelligence, however, had been well staffed and had produced excellent results — phenomenal penetrations of Japan's codes and an accurate, detailed picture of her war plans, which specifically identified Pearl Harbor as her target.

The administration's barricade was breached in 1944, when the Army Pearl Harbor Board and the above-mentioned Naval Court of Inquiry conducted investigations and reported warnings of the attack. But their reports were kept secret until a public congressional investigation held in 1945–1946 revealed some of the warnings. Military intelligence documents obtained by these tribunals — and published by Congress — confirmed that Pearl Harbor had been Japan's most likely target. Documents and testimony also showed that the intelligence had been withheld from Short and Kimmel. On that basis, the army and navy tribunals rejected the administration's position and charged leaders in Washington with negligence. The congressional investigation resulted in mixed findings about who was responsible for the lack of preparedness in Hawaii. But, despite the warnings of the Pearl Harbor attack it uncovered, its majority report largely upheld the administration's account.

Revelation of warnings received in Washington had little impact on the public, and by 1946 the myth of Pearl Harbor was well established, including that leaders in Washington had been deceived and had not expected the attack, and that Short and Kimmel had disobeyed orders to defend Pearl Harbor. Since 1946, even historians have been influenced by the myth and uncertain about the significance of warnings that Pearl Harbor would be attacked. What the warnings were, when they were received, and who knew about them are vital to understanding how the United States went to war, and will be examined in detail in later chapters. Here the point is that the claim of having been deceived — the key part of the myth — was at first simply patriotic rhetoric, typical of war announcements. Then, as the administration came increasingly under attack, it stuck to the story, even though government records contradicted it.

The claim that Japan attacked the United States without provocation was also typical rhetoric. It worked because the public did not know that the administration had expected Japan to respond with war to anti-Japanese measures it had taken in July 1941.

Criticism and justification of Roosevelt's acts are outside the purpose of this book. As president, he had a duty to set foreign policy in accordance with the nation's interests as he saw them. That included a duty to take measures risking war. He also had a duty to unify the nation for war after Japan attacked.

Roosevelt said that before December 7 the United States had negotiated in good faith while Japan, bent on attacking, had lulled the United States with false talk of peace and pretended to negotiate. The opposite is closer to the truth. Expecting to lose a war with the United States — and lose it disastrously — Japan's leaders had tried with growing desperation to negotiate. On this point, most historians have long agreed. Meanwhile, evidence has come out that Roosevelt and Hull persistently refused to negotiate — that, knowing Japan's September decision, they used the diplomatic talks to stall while they built up military forces in the Pacific. A few weeks after Roosevelt's speech to Congress, Hull said privately that he had "purposely prolonged the conversations with the Japanese in order to enable the Army and Navy to get men and supplies to the Far East."[35]

According to the myth, the United States offered compromises, but Japan refused to compromise. It was Japan, however, who offered compromises and concessions, which the United States countered with increased demands. Hull later wrote, "I credit Nomura with having been honestly sincere in trying to avoid war."[36] Despite the diplomatic records — which have long been in the public domain — this part of the myth also persists.

World War II left us with questions crucial to civilization. Why did a highly civilized nation give Hitler — a madman — the power to carry out his destructive obsession? What is it in charismatic mass killers that so beguiles followers to carry out their wishes? Why do people who are not beguiled ignore what is coming? Why do they obey destructive orders? Specifically, why did millions of ordinary people not only acquiesce to the Holocaust but also help carry it out? And why were European leaders blind to the menace Hitler posed, not only to start a world war and not only to commit genocide, but also to destroy Western civilization?

As Germany began to prepare for conquest, genocide, and destruction of civilization, the leader of only one major nation saw what was coming and made plans to stop it. As a result of Roosevelt's leadership, a planned sequence of events carried out in the Atlantic and more decisively in the Pacific brought the United States into one of the world's greatest cataclysms. The American contribution helped turn the war's tide and save the world from a destructive tyranny unparalleled in modern history. But the accusations against Roosevelt after the Pearl Harbor attack, and the defense mounted by his administration, obscured the way the United States entered the war.

In October 2000, Congress passed a resolution calling on President William Clinton to restore the reputations of Short and Kimmel. It provoked a flurry of accusations that Congress was usurping the job of historians, revising history, and reviving a long-discredited conspiracy theory. Clinton took no action on the resolution.

Wars begin and are fought with manipulation of information for patriotic and other purposes. Accounts provided during wartime are notoriously misleading and sometimes foster national myths. Government control of information decreases after war's end, facilitating the unearthing of secrets and writing of history. But patriotic myths tend to endure after they have served the needs that prompted them. The crisis of confidence that began on December 7 is long past, as are Roosevelt's needs to rally the nation and defend his administration. Most lay people and scholars now have a more detached view of the issues and events of 1941. Nonetheless, because the myth of Pearl Harbor has served as history for decades, this introduction and much of what follows may be surprising. As events sketched above are taken up, they will be documented, heavily for those still obscure or controversial. The myth still stands in the way of working out how the United States entered World War II and needs to be put in perspective before the sequence of events leading to the Pearl Harbor attack can be understood.

CHAPTER 2
ESTABLISHING THE MYTH

Pressed by friends and enemies for an explanation of why "our warships were caught like tame ducks," Roosevelt authorized quick navy and army inquiries. Navy Secretary Knox left to interrogate the navy command at Pearl Harbor. (An army officer also left to interrogate the army command there; but he died in a plane crash en route, and Knox took over his task.) Knox's inquiry was limited to what had happened in Hawaii. He later wrote about it: "Immediately the air was filled with rumors. There was a prospect ahead of a nasty congressional investigation," and his mission was intended to head it off.[1]

In Hawaii he asked Kimmel if a warning sent from Washington on Saturday night, December 6, had been received. Astonished by Kimmel's no, he asked Kimmel's staff, and then Short and his staff, the same question. All the officers — about a dozen — said no.[2] Sure that a warning had been sent, Knox would not drop the question.

Writers speculated that Knox made a simple error: when asking about a warning sent by the Navy Department Saturday night, he meant one sent by the War Department Sunday, December 7, at noon, Washington time. He did confuse the War Department's warning with one he was convinced the Navy Department had sent, but the error was not a simple one. Writers further suggested that his error was used wrongly to blame Roosevelt, as in: "Certain revisionists insinuate that this means a warning must have been prepared on the sixth but was suppressed in Washington."[3]

What happened to the War Department's warning is no mystery; it reached Short after the attack, as he told Knox. But Knox continued to ask about a message sent by the Navy Department. And after finishing his questioning of officers in Hawaii, Knox told his aide, Capt. Frank Beatty, to investigate what happened to the Navy

Department's warning when he returned to Washington.[4] Apparently there was no record of such a warning, and Beatty discovered nothing about it.

Returning to Washington on December 14, Knox presented his report to Roosevelt. It concluded that the commands in Hawaii were unaware of "the plain intimations of some surprise move, made clear in Washington, through the interception of Japanese instructions."[5] This referred to instructions from Tokyo (known as the "pilot message"), intercepted and sent in code to Washington and decoded by U.S. intelligence on Saturday, December 6. U.S. cryptographers took the message to mean that Japan was likely to attack the United States the next day.[6] Specifically, continued Knox's report, the Hawaiian commands had not received a warning sent them Saturday night. On the basis of earlier instructions, they had made thorough preparations, but not for an air attack. Kimmel had prepared for a submarine attack; Short, for sabotage. Despite being taken by surprise, the navy and army had performed well once the attack began.

Knox found no dereliction of duty by Kimmel, Short, their staffs, or their troops. According to a subordinate of Roosevelt, Knox and Roosevelt stayed up together through the night, going over the findings, which disappointed and depressed the president.[7] Knox's mention of the interception of Japanese instructions suggested a failure in Washington. The mystery of the warning not received would be spotlighted by congressional investigators four years later in questions to Marshall and Adm. Harold Stark, who were heads of the army and navy in 1941 — questions they would evade. And it would remain a mystery until 1973, when a friend of Knox would explain it.[8]

On December 15 Knox again discussed his report with Roosevelt, who gave him detailed instructions — "verbatim wording," according to Beatty — about what to make public.[9] The revised report omitted mention of intelligence received in Washington and a resultant warning not received in Hawaii, and said, "The United States services were not on the alert against the surprise air attack on Hawaii. This fact calls for a formal investigation." Knox added that Roosevelt was appointing a commission to investigate "any error of judgment which contributed to the surprise . . . any dereliction of duty prior to the attack."[10] Knox meant an error of judgment and dereliction of duty only in Hawaii, and he mentioned the possibility of punishment to follow the investigation. From then on administration statements would either assert or imply that laxity and dereliction of duty by Kimmel and Short caused the disaster at Pearl Harbor. And the administration would focus on Pearl Harbor, as if only there had the United States suffered a disaster that called for investigation.

On December 16, Roosevelt appointed a commission headed by Owen Roberts of the Supreme Court. Justice Roberts's high reputation inspired confidence in the American people. The *San Francisco Chronicle* wrote, "From such a board we shall learn the truth, the whole truth, and nothing but the truth, and whatever action it recommends will be just and fair and constructive."[11] Among those impressed was Representative Carl Vinson, who decided to forgo an investigation by his Naval Affairs Committee.[12]

Roosevelt personally instructed Roberts about his task, and he received further orientation from Knox and War Secretary Henry Stimson. Then members of the Roberts Commission received still further instruction from Marshall and Stark.[13] As critics of the commission later pointed out, its operation was shaped by people who were accused or suspected of responsibility for the disaster.

Marshall and Stark told the commission that they had kept Short and Kimmel fully informed of developments affecting their commands. On their orders, however, intelligence of Japan's coming attack had been withheld from Short and Kimmel.[14] The administration also withheld that intelligence from the commission. Because it specified Pearl Harbor as Japan's target, keeping it from the commission was crucial. Roberts later said he had mistakenly believed that the army and navy had given the commission "every document that could have bearing on the situation at Pearl Harbor."[15]

Roberts's instructions were to investigate whether the commands in Hawaii had shown poor judgment or dereliction of duty. What had happened in the Philippines, Samoa, Guam, Midway, and Wake — or in Washington — was outside the scope of his investigation. An unhappy member of the commission, Adm. William Standley, would later complain that Roberts ran it "as crooked as a snake" in order to bring in a predetermined verdict against Kimmel and Short.[16] Not only did the commission vindicate Marshall and Stark, it also gave them the opportunity to edit its findings about them![17]

As the commission brought in its report, Stark was relieved as head of the navy, for unstated reasons. His successor, Adm. Ernest King, became responsible for controlling secret naval intelligence documents and for controlling testimony given by naval officers to tribunals investigating the Pearl Harbor disaster.[18] He was in a position to know what was in the suppressed evidence, and later wrote that the Roberts Commission

> did not get into the real meat of the matter but merely selected a "scapegoat" to satisfy the popular demand for fixing the responsibility for the Pearl Harbor debacle . . . Admiral

Kimmel . . . and General Short were "sold down the river" as a political expedient.[19]

What later investigations brought to light supported Standley's complaint and King's conclusion.

Great Britain, too, had just suffered a series of stunning defeats by Japan's forces, and Churchill, like Roosevelt, was under pressure to produce explanations and lay blame. He responded in the House of Commons:

> no one is more accountable than I am. Why, then, should I be called upon to pick out scapegoats, to throw blame on generals or airmen or sailors? Why, then, should I be called upon to drive away loyal and trusted colleagues and friends to appease the clamour . . . [over] our reverses in the Far East, and the punishment which we have yet to take there? I would be ashamed to do such a thing . . . I feel entitled to come to the House of Commons and ask them not to press me to act against my conscience and better judgment.[20]

The House of Commons gave him a vote of confidence.

Britain had already been at war for two years, enabling Churchill to be more open with his people about war strategy than Roosevelt had been. For that reason, Churchill's long speech to Commons was rather candid, unlike Roosevelt's speeches to Congress after the Pearl Harbor attack. And clamor for scapegoats was stronger in the United States than in Britain, as were threats of investigations that Roosevelt might not be able to control. And the clamor in the U.S. for scapegoats came after prior efforts to impeach him. Under the circumstances, he dealt with threats to his administration much as other presidents have dealt with threats to theirs.

Restriction of the Roberts Commission investigation rested on a variety of considerations. Samoa, Guam, and Wake were small possessions of little importance. In planning for a coming war with Japan, the administration had conceded their loss and provided them only with small military forces. But the situation in the Philippines had been different, and no evidence of Roosevelt's reasons for excluding the Philippine disaster from investigation has come to light. With war raging there, an immediate on-the-spot investigation was impossible, but none was ever undertaken.

Reasons for sweeping the Philippine disaster under the rug may be inferred from what an investigation could have revealed—a disturbing chain of events that remains little known. Those events are described here in detail because strategy in the Philippines contributed to the Pearl Harbor disaster and because a look at the Philippine disaster provides a realistic balance to distortions that have framed the Pearl Harbor controversy since 1941. The events preceding the Philippine attack highlight how common sacrifice is in ordinary war plans and how top brass routinely mislead field commanders deliberately — and sometimes tragically — for strategic purposes. Finally, the Philippine story sheds light on political considerations in the punishment of Kimmel and Short.

The Philippine commands had received intelligence about Japanese war plans — intelligence withheld from Hawaii. The army commander in the Philippines, Gen. Douglas MacArthur, had received a warning that specified the Philippines as a likely target. And days before the attack there: "For many hours Japanese planes actually rehearsed their attacks on the Philippines, flying right to their allotted targets and back."[21] And hours before the main attack there, Japanese planes bombed a Philippine radio station and hit two planes and a tender. In addition, MacArthur's air chief, Gen. Lewis Brereton, received a warning from Army Air Corps Chief, Gen. Henry Arnold, that Japan was about to strike the Philippines. Arnold specifically cautioned Brereton not to be caught with his planes on the ground. And MacArthur received a similar warning from Marshall's assistant, Gen. Leonard Gerow, and assured Gerow that he was fully prepared to meet the attack effectively.

MacArthur had recently received a large force of new, long-range bombers. And Army Intelligence knew Japan had established a striking force of planes in Taiwan — three hours away — with the capability of bombing the Philippines. Despite all that and despite knowing for hours before the main attack on the Philippines that Pearl Harbor had already been hit — that war with Japan was on — army forces in the Philippines were taken as if by surprise, with their planes largely destroyed on the ground. For hours army pilots heard rumors about the Pearl Harbor attack but were not officially informed of it, or alerted for action, or given orders.[22] Then Japan invaded the Philippines, beginning a rout of the large army recently established there, and inflicting enormous civilian casualties.

Despite MacArthur's bungling, "One of the strange things in popular psychology is the different reaction of the American people to disaster at Pearl Harbor and to disaster at Manila."[23] The disasters were unequal. In Pearl Harbor, a large part of the U.S. Fleet was destroyed; in the Philippines, a few small warships were lost. The number of army planes destroyed was roughly equal in the two territories. Except for Pearl Harbor and some airfields, Hawaii was

nearly untouched and remained in U.S. hands. The Philippines suffered widespread destruction and was captured. Twenty-four hundred troops and seventy civilians were lost in Hawaii. In the Philippines, one hundred forty thousand troops were lost, and civilian
deaths — still unreported — are estimated to have been as high as
three million.[24] Nonetheless, the defeat at Pearl Harbor became a
wrenching tragedy, and the administration sacrificed the commanders there to restore public confidence, while the defeat in the Philippines became a noble defense. Despite devastation and loss of the Philippines, a public relations operation turned MacArthur into a hero
and he was promoted.[25] The public reaction is not strange, however, when seen in the light of government control of information —
a usual wartime practice.

Kimmel and Short stood officially accused of contributing to the
Pearl Harbor disaster by failing to cooperate with each other, but it
was in the Philippines that there had been a gross lack of cooperation.
And most observers attributed the lack to MacArthur's arrogant treatment of Adm. Thomas Hart, commander of the Asiatic Fleet, stationed
at Manila. Disclosure of MacArthur's performance was to be expected
in an investigation of what happened in the Philippines.

Hart had worked well with with MacArthur's predecessor. On
MacArthur's return from retirement to command the U.S. Army detachment in the Philippines, Hart made overtures to him for cooperation in military planning and operations. Instead of answering him,
MacArthur sent a letter to Hart's superior, Admiral Stark, complain-
ing about Hart as "arbitrary and illegal [and] dictatorial" — words that
more aptly described MacArthur than Hart.[26] Later MacArthur answered a proposal by Hart for joint action by insulting him directly:

> I find [your] proposal entirely objectionable . . . It would be
> manifestly illogical to assign . . . such a powerful army air
> striking force to an element of such combat inferiority as your
> command.[27]

Not surprisingly, Hart developed a negative attitude toward
MacArthur, which contributed to their lack of cooperation.

Stark brought MacArthur's high-handedness to Marshall's attention. Marshall then wrote to MacArthur, "I was disturbed to receive your note of November 7th transmitting correspondence between
Hart and yourself. I was more disturbed when Stark sent over to me
your letter to him of October 18th." This was a sharp rebuke, which
Marshall followed with an order for MacArthur to place some of his
forces under Hart's command.[28]

MacArthur was a brilliant military leader, and his postwar achievements as Supreme Commander of Allied Occupation Forces in Japan earned him a high place in history. His shortcomings are described only to emphasize political factors in the punishment of Short and Kimmel.

In 1941 MacArthur already had an international reputation, while Short and Kimmel were unknown to the public. MacArthur also had friends in high places and was known for his pugnacity. In 1933, then head of the army, he had been troubled by an impending reduction of its officer corps. To prevent this he had asked to see Roosevelt. In the ensuing quarrel, both were unyielding. Roosevelt angrily insisted the decision was his alone and MacArthur must accept that. MacArthur replied:

> **Mr. President, if you pursue this policy, which will lead inevitably to the destruction of the American Army, I have no other choice but to oppose you publicly. I shall ask for my immediate relief as Chief of Staff and for retirement from the Army, and I shall take this fight straight to the public.**[29]

MacArthur then walked out; it was Roosevelt who subsequently yielded. MacArthur's influence and combativeness may have been considerations in Roosevelt's decision about what the Roberts Commission should investigate. In addition Roosevelt needed MacArthur, and the public was not seeking scapegoats for what happened in the Philippines.

Roosevelt had long ago thought that, if war came, he would bring MacArthur out of retirement and give him a command again. In 1941 the United States made plans for combined military operations with forces of Great Britain and her commonwealths and the Dutch East Indies. After December 7 the Australian government suggested MacArthur be made Supreme Commander of Allied Forces in the southwest Pacific, and Roosevelt decided to do it. Consequently, while the Japanese were overrunning the Philippines, Roosevelt raised MacArthur's rank to prepare him for his new position and awarded him the Congressional Medal of Honor.

The United States had acquired the Philippines in 1898 by war with Spain. Problems in defending the new territory soon became apparent, and President Theodore Roosevelt said, "If we are not prepared to establish a strong . . . base for our navy in the Philippines, then we had better give up the Philippine Islands entirely."[30] But his successors had done neither. The Navy Department opposed independence for the Filipinos, considering a base there important to protect U.S. trade in East Asia. The United States had formally assumed the obligation of defending the Philippines but had not carried it out, stationing only a small military force there. The State Department did work out temporary agreements with Japan — the nation considered the main threat to the Philippines — in 1905, 1908, and 1917. Through these agreements, Japan accepted U.S. control of the territory in return for U.S. acceptance of Japanese control in areas of China.

From time to time, Washington began projects to reinforce the Philippines, and then dropped them. Meanwhile, in 1906, U.S. military planners had begun to develop strategies for a possible war with Japan. If it came, the fate of the Philippines would be a problem. The planners considered stationing a larger U.S. force there or creating a Filipino army. But if Japan invaded, neither force — nor both together — would be adequate for more than a holding action until a major force from the United States arrived. If one could be sent from a near enough outpost, it might arrive in time to defeat the invasion. But if one had to be sent from the United States — from seven thousand miles away — military planners expected it could not reach the Philippines in time.[31]

In 1919 Japan acquired Germany's Pacific islands called the Mandates, giving her potential bases nearer to the Philippines. In 1921 Japan and the United States agreed that Japan would not fortify the Mandates and the United States would not fortify the Philippines and some other Pacific islands (excluding Hawaii). When in 1925 Washington learned of Japanese plans to build oil tanks in the Mandates, war planners considered them — correctly — a step toward establishing naval bases there. The War Department then concluded that the Philippines were indefensible and a military liability.[32]

The United States normally kept her fleet on her own west coast. Occasionally the fleet went to Hawaii for war games. In the event of an invasion of the Philippines, if the fleet was in Hawaii it might be near enough to reach the Philippines in time. The Orange War Plan of 1924 projected an army force in the Philippines strong enough to hold out until relieved by the navy. ("Orange" in the title of the plan designated Japan as the enemy.) But fortification of the Philippines stopped, and no significant armed force was established. Subsequent Orange plans conceded to Japan loss of the Philippines, along with other small Pacific possessions at the outset of war, but not the Hawaiian Islands. During the 1920s and 1930s, those plans were hypothetical because no war between the United States and Japan was in prospect.

After completing his tour as commander of the Philippine Department in 1929, Gen. Johnson Hagood advised President Herbert Hoover:

> It is not within the wildest possibility to maintain or to raise in the Philippine Islands a sufficient force to defend it against any probable foe.[33]

Hagood's successor as commander there, Gen. Stanley Embick, advised in 1933:

> To carry out the present . . . plan [for war with Japan], with the provisions for the early dispatch of our fleet to the Philippine waters, would be literally an act of madness.[34]

The navy conducted large-scale Pacific war games in 1935, leading to the conclusion that defense of the Philippines would be impossible without a prohibitively expensive naval buildup.

Hagood's and Embick's strong language — rarely used by military officers in official reports — reflected their grave concern that Washington was not taking seriously the disastrous possibilities for the Philippines of a war with Japan. Planners may easily decide from afar to make only a token defense of a territory. A commander assigned to the territory, however, tends to take the situation seriously and to be troubled if its defense is impossible. MacArthur took defense of the Philippines very seriously.

Another who took the problem seriously was Philippine independence leader Manuel Quezon. He got an agreement from Roosevelt that "The United States would . . . negotiate with foreign governments for the neutralization of the islands" in case of war between the United States and Japan.[35] In hindsight the agreement was unrealistic; the U.S. made no such attempt.

Quezon was seriously troubled, anticipating that, if Japan went to war with the United States, she was likely to attack his country. In 1935 he turned to his old friend MacArthur, who was retiring as Army Chief of Staff, to ask if he thought a Philippine army adequate for defense could be built. MacArthur replied, "I don't think so. I know that the Philippines can be protected, provided . . . that you have the money." Asked if he wanted the job of building a Philippine army, MacArthur said, "there is nothing I would like more . . . America has a great responsibility for the future safety of the Filipino people. We cannot just turn around and leave you alone."[36] Upon arriving in the Philippines, he declared, "By 1946 I will have made of the Islands a Pacific Switzerland," meaning they would bristle with defenses strong enough to discourage a potential invader. The next year he told the Philippine nation that his mission was to build a defensive force so strong that "no Chancellory in the World . . . will ever . . . attack the

Philippines."[37] MacArthur viewed his task as vital to U.S. interests, declaring in 1939, "I must not fail! Too much of the world's future depends upon success here. These Islands . . . [are the key] to control of the Pacific . . . for America. I dare not allow that key to be lost."[38]

To an extent, MacArthur did succeed in building a Filipino army and obtaining more U.S. troops for the islands. (During autumn 1941 he would be misled by promises from Marshall of far more aid than he would get before Japan attacked.) But the combined increase in Philippine forces was still inadequate to meet a Japanese attack, and MacArthur relied on U.S. forces coming to his aid.

Quezon, who had become president of the Philippines in 1935, was well aware that Washington had not provided for their security. During 1938 he made trips to Japan in an unsuccessful quest for an agreement guaranteeing Philippine neutrality in case of war with the United States.[39]

In 1940 Roosevelt stationed most of the U.S. Fleet in Hawaii. In 1941 he ordered a major buildup in the Philippines. These two measures made successful defense of the Philippines feasible, provided war did not begin until March 1942 — the projected completion time for the buildup.[40]

In August 1941, trying to avoid war with the United States, Japan offered to respect Philippine neutrality. The United States rejected the proposal.[41] By November Quezon realized that his nation was about to be drawn into war, and under disastrous conditions. Not knowing that a decision to let the Philippines fall had already been made, he pressed Roosevelt harder, without success. Quezon then foresaw that the Japanese would overrun his nation, and he denounced Roosevelt for betraying the Filipinos. Nonetheless, when he heard of Japan's attack on Pearl Harbor, before her attack fell on the Philippines, Quezon issued a public statement: "I expect every Filipino — man and woman — to do his duty. We have pledged our honor to stand to the last by the United States."[42]

When the fleet at Pearl Harbor had been crippled by Japan, it could no longer aid the Philippines. With no U.S. forces coming, loss of the territory became a virtual certainty. Roosevelt, however, wanted Philippine resistance prolonged, and the War Department cabled MacArthur that U.S. forces were on their way to support his armies (see the afterword). But no such operation was in progress or even planned.

On February 2 Quezon asked the United States immediately to grant independence and negotiate Philippine neutrality with Japan, in order to save his people and land from further destruction. The request was supported by the U.S. commissioner in the Philippines,

Francis Sayre, and by MacArthur, who forwarded it to Washington, adding, "The temper of the Filipinos is one of almost violent resentment against the United States. Every one of them expected help and when it was not forthcoming they believe they have been betrayed."[43] Roosevelt did not accede; the sacrifice of the Philippines was part of U.S. war strategy — a sacrifice common in war.

To brace their morale, Roosevelt made a radio address to the Filipinos on February 28:

> I give the people of the Philippines my solemn pledge that *their freedom will be redeemed* and their independence established and protected. The entire resources, in men and in material, of the United States stand behind that pledge. It is not for me or the people of this country to tell you where your duty lies. We are engaged in a great and common cause. I count on every Philippine man, woman, and child to do his duty. We will do ours.[44] (Italics added.)

The phrase italicized here baffled Filipinos. It may have been a reminder of the 1934 U.S. agreement to grant the Philippines independence in 1946, used here to inspire Filipinos to fight on. Despite his earlier disappointments, Quezon still clung to hopes of U.S. forces coming to defeat Japan's invasion. Less credulous, Quezon's cabinet took independent action. Japan had offered the Filipinos independence if they stopped fighting. To compel Quezon's acceptance of Japan's offer, the cabinet informed him they were sending a cable to Roosevelt urging him to arrange a separate peace for the Philippines and that they were accepting the Japanese offer.[45] But the cabinet lacked effective power to accept the offer, and Quezon rallied his people to fight on. MacArthur, who had had a long, positive relationship with Filipinos, was sympathetic to the cabinet. Nonetheless, he obeyed Roosevelt and prolonged the fighting. The devastation of the Philippines continued.

These events are what an investigation could have revealed. In addition, secret strategic considerations had governed orders to MacArthur before Japan attacked, limiting his defense of the Philippines (see chapter 6). The orders were similar to orders that limited Short and Kimmel in defending Pearl Harbor.

A full investigation of the Philippine disaster would have embarrassed the administration and raised uncomfortable questions. Probably for this reason, the administration not only limited the scope of the Roberts Commission's investigation, but also manipulated evidence presented to it.[46] Army and navy officers were ordered to withhold certain data and to lie about it if pressed. General Miles, Chief of Army Intelligence, later said so in an affidavit and in testimony, and Marshall confirmed it (see chapter 5). The suppressed evidence was exculpatory to Short and Kimmel, and implicated officials in Washington.

The withholding of intercepted warnings of the coming Pearl Harbor attack from the Roberts Commission and Short and Kimmel was justified on the grounds of national security. The administration's idea was that if Short and Kimmel learned about the interception and decoding of Japanese messages, the Japanese might also learn of it and change their codes. The United States had, of course, an interest in keeping the code breaking a secret. But the justification was most puzzling in connection with Short and Kimmel before December 7, because their counterparts in Manila — MacArthur and Hart — were given access to the messages.

Lacking access to this suppressed evidence during the investigations, Short and Kimmel were unable to defend themselves adequately. With the restrictions placed on it, the Roberts Commission concluded that Short and Kimmel were responsible for the Pearl Harbor disaster, and it exonerated officials in Washington.[47] After the commission found Short and Kimmel guilty of grave errors of judgment and dereliction of duty, an outcry arose across the nation for them to be punished severely, and Roosevelt directed that court-martial charges be brought against them.

Because of Justice Roberts's prestige, because his investigation was the first, and because it provided a simple explanation for the Pearl Harbor disaster, his commission's findings were accepted by most people. The myth of Pearl Harbor — that because of Japanese deception the administration had not expected the attack and that Short and Kimmel had failed to carry out orders to defend it — was established as U.S. history. And although pieces of it were later controverted in very extensive investigations by the Army Pearl Harbor Board, the Naval Court of Inquiry, and a joint congressional committee, the Roberts Commission's report shaped the history of Pearl Harbor.

CHAPTER 3
WARNINGS OF THE PEARL HARBOR ATTACK

The crucial information withheld from the Roberts Commission was warnings of the Pearl Harbor attack. Defensive over criticism of his report, Roberts later testified that he had requested all documents bearing on the attack and been assured that—with the exception of intercepted Japanese diplomatic messages—the administration had provided all of them to him.[1] The administration also withheld most of the warnings from subsequent investigations by the Army Pearl Harbor Board, the Naval Court of Inquiry, and the joint congressional committee, while insisting it had not received them. The committee asked Adm. Theodore Wilkinson, who had been chief of the Office of Naval Intelligence (ONI) in autumn 1941, "Well, did you have any information, written or oral, prior to the attack, which specified Hawaii as a point of attack?" He answered, "Not the slightest."[2]

By December 1945 the committee had received copies of twenty warnings[3]—nineteen of which had come in during Wilkinson's tenure as intelligence chief—and he was asked the question over and over. He kept insisting that he had seen no warnings prior to the attack.

Even though the congressional committee's report contradicted such denials, they had an enduring effect. Histories written after World War II carried flat statements such as: "Nobody in Washington could warn Hawaii of something he neither knew nor suspected."[4] Then, as more and more warnings were uncovered, controversy about whether Roosevelt and his key subordinates had expected the attack became passionate. Some of his defenders dismissed the idea as unthinkable, as in: "There exists in law a rule that accusations which are beyond the capacity of human credence need not be refuted."[5]

General Miles explained that his division—Army Intelligence (G-2)—failed to anticipate the Pearl Harbor attack because Congress did not provide adequate funding for necessary intelligence.[6] Military intelligence had been, of course, only a fraction of what it grew to after Pearl Harbor. But even before the attack it had been large and provided many warnings of the coming attack.

Even with small staffs, foreign intelligence accomplished impressive feats. With a staff of about ten, Dutch intelligence in Java broke Japan's main naval code. With staff of a few hundred, British intelligence did the same.[7] Three Army units in Washington decrypted intercepted Japanese messages before December 7: G-2, with a staff of 425; the Signal Intelligence Service (a branch of the Signal Corps), with 330; and the smaller Army Air Corps intelligence unit. The army also had intelligence offices in Hawaii, the Philippines, Tokyo, Hong Kong, Shanghai, and the Dutch East Indies. ONI had a staff of seven hundred in Washington, aided by about one thousand intelligence workers in various naval districts. Those on the U.S. West Coast and at Pearl Harbor and Manila were devoted to information on Japan—particularly to intercepting and decoding Japanese naval messages. Combining all units, military intelligence had a staff of a few thousand in December 1941. In addition, military attachés and observers across the globe gathered intelligence, especially in Japan and her territories.[8]

Other U.S. government agencies also had intelligence units that focused on Japan's war plans—the Departments of Commerce and Agriculture, the Board of Economic Warfare, the Federal Bureau of Investigation, the Secret Service, the Customs Service, and the Federal Communications Commission. Some of these agencies sent spies to Japanese-occupied China and Korea or had informants in those places. The Treasury Department had several intelligence-type organizations. And Hawaii had a civilian intelligence corps. In addition, foreign governments—notably Great Britain, the Dutch East Indies, China, and the Soviet Union—provided intelligence to the United States in 1941.[9]

Additional sources of intelligence were ship masters' reports, business representatives abroad of the Rockefeller family, and a group of private citizens with extraordinary resources headed by businessman Vincent Astor. He had established an informal intelligence group called The Room in 1927, and expanded its operations in cooperation with the Roosevelt administration, renaming it The Club.[10]

In 1940 Roosevelt had called for a "special intelligence service"—not officially recognized, operating under cover as a private business—to coordinate ongoing intelligence gathering of government agencies and to recruit agents abroad. When Roosevelt established it later that year, he made Astor its coordinator. In February 1941 the State Department established an intelligence unit under John Carter, hiding its existence and Carter's identity by calling him Jay Franklin. From it and from diplomats, the State Department collected enough intelligence for the army and navy to send officers there daily to pick up new items.[11] In June 1941 Roosevelt established a new intelligence organization, the Coordinator of Information (COI), under William Donovan, who had been affiliated with The Room. It was budgeted for a staff of ninety-two, and Donovan increased it to six hundred by autumn.[12] (With the nation openly at war a year later, the COI was reconstituted under military direction as the Office of Strategic Services — the OSS, forerunner of the CIA.)

Records of what most of these agencies and individuals learned — if preserved — remain largely unavailable. Some vague summaries of or comments on undisclosed records indicate a coming attack on Pearl Harbor. In addition, many of the documents released were first censored. And a great many others were destroyed. Because of these limitations, no comprehensive picture of what all the intelligence sources produced is possible.

Throughout its long investigation, the joint congressional committee took pains not to expose the breaking of Japan's naval codes and what her naval messages revealed. It even handled the details of Japan's diplomatic codes carefully. When an ONI officer testified about them, a committee member interrupted, "I want to again protest revealing the mechanics or the details of how we broke the code. I do not see how it would help national security . . . or add anything to the inquiry." The committee's counsel responded, "Mr. Chairman, I have no intention of going into it," and directed the witness not to give such details. Another committee member then protested, "Mr. Chairman, that is absurd. . . . These matters are well known, well understood, have already been the subject of books and magazine articles."[13] (The war, of course, was over.)

Most controversial today are warnings in Japan's naval codes. Even the existence of these warnings remained hidden until President Jimmy Carter ordered intercepted Japanese naval messages released in 1979. The navy then turned them over to the National Security Agency (NSA), which processed the messages for release while minimizing their importance by saying over and over that they had been unreadable in 1941 (see more, following).

Among the defenses the administration offered, the hardest to evaluate is that the Pearl Harbor warnings did not stand out and therefore went unnoticed. It is impossible to put ourselves at the desks of intelligence officers and their superiors in 1941 and judge what stood out for them. The best known, most widely praised evaluation of what may or may not have been noticed was based on a study of the system by which intelligence was processed and communicated to high-level officials. Roberta Wohlstetter's theoretical analysis focused on how noticeable Pearl Harbor warnings might have been among other intelligence—a "signal-to-noise" type of communication analysis. She started with a problem crucial here:

> **Pearl Harbor provides a dramatic and well-documented example of an attack presaged by a mass and variety of signals, which nonetheless achieved complete and overwhelming surprise.[14]**

And she concluded—mistakenly—that no one in the intelligence community had been assigned to note items of special importance or to coordinate information received at different times. On the assumption of such a lack of personnel, her main conclusion was that the signals had been buried in the noise:

> **In short, we failed to anticipate Pearl Harbor not for want of relevant materials, but because of a plethora of irrelevant ones . . . of signs pointing in every direction.[15]**

Many writers relied on her findings. But Col. Rufus Bratton of G-2 was responsible in 1941 for noting important items and coordinating them with other intelligence. He discussed notable intelligence items with his counterparts in the navy—Commanders Arthur McCollum and Laurence Safford. The three of them concluded that Pearl Harbor was Japan's likely target, brought this to their superiors' attention, and tried to get warnings sent to Short and Kimmel.[16]

 In addition Roosevelt's new COI was responsible for collecting and coordinating intelligence on Japan's war plans. And during the weeks before the Pearl Harbor attack Donovan received at least two warnings that it was coming.

Wohlstetter emphasized another point germane to the following analysis—"the very human tendency to pay attention to the signals that support current expectations . . . To discriminate sounds against [a] background of noise one has to be listening for something . . . one needs not only an ear, but a . . . hypothesis that guides observation."[17] Amid a mass of information, what is expected is noticed; and what is unexpected is often missed. Accepting statements by some officers that they had not expected Japan to attack Pearl Harbor, she concluded that they consequently missed the warnings of it. Now so much is available about what was expected, what came in, and what was noticed, that a signal-to-noise analysis of what was theoretically noticeable is no longer relevant.

Most of those who testified that they had not expected an attack on Pearl Harbor had, however, written or said in the months preceding it that they did expect it. And their reports and memos saying so were preserved. The discrepancy between the records and their testimony was so striking that the Army Pearl Harbor Board commented sarcastically:

> We must . . . conclude that the responsible authorities . . . *all expected an attack on Pearl Harbor* . . . [but] when testifying after the Pearl Harbor attack, they did not expect it.[18]

The strategic idea that Japan's main chance to win a war against the United States lay in crippling the U.S. Navy by a surprise attack was an obvious one. A former U.S. intelligence worker wrote:

> For thirty-two years . . . Japanese naval strategy . . . envisaged [a naval] showdown with the Americans . . . For more than three decades the Japanese fleet trained and exercised for such an engagement . . . [specifically] an attack on the American fleet in Hawaiian waters at the outset of hostilities.[19]

After annual U.S. Fleet visits to Hawaii began, the fleet's commander, Adm. Frank Schofield, wrote in 1932:

> The enemy [Japan] will strike where the fleet is concentrated. The enemy will use carriers as the basis of his striking force. The enemy may make raids on Hawaiian Islands.[20]

And Schofield designed war games in 1932 and 1933 on the basis of his analysis, as did his successors and army commanders in Hawaii. Most of the games included attacks by carrier-based planes.

U.S. planners inferred—correctly, as it turned out—that, to escape detection, Japanese carriers would travel east across a hardly-used part of the north Pacific called "the vacant sea." Then, when near Hawaii, they would turn south and launch their planes from north of Oahu (the Hawaiian island containing Pearl Harbor). In the 1932 games "Japanese" carriers approached Oahu from the north, undetected, and "Japanese" planes attacked on a Sunday, achieving total surprise, destroying every battleship in the harbor and all U.S. planes before they could take off.[21] Reported to Japan, the result of the games contributed to reorganization of her navy, emphasizing carrier-based air power. Over the next years, war games in Hawaii produced similar results, and a War Department study in 1938 concluded that, if war came with

Japan, "there can be little doubt that the Hawaiian Islands will be the initial scene of action" by a surprise attack.[22] "U.S." defeats in the games heightened Washington's concern about Pearl Harbor's vulnerability and fed discussion of measures to safeguard the harbor and fleet.

After Roosevelt stationed most of the fleet indefinitely at Pearl Harbor in May 1940 — making it easier for Japan to attack it there — U.S. military planners became very concerned that Japan might do so. And in November, a British air attack on an Italian fleet at anchor in Taranto, Italy, still further heightened concern about the vulnerability of U.S. warships at Pearl Harbor. The sensational British victory was studied in Tokyo and Washington. It led Navy Secretary Knox to urge War Secretary Stimson to strengthen Hawaii's defenses. In 1941 there were three separate U.S. war games in which "Japan" attacked the fleet in Hawaii.[23]

Despite this background, Stark, Marshall, and other high officers testified after the attack that they missed warnings of it because they were not expecting an attack there. But Adm. Richmond Turner, chief of the navy's War Plans Division, testified that he himself, the Navy Department, and Stark did expect an attack on Pearl Harbor.[24] And the record supports Turner.

Even when not mentioned in a specific military study, Pearl Harbor was an ever-present concern, according to General Miles:

> Now an air attack on Pearl Harbor or any other attack on Pearl Harbor had been . . . a source of study for twenty years in Hawaii and in the War Department. It is not mentioned in this estimate of the situation presumably because it was so obvious . . . . That Hawaii could be attacked if Japan went to war was obvious to everyone.[25]

And even when intelligence indicated Japan would attack elsewhere, the presumption remained that she would also attack Pearl Harbor. Colonel Bratton testified that in 1941: "In various G-2 estimates submitted to the Chief of Staff over a period of many months an attack on Hawaii had always been listed."[26]

Thus before warnings came in, navy and army intelligence workers had good reason to expect a Japanese air attack on Pearl Harbor, and at least some of them did expect it. So did their superiors. On that basis, they should have been alert to the warnings detailed below.

When Admiral Yamamoto Isoroku began working on his plan to destroy the U.S. Fleet at Pearl Harbor in January 1941, he sent an outline to Navy Minister Oikawa Koshiro with a note that read: "For the eyes of the Minister alone: to be burned without showing to anyone else."[27] Despite his caution, Yamamoto's plan was not much of a secret in Japan.[28] Talk of it circulated in Tokyo and came to the attention of U.S. Ambassador Joseph Grew, including a boast by a Japanese government employee that "The American Fleet will disappear."[29] A member of Japan's Ministry of War confirmed to Grew that Japan was planning such an attack. Sent to Washington in January 1941, Grew's was the first warning of a coming attack on Pearl Harbor. The information was passed by the State Department to Roosevelt and to the Navy Department, which passed it to the War Department and preserved it in its files.

In June the army sent Maj. Warren Clear as an undercover agent to the Far East, seeking intelligence about Japan's war plans. He visited British intelligence in Singapore and reported Japanese plans to attack Hawaii, Guam, and the United States islands between them (which happened on December 7). In 1967 he wrote that "my evidence will show that Washington D.C. had solid evidence prior to P.H. [Pearl Harbor] that Japan would . . . [attack] Hawaii."[30] Also during June, the U.S. military attaché in Mexico City reported that Japan was building midget "submarines for attacking the American fleet in Pearl Harbor."[31]

In August Germany sent Dusan (Dusko) Popov to the United States and Hawaii, seeking intelligence. The Germans had given him written instructions, which included getting detailed information on military installations in Hawaii. The information could have been useful for sabotage or for a combat attack. Interviewed in August by the FBI, Popov said he inferred the information was for Japan's use in planning a combat attack on Pearl Harbor. According to Popov, his German superior confirmed this inference and said Japan was planning to use carrier-based torpedo bombers against the U.S. Fleet there.[32]

Popov was a British double agent whose alias was Tricycle. British intelligence considered the information he provided "a strong indication" of a coming air attack—so strong that "it seems incredible that Pearl Harbor should not have been on the alert for a surprise . . . air raid."[33] Popov also told the FBI that two Germans had shown Japanese naval officers around Taranto so they could learn how the torpedoing of ships at anchor in shallow water had been accomplished. One lesson was that the British planes had flown only thirty-five feet above water, so that the torpedoes they dropped would not dive to the bottom—a lesson Japanese pilots would apply at Pearl Harbor, whose waters were equally shallow.

According to widely accepted rumors, FBI Director Edgar Hoover was so disgusted by Popov's lustful and extravagant lifestyle that he gave no credence to his warning of an attack on Pearl Harbor and failed to pass it to responsible officials. That Hoover disapproved of

Popov's lifestyle was true; that he failed in his duty was not. Hoover passed Popov's material to ONI and informed Roosevelt.[34] Nonetheless, writers have used accounts of Popov's lifestyle to discredit him and, by implication, his warning, which some dismissed as "the Popov legend."

Warnings also came in from other foreign sources. In October, Richard Sorge, head of a Soviet spy ring in Japan, radioed Moscow, "Japanese air force attacking United States Navy at Pearl Harbor probably dawn November six. Source reliable."[35] It was his understanding that Moscow passed the warning to Washington.

Haan Kilsoo was an agent of the Sino-Korean People's League, an underground organization. Early in 1941 he told U.S. Col. George Patton of a Japanese plan to attack Hawaii. In March Haan sent a memo to Hull that Japan would attack Hawaii and other U.S. territories. By the beginning of October he informed the State Department that Japan planned to attack Pearl Harbor before Christmas.[36] On October 28 Haan again informed the State Department, where Stanley Hornbeck commented in a memo for Secretary Hull:

> In evaluating the information given by Mr. Haan, we must take into account the fact that Haan is a Korean, a bitter enemy of Japan, and a man who would like to see war between the United States and Japan. At the same time, the Koreans do have certain contacts in Japan . . . which enable them to get some information . . . Mr. Haan has from time to time furnished . . . information which proved authentic and also of value. We cannot dismiss Haan or information given by him.[37]

Haan got the impression that the State Department was uninterested and took his information to reporter Eric Sevareid and Senator Guy Gillette. Gillette informed the Departments of State, War, and Navy. According to Gillette's nephew, Thomas Gillette:

> [Guy] said that Haan had contacted him in late November, telling him that the Japanese Fleet had sailed under battle orders, east, not south, to attack Pearl Harbor or the Panama Canal.

Haan said he phoned Maxwell Hamilton of the State Department on December 4 with a tip that a Pearl Harbor attack was coming on the weekend.[38]

No records of Clear's, Sorge's, Haan's, or Gillette's reports have been found in government files. Hornbeck's memo confirms that the

State Department received at least one of Haan's warnings and that it was brought to Hull's attention.

Some of the above intelligence was sketchy and based on sources unknown to the U.S. government. Its validity could not be confirmed. It did, however, contain warnings which the administration denied receiving, while it withheld them from tribunals investigating the Pearl Harbor disaster.

As they did with Popov, writers dismissed Haan's warnings by impugning his character and calling his sources into question. They did this speculatively, without knowing Haan's character or his sources — without a basis. In view of the long-held presumption that Japan would try at the outset of war to cripple the U.S. Fleet, ignoring any warning of a Pearl Harbor attack — even if provided by a questionable source — was imprudent. Nonetheless, in perpetuating the Pearl Harbor myth, speculative denigration of informants and questioning of their sources continued and was used even against people of established reliability — Gen. Elliot Thorpe, Gen. Hein ter Poorten, Capt. Johan Ranneft, and the intelligence unit in the Dutch East Indies.

With the benefit of hindsight, we now know that most warnings of the Pearl Harbor attack had authentic sources and were valid. Nonetheless, writers continue to challenge warnings as impossible on the basis of two arguments. One is that only a handful of Japanese knew of the plan, and their discipline was so strict that leaks did not happen. The other, that the force en route to Pearl Harbor maintained "total" or "absolute" radio silence.[39] Therefore people who said they picked up messages from it and used them to locate or track the task force had to be mistaken. For example:

> the radios of ships in the task force had been sealed and sailors ordered to stay away from the equipment . . . measures had gone as far as removals of fuses from the transmitter circuits or the detaching and storing of keying equipment . . . placing of paper slips in keying mechanisms to prevent the electrical contacts used to generate Morse code signals.[40]

This was only partly true. When the task force assembled, its commander, Admiral Nagumo Chuichi, did indeed order total radio silence. But as it sortied, he modified the order:

> From November 26, all ships . . . will observe radio communications procedures as follows:
>   1. Except in extreme emergency, the Main Striking Force and its attached force will cease communicating.

2. Other forces are at the discretion of their respective commanders.

3. Supply ships, repair ships, hospital ships, etc., will report directly to parties concerned.[41]

The most flagrant misstatement about radio silence was by the editors of a book of Japanese documents on the Pearl Harbor attack:

A striking feature of revisionist literature on the Pearl Harbor attack is the concept that Franklin D. Roosevelt knew about it in advance, maintaining that the United States had broken the Japanese code and was picking up the task force's messages as it crossed the Pacific . . . Almost all the . . . documents in this volume . . . state positively that the task force never broke radio silence on the outward journey to Hawaii. Hence their messages could not have been intercepted.[42]

And if no messages could be intercepted, statements that decoded messages from the task force indicated its destination could not possibly be valid. Nor could statements that coded messages from it were used to track it by radio direction-finding. Nor, by implication, could statements that Roosevelt knew the attack was coming.

Despite the editors' vehemence, most of the documents in the book said nothing of the sort. And two documents in the book contain two radio messages sent by the task force while en route to Hawaii![43]

The following warnings came from authoritative sources — mainly from U.S. intelligence. The first group became known as bomb-plot messages because they provided information to be used in planning bombing runs at warships in Pearl Harbor. The word "plot" came from Japanese intelligence dividing the harbor into sections — what writers called a plot or grid — so that spies near the harbor could report precisely where ships were moored. Messages with this information were sent from Honolulu to Tokyo by diplomatic code. Intercepted immediately, decoding and translating them took from an hour to a month. Some were not fully translated until after December 7. The administration and sympathetic writers cited that delay in claiming that the messages were not understood in time as warnings of the Pearl Harbor attack.

Army and navy intelligence intercepted so many messages that they could not decode and translate all of them immediately. Consequently they screened intercepts to decide which could be held for delayed processing. According to an army intelligence worker, "That a message was not listed as translated [before a certain date] does not mean necessarily that it had not been *partially* broken or glanced at by some officer [for its] *gist*."[44] Some idea of the content of messages was to be noted before they were put aside for delayed decoding. Of 152 new Japanese diplomatic messages processed by Naval Intelligence on December 1, 3, and 5, 1941, gists were prepared for a third.[45] By projection, perhaps thousands of gists were prepared in 1941. (Only two have been found.)

According to Cdr. Alwin Kramer, who was in charge of translating Japanese diplomatic messages for the navy, excepting messages assigned for immediate processing, "all the others were looked over and a brief summary made by the translators."[46] Kramer was obsessively concerned that translations be highly polished. According to a subordinate, "Al would take even the most trivial piece of traffic and devote the same amount of time changing a comma here and a period there, as he would spend on an important message."[47] As a result, decoded messages were substantially delayed until Kramer was satisfied. And the official date of translation was the date when Kramer was satisfied. Delays resulting from his obsessiveness increased the need to convey a gist to responsible officers, and that was done. Finally there were dozens of bomb-plot messages; those marked as translated after December 7 were unnecessary to conclude that an attack on Pearl Harbor was coming.

In 1940 and 1941, Japanese officials abroad routinely gathered information about ships in various harbors and their comings and goings in many parts of the world, and reported the information to Tokyo in coded diplomatic messages. At first, intercepted messages about Pearl Harbor did not stand out from those about other ports. The crucial change to bomb-plot messages followed an order from Tokyo on September 24, 1941, intercepted and decoded in the United States, which asked for precise locations of warships at anchor.

Data collected pursuant to the order was useful for a combat attack or sabotage against ships in the harbor. The precise "grid" locations of warships particularly enabled attackers far away — pilots of submarines and planes — to plan their runs at targets. (Potential saboteurs in Oahu could see for themselves where warships were anchored.) The order and subsequent messages — when combined with intelligence already received — constituted a serious warning of a combat attack on the fleet in Pearl Harbor.

An intelligence officer who immediately noted the bomb-plot order's meaning was Bratton. He drew Stimson's, Marshall's, and Gen. Leonard Gerow's attention to it, and emphasized its importance. And Kramer brought the bomb-plot order to Capt. Alan Kirk, outgoing chief of ONI, and to Turner, Stark, Knox, and Roosevelt, along with a note that it was of special interest. Reportedly Kramer also brought it to the attention of the new ONI chief, Wilkinson, and they conferred over its significance.[48]

Some officers testified that the bomb-plot reports were the same as ships-in-harbor and coming-and-going reports gathered by Japanese observers across the world. But nothing comparable to the bomb-plot order was intercepted for any other port.[49] And the intelligence sent to Tokyo pursuant to the order was different from intelligence sent about other ports. Orders from Tokyo to send bomb-plot messages were marked "strictly secret," which also set them apart from most other diplomatic messages.[50] According to MacArthur's intelligence chief, Gen. Charles Willoughby:

> The sequence of messages . . . beginning with November 14th, would have led instantly to the inescapable conclusion that Pearl Harbor naval installations were a target for attack . . . for some sort of naval seaborne sortie.[51]

He explained that "co-ordinate grid is the classical method of pinpoint target designation; our battleships had suddenly become 'targets.'"

The order led to an increase in espionage messages about Pearl Harbor. For weeks, the messages gave warships' comings and goings along with their moorings. But after November 15, the messages went beyond information about ships in harbor to describe army and navy defenses against an air attack. For example:

> The Army ordered several hundred [barrage balloons] for training on . . . the American mainland. They considered (at that time) the practicality of their employment in the defense of Hawaii and Panama. Investigation of the vicinity of Pearl Harbor reveals no locations selected for their use or any preparations for constructing moorings. No evidence of training or personnel preparations . . . . Am continuing in detail the investigation of the non-use of nets for torpedo defense of battleships.[52]

Italics have been added in the following intercepts to identify details indicating a coming combat attack:

> 1. . . . *they have not set up [balloon] mooring equipment nor have they selected the troops to man them.* Furthermore there is no indication that any training for the maintenance

of balloons is being undertaken. At the present time there
are no signs of *barrage balloon equipment* . . . I imagine that
in all probability *there is considerable opportunity left to take
advantage for a surprise attack* against these places.
2. In my opinion *the battleships do not have torpedo nets.*[53]

The message specified "these places" as "the vicinity of Pearl Harbor,
Hickam, Ford and Ewa." Ford was an island in the harbor; Hickam
and Ewa were military installations on Oahu.

Intercepted messages received November 24 and later were
marked with translation dates after December 7; those received December 6 and later, with translation dates of December 8 or later. As
noted, gists had been prepared by December 7 for a third of the messages whose decoding was delayed (but for which third is unknown).

An intercept of December 3, after giving moorings of United
States warships in the harbor, ended with, "So far *they do not seem to be
alerted.* Shore leaves as usual." And one of December 5 said, "*No barrage balloons* sighted . . . *No indications of air or sea alert.*" And another of
December 6 included, "It appears that *no air reconnaissance* is being
conducted by the fleet air arm." Still another of December 6 read,
"There are *no barrage balloons up and there is an opportunity left for a
surprise attack* against these places."[54]

These messages told Tokyo that U.S. forces in Hawaii were unprepared for an air attack. The information was crucial because, if they
were prepared, the Pearl Harbor attack was to be called off. And according to Miles, G-2 had inferred that Japan would attack Pearl Harbor only if it was unprepared.

More dramatic than the bomb-plot messages are intercepted
Japanese naval messages, which were long kept from the public.
The government's secrecy and misdirection about them contributed
to the idea that they were a smoking gun, which they are not. After
1979 the two agencies in possession of the intercepts—the Naval
Security Group and then the NSA—continued to say they were
unaware of the documents' existence! And when acknowledging
their existence, the agencies claimed not to know the nature of Japanese naval intercepts in their possession.[55] Finally they released the
documents in censored form, which limits their use by researchers—
apparently a permanent limitation. According to the NSA:

When it has been determined a document can be released in
sanitized form, generally there is an unsanitized (classified)
true original of the document. However, an unsanitized true
original version of the "Pre-Pearl Harbor Japanese Naval

> Dispatches" can not be located. Therefore the redactions . . .
> can not be verified nor can be responded to *at any future
> date*.[56] (Italics added.)

"Sanitized" means censored; "redactions" means deleted parts. The statement says in effect, "Don't bother inquiring about what was deleted."

"Pre-Pearl Harbor Japanese Naval Despatches" is a partial set of intercepted messages from that period. The set was declassified in 1991 and released with the above explanation. Not only uncensored translations, but also decodings in Japanese, original coded intercepts, and worksheets used in decoding and translating them—more than one hundred thousand documents—apparently are missing. The statement implies they are missing permanently, and none have come to light since 1991.

Some of the intercepts provide indications that Pearl Harbor was to be attacked, and a few say so explicitly. The key question is which, if any of them, were decoded and translated during the weeks before the attack? In the circumstances, we may never know. The government's official position was that no Japanese naval intercepts were decoded before 1945—a position still accepted by most writers. However, some cryptographers who worked on Japanese naval messages contradicted the government's assertion. One in the Philippines wrote during November 1941, "We are reading enough current traffic to keep two translators very busy."[57]

On December 1 Japan made a minor change in its main naval code. Wilkinson testified about it, "I knew that there had been a change in certain of their codes which resulted in difficulty in our radio intelligence analyses at that time."[58] Cdr. Joseph Rochefort, chief of the naval intelligence unit in Hawaii, testified that his unit was reading one in ten messages.[59] (Other cryptographers' estimates ranged between none and nine in ten.) Using Rochefort's estimate, about 19 of the 188 messages indicating an attack on Pearl Harbor may have been read in whole or part by naval intelligence before December 7.

Victor Cavendish-Bentinck, chair of Britain's Joint Intelligence Committee (JIC) in 1941, wrote years later about the Japanese fleet that attacked Pearl Harbor:

> We knew that they changed course. I remember presiding
> over a J.I.C. meeting [on December 5, 1941] and being told
> that a Japanese fleet was sailing in the direction of Hawaii,
> asking "Have we informed our transatlantic brethren?" and

receiving an affirmative reply . . . [We had given] the U.S. authorities . . . ample time to at least send most of the fleet out of Pearl Harbor.[60]

By "changed course," he meant that the Japanese fleet, sailing east, had turned south to Hawaii on that day. The source of this British intelligence remains hidden; radio direction-finding seems its most likely basis. Another British intelligence officer confirmed Cavendish-Bentinck's statement. And American intelligence worker (and later chief of the CIA) William Casey wrote (without providing details): "The British had sent word that a Japanese fleet was steaming east toward Hawaii."[61]

Additional statements indicate not only that Japanese naval messages were decoded, but also that the decodings were shown to administrators. Undersecretary of State Sumner Welles testified that in 1941 "many" State Department meetings — sometimes attended by Roosevelt, Stimson, Knox, Marshall, and Stark — were held about the Pacific situation. "A very large part of those meetings was taken up with . . . intelligence which had come to us" about Japan. Welles said he routinely saw intercepted Japanese diplomatic messages and "occasionally, intercepts of a military character would also come to me."[62] No Japanese army codes are known to have been broken before the Pearl Harbor attack; evidently Japanese naval messages were what Welles meant by "military" intercepts. He also referred to them as "intercepted naval or military messages."[63]

Wilkinson confirmed Welles's evidence, testifying:

A book of radio intelligence was shown to the State Department, the White House, Chief of Naval Operations, Director of Naval Intelligence, Director of War Plans, and the Secretary of the Navy, daily or skipping a day if nothing pertinent was at hand.[64]

"Radio intelligence" meant intercepted Japanese diplomatic and naval messages.

And Churchill wrote:

From the end of 1940 the Americans had pierced the vital Japanese ciphers, and *were decoding large numbers of their military* and diplomatic telegrams.[65] (Italics added.)

Churchill had ordered millions of intelligence documents — about 90 percent of Britain's — to be destroyed and the rest sealed.[66] That prevented disclosure of specifics of British intelligence about the Pearl Harbor attack.

Better evidence than vague comments and estimates are actual decodings made in 1941. Naval intelligence prepared frequent summaries of information about locations of Japanese warships and projections about where they were headed, which sometimes quoted decoded Japanese naval message fragments. A summary of November 26 included these passages:

> In view of this force's operations and future—we definitely desire to be fueled before arriving at Palau . . .
> Suzuki (1776) is being sent to your headquarters on board the *Hiei* to report on inspection results.
>   Please arrange to have Suzuki (1776), who was sent to the 1ST AIR FLEET on business, picked up about 23 or 24 November at Hitokappu Wan by —— [unidentified ship] of your command.
>   Reply to your serial 622. He [Suzuki] will be taken on board the JUNAJIRI.
>   Will be in local circuits of below-mentioned Communications Zones as follows: Until 2000 the 20th, Yokosuka Communication Zone. Until 0800 the 22nd, Ominato Communication Zone. Thereafter, 1ST AIR FLEET Flagship Communication Zone.[67] (Dash in original where undecoded name of Japanese ship occurred.)

Palau, in the Mandated Islands, was where the fleet that hit Pearl Harbor refueled afterward. Commander Suzuki Sugeru had completed a trial run of the route to be taken by the fleet that would attack Pearl Harbor, and he was to provide the "inspection results" of his run to Nagumo. His identification number was 1776. Hittokappu Wan (Bay) was the attack fleet's departure point. The *Hiei* was a battleship in that fleet. Presumably the significance of these details (and some of the details themselves) were unknown to U.S. cryptographers in November 1941. The point here is that U.S. cryptographers were reading passages in Japanese naval messages during November 1941.

The first sentence was taken from a decoded Japanese naval message sent on November 26 (November 25, in the United States). It was decoded within 24 hours and, according to a postwar decoding, its correct translation was: "In view of this force's operations and future we definitely desire to be refueled before arriving at Palau."[68] The November 1941 message was decoded quickly and accurately. (In contradiction of claims that Japan's attack force maintained complete radio silence, this radio message was from one unit of the force to another.) And a more complete decoded message, also from November, 1941, is:

Today the House of Peers and House of Representative by means of a decision adopted the following resolution transmitted as follows:

1. Resolution of House of Peers—Expressed deepest thanks and emotion to Army and Navy for their glorious service over a long period to the Empire and expressed condolence, etc, for those fallen in battle.

2. Resolution of House of Representatives—Expressed thanks, etc., to all officers and men of Army, Navy and Air Force for 4 1/2 years service (in China affair) and for their contribution to the establishment of a permanent world peace. Gave prayers for well being of all hands, etc.[69] (Incomplete parentheses in original.)

None of the above decoded messages revealed a coming attack on Pearl Harbor. Whether any other messages decoded by Naval Intelligence before the attack did remains unknown.

To British cryptographers, intercepted Japanese naval messages were adequate warnings of a coming attack on Hawaii. Referring to them, the commander of British intelligence in Singapore called his staff together the day after the attack on Pearl Harbor and said, "With all the information we gave them. How could the Americans have been caught unprepared?"[70]

In summary, agents provided sixteen usable warnings of the Pearl Harbor attack. Twenty-five indications of it, ranging from vague to clear, came from intercepted bomb-plot messages, of which about twenty were decoded before the attack. And ten percent or more of the relevant Japanese naval messages probably were decoded as well. And radio direction-finding helped track the fleet moving to Hawaii. Given the U.S. Navy's expectation of thirty years that Japan would start a war against the United States with an attack on the fleet when it was in Hawaii, even one warning from a reliable source should have been taken seriously and alerted high-level officers for signs to come.

The Dutch naval attaché in Washington, Captain Johan Ranneft, often visited ONI, where he discussed the expected Japanese attack with ONI officers. He noted in his diary on December 2:

2-12-41. Conference at Navy Department, they show me on the map the *location of 2 Japanese carriers* departed from Japan on easterly course.[71]

Given the difficulty in decoding Japanese naval messages and the ease of radio direction-finding, and given the mention of the carriers' direction and location, radio direction-finding was probably the basis for this and the next items.

Ranneft later said a member of ONI commented, "This is the Japanese task force proceeding east," and that it was half way between Japan and Hawaii on December 2.[72] And on December 6, Ranneft wrote in his diary:

> At 1400 to Navy Dept., the department is closed, except the division O.N.I. where a night watch is kept. Everyone present at O.N.I. confer Director Admiral Wilkinson, Capt. Mac Collum, Lt. Cmdr. Kramer . . . At my request, they show me *the location of the 2 carriers* (see 2-12-41) west of Honolulu.[73]

Ranneft's diary notes and a translation were published by John Toland in his book *Infamy*. Toland asserted that ONI tracked the task force en route to Pearl Harbor, which he supported by Ranneft's notes. Historian John Costello attacked Toland's conclusion:

> Toland supported his thesis by quoting an erroneous translation of an entry in the diary of the Dutch naval attaché in Washington. That material was withdrawn from subsequent editions of *Infamy* without explanation by the author.[74]

Actually, Costello was wrong. In addition Costello wrote, "When confronted with the correct translation . . . during a public lecture . . . Toland fainted."[75]

This lurid discrediting of Toland served to dismiss Ranneft's evidence that ONI had warnings of the Pearl Harbor attack. Ranneft later confirmed the accuracy of Toland's translation, saying that ONI had tracked the task force en route to Hawaii. He added that the location shown to him on December 6 was less than three hundred miles northwest of Honolulu.[76] It is worth emphasizing that here—as in other dismissals of warnings of the coming attack—the people presenting the evidence (Popov, Haan, and Toland) were discredited without refuting the evidence itself.

Costello gave no basis for his assertion of an "erroneous translation" and he published no correct translation. His innuendo that because of Toland's embarrassment over publishing an inaccurate translation, "That material was withdrawn . . . without explanation," was speculation and wrong. The first (hardcover) edition of *Infamy* was followed by a paperback edition, in which the illustrations were changed. The page from Ranneft's diary was an illustration in the first edition, and contained Toland's translation in its caption. It is true that this illustration was omitted from the paperback edition. But Toland also had a translation of the diary notes in the text of *Infamy*, and retained this in the paperback edition.[77]

Seaman Robert Ogg of the navy's San Francisco office provided information similar to Ranneft's. (Ogg hid his identity from the public and became known as Seaman Z.) According to his account, when ONI lost track of Japan's carriers in late November, the San Francisco office was ordered to locate them. During early December, his superior, Lt. Ellsworth Hosner, and he tracked the task force to a point near Pearl Harbor by radio direction-finding. Hosner confirmed Ogg's information. Ogg also said their chief, Capt. Richard McCullough, gave the reports directly to Roosevelt.[78]

Additional warnings or indications that Japan was preparing to attack Pearl Harbor are so sketchy that their value is hard to judge. One is a report that Hans Thomsen, a German diplomat in Washington, told Donovan that Japan intended to attack Pearl Harbor.[79] Another is that reporter Edgar Mowrer, sent to the Philippines as a secret agent for Donovan, reported a coming attack on Pearl Harbor. Mowrer later wrote that in November 1941:

> **Ernest Johnson of the U.S. Maritime Commission, who had just arrived [in the Philippines from Tokyo told me] ". . . the Jap Fleet has moved eastward, presumably to attack our fleet at Pearl Harbor."[80]**

The task force left Japan on November 25; presumably Mowrer was informed of this between November 25 and 31. He wrote that he informed Donovan and other civilian and military officials, and told them that Japan was also going to attack Guam.

A third warning is a statement by Representative Martin Dies, who had chaired the House Committee on Un-American Activities:

> **Early in 1941 the . . . Committee came into possession of a strategic map which gave clear proof of the intentions of the Japanese to make an assault on Pearl Harbor. The strategic map was prepared by the Japanese Imperial Military Intelligence Department . . . I telephoned Secretary of State Cordell Hull and told him . . . he directed me not to let anyone know . . . and stated that he would call me as soon as he talked to President Roosevelt. In about an hour he telephoned to say that he had talked to Roosevelt and they agreed that it would**

> be very serious if any information concerning this map
> reached the news services . . . . I told him it was a grave
> responsibility to withhold such vital information from the
> public. The Secretary assured me that he and Roosevelt
> considered it *essential to national defense*.[81]

According to Dies, ONI made a copy of his map, but no copy has been found. He did not say how his committee obtained it or how it indicated a coming attack on Pearl Harbor.

A fourth warning is Gen. Elliott Thorpe's statement. He was the U.S. Army representative to the government of the Dutch East Indies, headed by Gen. Hein ter Poorten. After the war Thorpe wrote:

> the most important thing I ever did as an army intelligence
> officer was to notify Washington of the forthcoming attack
> on Pearl Harbor. . . . General ter Poorten . . . said to me, "I
> have something here of great importance to your government"
> . . . and handed . . . me . . . an intercept of a message from
> Tokyo to the Japanese Ambassador in Bangkok . . . [which]
> told of the upcoming attacks on Hawaii, the Philippines, Ma-
> laya, and Thailand.[82]

Besides showing an intercept to Thorpe, ter Poorten reportedly sent a warning of a Pearl Harbor attack to the Dutch army attaché in Washington, Col. F. G. Weijerman, who relayed it to Marshall.[83] Thorpe's and ter Poorten's warnings have been discounted by statements that the United States lacked confidence in Dutch intelligence, but no basis was given for such a lack.[84]

A fifth warning is Stimson's testimony:

> I was shown by General Arnold the letter about the telegram
> and an order; so that . . . [meant a Japanese attack] might
> fall on either Hawaii or Panama.[85]

The letter, telegram, and order have not been identified. A sixth warning is that Donovan received a Pearl Harbor warning from the British.[86]

Still others warnings are that radio operators on the U.S. commercial ship *Lurline*, en route to Hawaii, heard messages they took to be from a Japanese fleet northwest of Pearl Harbor, and that another U.S. commercial ship sighted Japanese warships near Hawaii. And lastly, at the end of November, navy "intelligence officers reported that a large Japanese force had sailed out into the Pacific."[87] "Out into the Pacific" meant eastward.

A record of Thomsen's information was found. The *Lurline*'s radio log was turned over to a navy office in Hawaii shortly before the attack on Pearl Harbor. There is evidence that the Navy Department retained the log, but it can no longer be found.[88] Records of Thorpe's, ter Poorten's, and Mowrer's warnings are missing. So are Ogg's and Hosner's reports and what Ranneft said he saw in ONI.

Of all the warnings described in this chapter, none were provided to Short, and only one—the rumor heard by Grew—was sent to Kimmel. It was accompanied by an evaluation:

> The division of Naval Intelligence places no credence in these rumors. Furthermore, based on known data regarding the present disposition and employment of Japanese naval and army forces, no move against Pearl Harbor appears imminent or planned for in the foreseeable future.[89]

At the time, the comment was reasonable. But as the months brought more and more warnings—credible ones from authoritative sources with increasingly specific information—Kimmel and Short got no hint of them. As Kimmel complained, "This estimate as to the improbability of a move against Pearl Harbor was never withdrawn."[90]

According to some scholars, those who controlled intelligence denied Roosevelt warnings of the Pearl Harbor attack. A widely accepted view is that the main culprit was the army:

> can you imagine that at such a critical period in history, with war approaching, our Army for several months denied our Commander in Chief [Roosevelt] the most vital intelligence he needed?[91]

Another scholar commented on the army's action:

> That the commander in chief could be denied details of vital intelligence for a whole month [repeatedly] . . . must once and for all cast doubt on the credibility of the argument that an omniscient Roosevelt had advance warning of the Pearl Harbor attack.[92]

That the army withheld some intelligence from Roosevelt is true. Army intelligence was properly concerned about protecting sources of its information and especially about preventing Japan from learning that her diplomatic messages were being read. According to one account, G-2 learned that Gen. Edwin Watson, Roosevelt's assistant, carelessly tossed into a waste basket a Japanese diplomatic intercept given to the president.[93] Army intelligence, therefore, decided to give Roosevelt no more intercepts, only summaries. However, the idea that any intelligence officer had authority to cut the president off is mistaken. Roosevelt acquiesced to not receiving Japanese diplomatic intercepts from the army during that time. That Roosevelt was thereby denied crucial intelligence is misleading. During the months in which the army withheld intercepts from the president, the Navy and State Departments provided them to him.[94] Apparently Roosevelt did not see all diplomatic intercepts during those months, but he did receive those considered important. And besides reading intercepts, he had daily briefings on intelligence.

Some writers with access to British intelligence documents concluded that Churchill withheld warnings of the Pearl Harbor attack from the United States. The conclusion is speculative, and, as noted, there is evidence that the British did provide warnings to the United States.

Direct evidence of what top-level officials did know about the coming attack is scanty. As noted, Seaman Ogg said Roosevelt knew about the San Francisco office tracking Japan's attack fleet, and Congressman Dies said Hull and Roosevelt knew about the coming attack. Joseph Leib, a reporter and friend of Hull, said:

> [Hull] on . . . November 29, 1941 . . . revealed to me and gave me a copy of an intercept which showed that he had information that Pearl Harbor would be attacked the following week. I asked him if Roosevelt knew about it and he assured me that he had discussed this with the president. I asked him if the FBI knew about it. He assured me that he had talked to Hoover about it.[95]

According to Leib, Hull told him that Roosevelt was willing to risk a surprise attack on Pearl Harbor in order to get the United States into the war.

Army Col. Carlton Ketchum wrote that, early in 1942, Hoover told him, Congressmen George Bender and Leslie Biffle, and Assistant Attorney General Joseph Keenan (in Ketchum's words):

> [The FBI] had warnings from repeated sources from early fall, 1941, to within a few days before the Pearl Harbor attack, that it was coming, and that these warnings became more specific from one time to another . . . [and] the President had warnings during all that time, in addition to those he received

from Mr. Hoover, from . . . a Dutch embassy and the Dutch
Secret Service in the Far East . . . a British businessman . . .
British Secret Services in Hong Kong . . . some governmental
agency in Japan . . . [and] at least one other source.[96]

According to Ketchum, Hoover said that in December he received information about a Japanese carrier force approaching Pearl Harbor.

Don Smith was director of War Service for the American Red
Cross. According to his daughter:

Shortly before the attack in 1941 President Roosevelt called
him to the White House for a meeting concerning a Top Secret matter. At this meeting the President advised my father
that his intelligence staff had informed him of a pending attack on Pearl Harbor, by the Japanese. He anticipated many
casualties and much loss, he instructed my father to send
workers and supplies . . . He left no doubt in my father's mind
that none of the Naval and Military officials in Hawaii were to
be informed and he was not to advise the Red Cross officers
who were already stationed in the area. When he protested
to the President, President Roosevelt told him that the American people would never agree to enter the war in Europe unless they were attack[ed].[97]

Workers and supplies were sent and ten emergency medical stations
were hurriedly established in Hawaii prior to the attack.

In summary, warnings of the coming Pearl Harbor attack were
enough to justify a conclusion that such an attack was likely — indeed,
far more than enough. The administration probably withheld them
from Short and Kimmel for strategic reasons. One may have been to
protect the secret of having broken Japan's codes — to keep Japan from
changing them — preserving the U.S. advantage of reading her messages and anticipating her naval operations. Another was to prevent
Short and Kimmel from putting their commands on combat alert, which
would have prevented Japan from carrying out her planned attack.
Both reasons are supported by testimony, and are taken up in later
chapters.

CHAPTER 4
CHALLENGES TO THE MYTH

The administration succeeded in suppressing warnings of the Pearl Harbor attack until 1944, when intelligence officer Laurance Safford revealed some of them. Ripples from his information spread to Congress and to army and navy tribunals.

Hoping to clear themselves, in 1942 Short and Kimmel had requested to be tried by court martial. People who believed them responsible for the Pearl Harbor disaster demanded their court martial so they could be convicted and punished further. Roosevelt, however, reversed his decision to put them on trial, saying that would harm national security by revealing to Japan that her diplomatic codes had been broken.[1]

In August 1943, Kimmel again requested a court martial, but received no answer from Knox. Some military officers expected trials to be held, and Captain Safford began preparing to testify. An intelligence specialist and head of a unit in naval communications during 1941, he had handled intercepted Japanese messages indicating the coming attack on Pearl Harbor, and he expected to be called as a witness. According to his account, Safford had made notes in 1941 about the messages, but then destroyed them on Adm. Leigh Noyes's orders. To be able to testify authoritatively, in late 1943 he searched navy files for documents he had handled, and found they were missing. After speaking to coworkers, Safford concluded the missing documents had been destroyed and that Kimmel had been framed. He then arranged to meet Kimmel in January 1944 and tell him.[2]

Kimmel passed the information about warnings of the Pearl Harbor attack received in Washington on to members of Congress, fueling calls for a congressional investigation. Perhaps as a result, in March 1944, Knox ordered a limited investigation of the Pearl Harbor disaster by Admiral Hart. Reportedly Knox did so out of sympathy for Kimmel, intending it as an alternative to granting his request for a trial and in hopes the Hart investigation would clear him.[3]

Hart's secret investigation heard Safford's evidence that Washington had advance knowledge of the Pearl Harbor attack from intercepted Japanese diplomatic messages. Hart made no official finding, but reportedly concluded privately that the Navy Department in Washington was responsible for the Pearl Harbor disaster.[4] The evidence Safford gave to Hart strengthened Kimmel's position, and Kimmel went back to Congress with it.

In the summer of 1944, Congress passed a joint resolution calling for full investigations of the Pearl Harbor disaster by the army and navy. The services responded immediately, and an army board and naval court conducted simultaneous investigations from July to October.

Meanwhile the presidential and congressional election campaigns began, and Republicans used rumors about Pearl Harbor, information leaked from the new investigations, and hints of secret evidence, to discredit the administration. In September Representative Forest Harness said in Congress that, three days before the attack, the Australian government had advised the United States that a Japanese carrier force was heading for Hawaii.[5] His allegation provoked much talk in Washington.

The administration then learned that Republican presidential candidate Thomas Dewey was about to reveal that the United States had broken Japan's diplomatic codes. He meant to discredit his opponent, Roosevelt, by showing that he had known in advance of the Japanese attack and done nothing. Hearing of this, Marshall sent his assistant, Col. Carter Clarke, to dissuade Dewey by appealing to his patriotism. Clarke told Dewey that Marshall's only purpose was to protect the most vital source of combat intelligence, and thereby to save troops' lives. He said, if Japan learned her codes had been broken and changed them, the U.S. war effort would suffer. Clarke also handed Dewey a letter from Marshall, which included:

> The vital element in the Pearl Harbor matter consists of our intercepts of the Japanese diplomatic communications . . . [from which] we possessed a wealth of information regarding their moves in the Pacific . . . but which unfortunately made no reference whatever to intentions toward Hawaii until the last message before December 7th, which did not reach our hands until the following day, December 8th . . . You will understand . . . the utterly tragic consequences if the present

political debates regarding Pearl Harbor disclose to the enemy . . . any suspicion of the vital sources of information we possess.[6]

Much of the letter was false. Clarke told Dewey that no diplomatic intercept identifying Pearl Harbor as Japan's target had been translated before December 7, and that Japanese diplomatic intercepts had enabled the United States to win her first victory in the naval battle of Midway and specifically to kill Japan's most important naval officer, Admiral Yamamoto.

Doubting what Clarke and Marshall told him, Dewey feared being manipulated. According to Clarke's official report of the meeting, Dewey said, "Franklin Roosevelt . . . knew what was happening before Pearl Harbor and . . . ought to be impeached."[7] Nonetheless, after consultation, Dewey agreed to Marshall's request. With the administration claiming that secrecy about breaking the diplomatic codes was vital to the war effort, he evidently feared that exposing it would make him vulnerable to attack as a traitor.[8] So the code-breaking remained secret from the public for another year.

Japanese diplomatic messages were only a minor source of military intelligence, and had played no role in the victory at Midway or the killing of Yamamoto. The most important source—the one that contributed to the previously mentioned and subsequent victories—was intercepted Japanese naval messages. Consequently the breaking of Japanese naval codes was a secret well worth keeping in 1944. Presumably Dewey did not know that secret. The main harm in his intended revelation was the harm he meant—discrediting Roosevelt during the election campaign.

Despite rumors and accusations that he had received advance warning of the Pearl Harbor attack, Roosevelt won a fourth term and the Democrats retained a majority in Congress. But the accusations did add to administration concerns. According to War Undersecretary Robert Patterson, Roosevelt "worried for fear there would be an adverse report by the [army board] just before Election . . . and was anxious to have termination of the inquiry postponed until after Election."[9] His fear was reasonable. The Army Pearl Harbor Board's report contained only moderate criticism of Short, putting most of the responsibility for the disaster on Marshall and his staff. And the Naval Court of Inquiry's report cleared Kimmel, putting responsibility on Stark. Stimson and Navy Secretary James Forrestal (replacing Knox, who had died in April) ordered publication of the reports—due two weeks before the election—to be delayed until afterward.[10]

On receiving an advance summary of the army board's report, Stimson noted:

> While I am not criticized explicitly in the report, the report does criticize Marshall and Gerow for things that I knew about and participated in and I have got therefore to be very careful not to be biased in the action I take.[11]

Nonetheless, in consideration of the harm to Roosevelt and Marshall the report could cause, Stimson took arbitrary action beyond delaying its publication.

Learning in November of the army board's still-secret findings, Marshall told Stimson they would destroy his usefulness and he would have to resign.[12] (Marshall had been an outstanding chief of staff before and during the war, and would go on to become secretary of state, contributing to the restoration of western Europe from the ravages of war.) Stimson noted in his diary, "I told him that was nonsense, to forget it," and added that Marshall "was very grateful for . . . the fight that I was making for him."[13] Although he did not specify "the fight," it may be inferred from what followed.

In discussing the army board's report with Roosevelt on November 21, Stimson said, "Congress could get after us, get at the papers and get at the facts."[14] According to Stimson, Roosevelt said, "we must take every step against that and we must refuse to make the reports public. He said that they should be sealed up."[15] Roosevelt meant the naval court's report as well as the army board's.

Stimson then took measures not only to prevent publication of the army board report, but also to overturn its findings. He impugned the character of board members and had Judge Advocate General Myron Cramer write an endorsement to the report, which concluded: "I am of the opinion that none of the Board's conclusions as to General Marshall are justified."[16] Stimson also appointed Maj. Henry Clausen of Cramer's staff to conduct an additional investigation that would change the evidence on which the army board had relied in reaching its findings.

The officially stated purpose of Clausen's investigation was to pursue "unexplored leads" in order to complete the record. Cramer gave Clausen a list of twenty-five leads. It included other officers' actions, but not Marshall's or Stimson's. Clausen later testified before the joint congressional committee that, in exploring one lead, he reviewed testimony Marshall gave to the army board,

and I suggested that this led to the White House . . . and I was

told that it was beyond the scope of my functions to investigate there.[17]

The lead to which he referred was a highly controversial secret
agreement made among the United States, Great Britain, Canada, and
the Dutch government in exile for joint military action (see chapter
10). (When rumors of the agreement had surfaced in 1941, the administration had vehemently denied them.) And in a book he wrote many
years later, Clausen made clear that the purpose of his investigation
was to exonerate Marshall and prove Short guilty.[18]

Stimson had read to the army board excerpts from his diary containing material damaging to the administration's position. During the
congressional investigation that followed, Clausen was asked if he had
read the diary.

> Clausen: No, sir.
> Question: Why not?
> Clausen: Well, you mean I should investigate the investiga-
> tor? That would be like the grand jury investigating the grand
> jury. You told him to do the job.[19]

By "investigate the investigator" Clausen meant that Stimson was in
charge of the investigation that he (Clausen) conducted — that Stimson
directed it. By "You told him to do the job" he meant that Congress
had put the investigation in Stimson's hands. Clausen was asked who
told him not to investigate members of the administration, and he said
Cramer did.[20] Clausen was implying that, if his investigation was bi-
ased, Congress was at fault. In calling for army and navy investigations, Congress had not specified that they be done by independent
bodies.

Forrestal was less sympathetic to Kimmel than Knox had been.
He made a public announcement that the naval court had decided to
keep its report secret. This reportedly led to an argument between
him and the court's head, Adm. Orin Murfin, who said the court meant
for its findings and proceedings to be published, except those parts
revealing the breaking of Japanese codes. Forrestal told Murfin to mark
the entire report secret. Murfin refused.[21] Then, on his own authority,
Forrestal suppressed the report.

In addition, Forrestal arranged for an endorsement to the naval
court's report to be written by the navy's judge advocate general, Adm.
Thomas Gatch, reversing the court's findings.[22] Still further, Forrestal
had Admiral King, then head of the navy, sign an endorsement to the
court's findings, reversing them. Reportedly King said after the war

that he did so without reading the evidence compiled by the court, that the endorsement he signed was written for him, and that he did not even read that. And in 1948 he withdrew the endorsement he had made in 1944.[23]

Gatch was also sympathetic to Kimmel. Perhaps for that reason, the endorsement he wrote was so strained and self-contradictory as to suggest he too was told what to write and was troubled about it. In the preface to his endorsement, he wrote that his proper role was to comment only on whether the court's findings were supported by its own evidence or not. And where there was evidence both for and against a finding by the court, "it is not within the province of the Judge Advocate General to substitute his evaluation for that of the Court."[24] Then Gatch discredited testimony about warnings received in Washington of a coming attack on Pearl Harbor by saying the witnesses "were not on duty in the Navy Department at that time" and,

> Their testimony is opinion evidence, *undoubtedly uncon-sciously colored by hindsight*, and arrived at by a process of selecting, from the great mass of intelligence reports . . . those which in the light of subsequent events proved "indicative."[25] (Italics added.)

He meant that intelligence that had not impressed officers beforehand as indicating that Pearl Harbor would be attacked did impress them in retrospect.

Gatch may have been right about the witnesses' unconscious mental processes but, since he had no evidence of their mental processes, his use of the word "undoubtedly" was rhetorical. The naval court had produced evidence for and against its finding that the Navy Department had had advance warning of the attack. By the above statement, Gatch offered his evaluation of evidence and rejected the naval court's evaluation, violating his own injunction.

In an endorsement to the report of a subsequent navy investigation by Adm. Kent Hewitt, Gatch recommended that "Admiral Hewitt's investigation be made available to Admiral Kimmel . . . that Admiral Kimmel be informed that he is free to make public anything contained in this record and in prior records."[26] As noted, King was also sympathetic to Kimmel, but he postponed Kimmel's access to the material until after the war.[27]

Informed that the naval court's unpublished report exonerated him, Kimmel asked Gatch what would happen if he (Kimmel) published an account of it, including "secret matter" — presumably Japanese diplomatic intercepts. According to Kimmel, Gatch replied, "You would be brought to trial before General Court Martial on charges you had divulged secret matter and you would be convicted, thereby confusing the whole issue and absolutely discredit[ing] you."[28] Kimmel asked Gatch's advice about publishing an account without the secret matter, and Gatch said that "the Navy Department would merely state that you are a liar and you would be unable to prove any of your contentions unless you reverted to the secret matter."[29] Kimmel dropped the idea.

The army board and naval court reports were kept secret for a year. But leaks indicated that they exonerated Short and Kimmel while putting responsibility on Marshall and Stark. To counter the leaks and to counter clamor for release of the reports, Stimson and Forrestal announced in December 1944 that releasing the reports would harm the war effort. They added — contrary to fact — that the army and navy investigations showed Short and Kimmel to be responsible for the Pearl Harbor disaster. But their failure was not dereliction of duty; it was only poor judgment, which did not justify court martial. Stimson and Forrestal said the investigations found that unnamed people in the War and Navy Departments in Washington had also shown "inadequacies" or "errors of judgment" contributing to the disaster — minor failings not calling for disciplinary action. The secretaries further said they were dissatisfied with the military tribunals' reports, and Forrestal added that he would investigate further.[30]

Their announcements failed to assure the nation; clamor for an independent investigation grew stronger. By the summer of 1945, with Germany defeated and Japan's surrender in sight, concerns about military security were fading. Democratic leaders in Congress finally decided to go along with Republicans' demands for a public investigation.

Meanwhile the secret investigations ordered by Stimson and Forrestal were proceeding. Forrestal chose Adm. Kent Hewitt, who was reportedly sympathetic to Kimmel. Hewitt later said that carrying out his investigation was a "very disagreeable duty," adding:

> Secretary Forrestal had some very set ideas . . . and he wanted me to find things which I could not find. I think he was disappointed that I didn't make a report in accordance with some of his ideas.[31]

Hewitt did not specify Forrestal's "set ideas"; indications of them may be seen in what follows.

Soon rumors arose that Clausen and Hewitt's counsel, John Sonnett, were coercing witnesses to change their testimony. The witnesses were military officers on whom the army board and naval court had relied in arriving at their conclusions. The rumors—which would prove true—increased the pressure on Congress. More shocking still was testimony in the Hewitt investigation that Marshall had ordered mass destruction of documents bearing on Pearl Harbor (see chapter 5).

The Clausen and Hewitt investigations set the stage for sensational hearings in Congress. They also increased polarization between Democrats and Republicans, which would hamper the congressional investigation. The Clausen and Hewitt investigations—contrary to their purpose—further loosened the lid on controversial administration strategies, operations, and other secrets. And despite its misgivings, Congress then plunged in. Besides conducting its own investigation, it published the still-secret reports of the prior investigations—Knox's original report, the Roberts Commission's, Hart's, the army board's, the naval court's, Clausen's, Hewitt's, and Clarke's two-part report. Clarke had first addressed allegations of tampering with army records and then the specific charge that Marshall ordered them destroyed.

The joint congressional committee arrived at mixed findings, which settled few major questions. Its majority report put most of the responsibility for the Pearl Harbor disaster on Short and Kimmel. Its minority report put most of it on officers in Washington. The congressional investigation did, however, produce an extremely valuable forty-volume record—a wealth of documents and some surprisingly candid testimony. The record became a rich source of data and of leads—a source still not exhausted. The data and the dozens of books on Pearl Harbor it spawned led to increasing pressure on succeeding administrations to release more documents, which they did slowly until President Jimmy Carter ordered hundreds of thousands of naval intelligence documents released. Material from all the investigations is taken up in later chapters.

CHAPTER 5
SECRECY AND COVER-UP

A cover-up began when Roosevelt changed Knox's report and controlled the Roberts Commission's investigation. Secrecy and cover-up — including manipulation of information, hiding it, and destroying it — have connotations of improper government practices and worse. Tampering with witnesses, perjured testimony, and suborning perjury are criminal in themselves and typically parts of criminal conspiracies. These activities are, however, commonplace in government operations across the world.[1] They are routine responses to serious charges against governments and do not set the Roosevelt administration apart from others.

Political controversy over Pearl Harbor and the investigations and research it fostered put operations of Roosevelt's administration under microscopic examination, which shows no sign of ending. Zealous partisans called him a traitor for government actions that ordinarily escaped scrutiny and criticism. Moral and legal judgments are outside the purpose here. Government secrecy and cover-up were, however, important in establishing the administration's accounts of Pearl Harbor as history.

As the Roberts Commission began its work, evidence was suppressed, at first by orders to military personnel against testifying about certain matters. Various officers collected documents and notes bearing on Pearl Harbor — some from central files, others from officers' individual files. Most of these records disappeared.[2] Some were destroyed, others hidden for a few years, and a great many remained hidden for thirty-eight years. And some are still classified as secret.

Miles testified before the Army Pearl Harbor Board in 1944:

> I am a little worried . . . because I was told, this morning, by
> Military Intelligence that there are numbered gaps in their

files today, and they do not know where those messages are.[3]

Safford testified that Adm. Leigh Noyes had called a meeting of communications division officers shortly after the Pearl Harbor attack and said, in Safford's words:

> if we knew anything *let it die with us*, pass that word to our subordinates . . . Furthermore, if you have got any notes or anything in writing destroy them."[4] (Italics added.)

And Noyes testified:

> I have no recollection of that particular meeting . . . but I would be perfectly willing to stand behind that order.[5]

When the Army Pearl Harbor Board was established in 1944, Marshall and his deputy chief of staff, Gen. Joseph McNarney, took measures preventing it from gaining access to documents bearing on the Pearl Harbor disaster.[6] They were so effective that, the board was concluding its investigation without awareness of Japanese diplomatic intercepts containing warnings of the attack until Kimmel drew its attention to them.[7]

When the army board asked him whether the War Department withheld information from it, Marshall said, "Well, I don't know." Perhaps to make the question gentler, a board member said, "I cannot imagine that it is intentional," and Marshall responded:

> The only thing I can think of . . . is that everybody concerned with this top secret thing is very cagey about saying anything about it . . . And naturally he feels no freedom whatever to speak about it unless he is especially authorized.[8]

But in later testimony to the congressional committee, Marshall said McNarney had arranged with Admiral King for military witnesses to withhold evidence. And Miles said about his appearance before the army board:

> I so limited my testimony . . . because . . . General Russell A. Osmun and then Colonel Clarke . . . transmitted to me instructions from the Chief of Staff [Marshall] that I was not to disclose . . . any facts concerning the radio intelligence.[9]

Osmun had also been designated to handle the army board's requests for army documents. He kept many documents from the board, while telling it he had provided everything requested.[10]

Navy witnesses had also limited their testimony before the Roberts Commission. Three decades later Adm. Arthur McCollum — then a commander in ONI in 1941 — wrote that before testifying to the congressional committee he had been ordered "not to reveal anything of a secret nature."

> I was told that I shouldn't discuss . . . codebreaking. The Judge Advocate General . . . [Oswald] Colclough said that at the direction of Admiral King he'd have to give me this warning . . . I was ordered . . . to talk with the chief of staff of the Atlantic Fleet . . . Commodore Oscar Smith, and he handed me a . . . secret document that had been issued by ComInch warning everybody of the penalty of being hung at the yard arm, not to discuss anything attendant upon code-breaking.[11]

"ComInch" meant "commander-in-chief," a term commonly designating the president, but which also could refer to a fleet commander, and apparently meant Admiral King in this instance. That evidence was kept from the congressional committee is better documented than that it was hidden from other tribunals. On August 28, 1945, when Congress was considering an investigation, the new president, Harry Truman, issued an order to the secretaries of state, war, and the navy, the attorney general, the joint chiefs of staff, and heads of other agencies:

> to take such steps as are necessary to prevent release . . . except with the express approval of the President . . . of . . . Information regarding . . . status, techniques . . . success obtained, or any specific results of any cryptanalytic unit.[12]

Congress passed its resolution to investigate the Pearl Harbor disaster in September. On October 5, the joint committee's chairman, Senator Alben Barkley, wrote to heads of government agencies and to Truman himself, asking them to appoint representatives to assist in obtaining documents and witnesses. Within ten days Barkley got replies from department heads and Truman, promising full assistance to the committee and designating representatives for the task. For example, War Secretary Robert Patterson replied:

> Lt. Col. Harmon Duncombe has been designated as the

representative of the War Department for the purpose of assisting the joint congressional committee to investigate the disaster . . . He will have full access to all pertinent files and records of the War Department . . . The War Department is prepared to furnish all information in its possession pertinent to the investigation.[13]

And Forrestal replied:

Please be assured that the Navy Department stands ready to render full assistance to the committee and its counsel, making available . . . all information material to the investigation.[14]

It is worth noting that these promises to cooperate fully with the committee were made while Truman's order limiting cooperation was in effect.

The committee saw a copy of Truman's order, and Congress put pressure on him to rescind it. In response, Truman modified it a few times, writing on October 23:

a specific exception to my memorandum dated August 28, 1945 . . . is hereby made as follows. The State, War, and Navy Departments will make available . . . any information in their possession material to the investigation, and will authorize any [personnel] . . . to testify concerning any matter pertinent to the investigation.[15]

But in a follow-up memo on November 9 — just before the committee began holding hearings — Truman specified that government personnel could give evidence "orally" but, "This does not include any files or written material."[16] And despite Truman's revised order, members of the administration continued coercing army and navy officers to suppress information.

Forrestal designated Colclough and Capt. John Baecher as representatives to the committee for supplying it with records. They also had the task — unknown to the committee — of preventing navy officers from testifying on certain matters. They did help the committee obtain thousands of government documents, but they also helped prevent it from obtaining tens of thousands of documents. ONI, for example, had received more than two hundred warnings of the Pearl Harbor attack; it provided twenty of them to the committee, continuing to hide the existence of the rest.

Baecher gave navy witnesses a memo:

> Admiral Colclough wants to be sure each witness . . . before
> the Joint Congressional Committee . . . has a copy of the Presi-
> dential Directives concerning testimony.[17]

Appended to the memo was:

> The Presidential Security Directive . . . prohibits . . . informa-
> tion regarding any specific results or degree of success ob-
> tained by any cryptanalytic unit. . . . The President modified
> his directive to allow any witness to testify . . . regarding
> cryptanalytic activities which had to do with . . . the Pearl
> Harbor incident.[18]

Despite Truman's modification, instructions to witnesses by Colclough, Baecher, and King served to suppress testimony and records about warnings of the Pearl Harbor attack.

The State Department had received warnings of the coming attack from informants and had seen warnings received by ONI. From what is known so far, the State Department provided none to the committee, nor did it inform the committee of their existence.[19] The FBI, administratively under the attorney general, provided the committee with documents containing hints of the coming Pearl Harbor attack— hints so obscure as not to be grasped. The FBI also had in its files clearer warnings of the attack, which it withheld from the committee.[20]

Other tribunals had smaller staffs than the congressional committee. The Army Pearl Harbor Board had a tiny staff and depended on government agencies to identify and supply needed documents. It noted:

> We have not had the opportunity, nor the organization, to
> comb personally and exhaustively the official files, but we
> have called for the pertinent letters, documents, and
> memoranda. We believe that practically all of them have
> been secured.[21]

One board member, Gen. Henry Russell, thought the opposite—that many intelligence documents had been withheld from the board.[22] And what came out in later years supported his impression.

As to warnings of the Pearl Harbor attack, the board wrote in a brief top secret report (separate from its main report):

> Information from informers and other means as to the activi-
> ties of our potential enemy and their intentions . . . [provided]

a reasonably complete disclosure of the Japanese plans and intentions . . . [and] potential moves against the United States. . . . This information showed clearly that war was inevitable and late in November absolutely imminent. The messages actually sent to Hawaii . . . gave only a small fraction [of] this information. . . . [Then] during the fateful period between November 27 and December 6, 1941 . . . numerous pieces of information came . . . indicating precisely the intentions of the Japanese including the probable exact hour and date of the attack. . . . Up to the morning of December 7, 1941, everything that the Japanese were planning to do was known to the United States except the . . . very hour and minute when the bombs were falling on Pearl Harbor.[23]

The report omitted who the informants were, what the "other means" were, and the particulars of their information. All that remains unknown. Probably it included some of the warnings in chapter 3.

The top secret report added that no message based on warnings received after November 26 was sent to Hawaii. Actually Marshall did send a warning to Short based on information received December 7, but delayed it despite strong urging by his staff. It reached Short after the attack.[24]

The number of hidden and missing navy documents alone was probably more than three hundred thousand.[25] And the War Department, the State Department, and other agencies had also destroyed records. According to a career officer in the State Department, in February 1942, his colleagues began destroying warnings of the attack on Pearl Harbor and altering "hundreds of documents" that contradicted the administration's account of events leading to it.[26] Testimony about destruction of records was given only in Hewitt's and Clarke's investigations.

The official justification for suppressing evidence was "national security." At first the phrase's meaning was limited to outcomes of combat during the war in progress. Intelligence obtained from Japanese naval messages did affect outcomes of combat until the end of the war, justifying keeping that code breaking secret. Suppressing codebreaking secrets also served the political purposes of shielding the administration and fostering national unity. Both political purposes could be argued as in the nation's interest during wartime. And such arguments could be countered. Meanings of "national security" other than the narrow one are arguable. The phrase has served presidents since World War II to disguise their suppression of records in protecting themselves from scandal and impeachment.

Most of the Pearl Harbor investigations were conducted during the war. By the time of the congressional investigation, however, the war was over. Nonetheless, King threatened navy personnel with severe punishment if they revealed the breaking of Japan's codes.[27] Earlier, after the army board completed its report, Judge Advocate General Cramer gave to Stimson a legal opinion about which army personnel—regular army, draftees, or reservists—could be court-martialed for having revealed classified information to the board. Cramer also pointed out that, regardless of army status, they could be prosecuted in federal courts for violating the Espionage Act![28]

The army board and naval court were partly aware that evidence was withheld from them. Kimmel had asked the Navy Department for access to warnings of the Pearl Harbor attack—a request denied. At his urging, the naval court asked for them, and the court's judge advocate reported:

> **The Secretary of the Navy replied . . . 10, August 1944, that the material requested "cannot be furnished as it is not in the public interest to introduce this type of material in evidence before the court of inquiry."[29]**

Kimmel then argued passionately that the documents were necessary to the court's purpose. He urged that, if it did not want to introduce them as evidence, the court should at least examine the documents in secrecy, even if he did not see them. Whatever followed was deleted from the court's report "in the interest of national security and the successful prosecution of the war." There are many such deletions from the court's record.[30] (Some of the deleted material was later restored.)

Harder to estimate is the congressional committee's awareness of what was withheld from it. McCollum said he did not reveal the restraint under which he testified. Nor did other military witnesses. As noted, many officers evaded questions about code breaking and its results without explaining their evasion. And when pressed, they lied. Other officers, however, testified candidly about code breaking.[31]

In administration efforts to control testimony and documents provided to the joint committee, the main issue was the extent to which government leaders knew about the coming attack. Some witnesses had testified to the army board and the naval court in 1944 about warnings. To get them to change their testimony, Major Clausen and counsel Sonnett used authority and coercion. For example, when confronting generals, Clausen showed them an order from Stimson, requiring their cooperation. Authority was particularly effective with career military officers, who feared that noncooperation would harm their careers.[32]

When the subject of witness tampering came up during the congressional hearings, Clausen and Sonnett vigorously denied any intention of getting witnesses to change their testimony or any coercion. Although they said so over and over, they had done both. According to Colonel Bratton, Clausen showed him his (Bratton's) testimony to the army board, along with affidavits contradicting it, and said:

> Now, after you have read these affidavits and considered the matter and tried to refresh your testimony, do you wish to make any comment on this point . . . in your testimony?[33]

Clausen confirmed Bratton's testimony, but denied improper intent.

In a memo about getting Bratton to revise his testimony, Clausen wrote that Bratton had originally testified that he had delivered a warning of Japan's coming attack to various top-level officials: "But in his affidavit to me made when his memory was more refreshed, he admitted he could not recall with any degree of accuracy, and that there were no records [of the deliveries]."[34] By saying Bratton's memory was "refreshed," Clausen meant he had confronted him with affidavits given by Bratton's superiors. Bratton had to choose between saying his superiors were wrong or changing his testimony. And Col. Otis Sadtler described Clausen using the same means to get him (Sadtler) to change his testimony.[35]

During the congressional committee hearings, evidence about attempts to change witnesses' testimony made little impression. Forty-seven years later, however, Clausen published a book about his investigation. On page after page, he described his intention and efforts to get witnesses to change their testimony, including attempts literally to terrify them. He boasted over and over about how much fear and anger he aroused in them:

> If an individual appeared reluctant to talk . . . I would open up my shirt and pull out . . . [a] document . . . That's what I did with Captain Layton, for example. The look of surprise on his face when I did my striptease act was worth the price of admission.[36]

The shock of Clausen's "striptease act" was enhanced by the fact that, in opening his shirt, he exposed an explosive pouch strapped to his chest, powerful enough to kill him and the witness. It was from this pouch that he pulled documents with which he confronted witnesses. He described himself as "a walking bomb" and added:

> Other people I interviewed flinched visibly when I first showed
> them the papers I was carrying. Others began to drip with
> sweat. The result was that one by one they changed or ampli-
> fied the stories they had told previously under oath.[37]

Clausen did not say if he told witnesses that the pouch contained
explosives. It was a standard explosive pouch, available in army stores.
Presumably some witnesses had seen such pouches before and recognized what Clausen's was. The words Clausen used in describing his
"striptease" suggest that they knew:

> I went to the bomb range at Fort Myer, I carefully packed the
> [pouch] with fifty carbon copies of unimportant letters and
> detonated it from a distance. It flared up, like a million
> matches going off at once. Not a shred of paper could be
> found. I also deduced that not much of me would be found,
> either. But at least it would be effective and quick.
> I then picked up another bomb pouch from supply and called
> on Maj. Gen. John Bissell.[38]

Clausen then described the fear and anger he aroused in Bissell.

The stated purpose of Clausen's pouch was to prevent Japanese
diplomatic messages he carried from falling into enemy hands if he
were captured when he entered war zones to interview witnesses. If
captured, he was to detonate the pouch. But he confronted Bissell in
Washington, far from any enemy and, according to his account, his
pouch contained no documents then — just explosives.

Much controversy developed over a matter of little importance.
Safford had drawn Kimmel's and tribunal investigators' attention especially to what became known as the "winds execute" — a message
he said was missing from navy files. On November 19, 1941, U.S. intelligence had intercepted a Japanese diplomatic message setting up a
special code for emergency use. If war with the United States, the Soviet Union, or Great Britain were about to begin, and if diplomatic
codes could not be used, Japanese diplomats abroad would be warned
using a winds code. One or more of three phrases would be inserted
in an ordinary Tokyo radio news program as if it were an ordinary
weather forecast. The phrases were:

Higashi no kaze ame. (East wind, rain.)

Kita no kaze kumori. (North wind, cloudy.)

Nishi no kaze hare. (West wind, clear.)

On hearing any of the three, Japanese embassy and consulate officials
in the indicated country were then to execute a prior order to destroy

code machines, codes, and other documents. Hence each of the three phrases was called a "winds execute" by U.S. cryptographers, who interpreted the phrases — correctly — to mean an attack on the United States (east), on the Soviet Union (north), and on British territories in Asia (west), based on the directions of those lands from Japan.

That a message establishing the winds code was intercepted and understood by U.S. intelligence is not in question. Whether an execute message was sent and received by the United States before December 7, 1941, became the subject of conflicting testimony and heated controversy. Safford told the Hart Inquiry and the naval court that a winds execute was received on about December 4 and that copies of it had been destroyed.[39] (A few years after the fact, lacking records, witnesses differed about the date on which they said a winds execute had come in, also giving December 3 and December 5. They also differed on what the Japanese words were.[40])

Military intelligence had taken the message setting up the winds code very seriously. Admiral Noyes had ordered several navy radio stations to monitor Tokyo radio for a winds execute. To ensure correct identification, he had provided radio operators with cards carrying the winds phrases in Japanese. And he had asked the Federal Communications Commission to have nonmilitary radio stations also listen for a winds execute. Army intelligence had also made a special effort to intercept it, as had British and Dutch East Indies radio stations.

The implications of Safford's testimony were that the Navy Department knew by December 5 that a Japanese attack was coming within a few days, that it did not inform Kimmel, and that it covered up having received the message. His testimony figured in the naval court's exoneration of Kimmel and placement of responsibility for the Pearl Harbor disaster on Stark. While Safford was testifying before the naval court, Sadtler of army intelligence testified before the army board about receipt of a winds execute. This contributed to the army board's substantial exoneration of Short and placement of responsibility for the disaster on Marshall. After the naval court and army board completed their investigations, the administration mounted a campaign to discredit witnesses who testified that a winds execute had come in, to coerce them to change their testimony, and to get other witnesses to contradict them.

When the message establishing the winds code came in on November 19, intercepting a winds execute had seemed vital. By December 5, however, the government had more specific information of an imminent Japanese attack, and intercepting a winds execute had lost much of its value. But the administration campaign made the alleged winds execute a major point of controversy in the congressional hearings and in books about Pearl Harbor. For sixty years, the controversy distracted attention from warnings that specified Pearl Harbor as Japan's target.

Hewitt's assistant, Sonnett, met with Safford three times before Safford testified during the Hewitt Inquiry. According to Safford, on each occasion Sonnett said:

> You are the only one who seems to have ever seen the Winds Execute message.
> It is very doubtful that there ever was a Winds Execute.
> It is no reflection on your veracity to change your testimony.
> It is no reflection on your mentality to have your memory play you tricks—after such a long period.
> Numerous witnesses that you have named [as having knowledge of it] have denied all knowledge of a Winds Execute message.
> You do not have to carry the torch for Admiral Kimmel.

According to Safford, Sonnett "attempted to make me believe I was suffering from hallucinations."[41]

By the time Sonnett testified, the congressional committee had already heard from other witnesses that a winds execute had come in. On that basis, Representative Frank Keefe challenged Sonnett:

> Sonnett: Captain Safford . . . had named certain people as having seen the winds-code message, the execute . . . We interrogated all of them and . . . none of them . . . saw the message . . .
> Keefe: Well, I don't agree with that at all. The testimony is quite to the contrary before the committee.
> Sonnett: Not the testimony I am referring to . . . The people named by Captain Safford as having seen the winds execute testified before us [himself and Hewitt] that they had not seen such a message.
> Keefe: Captain Kramer . . . certainly did not testify that he did not see this winds execute.
> Sonnett: Well, I don't know what he testified to here, Mr. Congressman; I haven't been following this inquiry that closely, but I do know that before Admiral Hewitt he was unable to testify or state that he ever saw a genuine winds-code message prior to the attack relating to the United States.[42]

The last qualifications brought Sonnett's testimony closer to the truth, but it was still basically misleading. Sonnett had interviewed officers who insisted they had seen a winds execute before December 7.

More disturbing than the challenge to Safford's sanity was a challenge to Kramer's, with the threat of mental hospitalization. Kramer had suffered a breakdown in 1942, during which he continued to report for duty but was incapable of work. Early in 1945, he had a brief mental hospitalization and a longer one after Sonnett's coercion of him. A neighbor and friend of Kramer, Adm. Robert Weeks, later said Kramer told him in 1945 that he was ordered "to speak right or undergo more mental treatment."[43] One of the matters on which he was told to change his testimony was the winds execute.

Kramer had testified with conviction before the naval court about seeing a winds execute before December 7. Asked if he or his coworkers had any doubt that the words heard on the radio were a winds execute, he answered, "This is very simple language and there was no doubt whatsoever" and that the message was *Higashi no kaze ame* (indicating war with the United States). He said he was "quite certain" of the words.[44] After coercion, Kramer's testimony became confused, vague, and self-contradictory. To the congressional committee he said that he had hardly glanced at the message, that he had read it, and that he was no longer sure what the words were.[45]

With coercion of witnesses, with contradictory, shifting testimony, and with records lacking, exactly what happened cannot be established. The Army Pearl Harbor Board concluded that a genuine winds execute had come in and:

> This original message has now disappeared from Navy files and cannot be found. It was in existence just after Pearl Harbor and was collected with other documents for submission to the Roberts Commission. Copies were in existence in various places but they all disappeared.[46]

Although it is unclear on what evidence the army board relied, it is established that several army and navy officers believed that during the days before the attack a winds execute did come in. They may have mistaken an ordinary Japanese weather forecast for a winds execute. But if an officer mistakenly believed an intercepted weather forecast was a winds execute, he was responsible for taking action on it, leading to a warning being sent to the Pacific commands. For example, Noyes heard what he believed at the time to be a winds execute, and had a warning to Pearl Harbor drafted. He said he learned later that the intercepted weather forecast was not a genuine winds execute. But that was not the reason for aborting the warning to Pearl Harbor. It was aborted by Stark — while the winds message was still taken to be a genuine execute — on the grounds that Pearl Harbor had already been warned enough and needed no new warning.[47] A telling fact is that officers who believed a winds execute came in did urge sending a warning, but their superiors refused. And that contributed to the naval court's and army board's findings that officers in Washington had withheld key intelligence and warnings from Kimmel and Short.

On the list Safford had given Sonnett of officers who said they had heard a winds execute or heard that one came in before December 7 was Warrant Officer Ralph Briggs, a radio operator. At Safford's suggestion, the congressional committee called Briggs as a witness. But he was ordered by his captain not to testify, and did not. (Army Maj. Warren Clear, who in 1941 had obtained intelligence of the coming attack on Pearl Harbor, was also ordered not to appear before the committee, and did not.[48]) Later Briggs went on record, saying himself had intercepted the winds execute. Also reported to have known of it, but not called as witnesses, were Thomas Mackie of U.S. Naval Intelligence, Commander Cedric Brown, and Lieutenant H. C. Dixon of the British navy. And Sonnett should have known that still others, including Adm. Royal Ingersoll, refused to budge from statements that they had heard a winds execute before December 7.

Noyes told the congressional committee that, four months before testifying, he knew that he, Safford, and Kramer would be called as witnesses. Knowing also that their testimony before the naval court was in disagreement, he had phoned Safford, suggesting a meeting of the three to try to come to an agreement about testimony they would give to the committee. Noyes added that he told Safford, concerning a winds execute:

> Why can't you get me something, if it is true; some record that we can get together on. He [Safford] said that [the winds execute] came in at Winter Harbor [Navy radio station] . . . and they have destroyed their records. *I didn't want to put any pressure on Captain Safford to change his opinion.* I just told him that I had no recollection of it, and *he would have to show me something* to indicate that there was an authentic execute.[49] (Italics added.)

Safford and Kramer were his subordinates, which gave his words authority, as if he said, "Find a record of a winds execute or stop saying one came in." Noyes himself had given orders to destroy records of intercepted weather broadcasts, and may have known Safford could not find a winds execute.[50]

As Safford was testifying before the committee, Sonnett gave a statement to the press:

> I discovered that Captain Safford was the only source of erro-
> neous rumors concerning the existence of [a winds execute]
> message . . . It should be borne in mind that, of the many
> people named by Captain Safford in previous testimony as
> having knowledge of the "Winds message," not a single one
> recalled the existence of such a message. It is impossible to
> believe that all these witnesses could be wrong.[51]

Despite the falseness of Sonnett's statements — despite available testimony (some of it in the congressional hearing record) refuting them — Sonnett was effective. A committee counsel confronted Safford with much the same words Sonnett had used:

> Now, it is a fact, isn't it, Captain, that every single witness
> who has testified on . . . having received or seen a Winds
> Execute message, testifies that they never saw one; isn't that
> a fact? Every single one of them.[52]

And the same argument was later used by writers to discredit Safford.[53]

Besides the winds execute, the administration took a stand against testimony that intelligence, understood by cryptographers to mean a likely Japanese attack on December 7, was delivered to ranking military officers on the evening of December 6. There is no question that a Japanese diplomatic message so understood was intercepted on December 6 and decoded that afternoon. The administration sought to prove that key officers did not receive it until the next morning.

The people responsible for delivering intelligence had been Kramer (to naval officers and the president) and Bratton (to army officers and the State Department). They both testified to the naval court and army board that they delivered the message during the evening of December 6. A civilian member of Kramer's staff, Eunice Rice, later said that Kramer was "instructed on orders from above to deny delivering the message."[54] Changing Bratton's testimony was Clausen's responsibility. According to Bratton, Clausen showed him his own testimony to the army board about making the deliveries, and then challenged him with ten affidavits contradicting it. As Clausen — who had been a prosecutor — described the confrontation in his book:

> [Bratton] seemed to grow smaller and he looked very sad and droopy, as if he had been caught . . . like an impaled fish. I had seen that look before: when I had a criminal dead to rights on the witness stand.
>
> Bratton had the same look on his face as he read the [affidavits]: Two-star General Deane, three-star General Gerow and three-star General Smith said Bratton had lied. He was trussed up like a Christmas goose.[56]

What the generals had said was that they had not received the intercept on December 6.

After this confrontation, Bratton gave the affidavit Clausen wanted, recanting what he had said to the army board. Then he repeated his recantation to the congressional committee:

> I testified before the Grunert [Army] Board that I had made delivery to [Colonel Walter Bedell Smith], to the night duty officer, or to General Gerow and to General Miles. That was my normal procedure . . . Since making that statement . . . I withdraw that statement . . . since making this statement to the Grunert Board I have been shown . . . affidavits by General . . . Bedell Smith, General Ralph Smith, General Gailey, General Gerow, and others . . . that they did not receive the [message] . . . Saturday night. Now I know all these men. I do not doubt the honesty and integrity of any one of them, and if they say I did not deliver these pouches to them that night, then my memory must have been at fault.[57]

Weeks later he said privately that he had, in fact, made the deliveries on December 6.[58] Gen. Walter Bedell Smith had testified before the army board that Bratton did make the delivery to him on the evening of December 6. When Clausen pressed Smith about that testimony, he signed an affidavit saying that he had left the office at 7 P.M. (which was before Bratton made his deliveries), implying that Bratton did not make the delivery to him. Clausen then used Smith's affidavit to persuade Bratton to change his testimony. Later Smith contradicted his own affidavit and affirmed his earlier testimony, stating again that Bratton did make the delivery to him on the sixth.[59]

Stark and Marshall testified that they did not receive the December 6 message until Sunday morning. When asked where they were at the time of the alleged delivery on Saturday evening, they said they could not remember. This aroused much speculation. Because Roosevelt and others who saw the message Saturday evening concluded it meant war within a day or so, people assumed Roosevelt got in touch with his top subordinates.[60]

Marshall—with a reputation for a "photographic memory"—was pressed on his activities during the evening of December 6 by the naval court. He answered, "I don't know where I was. I never thought of it until this instant."[61] He gave his most vehement testimony to the congressional committee in denying contact with Roosevelt during that evening and night. Asked if Roosevelt called him, he said, "I am quite certain that he did not." Asked, "And you are quite certain that you did not attend any meeting . . . at the White House that night?" he said, "I am absolutely certain of that."[62]

Stark was also asked by the congressional committee if he went to the White House that evening. In denying it, his testimony was more vehement than on any other point: "I am absolutely certain of that," and "I am certain the President did not call me that night."[63] To a question about a rumored top-level conference at the White House that evening, he answered:

> I never heard of such a conference, I know nothing now regarding such a conference, I was not present at it, I had never even heard anyone suggest such a thing until it was mentioned here . . . My honest opinion is that nothing of the sort took place. It was a complete surprise to Marshall that even the question came up. It was to me. I am certain that I did not leave the house after the Kricks left. I just can't think of any such thing as happening. Certainly I was not present, and Colonel Knox never mentioned any such thing to me.[64]

Later, evidence would come to light that Knox—Stark's immediate superior—was the source of an account of a conference at the White House on Saturday evening, attended by himself, Marshall, and Stark.[65]

The Kricks—Capt. Harold Krick and his wife, friends of the Starks—pointed out to Stark that his testimony before the congressional committee about that evening was wrong. Stark then asked the committee for an opportunity to amend his testimony, and testified that he and his wife had spent part of that evening with the Kricks and he had spoken to Roosevelt late that evening by phone.[66]

Privately, Stark said he had been evasive on orders from "higher authority." For that reason, his conscience was clear. Later he said the same in public.[67]

Similarly, while evading questions by the congressional committee, Marshall was overheard whispering to a senator that he could not say where he was during the night of December 6 because saying it would get "the chief" in trouble. By "the chief" he was understood to mean Roosevelt (who had died several months earlier). Years later he wrote that the committee's "political purpose [was] to embroil President Roosevelt," and said, "Remember that the investigation was intended to crucify Roosevelt, not to get me."[68]

Besides Stark and Marshall, so many military officers testified that they simply could not remember key events and had no idea where they were on the evening of December 6, that reporters commented sarcastically on an epidemic of amnesia in Washington. Also, officials simply did not answer troublesome questions put to them by investigators. They avoided some by invoking "national security," usually without explaining how the nation would be endangered by their answers. Hull and Stimson flatly refused to answer many questions. Military officers avoided answering questions by changing the subject. For example, asked by the congressional committee why the army withheld documents from the army board, Marshall brought up another subject. Asked again, he changed the subject again. Finally he gave a vague, speculative answer, as if he knew nothing about the withholding. The question was dropped.[69]

After thoughts of resigning when the army board found him responsible for the Pearl Harbor disaster, Marshall faced another accusation. William Friedman, a civilian in army intelligence, was asked during the Hewitt Inquiry what he knew about a winds execute coming in. Friedman answered that Otis Sadtler said he had heard about one, and added:

> I asked Colonel [Sadtler] whether he had a copy, had ever gotten or seen a copy of this message, and his answer was . . . that he hadn't himself seen a copy, but that he had been told . . . that the copies had been ordered . . . to be destroyed by General Marshall.[70]

Hewitt and Sonnett seemed to take no more notice than if Friedman had commented on the drinking water. Sonnett continued to ask Friedman about a winds execute, while Hewitt remained silent. Shortly afterward, Hewitt excused Friedman with polite thanks for his testimony. What Hewitt did do, however, was write to Marshall:

> Enclosed herewith for your information is a copy of Mr. Friedman's testimony . . . Since the statements referred to by Mr. Friedman . . . were allegedly based on information supplied to him by an officer of the Army, I am of the view that the matter should not be further pursued in my investigation.[71]

Hewitt's explanation — that he did not pursue the allegation because it came from an army officer — was probably for the record. He was also told by Safford that navy documents were missing — apparently destroyed — and did not pursue that either.

On receiving Hewitt's letter, Marshall assigned his assistant Clarke to deal with the allegation. Clarke held an investigation, calling Friedman to testify. Asked the source of the story about Marshall ordering destruction of records, Friedman repeated that Sadtler was. Called in turn, Sadtler named as his source Gen. Isaac Spalding. And in his turn, Spalding testified that in 1943, Gen. John Bissell was briefly under his command. They became friendly and, while drinking together, Bissell told him that he himself had destroyed army documents about Pearl Harbor.[72]

Bissell had been a member of Marshall's staff at the time of the alleged destruction. When called, he testified that he had destroyed no documents, nor had he ever spoken to Spalding about such a matter. He said that nothing he had mentioned to Spalding could be a basis for Spalding's testimony.

Clarke concluded his investigation with the finding that the alleged destruction of documents had not happened. He gave no basis for rejecting Spalding's testimony and accepting Bissell's. Nothing in Clarke's investigation record supported Bissell's testimony over Spalding's. Clarke, however, had personal knowledge bearing on the allegation. According to Marshall, in 1944, "Colonel Carter Clarke [had] charge of the most secret documents of the War and Navy Departments."[73] Years later — then a general — Clarke told historian Charles Tansill and Gen. Bonner Fellers that he had been present when Marshall ordered his staff to suppress evidence related to Pearl Harbor, adding, "Gentlemen, this goes to the grave with us."[74]

In Clausen's descriptions of people he interviewed, his questions disturbed Bissell the most by far. "He was not pleased to see me. He became furious when I . . . started to tell him what I needed." According to Clausen, Bissell wrote down Clausen's name to intimidate him, then picked up the phone to call Marshall and have him stop Clausen's investigation. In turn, Clausen threatened Bissell, who then stopped raging and offered to cooperate. What Clausen asked of Bissell was "every decoded Japanese message . . . intelligence evaluations for the twelve-month period before Pearl Harbor . . . anything that related to Pearl Harbor. Bissell turned puce while he listened."[75] If Spalding's testimony is valid, Bissell probably took Clausen to be asking for documents that Bissell had destroyed.

The congressional committee asked Marshall if he had ordered destruction of Pearl Harbor documents. Twice he did not answer and the third time he said, "I had no knowledge of it whatsoever."[76]

An important source of information about Japan's attack plans was British intelligence. Whatever it provided was also withheld from the Pearl Harbor tribunals. Senator Homer Ferguson of the congressional committee asked Marshall if "estimates" provided by British intelligence had been turned over to the committee, and he answered:

> I am quite certain that would not be in your records, sir, because we have been trying to keep that quiet as much as we could.

Seemingly shocked, Ferguson pressed Marshall, and he changed his answer:

> Ferguson: Now, then, General Marshall, do I understand we are not getting every bit, that certain things are being kept quiet, that we are not getting?
> Marshall: No, sir; I do not mean that at all.
> Ferguson: Have there been any instructions to G-2 that we were not to get all the files . . . relating to Pearl Harbor?
> Marshall: No, sir; none whatever.
> Ferguson: Then I do not quite understand that previous answer that that probably would not be given to us.
> Marshall: Well, I must have misled you.[77]

Ferguson may not have been as puzzled as he sounded, for Miles had already testified about orders from Marshall to withhold information.

The administration's cover-up included many important matters. The most important was that Washington had received ample warning of the Pearl Harbor attack. The cover-up's main effect was to maintain the position that Roosevelt and his subordinates had not known of the coming attack — that it had caught them by surprise.

CHAPTER 6
THE ACCUSED

The navy's judge advocate general had prepared charges against Kimmel that he failed

> to keep the ships of his . . . command ready for battle . . . to execute a defensive deployment . . . to provide . . . a proper and sufficient distant reconnaissance although means were available for such reconnaissance . . . to consult, confer and cooperate with [Short] with respect to measures to be taken . . . for joint defense . . . to put into effect . . . a state of alert and of readiness . . . [and that] shore batteries . . . and antiaircraft artillery on board vessels . . . were not manned and supplied with ammunition.[1]

The army's judge advocate general drew up similar charges against Short, but recommended against trying him because of difficulties in winning a conviction and "the defense would certainly attempt to pass part of the blame to the War Department."[2]

Short and Kimmel were not brought to trial, and the congressional committee's majority report, holding them responsible for the Pearl Harbor disaster, became the final official judgment of them by a tribunal. In this chapter, the question is: was the judgment against them warranted? Implications of the answer go far beyond the question.

The administration position was that it ordered them to defend Pearl Harbor by two dispatches sent on November 27, 1941, which were prompted by a crucial development the day before. On November 26, the administration decided to present a highly demanding note to Japan, expecting her to go to war against the United States in response. As Roosevelt made the decision to send the note, he directed the army and navy to send war warnings to commands in the Pacific. The one sent to Kimmel read:

> This dispatch is to be considered a war warning. Negotiations with Japan looking toward a stabilization of conditions in the Pacific have ceased and an aggressive move by Japan is expected within the next few days. The number and equipment of Japanese troops and the organization of naval task forces indicate an amphibious expedition against either the Philippines, Thai or Kra peninsula or possibly Borneo. Execute an appropriate defensive deployment preparatory to carrying out tasks assigned in WPL 46. Inform District and Army authorities. A similar warning is being sent by War Department. Spenavo inform British. Continental districts Guam, Samoa directed to take appropriate measures against sabotage.[3]

"WPL 46" was a detailed war plan defining the navy's tasks. "District" meant the Fourteenth Naval District, with headquarters in Hawaii — an autonomous administrative unit, commanded by Adm. Claude Bloch, somewhat under Kimmel's authority. "Army authorities" meant Short and his staff. "Spenavo" meant the U.S. special naval observer in London. And "continental districts" meant naval districts on the U.S. West Coast. Guam and Samoa are U.S. possessions between Japan and Hawaii.

For this analysis, key words were "war warning . . . Execute . . . defensive deployment . . . WPL 46." The obvious meaning of "war warning" was the intended one. Stark testified about the phrase:

> These words were carefully weighed and chosen after considerable thought and discussion with my principal advisers and with the Secretary of the Navy . . . we gave most careful consideration before making this a war warning."[4]

Their weighing of words centered on the question of how strong to make the warning, which they made weaker and weaker. "Defensive deployment" seemed obviously to mean that Kimmel was to go on full alert for defending Pearl Harbor. But, as will be seen, it did not.

The corresponding dispatch to Short (#472) was:

> Negotiations with Japan appear to be terminated to all practical purposes with only the barest possibilities that the Japanese Government might come back and offer to continue. Japanese future action unpredictable but hostile

action possible at any moment. If hostilities cannot repeat not be avoided the United States desires that Japan commit the first overt act. This policy should not repeat not be construed as restricting you to a course of action that might jeopardize your defense. Prior to a hostile action you are directed to undertake such reconnaissance and other measures as you deem necessary but these measures should be carried out so as not repeat not to alarm civil population or disclose intent. Report measures taken. Should hostilities occur you will carry out the tasks assigned in Rainbow five so far as they apply to Japan . . . Limit dissemination of this highly secret information to minimum essential officers.[5]

"Rainbow five" was the overall war plan.

Gen. Henry Russell of the Army Pearl Harbor Board wrote that the last sentence "was crippling in its effect" on army forces in Hawaii and fostered failures by personnel to respond to sightings of Japanese submarines and planes. He argued that, instead, Short should have been told to share the dispatch with all his personnel.[6] Another limitation was the order not to alarm civilians. And repetition of it — "not repeat not" — gave it emphasis.

Stating that negotiations with Japan "appear to be" terminated weakened the warning. A draft had said negotiations were terminated. No negotiations were in progress, but formally the diplomatic talks had not ended. Both governments expected hostilities to begin within days. Meanwhile, for strategic purposes, Tokyo and Washington continued to maintain the illusion that talks were to continue, which deceived Short and Kimmel.

For purposes of this analysis, the key words in the dispatch to Short were "let Japan commit the first overt act . . . defense . . . undertake . . . reconnaissance."

In accepting as valid the charge of disobedience against Short and Kimmel, the nation accepted the administration position that the two dispatches ordered them to defend Pearl Harbor against a surprise combat attack. In the popular view, it is taken for granted that the sender of a message knows what it means. And what the sender says it means is ordinarily taken to be true. If a misunderstanding arises, the receiver of a message is ordinarily presumed to be at fault. But that is only a presumption. As counsel to the congressional committee noted, the opposite presumption is equally valid, for "the man who wrote a document was the poorest man to interpret it, because he was always thinking of what he meant to say instead of what he did say."[7] And military manuals instructed officers in detail on how to make

orders clear, because misunderstandings might cause grave consequences. An army manual from the time included:

> Supervision of Execution. The responsibilities of the com-
> mander and his staff do not end with the issue of necessary
> orders. They must insure receipt of the orders by the proper
> commanders, *make certain they are understood*, and enforce
> their effective execution.[8] (Italics added.)

And understanding is not a simple matter because, as the Army Pearl
Harbor Board wrote:

> The vital [War Department] message of November 27 . . . can
> be understood and its proper place . . . determined only when
> we know the events which led up to its being sent . . . and the
> circumstances under which it was forwarded.[9]

Context determines the meaning of words; it can even change the obvious meaning of a word into its opposite. The more ambiguous a
message, the more important context is.

To scientists who study communication and specialists who practice it — notably military communication workers — a message is clear
(regardless of the sender's intent and even regardless of the apparent
meaning of the words used) *only if it is clear to the recipient*. Since the
lay view and the expert view differ, the point is worth emphasizing.
In operational terms, messages not understood by recipients are unclear messages. And not only Short and Kimmel, but also their staffs
took the November 27 dispatches to mean something rather different
than what the senders said they meant.

Communication workers use checks to insure that messages are
understood as intended:

> Do you understand? (In military jargon, "Do you read me?")
> What did I say?
> Report measures to be taken in response to this message.

In addition, key parts of messages are emphasized and repeated, and
messages themselves are repeated, sometimes with new phrasing. The
more vital a message, the more use of emphasis, repetition, and checks.

The check of having Short report measures taken was used, which
made the apparent failure of communication especially puzzling. Short
immediately reported the measures he took. Therefore his superiors
knew — or should have known — that the order which they insisted

meant to defend Hawaii against a military attack had been under-stood to mean defending it against sabotage by civilians. Nonetheless, they did nothing to correct him. And there is considerable evidence that the administration's declaration of what the messages meant was misleading.

One reason Washington sent different dispatches to Kimmel and Short was that they were assigned different tasks. Kimmel's were primarily offensive; Short's, defensive. The army detachment on Oahu had the responsibility of defending the island (especially Pearl Harbor) and Kimmel's fleet against attack—any form of attack. Expected forms were raid, invasion, and sabotage. Under some circumstances, Kimmel's fleet was to assist the army, but otherwise defense of Pearl Harbor was not his assigned responsibility.

The dispatches to Kimmel and Short will be taken up under three headings—reconnaissance, defense against sabotage, and defense against a military attack. In his dispatch, Kimmel was not told to conduct reconnaissance, but he and Short were required to share information and to cooperate. In addition, the Navy Department took the unusual measure of sending Kimmel a copy of the dispatch to Short.[10] Sending it emphasized that Kimmel was also responsible for reconnaissance.

Reconnaissance was undefined in the dispatch to Short, and the ambiguity was deliberate. General Gerow, mainly responsible for drafting it, so testified.[11] Both dispatches were written after thorough top-level discussion extending over a day and a half. Revised repeatedly, the dispatches involved an extreme level of attention—an obsessive concern—rare in writing orders. And during the revisions, the ambiguity of the dispatches increased. The main increase in ambiguity was about whether Short and Kimmel were to put their troops on combat alert or not.

Reconnaissance could take the form of patrol by planes, surface ships, and submarines. Approaching enemy ships could also be detected by radar and by intercepting radio messages from them. Radar—with a maximum range of 120 miles—could not provide warning of an approaching force while it was far enough away to stop planes from reaching Hawaii. Surface ships and submarines could provide reconnaissance far enough away, but could not cover the vast area around Hawaii.

"Reconnaissance" in Short's dispatch has been taken for six decades to mean long-distance plane patrol all around Hawaii, which is what Short and Kimmel were charged with failing to carry out. It was a reasonable reading of the dispatch based on the words. And Short's responsibility to defend Pearl Harbor and the fleet supported reading it that way. But in view of Short's lack of planes and of his standing orders *it was not a task he could perform.*

In January 1941, just before Short and Kimmel were assigned to Hawaii, the naval air chief there, Adm. Patrick Bellinger, had expressed his frustration about lack of equipment — especially planes — in an extraordinarily aggressive letter to Stark:

> I arrived here . . . with the point of view that the International situation was critical . . . and I was impressed with the need for being ready today rather than tomorrow . . . After taking command . . . I was surprised to find . . . we were operating on a shoestring . . . *This . . . indicates to me that the Navy Department does not view the situation in the Pacific with alarm* or else is not taking steps in keeping with their view.[12] (Italics added.)

Stark emphasized Hawaii's lack of planes to Marshall in February, but Marshall did not see it as crucial. In the spring and summer, he sent new bombers to the Philippines and Panama rather than Hawaii. According to the official record of a conference between Stimson and Marshall, "The Secretary of War asked if this would affect the impregnability of Hawaii. Marshall said it would not."[13] He had already assured Roosevelt in a long, detailed memorandum:

> The defense of Oahu, due to its fortification, its garrison, and its physical characteristics, is believed to be the strongest fortress in the world.
> *Air defense.* With adequate air defense, enemy carriers, naval escorts, and transports will begin to come under attack at a distance of approximately 750 miles. The attack will increase in intensity until when within 200 miles . . . the enemy forces will be subject to attack by all types of bombardment closely supported by our most modern pursuit [planes] . . .
> In point of sequence, sabotage is first to be expected and may cause great damage.[14]

He suggested that Hawaii's air defenses were substantial and would be increased, making "a major attack against Oahu . . . impractical."

Washington did not increase Pearl Harbor's defenses significantly. And in the autumn of 1941 the War and Navy Departments barred Short and Kimmel from taking active defense measures. Orders to them against intercepting approaching Japanese forces were vague, except for specific orders not to fire on approaching Japanese submarines. Despite the vagueness, the orders were effective in stopping them from taking measures to defend Pearl Harbor and other military installations in Hawaii against a combat attack.

The War Department considered a major increase of Hawaii's defenses until July 1941, when Roosevelt made a decision to arm the Philippines. According to Marshall, that decision meant no more long-range planes for Short — no more planes for distant patrolling around Hawaii or for bombing Japanese carriers before they launched their bombers.[15]

On assuming their commands, Short and Kimmel had their air chiefs do analyses of defense needs. The resultant report by Gen. Frederick Martin and Admiral Bellinger of March 1941 was approved in Washington. A remarkably accurate forecast, it included:

> It appears that the most likely and dangerous form of attack on Oahu would be an air attack. It is believed that ... such an attack would most likely be launched from one or more carriers which would probably approach inside of three hundred miles ... In a dawn air attack there is a high probability that it could be delivered as a complete surprise in spite of any patrols we might be using.

The report therefore advised:

> Run daily patrols as far as possible to seaward through 360 degrees to reduce the possibilities of surface or air surprise. This would be desirable but can only be maintained with present personnel and material for a very short period and as a practical measure *cannot, therefore, be undertaken* unless other intelligence indicates that a surface raid is probable within rather narrow time limits.[16] (Italics added.)

In July the War Department asked Short for a further study of his defense needs. The new report made the same points as before and emphasized:

> The only manner in which the Hawaiian area can be thoroughly searched for enemy surface craft, particularly aircraft carriers ... is to provide a sufficient number of aircraft to conduct daily search . . . during daylight hours with 100% coverage through 360 degrees.[17]

To search for and attack enemy carriers, the report recommended adding 180 long-range (B-17) bombers and thirty-six medium-range torpedo bombers to Short's air force.

The War Department allocated the recommended 180 B-17s to Short, but did not send them. Some were sent instead to the Philippines, passing through Hawaii en route. Awareness that planes were being sent to the Philippines, and not to Hawaii, contributed to Short's and Kimmel's impression that defense of Hawaii against an air attack had low priority in Washington. Martin and Bellinger apparently knew by the summer of 1941 that Marshall was describing Pearl Harbor as "impregnable," because they added to their report:

> It has been said . . . that Hawaii is the strongest outlying naval base in the world and could, therefore, withstand indefinitely attacks and attempted invasions. Plans based on such convictions are inherently weak and *create a false sense of security*.[18] (Italics added.)

Before the November 27 dispatches, responsibility for carrying out distant reconnaissance around Hawaii had not been assigned to Short or Kimmel by their standing orders or by specific orders. Short's standing orders emphasized defending Pearl Harbor by operating antiaircraft batteries and interceptor planes, by installing a radar system for detecting approaching enemy planes, by doing aerial reconnaissance *only up to 20 miles off shore*, by guarding against civilian sabotage and other subversive actions, and mainly by training his troops. When the attack would come, flight personnel at the army's Hickam Field would be engaged in training exercises. His standing order to carry on training would limit his forces' response to approaching Japanese planes. And he was not authorized to do long-distance reconnaissance all around Hawaii.[19]

The day before receiving his November 27 dispatch, Short had been ordered to send two planes on reconnaissance over Japan's Mandated Islands. The order was a long one, detailing exactly what the planes were to accomplish and how to carry it out, which marked it as especially important. Naval intelligence had detected warships assembling in those islands, which were west of Hawaii.[20] (The intelligence was correct in identifying submarines and small surface ships there. Its identification of two aircraft carriers there was wrong.) On receiving the November 27 dispatch, Short took its unspecified "reconnaissance" to mean the mission over the Mandated Islands. Apparently his take on it was correct. Gerow was asked by the Roberts Commission about the reconnaissance ordered in it, and said:

We had had reports of Japanese [navy] concentrations in the
Mandate Islands, and we felt that every effort should be made
to identify Japanese movements in that direction.[21]

(Before the congressional committee, however, Gerow testified as other
officers did: the reconnaissance ordered on November 27 meant patrol of the seas all around Hawaii.)

By written, standing orders, only Admiral Bloch was responsible
for distant reconnaissance around Hawaii. He carried responsibility
for coordinating his own, Kimmel's, and Short's forces for defending
the Fourteenth Naval District — an enormous area which included islands far from Hawaii. But the forces Bloch commanded were very
small. Bizarrely, distant reconnaissance remained his responsibility
even though he had no equipment with which to do it. In December
1940 he had written to Stark:

The Navy component of the local defense forces has *no planes*
for distant reconnaissance with which to locate enemy carriers, and the only planes belonging to the local defense forces
to attack carriers when located would be the Army bombers.[22]

(Bloch did not include the fleet's planes because, as far as he knew, the
fleet was only temporarily stationed in Hawaii.) Promised one hundred patrol planes by Stark, Bloch testified, "I did my utmost to implement my responsibility by demanding patrol planes for that purpose,
but I never had any; I never had one."[23]

He was entitled to borrow Short's and Kimmel's patrol planes,
but not before war broke out or Washington ordered War Plan 46 to
be executed — which did not happen before December 7. During 1941
Bloch repeatedly asked Kimmel for planes and Kimmel repeatedly
refused, once saying, "We'd have so many under maintenance if we
frittered them away in distant reconnaissance that we'd have none
ready for a real attack." With parts for repairs unavailable, running
daily patrol all around Hawaii would disable his patrol planes indefinitely. Besides, added Kimmel, he needed the planes to carry out training.[24] Testimony by Army Air Corps Chief Arnold supported Kimmel's
position: "We figured that they were wasting the striking force on reconnaissance missions so that when we had to use the striking force
they would not be available."[25]

In October 1941 Bloch wrote again to Stark, reminding him of
their correspondence about the need for planes and other equipment
for defense. To emphasize the situation's urgency, he noted, "Nearly
all the failures of the British . . . have been 'Too little and too late.' It is

hoped that we may profit from their errors."[26] Kimmel endorsed Bloch's plea. Stark replied that no planes and hardly any other equipment were available for Hawaii.

On November 24 Stark informed Kimmel that war with Japan was imminent, and the next day wrote to him:

> **The Department has no additional airplanes available for assignment to the 14th Naval District. Allocations of new aircraft squadrons which become available in the near future will be determined by the requirements of the strategic situation as it develops.[27]**

This meant Kimmel and Bloch should not expect to receive planes before war broke out, and they did not. It meant that maintaining distant reconnaissance all around Hawaii would continue to be impossible. It also implied that the Navy Department no longer expected a Japanese attack on Hawaii.

To detect approaching carriers in time for an effective defense required patrol of the seas for a distance of about seven hundred miles — patrol over about 1.5 million square miles of ocean. Assuming patrol crews could see as far as fifteen miles on most days, that required about 250 patrol planes.[28] In his May memo, Marshall had assured Roosevelt that an approaching Japanese carrier force could be attacked when 750 miles from Hawaii. For planes based in Hawaii to fly 750 miles to attack Japanese carriers required discovery before they came within nine hundred miles of Hawaii. That required patrolling about 2.5 million square miles of ocean. Marshall did not say how many patrol planes were required. By the projections above, it was more than four hundred — more patrol planes than the United States had.

Distant patrol required planes with a long range of operation — army bombers or navy patrol bombers (PBYs). But Short's and Kimmel's planes were mostly short-range fighters. Short had six planes capable of distant patrol. On paper he had twelve, but six were disabled indefinitely. Parts had been removed to repair the other six and to repair planes transferred to the Philippines. (Of Short's 149 fighter planes, sixty-nine were disabled for lack of parts.)[29]

Kimmel had eighty-one planes capable of distant patrol. But during the days before December 7, on Washington's orders, some of Kimmel's planes were assigned duties near the "outlying islands" around Hawaii and near other islands. Johnston Island, the nearest, was 820 miles away; Wake, the farthest, was 2,300 miles from Pearl Harbor. In addition, Kimmel had received orders to prepare to carry out air raids on Japan's Marshall Islands, and he held planes in reserve for that operation. The planes deployed in the outlying islands and held in reserve were unavailable for reconnaissance around Pearl Harbor. In addition, fifty-four of Kimmel's eighty-one patrol planes been delivered in autumn 1941 as replacements for obsolete ones. They "were experiencing the usual shakedown difficulties of new planes and their maintenance was hampered by an almost complete absence of spare parts."[30]

The War and Navy Departments were repeatedly informed of equipment shortages in Hawaii before November 27. In acknowledging the shortage of patrol planes there, the departments took responsibility for the Hawaiian commands' inability to carry out distant reconnaissance all around Pearl Harbor.[31]

Perhaps Washington's failure to supply planes for reconnaissance reflected a change in strategic thinking about what was required to defend Hawaii against a carrier-based attack. A War Department memo in 1936 had concluded:

> it would appear that long-range [planes] . . . while of assistance in the defence of Oahu, would not solve the problem presented and, therefore, would not justify the great initial and continuing expenses.[32]

And a Navy Department study had concluded that the speed of modern aircraft carriers and bombers made aerial patrol obsolete as a timely means of detecting an attack force. The study also concluded that developments in intelligence — particularly the breaking of Japanese naval codes in 1930s — enabled the navy to locate the entire Japanese fleet! Accordingly, an ONI report covering 1941 concluded:

> The greatly increased tempo of warfare which has come with aircraft, together with the vast areas over which hostilities have spread, have imposed upon our intelligence activities difficult problems never before encountered . . . The areas covered are so great that reconnaissance has become inadequate.[33]

On the other hand, according to the report, intelligence could not only detect the movements of enemy fleets but also reveal their intentions — their targets.

We lack direct evidence that the study's findings were adopted as the basis of Washington's planning for Pearl Harbor's defense. But in October 1940, Stark's assistant wrote to Pacific naval commanders that, by penetration of Japan's naval codes, "Every major movement of the Orange fleet has been predicted."[34] And while making no effective attempt to supply enough planes for patrol around Hawaii, the administration multiplied intelligence operations to discover Japanese war plans.

The September 1941 war games — the last games ordered by the Navy Department — were based on the premise that warning of Japan's approaching fleet would come from intelligence. Accordingly, during the games, Kimmel received simulated intelligence sent by the Navy Department and, in response, sent an order to units of his fleet playing the role of defenders:

> **Radio intelligence indicates [attack] force of considerable size heading for Pearl from position within 30 miles of latitude 26° 15' north longitude 161°00' west . . . Interpose and engage.**[35]

"Radio intelligence" meant intercepted Japanese naval messages. The position was about 350 miles north of Pearl Harbor.

Returning to the November 27 dispatch, distant reconnaissance all around Hawaii was impossible to carry out, even though the administration later said the November 27 dispatch directed it to be carried out. And when sending the dispatch to Short, Washington knew that it was impossible to carry out. Generals Marshall, Arnold, and Miles, and Admirals Stark, Ingersoll, and Turner testified that they knew about the crucial shortage of patrol planes in Hawaii.[36]

During wartime, impossible orders may be issued in desperation or haste, but such conditions did not apply. Even though the November 27 dispatch to Short was written with elaborate care, surviving drafts and testimony from officers who worked on it contain no hint that they considered the reconnaissance ordered impossible to perform — or even difficult!

With about thirty bomber and patrol planes available, Short and Kimmel were equipped to patrol an eighth of the seas around Hawaii — to maintain patrol in one direction only.[37] As noted, based on intelligence, Washington ordered Short to send patrol planes west, toward Japan's Mandated Islands, but the attack on Pearl Harbor came from a different fleet, north of Hawaii. Specific orders to Kimmel and amplifying letters to him from Stark carried no indication that he was ever expected to carry out reconnaissance to the north or all around Hawaii.

If the dispatch to Short meant reconnaissance toward the Mandates, it was not only feasible but also consistent with standing orders. An order to maintain distant reconnaissance all around Pearl Harbor would have contradicted Short's and Kimmel's standing orders to continue training. Consequently it would have called for the sender to mention the contradiction and tell them to disregard standing orders. Orders for Short and Kimmel to carry out training remained in force up to December 7. (Meanwhile, in late November, Washington ordered MacArthur's air corps to stop training flights and maintain readiness for an attack by Japanese planes based on Taiwan.[38]) And when asked why the warning sent to Kimmel November 27 had not been stronger, Stark testified, "Admiral Kimmel was confronted with problems, and very difficult problems, of training." And Stark wanted the training continued.[39]

For an effective defense of Hawaii and the fleet at anchor against a carrier-based air attack, it was necessary to detect approaching carriers and bomb them before they launched their planes — before they came within three hundred miles of Hawaii. But the dispatch to Short cautioned against these actions with the restriction "that Japan commit the first act." Although the restriction was qualified by the next sentence, it was crucial because of political considerations, which are taken up in later chapters.

Stark emphasized the first-strike limitation to Kimmel. In sending him a copy of the November 27 dispatch to Short, he added, on Roosevelt's instructions, "Undertake no offensive action until Japan has committed an overt act."[40]

To conclude on the charges involving reconnaissance, both Short and Kimmel interpreted the dispatch of November 27 to mean reconnaissance west of Hawaii. In the context of what reconnaissance the army and navy in Hawaii were equipped to do, and of the intelligence received about a Japanese fleet assembling in the Mandates, and of other dispatches about reconnaissance, theirs was a reasonable interpretation. To interpret the order to mean they should perform reconnaissance all around Hawaii — an impossible task that violated their standing orders — was unreasonable.

Kimmel's predecessor, Adm. James Richardson, had feared a Japanese attack on the fleet after it was stationed at Pearl Harbor (see chapter 9). Richardson had brought this danger to Stark's attention repeatedly, with increasing concern, but received only vague assurances. Finally he had informed Stark that "to provide a reasonable degree of security calls for employment of a great number of fleet units for security alone, which could otherwise . . . [be] used for training."[41] And Richardson had ended with a statement that he was issuing orders for full security measures. This violated his standing order to give training top priority, and prompted Roosevelt to remove Richardson from command and replace him with Kimmel. And at Stark's direction, Richardson had turned over to Kimmel his correspondence with

Stark.[42] That correspondence emphasized a basic fact: Kimmel had no authority to violate his standing order giving priority to training. Neither did Short.

"Defense" was also unspecified in the dispatch to Short. He was responsible for defense against all types of attack. On receiving the dispatch, he did nothing about defense against a raid or invasion. He did increase defense against sabotage to a wartime level by having sentries posted at bridges, roads, and utilities. Where sentries had already been posted, he doubled them. And he had planes bunched on airstrips so that sentries could easily watch them, preventing sabotage. The bunching delayed their take off when the attack came, and made them easy targets for Japanese bombers.

The dispatch gave Short no specific order to take these measures. And the literature on Pearl Harbor has carried the presumption that the dispatch's reference to defense meant against a raid or invasion. In fact, however, Short was implementing Washington's *known intentions*. A draft of the dispatch had included, "Needed measures for protection against subversive activities should be taken immediately."[43] ("Subversive activities" mainly meant sabotage, but included espionage and insurrection.)

It was the only instruction in the draft to be carried out "immediately" and the only one not qualified or left to Short's discretion. Other instructions were to be carried out at an indefinite future time ("Should hostilities occur . . ." and "Prior to a hostile action you are directed to . . ."). It was deleted from the November 27 dispatch and made the exclusive subject of a separate dispatch, giving it still more emphasis. And it added to the many, many orders Short had already received that gave priority to measures against sabotage.

Scholars accused Short of having a "preoccupation," a "fixation," an "obsession," and a "mania" with sabotage, which led him to misconstrue the word "defense" in the dispatch. These accusations had no basis. The most influential book on Pearl Harbor, Gordon Prange's *At Dawn We Slept*, has an index entry of "sabotage psychosis" for Short, citing nine pages of text. According to Prange, after receiving the November 27 dispatch, "Short's sabotage psychosis came into full play."[44] Prange's evidence that Short had a "sabotage psychosis" was that he took measures against sabotage—a circular argument. Nonetheless people accepted the imputation of irrationality to Short without considering the background of the dispatch or of the measures he took against sabotage.

Before Short's arrival, the FBI had dealt with anticipated subversion in Hawaii. Short considered his job to include fostering good relations with Hawaiians of Japanese descent, not taking measures against them.[45] Fear of harm from people of Japanese descent in Hawaii, especially in case of war with Japan, long preceded Short's arrival there. No evidence that Japanese Hawaiians posed a subversive threat has come to light. Probably the fear reflected belief in the "Yellow Peril," widespread in the United States and magnified by the growing number of Japanese in Hawaii — one third of the population by the late 1930s. Roosevelt, Marshall, Arnold, and Stimson feared sabotage there more than elsewhere, along with insurrection, espionage, and subversive teaching. Stimson said in 1944:

in Hawaii the danger of sabotage was stressed because of the large Japanese population, and General Short was expressly warned by the War Department against this danger.[46]

In 1936 Roosevelt had ordered that "every Japanese citizen or non-citizen on the island of Oahu who meets Japanese ships or has any connection with their officers or men should be secretly identified [for placement] in a concentration camp in the event of trouble."[47] As war with Japan loomed, administration fears of sabotage grew. A crank letter to Roosevelt in 1941, warning that Hawaiians — especially those of Japanese descent — posed a major sabotage threat, prompted him to order the FBI and other agencies to keep a close watch on them.[48] "Even [Japanese] Buddhist priests on Maui Island were kept under surveillance and their temple studied for wireless antennae." And Japanese Shinto temples in Hawaii were closed.[49]

Initially Short had taken the prospect of a Japanese air raid very seriously. According to Marshall's official biographer, "General Short's reports in the spring and summer of 1941 stressed particularly his preoccupation with the possibility of surprise from the air."[50] It was Marshall, however, who no longer considered an air attack to be a grave risk. He testified:

following General Short's assumption of command . . . there were a series of letters between General Short and myself . . . [which] gave me the most definite impression of an extreme sensibility to air and submarine attack. They did not give an impression of similar sensitivity to sabotage matters.[51]

Marshall then sent Short letters and dispatches giving priority to preventing sabotage.[52] These messages — which increased when Japan's attack became imminent — turned Short from measures against a combat attack toward measures against sabotage.

When Roosevelt proclaimed an "unlimited national emergency"

in May 1941, Washington's apprehension of sabotage became an obsession. Miles testified:

> Military Intelligence was specifically concerned, particularly concerned, and practically solely concerned with antisubversive precautions and operations. That was the reason I sent the G-2 message out.[53]

(The G-2 message, sent on November 27, reminded Short to guard against "subversive activities," which meant against sabotage.)

Earlier, to ascertain if army commands were taking heavy precautions against sabotage, the War Department had sent out inspectors. After studying Hawaiian precautions in July, Col. H. S. Burwell filed a long report which focused on army airfields, and concluded:

> In respect to the need for increased security for aircraft, supplies and installations . . . the prevailing attitude . . . to prevent the success of predictable acts of planned and ordered sabotage . . . must be reported as inadequate . . . Investigation indicates that a few bold, ruthless and intelligent saboteurs . . . could incapacitate Hickam Field or a similar large post on any predetermined night.[54]

Burwell's basis for anticipating "planned and ordered sabotage" was unstated. According to Stimson, the War Department's focus on sabotage came from the perception of Japanese Hawaiians as subversive by nature—a misperception.[55]

On Marshall's orders, Short had already instituted modest precautions against sabotage and later increased them to a level he considered reasonable. Burwell's finding of grave inadequacy may have shocked him. It troubled his air chief, Martin, who had to respond in detail to Burwell's report. Martin informed Washington that most of the many, many deficiencies alleged by Burwell had already been remedied or were being remedied.[56] That was untrue. Martin may have been trying to deflect War Department pressure for increased sabotage measures—measures which he considered inappropriate. To Short he wrote:

> Many of the opinions expressed by the inspecting officer [Burwell] are in conflict with established policies and Army organization and as such cannot receive remedial action . . . The vital installations on all Air Force stations are believed to be adequately guarded.[57]

Short and Martin were right; Burwell, Marshall, Stimson, and Roosevelt were wrong. No sabotage or other subversive activities occurred, nor is there evidence that any was even planned. Burwell's report may have prompted the further orders Washington sent Short to prevent sabotage — orders whose effect was to reduce precautions against an air attack.

Kimmel's thinking about the priority of defending Pearl Harbor and his fleet against a Japanese attack had also been changing. As Richardson had before him, Kimmel made repeated requests for personnel to bring his ships' crews up to full complement — to be ready for the outbreak of war. The response he got from the navy's chief of personnel in March was, "The President now feels so strongly that we will make our ships unhappy by overcrowding."[58] Roosevelt's idea seems to have been that putting aboard the number of sailors for which the ships were designed would be counterproductive. Bizarre in the context of getting ready for war, the explanation suggested that Washington did not expect war.

The above events are context for the November 27 dispatch to Short. He had no doubt about its meaning. After only a brief discussion with his chief of staff, he cabled Washington his report of measures taken:

Report Department alerted to prevent sabotage. Liaison with Navy. REURAD Four Seven Two Twenty Seventh.[59]

The "Department" referred to army troops in Oahu. "Liaison with Navy" probably meant that Kimmel and Bloch were cooperating in measures against sabotage, which was true. "REURAD Four Seven Two Twenty Seventh" was shorthand for "Re your radio message number 472 of the twenty-seventh." *This specified that it was the report requested by the November 27 war warning.* It provided the check on whether Short had understood the dispatch.

Gerow first testified about the November 27 dispatch to the Roberts Commission, that he and other drafters did, indeed, want Short to take measures against sabotage.[60] His later testimony, however, was in line with the administration's position: the November 27 dispatch meant for Short to take measures against a combat attack. Gerow's first testimony was consistent with instructions Marshall had been sending Short since March, and with instructions sent after November 27. If Gerow's first testimony is valid, Short's report of taking measures against sabotage should logically have been what the War Department expected. It should have been accepted — which it was.

A key question pursued by the congressional committee was: if the November 27 dispatch ordered Short to go on alert against a Japanese air attack, how could his report that he was taking measures only against sabotage have been accepted? At first no one at the War Department admitted to having seen Short's report. Later they testified that they had, but had not recognized it as a response to the November 27 dispatch, even though Short specified it was a response to that dispatch. They said they mistook it to be a response to subsequent dispatches telling Short to take measures against sabotage.[61]

Pressed repeatedly by the committee on how he and his subordinates could have failed to note that Short had gone on alert only against sabotage, Marshall testified that he did not remember having seen Short's report; that since he was shown a cover sheet stamped "Noted — Chief of Staff," he must have seen it; and that he had seen it.[62] His final explanation — which explained nothing — was:

> **So when this message came in this way I think everyone that had seen it was misled on what it meant or did not mean and that, I think, accounts for . . . the misunderstanding . . . The fact that it was merely sabotage did not register on anybody's mind.[63]**

Short's report was concise, on point, and unambiguous. With no rational explanation for the failure, Marshall's official biographer explained it away mystically, along with military officers not grasping the warnings they saw of the coming attack on Pearl Harbor. "No one in Washington noticed that fate, persistently against the United States in this period, had thrown dust in the eyes of officials in Washington."[64]

But Short's report had, indeed, struck Marshall as noteworthy, and he had forwarded it to Stimson, which he did not ordinarily do with reports from the field. Asked why by the congressional committee, Marshall answered, "Because I thought it was very important that he should see this particular message. It had been my custom always when there was anything up that was out of the ordinary that he might miss I always initialed it for him and had it taken directly to his room."[65] The committee did not ask what made it too important for Stimson to miss.

According to another biographer of Marshall, some members of his staff did note that Short's report was about defense against sabotage. On seeing it, Col. Walter Bedell Smith said to Col. Orlando Ward, "For God's sake, do you suppose he means that he is only acting to prevent sabotage?"[66] The biographer speculated that Smith and Ward did not bring the alarming observation to Marshall's attention. If they had failed to do so — and failed to bring warnings of Japan's coming attack to him — it is surprising no one was demoted, reassigned, or even reprimanded for these crucial lapses.

If Marshall and his staff had misconstrued Short's report, they had ample opportunities to correct their error. After November 27, Japanese spies in Hawaii sent a series of reports to Tokyo about Short's (and Kimmel's) forces not being on the alert against an air attack. Detailed in chapter 3, the reports included: "no signs of barrage balloon equipment," and "So far they do not seem to be alerted. Shore leaves as usual" and "no indications of air or sea alert" and "no air reconnaissance is being conducted." Marshall and Stark and their staffs saw these reports. If they believed the Hawaiian forces had gone on alert against a combat attack and were conducting distant reconnaissance all around Hawaii — as they claimed — logically, these Japanese messages should have shocked them and led to follow-up. *But they did not follow up on any of them.*

Whether Marshall's and his subordinates' explanations were truthful or not has no bearing on Short's and Kimmel's culpability. By War and Navy Department procedures, when a report from the field was received and not responded to, that meant the report was approved. Short and Kimmel had no basis between November 27 and December 7 to doubt that they were obeying orders correctly.

To conclude, the context in which Short received the key dispatch of November 27 supported his interpretation of it. And the measures he took were approved by the War Department. In those circumstances, his judgment was appropriate.

Controversy over the meaning of "defense" in the dispatch to Short was overshadowed by controversy over the meaning of "defensive deployment" in the dispatch to Kimmel. To many people the word "defensive" was clear on its face, but that, too, was a presumption. By 1941 "defense" and "defensive" were sometimes used as euphemisms for "offense" and "offensive." Naval officers gave different explanations of what "defensive deployment" meant.

Again context is crucial, and here a specific context was stated in the dispatch itself. The meaning of "defensive deployment" was qualified by "preparatory to carrying out tasks assigned in WPL 46." As noted, the main, long-standing mission of the Pacific Fleet was not defense of Pearl Harbor. And War Plan 46 — drawn up in 1941 — did not change that. It defined Kimmel's mission as:

> The United States . . . will employ the United States Pacific Fleet offensively in the manner best calculated to weaken Japanese economic power, and to support defense of the

Malay barrier by diverting Japanese strength away from Malaysia.[67]

Japan's economic power was to be weakened by a blockade. How Japan's military forces were to be diverted was spelled out in Kimmel's assigned tasks:

a. TASK. Support the forces of the associated powers in the Far East by diverting enemy strength away from the Malay Barrier, through the denial and capture of positions in the Marshalls, and through raids on enemy sea communications and positions;

b. TASK. Prepare to capture and establish control over the Caroline and Marshall Island area, and to establish an advanced fleet base in Truk;

c. TASK. Destroy Axis sea communications by capturing and destroying vessels trading directly or indirectly with the enemy;

d. TASK. Support British naval forces . . .

e. TASK. Defend Samoa . . .

f. TASK. Defend Guam . . .

g. TASK. Protect the sea communications of the associated powers by escorting, covering, and patrolling . . . and by destroying enemy raiding forces . . .

h. TASK. Protect the territory of the associated powers in the Pacific area and prevent the extension of enemy military power into the western hemisphere by destroying hostile expeditions . . .

i. TASK. Cover the operations of the naval coastal frontier forces . . .

j. TASK. Establish fleet control zones . . .

k. TASK. Route shipping of associated powers within fleet control zones.[68]

The "associated powers" were specified as the United States, the British Commonwealth (except Ireland), the Dutch East Indies, Greece, Yugoslavia, "Governments in Exile," China, and the "Free French." The "enemy" was Japan. The Malay Barrier was British territory. Truk was in the Carolines, a Japanese possession. The "naval coastal frontier forces" were the small fleet of the Fourteenth Naval District. And the tasks were in descending order of priority.

According to Admiral Turner, defending Samoa and Guam did not include shooting at Japanese invaders. It meant only preventing sabotage and blowing up whatever on the islands might be useful to Japan.[69]

Defense of Hawaii was not mentioned at all, but may have been implied under "h." The "territory of the associated powers" was undefined. It may have meant only territories of powers allied with the United States or it may have included U.S. territories. (Turner testified that it did include them.[70]) Samoa and Guam were tiny U.S. territories of far less military and other importance than Hawaii. Nonetheless War Plan 46 specified their defense, and not Hawaii's.

Pursuant to War Plan 46, in July, Kimmel issued WPPac 46 — his detailed orders for his Pacific Fleet. He divided the fleet into nine task forces; one had duties to defend Pearl Harbor, the others did not. Kimmel submitted WPPac 46 to Stark, who approved it. On November 15, Kimmel reported that he was preparing his fleet for offensive operations against Japan. On November 25, Stark approved that report.[71]

The November 27 dispatch ordered final preparation for the tasks assigned to Kimmel. Execution had to await a further order from Washington or a decision in Hawaii that war with Japan had broken out. The dispatch was ambiguous on a point that is crucial here. "Execute an appropriate defensive deployment" could have meant that Kimmel should take measures to prevent harm to his fleet while awaiting an order to carry out his offensive tasks. Or it could have meant that Kimmel should deploy his fleet in readiness to carry out offensive tasks on short notice.

Kimmel took the phrase in the second sense, acted accordingly, and was charged with not taking it in the first sense. His interpretation was reinforced by a dispatch he received the next day, which included a copy of Short's November 27 dispatch and ended with, "Be prepared to carry out the tasks assigned in WPL46 so far as they apply to Japan in case hostilities occur."[72] The messages to Kimmel immediately preceding and following the November 27 dispatch contained nothing about defense of Pearl Harbor or of his own ships. And the messages sent units of his fleet to positions — including Midway and Wake — which were so far away that those fleet units could not participate in defense of Pearl Harbor.

Asked by the congressional committee what the November dispatch ordered Kimmel to do, Turner said to put "into effect preparatory measures for the Rainbow-5 War Plan . . ."[73] Asked to define "appropriate defensive deployment," he said:

A "deployment" is a spreading out of forces . . . to spread out and make ready for hostilities. To get into the best positions from which to execute the operating plans against the enemy.[74]

Asked if the dispatch ordered Kimmel to take action, Turner answered, "Yes, sir . . . putting into effect preparatory measures for the Rainbow-5 War Plan."[75]

Stark was specifically asked:

Preparatory defensive deployment according to WPL-46 might well be construed to be some preliminary movement to carrying out that offense against the Japanese Mandated Islands, might it not?

He answered, "Yes."[76]

Congressional investigators also heard testimony to the contrary—testimony that the dispatch ordered Kimmel to defend Pearl Harbor and his own ships. Some members of the Navy Department went so far as to testify that Kimmel's sole responsibility under War Plan 46 was defensive! Stark and Turner sometimes said Kimmel's duties under the plan were defensive and at other times said they were offensive. Their most emphatic statements were (by Stark), "The Fleet primarily was in no way responsible for the defense of Pearl Harbor," and (by Turner), "So far as Admiral Kimmel was concerned, his part in [War Plan 46] was not defensive. It required a limited offensive through the Central Pacific Islands."[77]

Furthermore if, as Stark testified, the November 27 dispatch was intended as an all-out alert for an attack on Hawaii and the Pacific Fleet, it contradicted Kimmel's standing orders. If so, that called for drawing his attention to the contradiction and telling Kimmel to set aside the standing orders. The dispatch did not say so; instead it reminded Kimmel that War Plan 46—a standing order—governed actions he was to take.

These complexities involve arguable points and contradictory testimony. Beyond them remains a simple, uncontradicted point, which is worth emphasizing. On December 2, Kimmel sent Stark two long reports of dispositions he had made since receiving the November 27 dispatch. Almost all the dispositions involved operations far from Hawaii. The only defensive measure Kimmel reported was preparation against an attack by submarines on his ships in or near Pearl Harbor. He said nothing about defending against an air attack there. Earlier Kimmel had reported similar dispositions in response to orders from Stark, and Stark had approved them on November 28.[78] To his December 2 reports, Kimmel received no reply, which meant they were approved.

Indeed, a basic point in evaluating Kimmel's and Short's performance is that, until the attack, the measures they took were approved by their superiors. In the context of their orders and by Stark's and Marshall's approval of measures taken, Kimmel and Short interpreted the orders of November 27 appropriately and carried them out. Ironically the "'war warning' messages of November 27 left Hawaii less ready for a Japanese attack then it had been before the dispatches arrived."[79]

In my view, this is enough to judge Kimmel and Short on the charges brought against them. If they carried out their orders, responsibility for the Pearl Harbor disaster lay elsewhere. Nonetheless some misunderstanding does seem to have developed in Washington about what Kimmel and Short were doing. Going further into the background of the November 27 dispatches may help explain a misunderstanding that could have contributed to disappointment with Kimmel's and Short's actions and to their becoming scapegoats for the disaster.

Until the late 1930s, the U.S. government gave little serious consideration to war with Japan. The Orange war plans were exercises in contingency analysis. After World War I, with the expectation of remaining at peace, "enemy" nations were designated somewhat arbitrarily in strategic planning—Japan (called Orange), Germany (Black), Great Britain (Red), and Mexico (Green).

By 1940 the European war had become the administration's main concern. That made War Plan 46 obsolete by the time it was adopted in May 1941. Like the Orange plans from which it was derived with little change, the part governing action in the Pacific involved waging an aggressive war against Japan. But planning in Washington had changed the role of fleet units remaining in the Pacific to a defensive one, in which offensive operations had a defensive purpose—not to win victories, but to limit losses.

Leaders in Washington did not share this knowledge fully with commanders in the Pacific. Neither documents nor testimony on why strategic planning was withheld from them are available. Perhaps Washington's evolving strategy was withheld to avert morale problems likely to arise from informing Pacific commanders that, for an indefinite period, they were to fight a losing battle—and take heavy losses—against an enemy considered militarily inferior.[80] In any case, the strategy was not made clear to Kimmel, Short, or MacArthur.

Administration leaders had not conceded loss of the Pacific Fleet. Perhaps they expected that, as Hart did, Kimmel could save most of his fleet. The heavy destruction it suffered was a shock to them as well as to the nation. Besieged by criticism and threatened with a congressional investigation, they were angry and seem to have felt let down by their forces in Hawaii. Ordinarily people with unspoken needs half-consciously expect others to grasp and meet them—especially when they have given hints. And when others fail to meet unspoken needs, resentment and punitive impulses are as common as they are irrational. Capt. Charles Wellborn, an aide to Stark in 1941, later wrote, "I think it's worthy of note that Admiral Hart very accurately *interpreted* the intent of all those messages, and I think he did exactly what was expected of him."[81] (Italics added.) What Hart did was to save most of his fleet by taking it out of harm's way and not participating in the defense of the Philippines. Kimmel and Short did not interpret their messages as Hart interpreted his, and that may have contributed to criticism and punishment of them and to later disagreement about what the dispatches of November 27 meant.

The best hint given to the Hawaiian commanders of Washington's strategy was in the November 27 dispatch to Short: "the United States desires that Japan commit the first overt act." As is shown in chapters 13 and 14, this policy was crucial for political reasons. The administration's unspoken wish was for Pacific commanders to do what they could to save their forces from Japan's coming attack without taking action against Japan's forces until attacked.

Asked whether a Japanese fleet one thousand miles from Hawaii could be attacked, Stark testified, "That certainly is one hypothetical question. I think if I were out there and saw them I would keep them under surveillance."[82] Stark conveyed his understanding of the policy to Kimmel by specific instructions: if Japanese submarines came to Hawaii, they were to be kept under surveillance and not fired on. Other Pacific commanders operated under the same restriction. MacArthur, who prevented his forces from going beyond surveillance of approaching Japanese planes, later explained, "My instructions from Washington were not to initiate hostilities under any circumstances."[83]

The policy also discouraged lesser defensive measures. Even going on combat alert—like mobilization—has long been considered a warlike act that could justify an attack by a potential enemy. According to an official navy history, the dispatches of November 27 "effectively tied" the hands of Kimmel and Short. For them to have gone on combat alert "would have been contrary to the basic policy of taking no steps that might be looked upon as provocative."[84]

Stimson had participated decisively in drafting the dispatch to Short, and he testified:

> [It] presented with the utmost precision the situation with which we were all confronted and in the light of which all our commanding officers, as well as we ourselves in Washington, had to govern our conduct. The situation was admittedly

delicate and critical . . . we needed the Japanese to commit the first overt act . . . that nothing would be done, unless necessary to the defense . . . to precipitate an incident and give the Japanese an excuse to go to war . . . and say that we had committed the first overt act.[85]

Marshall's effort to shift Short's preparations toward sabotage and away from a combat attack has been described. Stark made no such effort with Kimmel, but subtler factors — including Washington's failure to meet his, Short's, Bloch's, and Richardson's defense needs — influenced Kimmel to believe Washington no longer expected an air attack there.

In March Short wrote to Marshall, "I feel that . . . anti-aircraft defense is the most serious problem that we have to face." Marshall replied, "I am hopeful of arranging for the early augmentation of your anti-aircraft garrison."[86] But significant augmentation was not provided. Nor did Washington provide for Short's other defense needs.

Not receiving antiaircraft or reconnaissance equipment, the Hawaiian commands were left with lesser means of defense. Receiving intelligence of a coming attack became most important. Kimmel had no cryptographers and was unable to decode Japanese messages that his radio operators intercepted. He did receive information from Bloch's intelligence unit; however, it had been ordered by the Navy Department to switch its decoding from Japan's most-used naval code to a little-used one.[87] As a consequence, Kimmel got less intelligence than before.

On assuming his command in January 1941, Kimmel wrote to Stark, emphasizing his need for Washington to supply crucial intelligence. Not satisfied that he was getting it, in February he wrote again to Stark:

I have recently been told by an officer fresh from Washington that ONI considers it the function of [War Plans] to furnish the Commander-in-Chief with information of a secret nature. I have also heard that [War Plans] considers the responsibility for furnishing the . . . information to be that of ONI . . . if there is any doubt as to whose responsibility it is to keep the Commander-in-Chief fully informed . . . will you kindly fix that responsibility so that there will be no misunderstanding?[88]

The "Commander-in-Chief" was Kimmel. The question of who disseminated information was a sore point in the Navy Department.

ONI had long carried responsibility for sending information to outposts. But since Turner had become director of the War Plans Division, he had been aggressively taking over functions outside his division. The problem that troubled Kimmel came from Turner's attempt to take over evaluating intelligence and controlling its distribution. Turner had had angry confrontations about it with Capt. Alan Kirk, Director of ONI.[89] Although Stark favored Turner generally, he had not taken sides in their dispute over control of intelligence.

Perhaps the dispute was why it took Stark until March 22, 1941 to answer Kimmel:

> With reference to your postscript on the subject of Japanese trade routes and responsibility for furnishing of secret information to [you] Kirk informs me that ONI is fully aware of its responsibility in keeping you adequately informed concerning foreign nations, activities of these nations and disloyal elements within the United States . . . the location of all Japanese merchant vessels . . . Japanese trade routes, the commodities which move over these trade routes, and the volume of shipping which moved over each route.[90]

This ignored Kimmel's concern about receiving "information of a secret nature," especially about Japanese war plans and fleet movements.

While awaiting Stark's reply, and perhaps to avoid pressing him on the sore point, Kimmel had already asked his intelligence officer, Cdr. Edwin Layton, to use his contacts in ONI to ensure receiving crucial intelligence. And Layton had written on March 11 to his friend and former chief, Cdr. Arthur McCollum. It took McCollum until April 22 to reply:

> Dear Eddie: Sorry to be so late in replying . . . *I have taken up the matter . . . and hope that this matter will be adjusted in the very near future*, but I cannot be certain as another division handles the mailing and distribution . . . I thoroughly appreciate that you would probably be much helped . . . if you had at your disposal the DIP [DIP meant diplomatic messages]. This, however brings up matters of security, et cetera, which would be very difficult to solve. While I appreciate your position fully in the matter, still I cannot agree that this material should be forwarded to you in the way you suggest. It seems reasonable to suppose that the [Navy] Department should be the origin for evaluated political situations as its availability of information is greater than that of any command afloat . . . its

staff is larger and it should be in a position to evaluate the political consequences. Therefore it would seem that the forces afloat must rely on the Department for evaluated views of political situations. I should think that the forces afloat should, in general, confine themselves to the estimates of the strategic and tactical situations with which they will be confronted when the time of action arrives. The material you mention can necessarily have but passing and transient interest as action in the political sphere is determined by the Government as a whole and not by the forces afloat . . . I appreciate that all this leaves you in rather a spot . . . I believe, however, that a sharp line should be drawn . . . between information that is of interest and information that is desirable to have on which to base action. In other words, while you and the Fleet may be highly interested in politics, there is nothing you can do about it. Therefore, information of political significance, except as it affects immediate action by the Fleet, is merely a matter of interest to you and not a matter of utility.[91] (Italics added.)

The letter confirmed Kimmel's apprehension that intelligence was being withheld from him. It is quoted at length because it indicates that, after discussion in the Navy Department, a decision was made to withhold from Kimmel the intelligence he was requesting—a decision that McCollum hoped would be reversed. McCollum's letter contradicts statements by top-level navy officers that they meant to withhold nothing from Kimmel and that they were unaware that significant information was withheld from him. As will be seen, the decision to withhold intelligence from Kimmel remained in effect up to the Pearl Harbor attack, and a parallel decision was made to withhold information from Short. Some officers—including Turner—denied such a decision had been made, and claimed to have been unaware of which commanders received intelligence. Admiral Noyes, however, testified that who received intelligence from the Navy Department was:

a matter of continual discussion [among himself, Turner, and Wilkinson] . . . we conferred almost daily on the question . . . and I thought that Admiral Turner had a clear understanding of what was being received in Pearl Harbor . . . and what was not."[92]

In April diplomatic messages only occasionally contained indications of upcoming Japanese military moves. After September they carried the bomb-plot warnings of a coming attack on Pearl Harbor. But that change did not affect what had become a policy of withholding intelligence from Kimmel and Short. One intelligence officer said he remembered a written order to withhold intelligence from the Hawaiian commands, while others cited an unwritten policy. Asked who made the decision to withhold intelligence from Short, Miles testified:

> That followed from the general policy laid down by the Chief of Staff [Marshall] that [Japanese diplomatic] messages and the fact of the existence of the messages or our ability to decode them should be confined to the least possible number of persons.[93]

The policy can be viewed as a reasonable effort to ensure that Japan did not discover her codes were broken and thus maintain the advantage of being able to read Japanese diplomatic and naval messages. But Miles's answer did not explain why MacArthur got much intelligence — specifically including Japanese diplomatic messages indicating a coming attack on Pearl Harbor — while Short got none. Nor did it explain why MacArthur was warned to expect a combat attack, while Short was not. Miles and other intelligence officers who testified about restrictions on intelligence to Short and Kimmel were not asked these questions, perhaps because the investigations were devoted to Pearl Harbor and largely ignored what happened in the Philippines.

McCollum's letter got increasingly hostile, going from a vague mention of security problems to suggesting that Layton lacked the ability to evaluate diplomatic messages. Layton reasonably took the last part as telling him diplomatic messages were "none of Pearl Harbor's business."[94] The hostility in his letter to an old friend — together with McCollum's hope that the withholding would be "adjusted" — suggest that he was troubled about withholding intelligence from Kimmel.[95]

By April ONI had heard only rumors of Japan's preparation to attack Pearl Harbor. But in autumn, when it received extensive intelligence of the coming attack, McCollum tried hard to send warnings to Kimmel, but was prevented from doing so. Similarly, Bratton and Sadtler of army intelligence tried to send Short intelligence and warnings, but were prevented from doing so (see chapter 14).

During investigations of the Pearl Harbor disaster, Stark persistently denied any intention of withholding intelligence from Kimmel, insisting he had believed — mistakenly — that Kimmel was receiving all the intelligence available in Washington. Marshall was more candid, testifying that withholding intelligence from field commanders was normal procedure.[96] Stark did, however, join Marshall in stating a crucial policy that governed what intelligence and warnings Kimmel and Short were to receive: nothing that might prompt them to take aggressive *or defensive* action.[97]

Frustrated, Kimmel kept requesting intelligence, and Stark kept assuring him that he was getting everything relevant to Hawaii's situation.[98] In May Kimmel sent a strongly worded protest to Stark. They were old, good friends. Commonly Stark addressed Kimmel not by his title and name, but as Mustapha (from the similarity of the name Kimmel to the name of Turkish leader, Mustapha Kemal). And Kimmel addressed Stark as Betty (long a nickname of men in the Stark family, used by friends). They referred to themselves in the first person, and signed letters "Mustapha" and "Betty." But on this occasion Kimmel wrote to Stark in formal language, which emphasized again that he was seriously troubled:

> The Commander-in-Chief, Pacific Fleet, is in a very difficult position. He is far removed from the seat of government in a complex and rapidly changing situation. He is, as a rule, not informed as to the policy, or change of policy, reflected in current events and naval movements and, as a result, is unable to evaluate the possible effects on his own situation . . . [which undermines] the conduct of military operations.

Kimmel then said he understood that some information must be withheld from him, but argued and pleaded for more, ending with:

> It is suggested that it be made a cardinal principle that the Commander-in-Chief, Pacific Fleet, be immediately informed of all important developments as they occur.[99]

To emphasize the point further, Kimmel brought a copy of the letter when he visited Stark in June for a discussion of his defense needs. He pointed out that the congestion of ships and facilities in the harbor invited an air attack and that the fleet would need three hours warning to get out of the harbor because the entrance was long and narrow.[100] (It allowed only one capital ship to pass at a time.) Therefore, the fleet could only be saved by not being in harbor when an attack came.

Stark continued to promise Kimmel that he would get the intelligence he needed. For example, in August he told Kimmel, "You may rest assured that just as soon as I get anything of definite interest, I shall fire it along."[101] Nonetheless, Stark prevented his subordinates from sending Kimmel warnings that Japan was planning to attack Pearl Harbor. And in December, he prevented them from sending warnings that she was expected to attack within days. And Marshall prevented his subordinates from sending such warnings to Short. The lack of these warnings probably contributed more than anything else to the unpreparedness of Kimmel's and Short's forces.

Short also had no way of decoding Japanese messages that his radio operators intercepted. His request for such help was refused, and he devoted himself to other ways of detecting an approaching Japanese attack. His experience in trying to build radar stations was especially frustrating.

Early in 1940, the War Department had instructed his predecessor, Gen. Charles Herron, to make preparations for use of radar equipment, due to arrive the next year. Six radar units were to be mobile and three to be installed in fixed structures. The fixed units were to provide maximum range by having their antenna towers placed on high points. Herron's engineers recommended sites on National Park lands.

The highest was on Mount Haleakala. In July 1940, Herron informed the national park superintendent in Hawaii that requests would follow to make surveys of Haleakala, to build a road up the mountain, to take over a section of the mountain, and to build a structure on it. The superintendent granted permission for the surveys, forwarded the other requests to the director of the National Park Service in Washington, and suggested that sites not on park lands would serve Herron's needs. In November the superintendent suggested to Herron a specific site not on park land. Herron replied that any site other than Haleakala would greatly reduce the range covered by a radar unit. The park service then requested that construction plans be submitted before it made a decision.

On replacing Herron in February 1941, Short found the request to use Haleakala and the counter request for construction plans to be pending. Delays of military projects were common, but administrators had means of expediting them. Short anticipated a long delay. (When he submitted plans, the park service could request modification and resubmission of plans, with no assurance of approval in the end.) And the radar equipment was due to arrive in June. On March 6, Short wrote an extraordinarily aggressive letter to Marshall:

> One of the first projects which I investigated . . . was the aircraft warning service . . . At the present time *the maximum*

distance an approaching airplane can be detected is about five miles. The radio detector equipment [radar] . . . increases the distance to one hundred and twenty miles . . . [But] a radiogram of 3 March 1941 . . . from the Adjutant General regarding the Haleakala installation . . . indicates to me that the seriousness of this situation has not yet been appreciated by the War Department. It lists certain restrictions regarding construction, and if it is necessary to comply with these, the completion of this construction will be unduly delayed . . . its commanding [location] gives it greater coverage than any of the others, and its early completion is vital. I believe that this matter is sufficiently important to be brought to the attention of the Secretary of War to see if permission can not be obtained from the Secretary of the Interior to construct the Haleakala installation without the necessity of submitting detailed plans . . .

Defense of these islands and adequate warning for the United States Fleet is so dependent on the early completion of the Aircraft Warning System that I believe all quibbling over details should be stopped at once.[102] (Italics added.)

Marshall's deputy, Gen. William Bryden, replied on March 15:

The matters referred to . . . have been given careful study . . . it will be necessary to comply with certain fixed regulations . . . where facilities are to be established on [Park] lands . . . The National Park Service officials . . . will not waive the requirements as to the submission of preliminary building plans . . . They are also very definitely opposed to permitting structures of any type to be erected at such places as will be open to view and materially alter the natural appearance of the reservation . . . It is not believed . . . advisable to attempt to alter the informal decisions of the Department of the Interior by carrying this matter to higher authority.[103]

Marshall did change his mind in May, intervening with Interior Secretary Harold Ickes, and Short got permission to proceed with work on Haleakala. However, other delays followed, beyond the control of the War Department. On December 7 the Haleakala radar unit was still not operating. Neither were the other fixed radar units. The mobile units were operating, but, in accordance with standing orders, they were being used only for training operators.[104]

Despite limitations on the defense Short and Kimmel were

equipped and permitted to make, a remaining question is: why did they not do better with the resources they had in taking routine precautions against an air attack? During the days between November 27 and December 7, Short's radar operators, during training, detected approaching U.S. warships and planes. On December 7, before the attack began, a radar operator detected approaching planes and reported them to his superior.[105] Having been informed of U.S. planes due in Hawaii that day, and not expecting a Japanese attack, his superior did nothing with the report. The planes, however, turned out to be Japanese.

Probably the superior officer's nonresponse to the radar warning reflected the fact that Short, Kimmel, and their staffs no longer expected a Japanese air attack. Orders and information from Washington had stopped mentioning the likelihood of an air attack on Hawaii. Starting in February 1941, Stark had been writing to Kimmel that the administration was working for peace with Japan.[106] And after that policy was reversed in July, Stark continued writing to Kimmel in the same vein. Meanwhile some refusals of equipment for defense cited only cost or limited availability, while other requests were refused or ignored for no apparent reason. The accumulation of information, orders, actions, and nonactions—most notably withholding warnings of Japan's coming attack—seems sufficient to account for Kimmel's and Short's belief in late 1941 that Washington no longer expected an air attack on Hawaii.[107] As noted, Admiral Bellinger had written in January that Hawaii's lack of equipment for defense indicated that the Navy Department had little concern about an attack on Hawaii (which was untrue). By autumn the indication was stronger still.

Besides assessing Kimmel's and Short's responsibility, this account has touched on secret government policies and strategies that contributed to the Pearl Harbor disaster. Working them out is the main task remaining.

CHAPTER 7
BACKGROUND
TO WAR BETWEEN JAPAN
AND THE UNITED STATES

Ninety years before her attack on Pearl Harbor, Japan was an extremely isolated nation, still feudal, lacking industrialization, and militarily weak. The United States, although active in foreign trade, was still adhering substantially to George Washington's advice against political entanglement abroad, which somewhat isolated her. The United States had just won a war with Mexico, extending her frontier to the West Coast. To ambitious Americans, the Far East beckoned as a market for trade and an area for conquest.

While moving toward a position as a world power, the United States forced Japan to her knees and then led her out of her isolation into the arena of power politics. Later, as Japan struggled to regain her independence, she too embarked on a course of empire. At first the United States and Japan cooperated in building their empires, but their expansion and involvement in the affairs of other nations would bring them to war with each other in 1941.

Early in the nineteenth century, expansion-minded Americans had turned to Texas, California, and New Mexico—then parts of Mexico. While various administrations and Congress were cautious about taking action beyond purchasing territory in the west, adventurers—usually without government support—took steps in expanding the nation. Some settled in Texas, wrested it from Mexico, and sought incorporation as a state in the Union. Others moved into what are now California and New Mexico with similar aspirations.

With the status of Texas unsettled, President James Polk sent an army to the Rio Grande, recognized by the United States in the Adams-Onis treaty of 1819 to be within Mexico. Mexican forces attacked, and

113

a one-sided war followed, ending with Mexico's agreement in 1848 to U.S. acquisition not only of Texas, California, and New Mexico, but also of Arizona, Nevada, and parts of Oklahoma, Colorado, Utah, Wyoming, and Kansas. The United States gained more than half of Mexico, an enormous territory.[1]

When westward expansion reached the Pacific Ocean, some Americans began to think of conquest beyond the hemisphere. Meanwhile, as industrialization advanced, U.S. merchant ships began to visit China in 1840, and the United States signed a trade treaty with her in 1844. Acquisition of California ports eased trade with China by shortening the sea route.

Growing trade with China and operations by U.S. whalers in the western Pacific made Japan potentially useful as a way station for ships and a refuge for shipwrecked sailors. In addition, some traders saw Japan as a new market for their goods.[2] As a result, the United States made overtures to open diplomatic and commercial relations with Japan, but was rebuffed, as other nations had been. To force the issue, in 1852 President Millard Fillmore sent Cdr. Matthew Perry with a naval squadron to Japan.[3]

His mission was announced in advance, and Tokyo alerted clans along the coast. But lacking modern armaments, neither the clans nor the Imperial army had the power to repel a naval attack. One clan lined its shore with bronze temple bells, hoping Perry might mistake them for cannons and be frightened into aborting his mission.[4]

On arrival in 1853, Perry was the first envoy not to be rebuffed. Unlike others who landed in outlying places, he sailed his squadron into Tokyo Bay, almost to the capital, which he threatened to destroy with his warships' cannons.[5] Because most of Japan's buildings were made of wood and paper, bombardment could wipe out a city by setting it on fire. The Japanese said they needed time to consider his demands, and Perry said he would return for their answer with a larger fleet—a greater threat. Adding to the menace, Perry's black-painted ships—the first steamships Japan had seen—belched dark smoke. To the most superstitious Japanese, they appeared to be monsters from the sea.[6]

Perry's demands for commercial and diplomatic relations required Japan to break from a long-established policy against contact with foreigners—a policy based on her sense of vulnerability. Centuries of civil war had fostered a warrior mentality, but limited her population and prolonged her disunity. Although nominally a nation under one emperor, Japan was effectively still a collection of clans.

Early in the seventeenth century, the Tokugawa clan came to power as the hereditary military dictators (shoguns), ruling in the name of the emperor. Moved by the devastation of civil wars, the Tokugawans' main goal was domestic peace. To ensure it, they increased central control of the nation and regulation of daily life.[7] They also began to modernize Japan, but slowly, within the confines of the conservatism they imposed.

At first, they allowed Portuguese and Spanish traders, already in Japan, to stay and continue commercial activities. These traders had brought Christian missionaries, whose work was seen as a threat to tradition and order — both long viewed as essential to the nation's existence. The Tokugawans largely confined the Europeans to the port city of Nagasaki, and alternately tolerated and suppressed proselytizing.[8]

The Tokugawa peace and order were soon broken by the Shimabara rebellion. Like many earlier rebels, the Shimabarans rose up against feudal tyranny and privations suffered under it. But unlike earlier rebels, they were also united by Christianity. After putting down the rebellion, the shogunate increased adherence to traditional ways, regulation of life, and exclusion of foreigners to an extreme. The Portuguese and Spanish were expelled. A few Dutch and English traders — who had not brought missionaries — were allowed to stay, but confined to an island off Nagasaki. And except for them, the borders were closed tightly. The shogunate kept out foreigners and their influence, and forbade Japanese to leave. And if they left, they were forbidden on pain of death to return.[9] For centuries, Japanese had studied in China, whose culture they considered superior. This outside influence was also curtailed. Exclusion of foreign influence and enforced adherence to tradition sharply limited modernization and other change.

The Tokugawans succeeded. Their rule was crowned by an unprecedented two hundred years of domestic peace. As a result, the population grew toward a level of crowding that later would spur emigration and acquisition of foreign lands for Japanese settlers. But the price of tranquility was scientific, technological, military, and cultural stagnation. Bypassed not only by industrialization, but also by the Renaissance, democratization, and empire building — and not yet even a unified nation — the warlike Japanese became militarily powerless in comparison to European nations. Knowing this, they tried to discourage foreign contact by a truculent attitude toward visitors. From time to time, visitors and castaways were assaulted or killed. It was to this vulnerable, bristling, and rigid society that Perry presented his demands and threats. It was a society shaped by facing the constant threat of overwhelming power.

Since the beginning of recorded history, Japan has been devastated frequently by volcanic eruptions and earthquakes.[10] The frightening thunder of those cataclysms and the chaos and destruction that follow are hard to imagine without experiencing them. Eruptions also produce dust so heavy that it turns day into night—a night that people fear may never end. (The 1923 earthquake lasted six days, killed one hundred thousand people, and destroyed the cities of Tokyo and Yokohama.) Even tremors that subside after little or no damage may make ominous rumbling and crashing noises, arousing terrible suspense. And Japan, in addition to her many eruptions and earthquakes, experiences thousands of tremors a year—reminders of the devastating power in unpredictable forces.

Other disasters—also frequent—fires and typhoons. The Japanese word *tsunami* has been adopted in other Pacific lands for the most extreme of typhoons, but the *tsunami* wave—sometimes reaching a height of one hundred feet—is not caused by windstorm. Rather, it comes from an underwater volcanic eruption. From her history of destruction by volcanic forces grew an adaptation—reinforced by the Mongol invasions—that would influence Japan's actions in confrontations with the United States during the twentieth century.

In a country that still experienced about three tremors a day, an appreciation of silence and order, which flowered under Tokugawa rule, is hardly surprising. The book *The Japanese Cult of Tranquility*, coveys the dependence on silence and order that became an enduring feature of Japanese life.[11] Harder to understand may be Japan's embrace of overwhelming threats. Along with a general love of nature and its forces, the Japanese particularly loved and worshipped their volcanoes, even when they were active. Mount Fuji has long been revered as "the beginning of heaven and earth, pillar of the nation."[12]

The Japanese had also embraced China, their neighbor, who was a superpower during most of Japan's recorded history. They not only paid tribute to China, but also studied her ways. Aspiring artists, scholars, and priests went there as students, and Japanese adopted China's written language, religions, artistic forms, and learning.

The Japanese shared with their Asian neighbors a fatalistic and often fairly contented acceptance of forces and consequences beyond their control, but were less passive. For they were also inclined to bold, reckless, even suicidal action in the face of overwhelming threats.[13] They wondered, like Hamlet, "Whether 'tis nobler . . . to suffer the slings and arrows of outrageous fortune, or take arms against a sea of troubles . . . ?" Usually they chose action as the nobler path, even when doing so risked everything. And they often chose suicide as an alternative to bearing humiliation.

Like other peoples, ancient Japanese believed gods controlled eruptions, earthquakes, and storms. (In the United States, calling such events "acts of God" is a vestige of such beliefs.) They also believed people could win favor with the gods by bold, self-sacrificing acts of duty. And such acts did not need to be reasonable. Japan carried into the twentieth century a special fondness and reverence for the hero who lost his life by foolish action in a hopeless cause.[14] Such acts and other ancient ways of dealing with grave threats had been reinforced by dramatic events of the thirteenth century, which provided a lesson the nation would apply in war with the United States.

A decline of China's power had been reversed by the Mongol dynasty, and in 1268 Kublai Khan demanded renewal of Japan's tributary status, which had lapsed in the ninth century. Japan ignored his first demands and rebuffed his more insistent ones that followed. To force his demands, in 1274 Kublai Khan sent an invasion fleet of 450 ships carrying fifteen thousand troops—a great force compared to what Japan could muster. Although militarily outclassed, Japanese troops fought to the last man on outlying islands and then on the home island of Kyushu, delaying submission to Chinese forces, which seemed inevitable. Suddenly, a typhoon destroyed half the invasion fleet along with invading troops quartered on ships. The survivors returned to China.[15]

In 1275 Kublai Khan sent a new envoy demanding Japan's submission. He was beheaded on arrival, and another Chinese envoy was killed in 1279. Then, in 1281, Kublai Khan sent a fleet of one thousand ships carrying about seventy-five thousand troops—an enormous force. On arrival, it was destroyed by another typhoon.[16]

The Japanese called the typhoons *kamikaze* (divine wind). They believed the gods sent the wind to destroy their enemies, thus rewarding their brave stand against overwhelmingly powerful forces. This idea became a model for heroism in the face of disaster. (Conversely, an earthquake in 1854 was widely taken to be divine punishment for yielding without a fight to Perry's threats.[17])

These beliefs influenced Japanese military thinking during World War II. When the tide of war turned decisively against Japan, as U.S. forces gained overwhelming superiority, Japanese leaders gave military priority to a suicidal strategy. Army units on outlying islands were ordered to fight to the last man. Individual soldiers, loaded with explosives, hurled themselves against tanks. And a group of pilots was established to ram attacking warships with specially built explosive-laden planes. The Japanese called these measures and the men who engaged in them *kamikaze*. They hoped that the ferocity demonstrated would discourage the United States from invading their home islands. They also hoped that this self-sacrificing bravery would summon divine forces to defeat the United States, as they had twice defeated China.

In 1854 when Perry returned for an answer to his demands, Japan's leaders were less mystical and defiant than their ancestors in the thirteenth century. Technological advances gave the United States an awesome superiority, more so even than the Mongols had enjoyed. And Perry did not demand tribute or submission to U.S. domination, but only trade and diplomatic relations. Japan's leaders submitted, agreeing to a treaty with the United States, but asked that its implementation be gradual, so that it would appear to the people as something intrinsically good, done voluntarily, rather than a humiliation forced on them.[18]

The treaty began with:

There shall be a perfect, permanent, and universal peace, and a sincere and cordial amity, between the United States of America . . . and the Empire of Japan . . . and between their people . . . without exception of persons or places.[19]

The words were decorative. Despite the pledge of peace and amity, Japan began a program of military development so she could acquire the power to throw out "the barbarians." Despite the pledge, the United States threatened war again and again to extort additional benefits — extraterritoriality, control of Japan's tariffs, and control of some Japanese ports. Despite words suggesting equality, the treaty of 1854 and those that followed established a semi-colonial relationship.

Japan was then forced to submit to similar treaties by Great Britain, Russia, Holland, France, and even Mexico — the "unequal treaties" that would rankle until she was able to end them between 1894 and 1911. As the treaties accumulated, Japan was approaching the humiliated position of China, who had fallen so low that she could not stop Western powers from taking whatever land they coveted. China could not even maintain control over what was left to her, as local warlords gained independence from the central government and made their own treaties with foreign nations. The helplessness of once-great China served to remind the Japanese of the fate they could expect unless they became powerful quickly. And their perceptions of material danger from Western powers were magnified by the traditional belief that passivity and moral weakness were evils, putting them at risk of abandonment by the gods, and therefore of extinction.

The perceived combination of material and mystical threats left them little time for industrialization and the building of a modern military force. The decisions to submit to Western nations aroused mounting apprehension and intolerance of delay, especially among the samurai, to whom bold action was needed immediately.

Hereditary knights and members of Japan's highest social class, the samurai personified their nation's ideals and traditions.[20] To them, submission to Western powers was more than a humiliation; it was a defilement of the nation. The Choshu and Satsuma — militant clans in which the samurai spirit was particularly strong — decided to drive out the foreigners.[21] In 1863 they bombarded U.S., French, and Dutch shipping in Japan's seas. Easily crushed by U.S. and French fleets, the Choshu and Satsuma then attacked individual foreigners in Japan. Partly in reprisal for the killing of an Englishman, a British fleet laid waste in 1864 to Kagoshima, the Satsuma capital.[22]

Nonetheless the samurai — especially the younger ones — remained determined to drive out the foreigners. They decided a change of government was necessary to save Japan, and in 1868 led the Choshu and Satsuma in rebellion, ending Tokugawa rule and restoring administrative power to the new emperor, Meiji. The resultant government and the sweeping changes it introduced became known as the Meiji Restoration.[23] Japan's lords were ordered to yield their vast estates to Meiji, and almost all of them did so voluntarily. The changes were presented as a restoration because calamity was believed to be caused by abandonment of ancient ways. Therefore solutions to national problems were usually called a return to those ways.

Meiji took up the modernization begun under Tokugawan rule and accelerated it greatly.[24] To rush change, he and the parliamentary government he established directed a revolution from the top. It was a marvel of ambition and speed of achievement. Meiji quickly ended illiteracy and expanded higher education. Western advisers were brought in and Western methods and technology were adopted. Manufacturing was spurred by Imperial demands and funds, along with grants of monopolistic rights, resulting in quick growth of industrial giants. And a national army and navy were created by conscription and provided with modern equipment.

Japanese leaders understood that Western powers perceived them, along with other Asians, as inferior, suitable for exploitation. To change the perception and improve their position, they sought — and in time won — alliances with Western powers by which they were equals on paper. For example, in a 1905 agreement, Japan recognized U.S. domination of the Philippines in return for recognition of Japanese domination of Korea. Such agreements resembled those between European nations, recognizing each other's spheres of influence. In addition, acting as an ally of the United States and Great Britain, Japan sent troops to China, helping suppress outbreaks of resistance to Western oppression. Then she began to seize pieces of China for herself.

As she grew in military strength, Japan began to expand tentatively, careful not to offend Western powers. Her aims were acquiring additional lands for her growing population, fulfilling dreams of empire, and emulating Western nations in colonial expansion. Shortly before the turn of the century, Japan's foreign minister said, "The nation and the people must be made to look like European nations and European peoples."[25] Japanese leaders thought that, if they imitated Western powers, Japan might be accepted as an equal. Then the powers would be less likely to destroy Japan and might even agree to cancel the unequal treaties.

Joining Western powers in exploiting China ran counter to the belief that the Chinese were a noble people, creators of the world's greatest civilization, while Westerners were barbarians. Some leaders justified seizing parts of China with the idea that they were saving them from the barbarians.

Up to a point, the strategy of joining and emulating Western powers worked. The United States and Great Britain appreciated the availability of Japanese troops to protect their commercial interests in China against rebels and bandits. U.S. leaders spoke admiringly of the Japanese as a "civilizing" influence in China, because they helped maintain order there. The United States and Great Britain encouraged Japan's colonial expansion in China, and at first China did not fight it.

Japan's expansion began in 1876 by the annexation of the Bonin Islands—a lightly settled, unclaimed group. China permitted extension of Japanese influence in Taiwan (a Chinese territory) and Korea (a kingdom tributary to China). But when Japan tried to end China's domination of Korea in 1894, China sent troops in. Japan did also and defeated China in a limited war. By the peace treaty, Japan gained Korea as her tributary, Taiwan as her territory, and additional territories—the Pescadore Islands and part of China's Liaotung peninsula in Manchuria.[26]

Subsequently, some fruit of this victory was taken away. France, Germany, and Russia pressured Japan to return the Liaotung territory to China.[27] Their high-sounding justification—preserving China's territorial integrity—was undercut five years later, when Western powers seized additional pieces of China. Japanese resented them for prohibiting to Japan what they took for themselves; increasingly they viewed Western statements of principle as two-faced. According to an influential writer:

> **Say what you will, [the loss of Liaotung] happened because we weren't strong enough. What it came down to was that**

sincerity and justice didn't amount to a thing if you were not strong enough.[28]

While Japan's victory over China impressed Western powers, her subsequent victory over Russia impressed them far more.[29] In their eyes, China was weak — a victim for prey — while Russia was a European power with a great empire. Although Japan's smashing victory over Russia in 1904–05 was a shock to the West, it still did not mark her fully as a world power in Western eyes. It impressed the United States enough, however, to consider Japan a potential military rival in East Asia and to draw up the first Orange war plan.

Victory over Russia also strongly impressed the Japanese, adding to their mystical faith in bold, reckless action. The defeat of Russia, "aging into legend with each passing year . . . fostered the deeply held belief in the unconquerable samurai spirit and its divinely bestowed right to victory."[30]

Japan had started her war with Russia by a surprise attack on Port Arthur. It is noteworthy for the Pearl Harbor myth that U.S. leaders did not view this as an act of treachery. On the contrary, they praised Japan for showing military sophistication by attacking before declaring war. She won praise as "a model belligerent that abides strictly by international law almost all the time."[31] But the surprise attack was not forgotten; when anticipating war with Japan in 1941, U.S. leaders would remind each other to expect another Port Arthur (see chapter 14).

Emulating the United States was not only a calculated way of acquiring power and territory, it was also a spontaneous expression of growing attachment. A bond commonly develops between a colonial power and the nation she dominates, and this kind of relationship happened between the United States and Japan. As Japan had turned to China centuries earlier, so she now turned to the United States as a source of wisdom and culture. As Chinese words had been taken into Japanese over the centuries, English words now became part of her language, brought home by students who flocked to the United States before World War I. American tastes and ways became popular and teachers from the United States were brought in. While Americans were still resented as barbarian intruders, the resentment was more than balanced by admiration and affection — so much so that subsequent rebuffs by the United States were especially painful. And U.S. leaders developed affection for the Japanese and pride in their protégé's accomplishments, along with lingering contempt.

Common interests aided the growing bond. Both nations had embarked on the intoxicating course of conquest and empire, and the

United States was also acquiring islands in the Pacific. Some were tiny and unpopulated; others were independent or subject to other nations' control until taken over directly, still others were acquired by defeating Spain in the war of 1898. U.S. acquisitions included Howland and Baker in 1857; Midway, Johnston, and Palmyra in 1859; Hawaii, the Philippines, and Guam in 1898; and Samoa and Wake in 1899.[32]

Japan joined the Allies in World War I, declaring war on Germany. Jointly with a British force, she defeated the Germans in their territory of Shantung, China. On her own, Japan occupied three Pacific island groups recently acquired by Germany—the Carolines, Marianas, and Marshalls. In addition, her fleet joined a British one in fighting a German fleet in the Pacific, and she sent a squadron to convoy Allied shipping in the Mediterranean.[33] While she declined a request for troops to fight in Europe, she had done enough to join the victors in claiming spoils at the peace table. The German island groups were mandated to Japan, and became known as the Mandates. Part of Shantung was also awarded to Japan. These were her last acquisitions approved by the United States and Great Britain.

After the war, Japan was recognized as a world power by a permanent seat on the council of the new League of Nations. This seemingly made her the equal of Western powers. But when the Japanese delegation proposed—with the encouragement of U.S. President Woodrow Wilson—that a declaration of racial equality be included in the League's Covenant, its rejection by delegates of Great Britain *and the United States* was a shock.[34] The Japanese took this action as a racial insult and a sign that their nation would not be accepted fully. It became a step in turning their fondness for the United States back toward hatred.

During the nineteenth century, a vague racism had influenced United States policy toward Japan. Few people knew the grand dream in Perry's mind when he extorted rights from her. To expansionists in the United States, domination of Japan was a step toward conquering East Asia. Perry was an avowed expansionist, and said in 1855:

> It requires no sage to predict events so strongly foreshadowed to us all . . . the people of America will, in some form or other, extend their dominion and their power, until they shall have brought within their mighty embrace the multitudes of the Islands of the great Pacific, and placed the Saxon race upon the eastern shores of Asia.[35]

He added that, in Asia, the United States would confront her main rival in expansion—Russia—"and then will be fought the mighty battle

. . . [for] the freedom or slavery of the world." Most Americans lacked Perry's enthusiasm for an apocalyptic war, but ideas of Anglo-Saxon supremacy were growing in the United States.

After Perry's mission, the United States had welcomed Japanese as diplomats, visitors, and students. But in the early 1900s, Japanese immigrants alarmed people—especially in California, where most of them settled—as an economic threat because they worked for low wages, weakening the position of native laborers, especially during hard times. More dangerous seemed the imaginary threat of the "Yellow Peril"—Japanese and Chinese immigrants as advance agents for an invasion of the West Coast. With growing fear and animosity toward them, Californians of European descent rioted against the newcomers. They also passed laws barring Japanese children from public schools and adults from owning or leasing land.[36] Besides the racism, the discriminatory laws were deeply offensive to Japanese immigrants for mystical reasons. Tolerating contemptuous treatment meant inviting abandonment by the gods.

Theodore Roosevelt and his successors as president realized that Japan's growing military power exceeded what the United States deployed in the far Pacific. They therefore followed a policy of avoiding war with her. When Japanese planes sank the U.S. gunboat *Panay* in China in 1937, and hotheads demanded war to punish Japan, Franklin Roosevelt quickly accepted monetary compensation to end the incident.[37]

By the time the United States condemned her territorial expansion in the 1930s, Japan had turned from defensive dependence toward its opposite—toward becoming the dominant power in Asia and even the ruler of that quarter of the globe. Striving for superiority ordinarily reflects a sense of inferiority and vulnerability. Volcanoes and storms had terrorized Japan's early settlers. Their mythology and other writings reflected catastrophic fears and vulnerability, while also proclaiming themselves to be the chosen people of the gods, the greatest race on earth. But no amount of self-puffery and of presenting a ferocious face to enemies can eliminate an established sense of vulnerability. Western insults and threats—real and imagined—brought out Japanese fears and the need to counter them boldly, in a superior manner. Japan's turn toward becoming a superpower involved no basic change of character.

A common interest between Japan and the United States also developed from their wariness of Russia, intensified by her Communist revolution. Horror of communism ran strong in both nations, fostering a brief de facto alliance and joint invasion of the new Soviet Union to destroy the Communist regime.[38] But in the end, common interests failed to stop deterioration in relations between Japan and the United States. Japan's independent, bold moves into Manchuria in the 1930s aroused strong Western opposition. And her joining with Germany in the Anti-Comintern (anti-Soviet) Pact of 1936 alarmed Roosevelt, who viewed Germany as a graver threat than the Soviet Union.[39] His alarm increased in 1940, when Japan joined Germany and Italy in the Axis Pact, which Roosevelt saw as a charter for world conquest.

When Japan decided to follow an independent course in the 1930s, she was powerful enough to risk displeasing the West. Her leaders calculated — correctly — that the United States and Great Britain would not go to war over her expansion on the Asian mainland, even if it threatened their interests in China. The events sketched here set the stage for war between Japan and the United States, but do not provide a sufficient cause for it. As Japan became involved in a long war with China, the United States was about to be drawn again into a European war. These separate courses of events crossed in 1941.

CHAPTER 8
JAPAN'S MOVES TO DOMINATE EAST ASIA

Even though samurai led the Choshu-Satsuma revolt that brought down the shogunate, its fall was their death knell as a class. When Emperor Meiji ended feudalism in 1871, formally abolishing the clans, the change was hardest on ordinary samurai. Those who were lords continued to function as local rulers by accepting Imperial appointments as non-hereditary governors of their prior domains. Funds and monopolistic rights from the emperor aided some samurai to become giants of industry. And they retained their titles of nobility. Other samurai, however, lost their function when Meiji established a modern army and navy by conscription. Some became leading officers in the new armed forces, but there were four hundred thousand samurai and only a few thousand positions for officers. During the Tokugawan peace, a shift of samurai from military units into bureaucratic jobs had begun. Meiji continued the shift and tried to inspire gentleness in former samurai, many of whom entered a greatly expanded national civil service. Others went into business and civilian professions.[1]

That still left many idle former samurai, pensioned off by the government, restless and resentful. Between wars, samurai had served as peace officers with the authority to mete out instant justice by beheading offenders on the spot. Now, no longer knights and no longer accorded the rights to carry their swords in public and to judge and punish citizens, they had no legitimate outlets for the violence to which they were conditioned. And they were no longer officially entitled to respect as Japan's highest social class, the bearers of her sacred values.

Many who had been made masterless and jobless by the end of feudalism joined the Satsuma, the most dissident and militant of the clans, which resisted clan abolition. Even though they had helped restore Imperial power, the Satsuma found Meiji's changes too radical a

125

departure from tradition. The more Meiji changed Japan, the more troubled they became, believing the nation had lost her guiding values. The Meiji revolution—like other revolutions—loosened established restraints, freeing pent-up impulses, particularly destructive ones. Former samurai who did not fit into the roles available to them in the new Japan, or did not find satisfaction in those roles, increasingly used violence for political purposes. In 1875, two hundred former samurai formed the League of the Divine Wind and rebelled against the new ways. The army quickly put down the rebellion.[2]

Satsuma dissatisfaction over the changes again came to a head when the government hesitated about going to war against Korea over an insult. Japan had sent a trade mission to Korea, which the Koreans had rejected contemptuously. The Japanese government took no action—a failure which Satsuma leader Saigo Takamori saw as cowardly and fatal paralysis. He proposed that Tokyo send an envoy to Korea who would provoke the Koreans to kill him, providing a pretext for war, and he volunteered to be the envoy. When the government ignored his proposal, Saigo led another Satsuma rebellion in 1877. After a bloody civil war, the new conscript army beat his large samurai army, and Saigo committed suicide.[3] With the defeat, his samurai lost their last employment as knights.

The public, however, retained its veneration of samurai, treasuring especially stories of those from the past who died fighting for their lords' honor or their own. The Japanese admired those who defied the law by an act of conscience—often to exact vengeance—and then committed suicide. They honored rebels—even those in hopeless causes. Often they admired heroic failures more than successes; "losers, mythical or historical, have provoked a far greater amount of sympathy, adulation, and exaltation than the winners." This admiration persisted even into the twenty-first century.[4] Such heroes were usually isolated figures, committing suicide if not killed by enemies. Saigo had achieved a long record of humanitarian and government service. However, it was for committing suicide after leading a hopeless revolt that he was remembered as "the great Saigo," the last true samurai.[5]

Honoring rebelliousness and disregard for the law may seem surprising in a culture that stressed adherence to authority and rules. But rigid adherence came from the Tokugawa era, while adoration of failed heroes was an older tradition on which the samurai code was based. The key virtue of a failed hero was *makoto* (sincerity of spirit), which had connotations of loyalty and devotion:

> **Sincerity precedes not only . . . demands of established authority but also conventional rectitude; for its ultimate criterion**

> is not the objective righteousness of a cause but the honesty
> with which the hero espouses it . . . his noble renunciation of
> everything temporal and impure disposes him to defeat.[6]

By contrast, insincerity and corruption were seen as contributing to material success. Therefore, success made a man morally suspect.

A famous samurai said, "One's way of dying can validate one's entire life." According to the samurai "bible" — the *Hagakure* — "*Bushido* [the Way of the Warrior] consists in dying."[7] And a key to virtue was immediate performance of duty, without regard to consequences. Yoshida Shoin, a famous samurai of the Tokugawa era, wrote:

> If a general and his men fear death and are apprehensive
> over possible defeat, then they will unavoidably suffer defeat
> and death. But if they make up their minds, from the general
> down to the last footsoldier, not to think of living but only of
> *standing in one place and facing death together*, then, though
> they have no other thought than meeting death, they will in-
> stead hold on to life and gain victory.[8] (Italics added.)

The image of standing in one place, standing on one's feet, and facing death together would recur in statements by Japan's leaders about embracing the necessity of war with the United States. To Japanese people, it was an inspiring image from early times. Perhaps the image came from the predicament of being caught in an earthquake, when people are thrown to the ground and standing is difficult and frightening. Nonetheless, a constructive response may require ignoring the prospect of death and getting to one's feet for concerted action.

When Japan was helpless against foreign military threats — when she needed quickly to build up her armed forces — Meiji had given leaders of the army and navy (former samurai) extraordinary powers, perhaps to pacify them. They were not subject to civil authority. Later, when Japan was more secure against foreign military threats, that independence was taken from them. But having had it was a precedent for independent action by military leaders in the 1930s, which destabilized the government. A second privilege given heads of the armed forces was veto power over who could be chosen as minister of the army or navy. This enabled them to prevent formation of a cabinet unsatisfactory to them by refusing to accept a designated military minister. Similarly, they could bring down a cabinet by ordering the minister of the army or navy to resign. And by threatening to do so, they could influence cabinet decisions. During Meiji's rule the army and navy usually accepted whoever the prime minister chose as ministers.

But later the army increasingly exercised this extraordinary power (the navy rarely used it) to advance political goals.

The new parliamentary government structure carried over from the past only the figure of the semidivine emperor. Lacking any history of democracy or of political parties, the institutions of parliament and cabinet were taken from Western models. Without tradition or experience, parliament members and cabinet ministers had little besides the emperor to guide and restrain their actions or provide stability. Corruption became widespread. Cabinets — disgraced, or only suspected of corruption, or simply ineffectual — were short-lived, as former samurai urged their replacement by leaders who were above political parties, by princes and military heroes.

Former samurai also sought to influence government policy by education and propaganda. For this purpose, in 1881 they organized the political society Genyosha (meaning Children of the Sea of Genkai, which separated Japan from China). The name reflected a goal of expansion in China.[9] Concluding that working through the parliament and political parties was futile, in 1901 the Genyosha organized an action group, the Kokuryukai. The actions undertaken were killing national leaders considered evil or obstacles to the nation's grand destiny.[10]

"Kokuryukai" has been translated as both Black Dragon Society and Amur River Society. The Amur River, in Manchuria, represented the members' goal of winning and colonizing that land for Japan. Some Japanese believed their ancestors came originally from Manchuria; for them, acquiring it meant regaining their ancient homeland. To the most idealistic, who saw Japan as gravely corrupted, a return to that homeland was a return to purity.

Many similar patriotic societies sprang up, working for elimination of Western ways, for a return to purity and tradition, for elimination of inequities, and for elevation of Japan to the supremacy they saw as her destiny. Imbued with the samurai spirit, but lacking the mental discipline that had been a daily feature of samurai life, they were not much limited by the samurai code or other traditional restraints. With fanaticism, they turned to intimidation and the killing of military and cabinet officers and business leaders, and then to coups.[11] Young military officers in the societies laid claim to the legacy of the young samurai who had brought about the Meiji Restoration.

Some of these action groups called themselves Sakurakai — Cherry Blossom Society — taking as their spiritual ideal the cherry blossom tree. Beloved in Japan, the tree's striking feature is its spring blooming — brilliant but short-lived, as the petals quickly fall to earth.[12] The image conveys a traditional Japanese aesthetic sensibility — *aware* — the pathos aroused by natural beauty, as one realizes that it will soon be lost. The realization is a reminder that everything in the world — and the world itself — is ephemeral.[13] The sense of fragile transience was stronger in Japan than in other nations.

Translated into political affairs, the cherry blossom ideal meant that the noblest act a young man could perform was to express his purity and then die for it. Concretely, he should carry out an act of sincere violence and then — if he survived — commit suicide. In this way, the societies combined the symbolism of the cherry blossom with the kamikaze myth to deal with what they saw as threats to Japan's existence.

These images would dominate the thinking of kamikaze pilots during World War II. Before taking off on the missions that usually ended their lives, they would write poems in the vein of:

If only we might fall
Like cherry blossoms in the Spring—
So pure and radiant![14]

And some named their planes "Cherry Blossom."

The numerous patriotic societies were small, and their combined membership also small. But because they embodied ancient traditions, they exercised influence far beyond their numbers. The nation viewed patriotic assassins and coup leaders as heroes, and many thought they should not be punished. Because of regard for the tradition and awareness of public sympathy for patriotic activists, government leaders hesitated to prosecute or even arrest assassins and participants in coup attempts.[15] During the 1920s and 1930s, small army units joined in coups. And in China, army units took independent action to force Tokyo's hand or to accomplish what they thought administration leaders wanted, but were too cowardly to carry out. Facing frequent assassinations, coups, and attempts at both — and more frequent threats and rumors of such plots — government leaders were often intimidated, and cabinets went from crisis to crisis, as controlling the army became a constant concern. A Western reporter called the chaotic conditions under which administrations tried to rule "government by assassination."[16]

The main effect on foreign affairs was to move still-cautious administrations toward war with China, the Soviet Union, Great Britain, and the United States. It was a drift toward total war, pictured by a Japanese official as the course of a rudderless ship beset by storms (army violence), with its crew confused and so intimidated that no one was willing to take charge.[17] Cabinet officers and advisers to the emperor talked endlessly about grave problems created by runaway elements of the army without confronting them, and ended by substantially abdicating responsibility.[18]

Japan had begun her climb to world power by acquiring territories from China. In 1905, on winning rights in southern Manchuria by defeating Russia, Japan took over the Russian-built railroad there, stationed troops along it, invested in other enterprises, and began to move in colonists. Manchuria was ruled by warlord Chang Tso-lin, who now found himself needing to please three nations contending for power over his domain: China, Russia, and Japan. Despite the stresses, for sixteen years, incidents among troops of the four sovereignties were minimal. Meanwhile Japan used threats against China to win additional rights in Inner Mongolia, which adjoined Manchuria.[19]

During the 1920s, Japanese troops in southern Manchuria—called the Kwantung Army—became a center of superpatriots who plotted military ventures. In order to make Tokyo safer, army leaders in Tokyo contributed to the concentration of plotters in the Kwantung Army by transferring to it soldiers who had participated in assassination and coup plots in Japan. In 1928 a bomb set by officers of the Kwantung Army killed Chang as part of a plot to take over Manchuria fully. While Japan's leaders saw to it that the plot was aborted, strong tension arose in Tokyo between superpatriots and moderates over how far to go in China. When Chang's son and successor, Chang Hseuh-liang, announced his allegiance to China, Japan's superpatriots grew determined to have a more militant policy in China. This led to increasing conflict between the Kwantung Army and Chang Hseuh-liang's forces, and, in Tokyo, to a failed army coup in 1931.[20]

Later that year, Japan's administration discovered a plot to stage another incident, giving the Kwantung Army a pretext for decisive military action in Manchuria. The cabinet gave orders to stop the plot—orders not carried out. The Kwantung Army set off an explosion, claimed Chinese troops had set it off to sabotage the railroad, and proceeded to occupy Mukden, the Manchurian capital, and advance against Chang Hseuh-liang's forces.[21]

Japanese field commanders traditionally had wide discretion, but the Kwantung Army's actions shocked some cabinet members, while provoking Western condemnation. As the Kwantung Army was advancing, Tokyo gave repeated assurances that Japan would not extend her control in Manchuria, and ordered her troops to return to positions they held before the incident. Defying these orders, the Kwantung Army continued on and, by 1932, was in control of Manchuria. Tokyo then established a puppet state there—the "independent" kingdom of Manchukuo under Pu Yi, the last Chinese emperor.

(He had lost his throne when the Chinese republic was established in 1911.) In doing this, Tokyo carried out the Kwantung Army's plan. Earlier Kwantung officers had contacted Pu Yi and brought him to Manchuria for this purpose.[22]

Conquest of Manchuria, added to earlier victories over China and Russia, created "a new pantheon of national heroes . . . and sanctified Japanese rights and interests [in Korea and Manchuria] as a matter of national honor."[23] Cabinets and more responsible army leaders found it harder and harder to rein in field officers who violated orders, especially when they succeeded in winning valuable territory for Japan. And the cabinet found its fear of foreign reactions offset by the easy success of the Kwantung Army.

The United States and Great Britain condemned Japan's seizure of Manchuria, as did the League of Nations, prompting Japan to leave the League. Action against Japan was limited, partly because U.S. and British leaders saw Japan as a bulwark against the Soviet Union and the spread of communism to China. The Soviet Union, however, accepted the seizure, sold her railroad in northern Manchuria to Japan, and withdrew. Manchuria—a vast, rich land—was won at a cost of little more than foreign criticism.[24] By 1933 Japan was isolated again, but this time she was militarily powerful and prepared to continue her expansion without consideration for pleasing the West. Subsequent campaigns in China were authorized by Tokyo.

The crucial one began in 1937 with an incident. Again Japan intended only a limited war; after quick victories, peace was to be negotiated giving her control of additional provinces near Manchuria. Japan did win a series of victories and proposed peace. China's ruler, Chiang Kai-shek, considered the proposal, but was encouraged to continue fighting by a U.S. promise of aid. The aid did not come in time and, after further defeats, Chiang offered to accept Japan's terms. But by then Japan wanted more, for she had become committed to a grand plan of domination to establish her "East Asia Co-prosperity Sphere." She saw herself as destined to lead a resurgence of East Asian civilization and power. The superpatriot Okawa Shumei projected Japan's future role:

a struggle between the great powers of the East and the West which will decide their existence is . . . absolutely inevitable if a new world is to come about . . . not . . . that a united Asia will be pitted against a united Europe . . . Actually there will be one country acting as the champion of Asia and one country acting as the champion of Europe, and it is these who must fight in order that a new world may be realized. It is my belief

that Heaven has decided on Japan as its choice for the champion of the East.[26]

Many Japanese, particularly officers of the Kwantung Army, shared
his view of an apocalyptic war. That army's General Ishiwara Kanji
lectured on the theme at Japan's National War College, identifying
the United States as the champion of the West.[27]

The campaign in China went on, with Japan winning more
battles while offering peace terms. Japan did not commit her armies
fully, holding most in reserve against the possibility of war with a
Western power. And Chiang no longer wanted peace at the price of
Chinese territory, for his position was now stronger. In 1927 his drive
against the warlords had faltered after he had ousted Communists
from his government (the Kuomintang) and tried to wipe them out.
The Communists established their own army, and civil war ensued,
limiting the fight either side could put up against the Japanese until
1937. But Japan's invasion brought the Kuomintang and Communists
together again in a fragile truce with limited cooperation, which lasted
through the war. The invasion also brought considerable aid to Chiang
from the Soviet Union, including a "volunteer" air force. Japan's China
campaign—the Japanese continued to call it "the China incident"—
went on and on. She conquered an enormous territory but—because
of China's gigantic area, population, and natural resources, as well as
her newfound spirit and foreign aid—her resistance grew stronger.
The "incident" had become a major war with no end in sight.

Despite growing animosity toward China, some Japanese still
managed to see themselves as rescuers of the Chinese and other Asians
from Western oppression. In a radio address to his nation in 1940,
Foreign Minister Arita Hachiro said the sword drawn in China "is
intended to be nothing other than the life-giving sword that destroys
evil and makes justice manifest."[28] In his propaganda for the war, he
invoked the tradition of the samurai sword as an instrument of purifi-
cation and justice.

Japan's armies, however, failed to live up to the tradition. In contrast to their disciplined conduct in the 1904–05 war with Russia, they
went on rampages in China—most notably, raping and slaughtering
civilians when they captured the Kuomintang capital of Nanking.[29]
The atrocities fed U.S. animosity toward Japan, but substantial measures against her were slow to come. It would be the menace of Hitler's
Germany that would move Roosevelt toward high-risk measures
against Japan in 1941.

CHAPTER 9
ROOSEVELT'S TENTATIVE MOVES AGAINST GERMANY

Franklin Roosevelt was inaugurated as president in 1933, weeks after Adolf Hitler was appointed chancellor of Germany. Roosevelt was the exception among world leaders in seeing early and taking seriously the menace of Hitler. Not only did he grasp Hitler's intentions, Roosevelt also considered him extremely dangerous—a "madman" who, as leader of Germany, was now in a position to do grave harm.[1] During the following years U.S. diplomats in and around Germany kept Roosevelt informed about destructive plans of the Third Reich. A 1937 report from Berlin said Reich leaders were clinically "psychopathic cases," confirming Roosevelt's impression that they were dangerously deranged and his decision to prepare for war.[2] After World War II, as the Holocaust and other wanton destruction Hitler perpetrated became known, Stimson wrote, "No statesman in the world saw and described the Nazi menace more truly than Franklin Roosevelt."[3]

He would die a few weeks before Hitler did, making their terms in office almost the same. During those twelve years they would often think about each other with contempt, anticipating the day when they would lead their nations against each other. But in 1933 that confrontation was remote. Roosevelt's and Hitler's initial challenges were domestic—overcoming severe economic depressions.

Hitler had made his vision of world conquest clear enough in his book *Mein Kampf* and in fiery speeches. British Prime Minister Neville Chamberlain's perception of Hitler's personality—hate-filled, mad, reckless, and extremely dangerous—was very like Roosevelt's. In 1934 Chamberlain wrote, "The *fons et origo* of all our European troubles and anxieties is Germany."[4] (The Latin words *fons* and *origo* both mean "source"; the repetition added emphasis.) He also wrote, "I hate Nazism, and all its work, with a greater loathing than ever."[5] Nonetheless he and Roosevelt dealt with Hitler rather differently. Chamberlain went all-out for peace; Roosevelt planned for war.

Chamberlain has been ridiculed for disregarding Hitler's record and accepting promises of peace Hitler made to him personally. But many others were also taken in, including most Germans — people who knew Hitler best. Denial of the threats he posed was massive. Former British Prime Minister Lloyd George met with Hitler for three hours in 1936 and came away convinced that he was "a great man."[6] Winston Churchill earned a reputation for hardheaded political judgment, but he too was taken in at first, devoting a chapter to Hitler in his 1933 book *Great Contemporaries*.[7] The gullibility of Chamberlain and many other leaders in seeking security through agreements with Hitler was in sharp contrast to Roosevelt's exceptionally realistic perception of him and determination to fight him.

Shortly after taking office, Roosevelt secretly made a vague offer to join France in collective security against Germany. A year later he urged that France, Great Britain, and the United States send a joint commission to investigate alleged German armament violations of the Versailles Treaty. If Hitler refused, the three nations would stop trading with Germany. In 1935 he proposed that, if German aggression prompted France, Britain, and Italy to boycott Germany, the United States would join them. To an adviser, Roosevelt said the United States could even join a blockade of Germany — an act of war — by executive order, without Congressional approval. Germany had not yet made an aggressive move, and leaders of France and Great Britain largely ignored Roosevelt's early proposals. And when they did respond to later ones, asking for a commitment from the United States, Roosevelt held back because Americans strongly opposed intervention.[8]

Meanwhile Roosevelt devoted himself to educating the nation about the menace of Hitler, to persuading it that war against Germany was necessary, and to unifying it. And he developed war plans in secret. Despite the hesitancy of his steps, his goal did not change. A biographer described Roosevelt's predicament as requiring him to "make upon the public mind a . . . self-contradictory [impression] of a strong, bold leader who is . . . forced by circumstances into actions he is reluctant to take. Above all, he must avoid like the plague . . . Woodrow Wilson's great mistake . . . of . . . outstripping his public support."[9] This is the same impression Presidents Polk and Lincoln had given in leading the United States into war, as have presidents after Roosevelt.

Like Wilson — whom he admired greatly — Roosevelt was an internationalist at heart.[10] In his inaugural address he said, "Our international relations, though vastly important, are in point of time and necessity, secondary to the establishment of a sound national economy."[11] But he began to staff the State Department and diplomatic corps with people who favored intervention against aggression abroad.[12]

A major obstacle to intervention was his promise to bring the United States out of the depression — a promise he took seriously. And some of his herculean economic measures aroused strong congressional opposition. Many conservatives came to hate him for his New Deal, and their hatred would later contribute to calls for his impeachmnnt over foreign policy.

To win support for economic measures from resistive legislators — many of whom opposed U.S. involvement in European affairs — Roosevelt adopted a noninterventionist posture, pledging to keep the United States out of a new European war. According to insider Robert Sherwood, such pledges were "what Roosevelt felt compelled to say in order to maintain influence over public opinion and over Congressional action."[13] In maintaining this posture, he accepted congressional adoption of the 1935 Neutrality Act, which prohibited selling arms to nations at war. That same year, even though the United States was still deep in the depression, he told a reporter that foreign affairs concerned him much more than domestic ones. Nonetheless, and despite being even more troubled by foreign affairs during 1936 and 1937 and more determined to help attacked nations, he accepted amendments strengthening the Neutrality Act.

Roosevelt's tentativeness and indirection in taking controversial action also reflected his personality. When he was growing up, the "law" in his home was his mother, Sara. She used heavy threats to control him — even when he was an adult — and he adapted by avoiding confrontations with her. When determined to have his way, he found ways to get around her. For example, he seemingly accepted Sara's actions to separate him from his cousin Eleanor Roosevelt, while secretly becoming engaged to her.[14] In this way, he was able to marry the woman of his choice despite Sara's opposition.

While serving as assistant secretary of the navy, Roosevelt had witnessed Wilson's difficulties in leading the United States into World War I. Despite long-standing isolation from European wars, the American public had been moved toward the goal of fostering democracy and freedom from oppression throughout the world by Wilson's infectious idealism. But idealism had not been enough, and Wilson had turned to rousing speeches, inciting anger at Germany for her attacks on ships of non-belligerent nations — especially the sinking of the *Lusitania* and especially when U.S. lives were lost. And most effective in arousing the public for war had been publicizing the "Zimmermann telegram" — an intercepted coded German message to Ambassador

Arthur Zimmermann in Mexico, telling him to feel out the Mexican government about an alliance against the United States.[15] By seizing on these incidents, Wilson finally won his battle to enter his reluctant nation into World War I. Roosevelt would similarly seize on incidents at sea, and he would publicize German documents — including forged ones — to arouse the public for war against Germany.

Roosevelt was, of course, limited in taking action against Germany by the Constitution and Congress, as well as by public opinion. Leaders of European nations, less restricted by their constitutions than he, sometimes grew impatient with what they saw as his indecisiveness in opposing German aggression. Presidents before Roosevelt had gotten around restrictions, manipulating the United States into wars. Perhaps the memory of those manipulations contributed to a congressional resolution in 1938: except if the United States were attacked directly, she could go to war only with the approval of a national referendum.[16] It lost by a narrow margin, but emphasized to Roosevelt the opposition to be overcome in going to war against Germany.

Italian Prime Minister Benito Mussolini prompted Europe's first war crisis. His heart set on building an empire, on restoring a measure of ancient Roman glory, he ordered military studies begun in 1933 for an invasion of Ethiopia in 1935. In a 1934 memo to his army chief he wrote:

> The problem of Italian-Abyssinian [Ethiopian] relations has very recently shifted from a diplomatic plane to one which can be solved by force only: like all historical problems of this kind, it admits of one solution: a resort to arms.[17]

What had shifted the situation was Mussolini's conclusion that France, Great Britain, and the League of Nations would not take decisive counteraction. He added:

> there will be no need for a declaration of war and . . . we must emphasize the purely defensive character of operations. *No one in Europe would raise any difficulties provided the prosecution of operations resulted rapidly in an accomplished fact. It would suffice to declare to England and France that their interests would be recognised.*

Conquering Ethiopia proved more difficult than he anticipated, but he was right in judging that European powers would allow him to carry it out.

When Italy attacked, Roosevelt urged British Prime Minister

Stanley Baldwin to take joint military action with France in defense of Ethiopia.[18] France, however, had already given Mussolini a free hand to invade, in return for an alliance with Italy that offered security against aggression by Germany. Britain protested the Ethiopian invasion, but remained equivocal. And the League of Nations imposed limited trade sanctions on Italy, but took no action on a proposed oil embargo. (Mussolini later said, had an oil embargo been imposed, "I would have had to withdraw from Abyssinia within a week. That would have been an incalculable disaster for me."[19])

In 1936 German troops — only twenty-two thousand strong — occupied the Rhineland, violating the Versailles treaty clause that made it a demilitarized zone. Roosevelt then urged to King George of England that Britain join in a blockade against Germany. The nations most concerned — France, Belgium, and Britain — took no action. (Hitler later said that, "at that moment I risked a great deal. If France had marched then, we would have been forced to withdraw."[20])

Onset of the Spanish civil war in 1936 provoked heated political controversy in the United States. Spain's army-based rebels ranged from conservative to fascist; her government, from liberal to Communist. European powers lined up accordingly: help for the rebels — supplies and soldiers — came from Germany and Italy; help for the government, from the Soviet Union and then from Britain and France. The same European alignment would develop in the war to come: Germany and Italy against France, Britain, and the Soviet Union.

Roosevelt wanted badly to help the Spanish government. The Neutrality Act applied only to wars between nations, and did not prohibit arms sales to a government during a civil war. But he feared alienating Catholic voters, a traditional bulwark of the Democratic Party.[21] While Catholics in the United States were divided in their support between the Spanish government and the rebels, the "Catholic" position proclaimed by some archbishops was so strongly pro-rebel that Roosevelt held back. Hull announced that the United States would "scrupulously refrain from any interference whatever in the unfortunate Spanish situation," and in August 1936 the State Department discouraged a manufacturer from selling planes to her government.[22] As the Spanish government's position became precarious, Roosevelt again considered aiding it. But in January 1937, Congress banned arms sales to both sides in Spain. Roosevelt then sent supplies to the Spanish government surreptitiously.[23]

When Japan invaded China in July 1937, Roosevelt began to consider an embargo combined with a partial blockade of Japan, in cooperation with Great Britain.[24] In October Roosevelt made a powerful public statement, known as his "quarantine" speech:

> Without a declaration of war and without warning or justifica-
> tion of any kind, civilians, including vast numbers of women
> and children, are being ruthlessly murdered with bombs from
> the air. . . . If those things come to pass in other parts of the
> world, let no one imagine that America will escape, that
> America may expect mercy, that this Western Hemisphere
> will not be attacked and that it will continue tranquilly . . . to
> carry on. . . civilization. . . . The peace-loving nations must
> make a concerted effort in opposition. . . . When an epidemic
> of physical disease starts to spread, the community . . . joins
> in a quarantine. . . . War is a contagion, whether it be de-
> clared or undeclared.[25]

The first words were understood to refer to Japan, and "other parts of the world" to Germany and Italy. In the light of his earlier and subsequent thinking about a blockade, he may have meant these nations in his mention of a quarantine. According to an associate, Roosevelt intended the quarantine speech as a trial balloon, hopefully leading to joint sanctions against aggressor nations.[26]

The speech aroused strong opposition; noninterventionists charged Roosevelt with preparing to plunge the nation into war, and members of Congress angrily spoke of impeachment.[27] Roosevelt told an adviser, "It's a terrible thing to look over your shoulder when you are trying to lead — and find no one there."[28]

In private Roosevelt spoke of a "peaceful blockade," which was a euphemism inasmuch as a blockade had long been classified as an act of war. And the war plan developed shortly after the quarantine speech included a blockade of Japan. The phrase suggests Roosevelt was straddling the question of war.[29] Months later he said privately:

> Since the Germans, the Italians and the Japanese have in-
> vented a new method [of war] which consists of carrying on
> military operations without declaring war, why not do like-
> wise? . . . It is possible that Germany and Italy in case of a
> blockade, would go to war, but it would not be us who would
> declare it.[30]

In March 1938 Hitler annexed Austria and began to threaten Czechoslovakia. A reporter asked Roosevelt if he might take concrete action against further aggression. He replied whimsically that, if he had such a secret plan, he certainly would not announce it at a press conference.[31] Roosevelt's words were not taken seriously. He had, however, ordered steps leading to a military alliance with Great Britain, which may have been behind his mention of a secret plan.

In August the United States informed Japan that their trade treaty of 1911 would be terminated in six months.[32] That troubled Japan's leaders more than protests of her invasion of China and her atrocities there. They took it as a sign of the embargoes to come, fearing U.S. power to throttle Japan economically.

With France and Britain at peace, there was no legal barrier to helping them arm, and Roosevelt devoted himself to that task. He had, however, considerable opposition from his own military leaders. They agreed with him on the threats Hitler posed and on the need to arm for war, but considered weapons production insufficient even for meeting projected U.S. needs.[33] France needed warplanes desperately, but Army Air Corps Chief Arnold vigorously opposed selling her any. Military leaders' public statements against sending arms to Britain and France encouraged opposition to it in Congress. Roosevelt therefore silenced his generals and arranged to sell arms secretly.[34]

When France considered buying a new U.S. warplane in January 1939, a French aviation expert went on a test flight. The plane crashed, injuring him (or, by another account, killing him). The first report identified him as a U.S. aviation mechanic.[35] When his true identity was exposed, so also were U.S. warplane sales to France.

As a result, the Senate Military Affairs Committee considered an investigation of arms sales to France and Britain. To prevent it, Roosevelt invited the committee to the White House, giving members a report of intelligence on Hitler's war plans. According to a White House transcript of the meeting, in projecting the danger of an attack on the United States, Roosevelt referred to our "first lines of defense" in Europe, guarded by France and Britain.[36] According to a committee member, he said "the frontiers of the United States are on the Rhine."[37] Reported to the press, the latter words prompted an outcry, which Roosevelt tried to silence by calling them a "deliberate lie."[38]

According to Sherwood, whatever words Roosevelt used, "he most certainly did believe that America's eastern frontier was on the Rhine," and he acted accordingly.[39] Because of the vigorous protest aroused, he then used greater secrecy and misdirection in supplying France and Britain. In all, about five hundred U.S. planes were sold quietly to France — far short of what she needed to make a stand against the German air force.[40]

Many political leaders in Europe and the United States expected Hitler's territorial demands of Czechoslovakia to result in war. Because of armament lacks and extreme domestic dissension,

French Premier Edouard Daladier and his cabinet were divided about whether to honor their treaty, committing France to defend Czechoslovakia if she were invaded. To the public Daladier declared, "The solemn pledges made by France to Czechoslovakia are unequivocal and sacred," and perhaps he was sincere at the moment.[41] But he had been premier in 1934 — a time of extreme domestic political strife, with rioting and danger of civil war — and "had been unable to foresee or forestall anything . . . unable to take command in the moment of crisis."[42] Paralyzed, he had resigned. Again premier during the crisis over German demands of Czechoslovakia, Daladier's actions fell far short of his words; he tried to appease Hitler at Czechoslovakia's expense.[43]

Baldwin and his successor as prime minister, Chamberlain, were pacifists, well aware of Britain's anti-war mood and military unpreparedness for war with Germany. They also chose a course of appeasing Hitler. If war came nonetheless, they meant to rely on a blockade to starve Germany into giving it up.

On becoming prime minister, Chamberlain was more realistic than Baldwin about the menace Hitler posed, but extremely hesitant to confront it. When Hitler threatened and then annexed Austria, Chamberlain did nothing. When Hitler threatened Czechoslovakia in 1938, the Soviet Union proposed extending her pact with France into an alliance that would include Great Britain, to defend Czechoslovakia against Germany. Churchill, still influential although no longer in the cabinet, urged such an alliance, but Chamberlain rejected it.[44] He seems to have distrusted and feared Stalin more than Hitler.

Most revealing about Chamberlain's reaction to having his ideas contradicted was his response to a 1938 book, *The House That Hitler Built*. He wrote in his diary that, "if I accepted the author's conclusions, I should despair, but I don't and won't."[45] The author had spent a year and a half in and around Germany, compiling much data on Hitler and the Third Reich. His remarkably perceptive conclusion was:

> From whichever angle we approach the question . . . we come
> to the inevitability of war . . . Hitlerism cannot achieve its aims
> without war; its ideology is that of war.[46]

Chamberlain, who had never visited the Third Reich or met Hitler, not only dismissed the conclusion but also the data on which it rested.

He believed that Hitler and Mussolini were subject to moods, and if caught in a good mood they would give him what he wanted. Accordingly, he tried putting or keeping them in a good mood and ingratiating himself by speaking well of them, acceding to their wishes, and supporting their actions when possible — including their seizures of territory.[47] He saw his task as propitiating them as if they were mercurial gods. Hitler and Mussolini were, in fact, moody and susceptible to flattery. But Chamberlain seemed not to grasp that, when their good mood passed, they might go back on what they promised him. Nor did he see that, out of low self-esteem, they were insatiable. Concessions reinforced their contempt of British and French leaders. Disappointed over and over, Chamberlain nonetheless persuaded himself that they could be trusted. According to his foreign secretary, Anthony Eden, "He believed the dictators to be anxious for genuine agreements and himself to be the only man who could negotiate with them."[48] In 1937 Chamberlain had said, "If only we could sit down at a table with the Germans and run through all their complaints and claims . . . this would greatly relieve all tension."[49] In September 1938, when Hitler's designs on Czechoslovakia seemed about to plunge Europe into war, Chamberlain turned to personal diplomacy in a last effort to avert it. On his initiative, he met three times with Hitler.

Hitler was a master of manipulating people by offering them what they most wanted, but had no basis in reality to expect. This skill had won him the support of Nazis, of many conservative political and industrial leaders in Germany, and of the public, making him ruler of the nation. His was the art of the confidence man, tempting the mark with an offer of what no one else could have. In addition, as Anthony Eden put it:

> Hitler's technique was to accompany each blow with an offer nicely calculated to tempt the victim. Even if the offer did not compensate for the blow, it made it all the more difficult to strike back.[50]

And in making himself ruler of Europe, Hitler was using these techniques on leaders of nations around Germany.

After their first meeting at Hitler's home in Berchtesgaden, in which Hitler was friendly, Chamberlain returned to England euphoric. He told his cabinet that he thought he had developed an influence over Hitler and "in spite of the hardness and ruthlessness I thought I saw in his face, I got the impression that here was a man who could be relied upon when he had given his word."[51] Hitler's word was that he wanted the Sudetenland — the part of Czechoslovakia where ethnic Germans lived — and nothing more.

After consultation with French leaders, who still had made no decision against honoring their treaty with Czechoslovakia, Chamberlain pressured Czech leaders, obtaining their consent to an Anglo-French proposal by which Hitler would get the Sudetenland if a plebiscite in the region favored unification with Germany. He then presented this proposal at a follow-up meeting with Hitler in Godesberg. Hitler interrupted, saying, "I am sorry, but that no longer applies." He went into a tirade of allegations against the Czechs that required immediate redress, and increased his demands. Shocked, taking this to mean Hitler had broken his word, Chamberlain protested. Hitler then said, "You know, you're the only man I've ever made a concession to."[53] (Hitler had, however, made many concessions in his rise to power and since then). On returning from Godesberg, Chamberlain reported to the House of Commons:

> I had been told [by Hitler] at Berchtesgaden that if the principle of self-determination were accepted [for the Sudetenland], Herr Hitler would discuss with me the ways and means of carrying it out. He told me [at Godesberg] that he never for one moment supposed that I should be able to come back and say that the principle was accepted. *I do not want the House to think that he was deliberately deceiving me . . .* but . . . I expected that when I got . . . to Godesberg, I had only to discuss quietly with him the proposals that I had brought back with me, and it was a profound shock to me when I was told at the beginning of the conversation that these proposals were not acceptable, and that they were to be replaced by proposals of a kind which I had not contemplated at all.[54] (Italics added.)

Chamberlain also said Hitler "would not deliberately deceive a man whom he respected," and clung to the belief that Hitler especially respected him.[55] Therefore he could best deal with Hitler.

On that basis, Chamberlain decided to make a final effort, and Daladier joined him in September 1938 at Munich, where Czechoslovakia's fate was decided without her being represented. The resultant Munich Pact gave Germany the Sudetenland in return for Hitler's agreement to no further territorial acquisitions.

Chamberlain again returned in euphoria, waving a separate agreement he had made with Hitler, and declared, "It is peace in our time. See, here is a paper that bears his name."[56] And much of the world, yearning for peace, took the Munich Pact with relief, while perceiving it as a victory for Hitler. (One who did not was Hitler himself, who complained privately that Chamberlain had cheated him out of his war.)

Daladier, who had kept in the background at Munich, considered

Chamberlain's euphoria most unrealistic. Cheered by a crowd on his return to Paris, Daladier reportedly said, "The imbeciles, if only they knew what they were acclaiming."[57] And he was not surprised when two members of his cabinet resigned in protest. By contrast, Chamberlain was shocked when members of his administration below cabinet-level resigned over Munich. And then his war minister, Duff Cooper, resigned with an angry protest. Nonetheless, Chamberlain remained convinced he had done the right thing, writing to the Archbishop of Canterbury, "I am sure that some day the Czechs will see that what we did was to save them for a happier future."[58] Chamberlain's poor judgment is detailed here because, although extreme, it was shared by leaders in many nations.

The appeasement and betrayal of Munich had broken the Czechs' will to resist. Perhaps they relied on a rider to the Munich Pact: "His Majesty's Government [Britain] and the French Government . . . offer an international guarantee of the new boundaries of the Czechoslovak State." Germany and Italy were also listed as guarantors.[59] But a few days after the pact was signed Poland seized a piece of Czechoslovakia, and neither the Czechs nor the nations designated in the pact as guarantors of their territorial integrity did anything. Then Hungary made demands for Czech territory, and Hitler and Mussolini decided how much she was to take, while Britain and France did nothing.

Roosevelt had lent some support to the Munich appeasement.[60] Quickly, he regretted it. Hitler's persecution, maiming, and killing of Jews, beginning with his appointment as chancellor, had been escalating. Two months after Munich, he carried out the pogrom known as *Kristallnacht* (the Night of Broken Glass), which apparently stiffened Roosevelt's conviction that Hitler must be defeated by military force. The German government declared the pogrom to be a spontaneous popular action, which fooled few people.

This beating and killing of Jews, along with destruction of their temples, stores, and homes, prompted Roosevelt's strongest measure against Germany until then: he denounced *Kristallnacht* at a press conference, adding, "I myself could scarcely believe that such things could happen in a twentieth-century civilization." And he dramatized his condemnation by recalling the U.S. ambassador in Berlin, which shocked Germans.[61] Despite widespread anti-Semitism in the United States, the pogrom so horrified people that a poll showed 72 percent supporting Roosevelt.[62] He then told Chamberlain that he wanted no more "Munichs" and that the industrial resources of the United States would back Britain in the coming war against Germany.

Although Roosevelt's words had no apparent effect, Hitler's

subsequent dismemberment of Czechoslovakia did. Before his negotiations with Chamberlain, Hitler had told his generals, "I am utterly
determined that Czechoslovakia should disappear from the map."[63]
Months after Munich, Hitler took over half of Czechoslovakia, made
the other half into a puppet state, and began to exterminate Czech civilians. Later, when planning the invasion of Poland, he told his generals, "I
experienced those poor worms Daladier and Chamberlain in Munich.
They will be too cowardly to attack. They won't go beyond a blockade."[64]

After the dismemberment of Czechoslovakia, Roosevelt used
diplomacy to unite the United States and much of the world against
Germany. He sent Hitler and Mussolini a list of thirty-one nations,
asking for an assurance not to attack any of them for ten years.[65] Hitler
and Mussolini did not take the request seriously and made no reply.
Apparently Roosevelt expected none; the request — and publicizing it —
amounted to pointing dramatically at the threat they posed to other
nations.

Roosevelt was well informed of events leading to Hitler's invasion of Poland, which prompted France and Britain to declare war on
Germany. In March 1939 — six months before the invasion — he told a
friend that, unless Britain and France faced defeat, he would keep the
United States out of the coming European war. But if their defeat appeared imminent, he would consider entering the war.[66] According to
another friend, by then, "Roosevelt knew that, barring an unforeseen
collapse of the Nazi forces, Hitler was a threat to the very existence of
our country, and that war was inevitable."[67]

That would not be much of a secret by the end of 1940. Roosevelt
began hinting at it in public speeches, and top-level military leaders
often discussed it and included it in memos on strategy and in war
plans. Even mid-level officers discussed the inevitability of war with
Germany and worked on plans for it.[68]

The invasion of Poland shattered remaining hopes that Hitler's
talk of war had been only bombast. It prompted Chamberlain to write,
"We have to kill one another just to satisfy that accursed madman,"
and "it is to restore the possibility of any civilised life at all that we
have got to put an end to Nazi policy."[69] It also prompted Roosevelt to
order new war plans based on the assumption of U.S. entry into the
European war, with that war given priority over a possible war in the
Pacific. Subsequently, the assumption was spelled out in military documents. The Joint (army and navy) Planning Committee recommended
in December 1940 that the United States "should not willingly engage
in any war against Japan," but if that happened, Pacific operations
should be restricted "so as to permit use of forces for a major offensive
in the Atlantic."[70]

On learning that the invasion of Poland was imminent, Roosevelt decided to sell Britain and France three-eighths of arms being produced in the United States. This aroused opposition in Congress and among Roosevelt's military advisers. But the decision had no effect because days later Hitler launched his invasion, and Britain and France declared war on Germany, making arms sales to them illegal. Roosevelt then called Congress back into session and, after he urged staying out of the European war, added, "Fate now seems to compel us to assume the task of helping to maintain in the western world a citadel wherein civilization may be kept alive."[71] And he asked for a major revision of the Neutrality Act—a virtual repeal. To his attorney general he said, "If we fail to get a [new] Neutrality Bill, how far do you think I can go in ignoring the existing act?"[72] He failed to get the revision, but Congress gave him authority to sell obsolescent warships and warplanes to belligerent nations. Under this compromise, he arranged for sales to Great Britain, and included military craft that were not obsolescent.

Hitler's invasion of Poland also prompted Roosevelt's first naval measure against Germany—the establishment on September 9, 1939, of a "Neutrality Patrol" in the Atlantic. In October Germany and Italy were warned to keep their warships out of the patrolled area. Operating outside U.S. territorial waters, the patrol force would be built up over the next two years to cover most of the North Atlantic, protecting British shipping against German and Italian submarines. It was the first step in what would become known as Roosevelt's "undeclared war" in the Atlantic.

Congress's refusal to repeal the Neutrality Act may have confirmed Roosevelt's belief that he could not win enough support to enter the European war openly or even provide enough arms to Britain and France openly. Over the next two years, Congress would allow some aid to Great Britain, and he would go beyond what it allowed by providing secret or misleadingly labeled aid. By hindsight, he seems to have been unnecessarily cautious and devious. Noninterventionists made much noise, although their influence was shrinking. Despite ringing speeches of opposition during debates, Congress passed almost all Roosevelt's subsequent measures to arm Britain and the United States. But Roosevelt asked for approval only of modest measures.

Three of Roosevelt's militant cabinet members—Knox, Stimson, and Ickes—urged him to lead the United States forthrightly into war, assuring him the nation would follow. Throughout history it was rare for nations not to rally behind leaders who took them into wars. Nations even followed insane rulers who arbitrarily did so for personal reasons. And opinion polls showed more and more people accepting the probable necessity of war against Germany, while still wishing it could be avoided.[73] But Roosevelt lacked confidence in the nation and Congress on this matter. He told Ickes that he planned to "slip a noose around Japan's neck and give it a jerk now and then," while he took measures to foster an incident in the Atlantic.[74]

A week after Germany invaded the Low Countries and France in May 1940, Roosevelt told Treasury Secretary Henry Morgenthau that "we will not be in it for *60 or 90* days."[75] And ten days later he told Philip Kerr (Lord Lothian, the British ambassador), in Lothian's words:

> As things were going, it seemed likely that Germany would challenge some vital American interest in the near future, which was the condition necessary to make the United States enter the war with the necessary popular support.[76]

Germany's easy conquest of Denmark and Norway in the spring of 1940 had had no significant effect on the United States, but her invasion of the Low Countries and France did. Holland and Belgium fell quickly, and within a few weeks it was apparent that France too was falling. This was a profound shock because France had long anticipated war with Germany, had mobilized heavily, and had an army widely — but mistakenly — considered the best in the world. Roosevelt now expected that, if France surrendered, Great Britain would also fall. That would leave Hitler astride most of Europe, with its enormous human and industrial resources, enabling him to invade the western hemisphere when he chose to.

Munich had not only cost Chamberlain the support of many in his own Conservative Party, but also aroused the enmity of Labour Party leaders. Hitler's subsequent seizures of Poland, Denmark, and Norway, and his expected invasion of western Europe moved Conservative and Labour leaders to force his resignation.[77] They did so on May 10 — hours before Germany launched her invasion of Holland, Belgium, and France — and Churchill became Britain's prime minister, telling the House of Commons:

> I have nothing to offer but blood, toil, tears and sweat . . . our policy is to wage war, by sea, land and air with all our might . . . against a monstrous tyranny, never surpassed in the dark, lamentable catalogue of human crime.[78]

Eight days later his son asked him how he would save Britain, and Churchill replied, "I shall drag the United States in."[79]

Even though formally at war with Germany since the prior

September, Britain had kept most of her troops in her colonies, far from England. On taking office Churchill sent almost all the troops and tanks he had in the home islands—about a quarter of the army—to France. And he began to plead passionately with Roosevelt for more arms.

In contrast to Chamberlain, Churchill understood the constraints on Roosevelt. He also better understood Roosevelt's ways and felt closer to him. Chamberlain gave up on Roosevelt; Churchill persevered in doing whatever he could to draw Roosevelt and the United States into the European war. In addition, Germany's easy victories made the need for cooperation between Great Britain and the United States more urgent and more feasible. Cooperation between the two nations then became effective.

So also did U.S. cooperation with Canada. In 1937 Roosevelt had begun talks with Canada's Prime Minister Mackenzie King about joint planning for war against Germany. They focused on defending the western hemisphere at first, but also considered helping Britain in a European war. For example, if the United States took over defense of Canada's Atlantic provinces and the Dominion of Newfoundland, that would free Canadian and British forces for combat in Europe.[80] (Before the United States entered World War I, Canada sent troops to fight in Europe with the understanding that they were not needed at home because the United States would take responsibility for Canada's defense.)

In June 1939 Roosevelt had told Britain's King George that if London were bombed, the United States would enter the coming war.[81] The same month—weeks before the invasion of Poland—Roosevelt and Mackenzie King had talked about cooperation in the impending war, and the Canadian leader may have read too much into Roosevelt's words. When Hitler invaded Poland and Roosevelt declared the United States was remaining neutral, King wrote in his diary that he was very disappointed. "America [was] keeping out of this great issue, which affects the destiny of mankind. And professing to do so in the name of peace when everything on which peace is based is threatened."[82] King did, however, send most of Canada's small army to England, relying on U.S. forces to guard against an invasion of his homeland.

In August 1940 Roosevelt and King announced the formation of a "Joint Board on Defense and what amounted to an alliance."[83] After the invasion of Poland, Canada declared war on Germany which prevented a full alliance with Canada. Roosevelt stressed that the agreement reached was for defense of the western hemisphere, and the American public accepted it. A poll showed 84 percent favoring it, and only 5 percent opposed.[84] (At the time, about 80 percent still opposed U.S. participation in the European war.) Roosevelt did not tell the public that the agreement with Canada also involved cooperation in the European war.

Congress then agreed to supply Britain with arms on a "cash and carry" basis. The cash provision reflected lingering resentment over the belief that Britain had manipulated loans from the United States during World War I to profit from them. The carry provision reflected unwillingness to lose U.S. lives and ships delivering arms; it required Britain to pick them up in the United States.

On taking office Churchill had asked for fifty destroyers, and Roosevelt had refused. By the middle of June 1940, with France's armies in a disorganized retreat, Churchill pleaded for the destroyers, and Roosevelt suggested sending them to Canada, in the expectation that Congress and the public would hardly object to that. Canada could then turn them over to Britain.[85] Meanwhile he made a rousing public speech, announcing two policies. The United States would rearm and she would assist victims of aggression—France, Great Britain, and China. He then got around the Neutrality Act by having the army sell arms to a private company, which then resold them to Britain.[86]

In the spring, expecting a German invasion of his country, Daladier had resigned. His successor, Paul Reynaud, tried vigorously to prepare for the invasion, bringing militant Charles de Gaulle into his administration. But they were too late. German armies swept through France, and when her collapse became imminent, Roosevelt urged her to go on fighting, vaguely promising additional arms. As none came, Reynaud sent Roosevelt a telegram pleading for a major supply of arms, pledging that, if he received them:

> We shall fight in front of Paris; we shall fight behind Paris . . . and if . . . driven out . . . we shall establish ourselves in North Africa to continue the fight and if necessary in our American possessions.[87]

On June 13 Reynaud sent his last appeal to Roosevelt:

> At this most tragic hour of its history France must choose. . . . We can choose . . . [continued] resistance, only if a chance of victory appears in the distance. . . . [If France falls, probably England too will fall.] The only chance of saving the French nation . . . and through her to save England . . . is to throw into the balance, this very day, the weight of American power. It is the only chance also of keeping Hitler . . . from attacking America. . . . if you cannot give to France in the hours to come

the certainty that the United States will come into the war within a very short time, the fate of the world will change.[88]

Churchill pleaded with Roosevelt to give Reynaud a definite assurance. Roosevelt answered Reynaud on June 15, promising additional arms, expressing sympathy, but also making his limitations clear. "I know that you will understand that these statements carry with them no implication of military commitments. Only the Congress can make such commitments."[89] Then, after his cabinet refused to support moving the government to Algeria, Reynaud resigned on June 16. On the next day, his successor, Marshall Henri Petain, asked Germany for an armistice.

Churchill and Roosevelt now considered England's situation desperate. With most of her troops far away, with only a demoralized remnant of the beaten troops she had sent to France back in England after the Dunkirk evacuation, and with few guns and very few tanks, she had almost no defense against German troops if they landed on her soil. Churchill made stirring speeches to rally his people, although he himself saw little hope. After the Dunkirk evacuation he declared:

> We shall go on to the end . . . we shall defend our Island, whatever the cost may be; we shall fight on the beaches, we shall fight on the landing-grounds, we shall fight in the fields and in the streets, we shall fight in the hills; we shall never surrender, and even if . . . this island were subjugated and starving, then our Empire . . . would carry on the struggle, until . . . the New World, with all its power and might, steps forth to the rescue and liberation of the old.[90]

After this moving declaration, he reportedly put his hand over the microphone, so that only people in the radio studio could hear, and added, "And we will hit them over their heads with beer bottles, which is all we have really got."[91]

As France was falling he made his most memorable speech:

> the Battle of France is over . . . the Battle of Britain is about to begin. . . . The whole fury and might of the enemy must very soon be turned on us. Hitler knows that he will have to break us in this Island or lose the war. If we can stand up to him, all Europe may be free . . . but if we fail, then the whole world . . . will sink into the abyss of a new Dark Age. . . . Let us therefore brace ourselves to our duties, and so bear ourselves that . . .

[in] a thousand years men will still say, "This was their finest hour."[92]

He told his people they were well equipped with troops, while he set about building an army. He told them the troops were well armed, while he pleaded with Roosevelt for planes and ships during the next year and a half. As he later described England's situation, "Never has a great nation been so naked before her foes."[93] (Harold Nicolson, a member of his cabinet, said "all we can do is lie on our backs with our paws in the air and hope that no one will stamp on our tummies."[94]) But by his rousing speeches Churchill succeeded in building a tenacious determination to fight in a people who had lost their spirit for it after World War I.

Roosevelt then resolved to send major aid to Britain even though it was against the law and even though the arms he sent were needed at home to prepare for war. He sent to England rifles, machine guns, bullets, cannons, shells, bombs, and explosive powder. The British Home Guard was a part-time paramilitary force, equipped with hunting rifles, pitchforks, and flails. It performed guard duty, freeing army units for combat training and other duties, and it prepared for action against a German invasion. At last it had military guns, supplied by the United States. And Churchill literally had the explosive powder from the United States put into beer bottles, making anti-tank bombs to hurl at the expected invaders.[95]

Actually England was not in the immediate danger that Churchill and Roosevelt believed. Information available only after the war -- and still little known in the United States — showed she was not facing an imminent invasion because Hitler had other plans. As France fell, Hitler made his decision to start the extermination of Jews. His generals estimated that their troops could overrun England within three weeks of landing there. But to carry out the Holocaust, he needed the cover of war for three more years, which his technicians estimated to be how long the extermination would take. He decided to prolong the war by holding off on invading England and invading the Soviet Union instead.[96]

Unaware of Hitler's decisions, Churchill and Roosevelt expected an invasion of England at any time in June, July, August, and September. Roosevelt therefore became determined to increase arms deliveries to Britain, even at the risk of political repercussions at home. Then in October, he and Churchill learned from intelligence of German plans to invade the Soviet Union and that an invasion of England was not imminent.

After declaring war on Germany in September 1939, Britain had begun convoying her merchant ships carrying supplies from North America. German submarine attacks on them were rather limited, and the first British ship was not sunk until the following February. Losses of merchant ships continued to be minimal until France fell in June 1940, giving Germany bases on the Atlantic from which to send out her submarines and surface warships. As a result, the German navy was soon exacting a heavy toll on British merchant ships and their crews. During the second half of 1940, Britain lost four hundred ships — a quarter of her merchant fleet. (After replenishment, she would lose a quarter of her fleet again in 1941.) And during the Dunkirk evacuation, Britain lost many destroyers. Unable to carry on without ship-born supplies, Churchill said, "The decision for 1941 lies upon the seas." His ally, French resistance leader Charles de Gaulle, agreed, saying, "Tonnage became an obsession, a tyrant dominating everything. The life and glory of England were staked every day upon the sea."[97]

Aware of Britain's requests for destroyers, Congress had put a new restriction on supplying major equipment to her; the head of the army or navy must first certify that it was "not essential to defense of the United States."[98] The requirement came into play when Roosevelt designated fifty old destroyers for Britain and asked Stark to certify that they were unessential for defense. Stark said that was impossible to certify.[99] In addition, Congress had added the restriction that arms sales must be paid for immediately. This blocked sending destroyers to Britain because she was no longer in a position to pay. Roosevelt asked his attorney general, Robert Jackson, for a legal opinion: if a swap could be arranged to give the destroyers to Canada in exchange for U.S. acquisition of Canadian and British bases, could Stark judge that the risk to U.S. defense would be offset in such an arrangement? Jackson said yes.[100] Roosevelt arranged the swap, and Stark certified that the destroyers were unessential for defense. To his secretary, Roosevelt confided, "Congress is going to raise hell about this, but even another day's delay may mean the end of civilization."[101]

The swap also included an agreement for the United States to build merchant ships for Britain. Known as Liberty Ships, they made a major contribution to replenishing Britain's merchant fleet. Despite Roosevelt's fear of trouble from legislators, when notified of the destroyer transaction, Congress accepted it. The shocking fall of France had shifted opinion decisively.

The transaction meant much more than equipment for Britain. In acquiring the bases, "Roosevelt openly placed the United States on the side of Britain in the fighting."[102] As an official army history put it, "The United States had obviously abandoned neutrality and . . . had entered upon a status of 'limited war.'"[103] While this act of alliance and step closer to war was obvious to some writers afterward, except by noninterventionists, it was hardly noticed by the public. The *St. Louis Post Dispatch* angrily declared, "Mr. Roosevelt today committed an act of war . . . an agreement that amounts to a military . . . alliance with Great Britain."[104] For by staffing the bases obtained in the swap, Roosevelt put troops in a position that made their cooperation in defense of British territories likely. During the next year—months before the attack on Pearl Harbor—the alliance secretly became explicit. Marshall ordered troops on those bases to join in defending the British territories, even if U.S. bases on them were not attacked.[105]

The congressional certification requirement came up again in November 1940, when Roosevelt decided to supply new Liberator (B-24) bombers to Britain for defending her convoys against submarines. Marshall was asked to certify the Liberators as unessential, using the rationale that Britain had contributed to their construction by supplying the secret design for their engines. The idea was that, without Britain's contribution, the United States would not have the Liberators. Marshall said he was unprepared to give certification without study.[106]

Along with the Liberator, the United States was developing on her own another, more-powerful bomber, the Flying Fortress (B-17). Roosevelt proposed to advisers that Flying Fortresses be sent to England for testing by U.S. crews—for testing in combat! He said that was "the only peg on which we could hang the proposition legally"— that is, to supply them to Great Britain.[107] Stimson submitted the proposal to the State Department, and then it went to the Justice Department, where it was judged illegal. While not implemented, the proposal did lead, prior to the Pearl Harbor attack, to U.S. flight officers serving in combat operations under British commanders (see chapter 10).

In rejecting the Flying Fortress proposal, the Justice Department suggested supplying them as substitutes for obsolete bombers already on order by Great Britain. Marshall agreed to certify the Flying Fortresses as unessential on that basis, and they were supplied to Britain.

In detailing Roosevelt's deceptiveness, no implication that it was deviant among presidents is intended. President Ronald Reagan's aid to Nicaraguan rebels was a more direct violation of congressional injunctions, involving greater deception. And before Roosevelt, Presidents James Polk, Abraham Lincoln, and William McKinley had concluded that U.S. interests justified war even though Congress and the public opposed it. They manipulated events toward an incident, enabling them to go to war. In deceiving the nation about Mexico's attack on a U.S. army, Polk had outdone Roosevelt.[108]

Lincoln's manipulation served to preserve the nation—a purpose comparable to Roosevelt's. Polk's and McKinley's manipulations were for lesser purposes (see the afterword). Roosevelt's deception was not a well-kept secret, nor does it seem to have been intended as one. While hiding some measures to arm Britain and France, he hinted at others and was open about still others.

As 1940 ended, Britain's ability to pay for expensive equipment was exhausted. Congress then accepted the cost as well as the risk of war. In March 1941, it approved by a large majority Roosevelt's proposal for Lend-Lease aid to Britain, innocuously titled "A Bill to Further Promote the Defense of the United States and for Other Purposes."[109] His manager of the bill in the Senate wrote, "We had to admit to opponents that little of what we would lend or lease . . . would ever come back."[110] Equipment supplied remained U.S. property on paper, but Britain was not expected to replace ships or planes that went down or were damaged beyond repair, for "it was clearly understood by both Roosevelt and Churchill that what was lent would never be returned and what was leased would never be paid for."[111]

Lend-Lease was widely viewed as a major step into war with Germany. According to an official army history, it "meant the abandonment of any pretense of neutrality," as Stimson said to army supply chiefs, adding that it constituted "a limited alliance."[112] And Marshall wrote in a memo about Lend-Lease:

> **Such a program cannot be sustained . . . unless we are willing to state that we are preparing for an *offensive* campaign in the air against a foreign power.[113]**

Besides saving Britain, Roosevelt would use Lend-Lease to forge a broader alliance against Germany. By offering Lend-Lease aid to other nations in 1941—neutral nations, mainly in the Americas, not facing an immediate German threat—he would win assurances to support the United States in a later war against the Axis powers. By December, when the United States formally entered World War II, Roosevelt had such arrangements with thirty-eight nations, who then declared war on Germany.

As the United States sent more supplies, the British became less able to transport them. To help them reach England, the U.S. Navy began to escort British merchant vessels, and then U.S. merchant ships began to carry supplies. The administration began these measures without a public announcement, although they did not remain secret long. And when the British air force could no longer spare pilots to pick up planes, Roosevelt had U.S. pilots deliver them surreptitiously.[114]

Roosevelt's commitment to saving Great Britain and defeating Germany made Japan, Germany's new ally, a potential enemy of the United States. Japan was also considered a particular threat to Britain's Asian territories. In turn, that threat made China's resistance valuable in tying down Japan's armies, thereby providing some security to Britain. Roosevelt "was particularly concerned with the Far East only as it affected the European war."[115] After France fell, U.S. aid to China became substantial, and there is evidence in War Department documents that the need to save Britain influenced the decision to increase aid to China.[116] U.S. policy toward China and Japan in 1940 and 1941 depended on what the administration considered useful in defeating Hitler.

In September 1940, Japan joined in the Axis Pact (also called the Tripartite Pact) with Germany and Italy. Roosevelt and his advisers viewed it as an alliance for world conquest, and with good reason. A year later the pact would be discussed at the White House in an opposite sense, for it provided the administration with the means of entering into war with Germany through Japan. The discussions would center on the probability that, if war broke out between the United States and Japan, Germany might declare war on the United States (see chapter 13). Then Congress would declare war on Germany.

The Axis Pact prompted Roosevelt to order an embargo against Japan in two parts. He restricted sales of steel and scrap iron, and asked firms voluntarily not to sell Japan other materials useful for war. (The voluntary part became known as the "moral embargo," and the phrase was used later for the embargo as a whole, to distinguish it from the oil embargo of 1941.) In his public announcement, Roosevelt also mentioned the possibility of a future oil embargo, and this prospect alarmed Japan the most. A large oil supply was necessary to carry on her war in China. Having no oil deposits of her own, Japan bought from the United States not only most of her oil, but also 80 percent of her petroleum products — including 90 percent of her gasoline, particularly aviation gasoline. The mention of a future oil embargo was a step in turning Japanese leaders toward serious consideration of war against the United States. The possibility that Roosevelt intended this effect is supported by other actions that began in May 1940.

Up to 1941, the United States officially had one fleet, stationed on her West Coast. A squadron had been stationed in Manila and named the Asiatic Fleet. Beginning in 1940, other units were detached for patrol and other action in the Atlantic. At the beginning of 1941, they would officially be named the Atlantic Fleet. Meanwhile, in April 1940 Roosevelt decided to station most of the fleet in Hawaii. He told

Stark the transfer was to deter Japan from new aggression. At the time there was no specific act by Japan to deter — no activity preliminary to new aggression and no intelligence of a coming move. Because of the priority given to the European war, stationing most of the fleet in Hawaii hindered training, deprived it of logistical support, and exposed it to a Japanese attack, and because they believed stationing a fleet there might provoke Japan to war, the Joint Army-Navy Board and Marshall and Stark opposed the transfer.[117] The decision to move the fleet led to the Pearl Harbor attack, and will be examined in detail.

As in prior years, a fleet was scheduled to go to Hawaii for war games in April and return in May. Stark sent the fleet's commander, Adm. James Richardson, a preliminary notice of the transfer in words the president chose himself. Roosevelt rarely provided the wording for military orders; when he did, it marked them as extraordinarily important. The dispatch said:

> In view of the possibility of *Italy becoming an active belligerent in May*, you may receive instructions to remain in Hawaiian waters. . . . Utmost secrecy is desired for the present.[118] (Italics added.)

And the dispatch ordered Richardson to acknowledge receiving it.

Richardson did not know the background or purpose of prolonging his stay in Hawaii and was troubled that it made his fleet vulnerable to a Japanese attack. He had taken Stark's earlier warnings seriously, particularly a recent one:

> I believe the situation in the Far East is continually deteriorating as far as our relations with Japan are concerned. . . . I think you should continually keep uppermost in your mind the possibility of trouble in the Orient, and the means to meet it.[119]

The transfer dispatch also seemed inconsistent with the new war plan, which gave priority to naval operations in the Atlantic-European theater. On May 7 — two days before the fleet's scheduled return to California — Richardson received additional orders:

> CINCUS make immediate press release instructions as follows. "I request permission to remain in Hawaiian waters to accomplish some things I wanted to do while here. The Department has approved this request."[120]

"CINCUS" was the navy's abbreviation for "Commander in Chief,

U.S. Fleet," meaning Richardson. The dispatch put him in the position of having to carry out orders he considered dangerous, and of taking responsibility for them. Since the fleet had arrived in Hawaii, Japanese submarines had shadowed it. Occasionally the submarines were spotted, probably adding to Richardson's concern.[121] If harm befell the fleet, the onus would be on him. Despite his concerns, Richardson issued the press release.

Then Richardson received a letter from Stark, explaining:

> Of course you know the thought behind [the order to stay in Hawaii] and that is that the Italian situation is extremely delicate, the two weeks ahead regarded as critical; then - - - ? ? ? ? ? nobody can answer the riddle just now.[122]

Stark explained further in a letter of May 22:

> When we sent our dispatch it looked as if Italy were coming in almost immediately and that a serious situation might develop in the East Indies, and that there was a possibility of our being involved.[123]

Stark went on to mention the danger of "a complete collapse of the Allies, including loss of their fleets . . . [resulting in a] far more serious situation."

On the basis of intelligence, the administration expected Italy to join Germany's coming invasion of the Low Countries and France. If that happened Holland and France would be in no position to defend their Asian territories against a Japanese invasion, and the U.S. Fleet might serve as a deterrent to Japan or even come to the aid of those territories. Those projections were behind the orders to Richardson.

When Stark sent the order to stay in Hawaii, of which he had given Richardson advance notice, he added:

> Just hung up the telephone after talking with the President and by the time this reaches you you will have received word to remain in Hawaiian Waters for a couple of weeks.
>
> When the Fleet returns to the Coast (and I trust the delay will not be over two weeks, but I cannot tell) the President has asked that the Fleet schedule be so arranged that on extremely short notice the Fleet be able to return concentrated to [Hawaiian] Waters.[124]

Despite this letter, the fleet's stay in Hawaii became indefinite, without explanation to Richardson. On May 22 — now seriously troubled — he wrote to Stark that the stay required planning fleet activities for a few months, and "To do this intelligently, however, it is necessary to know more than I know [now] about why we are here and how long we will probably stay."[125] He proceeded to question whether a deterrent plan was realistic in view of the fleet's deficiencies and its vulnerability at Pearl Harbor, and whether he should continue "carrying out normal training" or prepare to take belligerent action. The two alternatives were incompatible.

Stark replied:

> First . . . I would like to say that I know exactly what you are up against, and to tell you, that here in the Department we are up against the same thing. Why are you in the Hawaiian Area? Answer: You are there because of the deterrent effect which it is thought your presence may have on the Japs going into the East Indies. In previous letters I have hooked this up with the Italians going into the war. The connection is that with Italy in it, it is thought that the Japs might feel just that much freer to take independent action . . . In the Dutch East Indies.[126]

If that happened, said Stark, he did not know what the United States would do.

The prefatory comment suggested that the Navy Department, including Stark himself, was also being kept in the dark. And about how long the fleet was to remain in Hawaii, Stark added, "Like you, I have asked the question, and also — like you — I have been unable to get the answer."[127] Apparently Roosevelt had told Stark that, by being in Hawaii, the fleet would deter a Japanese attack on the Dutch East Indies, and Stark may have been unsure of Roosevelt's judgment or his sincerity.

In 1941 Japanese leaders would consider seriously an invasion of the Dutch East Indies, to give their nation its own oil supply. In the spring of 1940, however, the Japanese had no compelling reason to do it because the United States was still supplying almost all their needs for oil and gasoline. And Stark's opposition to deterrent use of the fleet in the Pacific was on record.[128] His phrase "it is thought" probably referred to people other than himself — Hull and Roosevelt.

If anything, the letter seems to have increased Richardson's worry about the safety of the fleet. Meanwhile, Italy invaded France, and France fell. Then on June 22, Stark informed Richardson that the fleet would remain at Pearl Harbor indefinitely.[129] At this point, to emphasize his concerns and to find out what was going on, Richardson asked permission to visit Washington, which he did in July. But his talks with Stark and Roosevelt apparently resolved little.

At Knox's request, he visited Washington again in October and took the occasion to confront Roosevelt. His recollection of their long, tense discussion was largely supported by Roosevelt's friend, Adm. William Leahy, who was also present.[130] Richardson and Roosevelt restated positions they had taken during the July visit. Richardson urged returning the fleet to the West Coast because of its vulnerability at Pearl Harbor. Roosevelt said the fleet was needed in Hawaii to deter Japan. Richardson said it was too weak to be an effective deterrent, and the Japanese knew that. Roosevelt replied:

> **Despite what you believe, I know that the presence of the fleet in the Hawaiian area has had, and is now having, a restraining influence on the actions of Japan.[131]**

(The basis of this statement is unknown. It was not supported by intercepted Japanese diplomatic messages or other intelligence that has come to light.)

Both Roosevelt and Richardson made the same arguments over and over, becoming angry and challenging each other. Suspecting the fleet's transfer might be part of a hidden plan, Richardson finally broke the stalemate by asking if Roosevelt meant to go to war with Japan. That, the president answered, depended on where Japan attacked. If she attacked Thailand or the Dutch East Indies, the United States would not go to war. If she attacked the Philippines, the United States probably would not go to war, but (in Richardson's words),

> **[the Japanese] could not always avoid making mistakes and as the war continued and the area of operations expanded sooner or later they would make a mistake and we would enter the war.[132]**

The only U.S. territory in the Pacific more important than the Philippines was Hawaii. By inference, a Japanese "mistake" meant an attack on Hawaii or on the fleet; either one would enable Roosevelt to enter the war.

On October 7, the day before his argument with Richardson, Roosevelt had received an ONI memo, written by McCollum containing proposed measures to help save Great Britain and ultimately to defeat Germany:

> Make an arrangement with Holland for the use of base facili-
> ties . . . in the Dutch East Indies. . . . Send a division of . . .
> heavy cruisers to the Orient. . . . Send two divisions of subma-
> rines to the Orient. . . . Keep the main strength of the U.S.
> Fleet . . . in the vicinity of the Hawaiian Islands. . . . Insist that
> the Dutch refuse to grant Japanese demands for . . . oil. . . .
> Completely embargo all U.S. trade with Japan, in collabora-
> tion with the British Empire.[133]

It is worth emphasizing that measures to defeat Germany were directed against Japan. And the memo ended with, "If by these measures the Japanese could be led to commit an overt act of war, so much
the better."

Administration officers considered a blockade of Japan even more
likely than the above actions to move her to war. Roosevelt had already stationed the fleet in Hawaii and ordered a partial embargo; he
was considering a blockade and was beginning to implement other
measures in the memo. Presumably the measures and what they might
lead to were in his mind on October 8, when he spoke to Richardson.
On the same day, Roosevelt told an unidentified visitor:

> this country is ready to pull the trigger if the Japs do anything.
> I mean we won't stand any nonsense, public opinion won't,
> from the Japs, if they do some fool thing. . . . The only thing
> that worries me is that the Germans and the Japs have gone
> along, and the Italians, for . . . five, six years without their feet
> slipping. . . . Now the chance you could get from doing that all
> the time may be to do something foolish. And the time may
> be coming when the Germans and the Japs will do some fool
> thing. That would put us in.[134]

By "this country is ready to pull the trigger if the Japs do anything,"
he may have had in mind growing public animosity toward Japan
after her invasion of China and her atrocities there, or spontaneous
outcries for war against her when she attacked the U.S. gunboats *Panay*
in 1937 and *Tutuila* in 1939. (Determined to avoid war with Japan then,
Roosevelt had accepted peaceful resolutions of the gunboat incidents.)

After his meeting with Roosevelt, Richardson met with Knox,
Hull, and Welles, whom he told that the fleet was at heavy risk in
Hawaii. Knox brought up the Burma Road, a supply lifeline for China.
Under pressure from Japan, Britain had closed it in July, but intended
to reopen it shortly. Knox told Richardson that, if Great Britain
reopened it, Japan might take drastic action. And if she did, Roosevelt

might order the fleet to blockade Japan. Richardson said the fleet was ready neither for a blockade nor for war with Japan resulting from a blockade. Nonetheless, Knox told Richardson to draw up a blockade plan. Hull and Welles also told him that diplomatic considerations required keeping the fleet in Hawaii.[135]

Military leaders are troubled by measures that put armed forces at risk for diplomatic or political purposes. In such measures, the safety of the forces may have low priority, and that struck Richardson as the case.

Subsequently Richardson and his successor, Kimmel, would receive orders to send fleet units out, as proposed in McCollum's memo. The memo and Roosevelt's October conversations are the first signs that he was considering provoking Japan.

In any case, the glimpse of strategy Richardson received from Roosevelt and Knox did not reassure him; on the contrary, considering the fleet to be in grave danger, Richardson returned to Hawaii more troubled than before. He understood that the fleet would remain in Hawaii; he expected that it would not be strengthened enough to hold its own against a Japanese attack; and he may have suspected that part of the fleet was to be sacrificed.

In the past, Stark and Richardson had corresponded informally as old friends, using the names Betty and JO (for James Otto). But on returning to Pearl Harbor, Richardson wrote Stark a long letter in stiff words, referring to himself as "the Commander-in Chief" and Stark as "the Chief of Naval Operations."

> Since the return of the Commander-in-Chief, U.S. Fleet, from his recent conference in Washington, and in view of the conversations that took place there . . . the Commander-in-Chief, U.S. Fleet, feels it to be his solemn duty to present . . . certain facts and conclusions in order that there may be no doubt in the minds of higher authority as to his convictions in regard to the present situation. . . .
>
> On the occasion of his first visit to Washington, in July, and in personal letters to the Chief of Naval Operations, the Commander-in-Chief stressed his firm conviction that neither the navy nor the country was prepared for war with Japan. . . . He left Washington with three distinct impressions:
>
> *First.* That the Fleet was retained in the Hawaiian area solely to support diplomatic representations and as a deterrent to Japanese aggressive action;
>
> *Second.* That there was no intention of embarking on actual hostilities against Japan;

Third. That the immediate mission of the Fleet was accelerated training and absorption of new personnel.[136]

Richardson noted that the international situation had changed "materially," and,

it now appears that *more active, open steps aimed at Japan are in serious consideration and . . . may lead to active hostilities.* It is in connection with this eventuality that the Commander-in-Chief is constrained to present his present views. (Italics added.)

After reviewing more background and stressing fleet deficiencies in the face of imminent war, he continued, "I know of no flag officer who wholeheartedly endorses the present ORANGE Plan" as adequate in the changed circumstances.[137] (Other navy leaders agreed. Turner would later testify, "I shared the opinion with many others that the war plans which were in effect during 1940 were defective in the extreme. They were not realistic."[138])

Richardson's letter concluded:

There is no intention or desire on the part of the Commander-in-Chief to evade his legitimate responsibilities nor is it desired that anything in this letter be so construed . . . At the same time, it is most strongly believed that the Commander-in-Chief must be better informed than he is now as to the Department's plans and intentions if he is to perform his full duty.

And he added, "Please acknowledge receipt of this letter by despatch."

Stark replied in two letters, mostly with vague strategic considerations, good intentions, and hopes that Japan would not go to war against the United States. He said he could not give Richardson a definite answer about coming changes in the war plan because Roosevelt had not yet made up his mind. He mentioned prospects of strengthening the fleet and a specific plan for the Fourteenth Naval District and army forces in Hawaii to provide protection for it.[139] On Richardson's suspicion of "more active, open steps" that might provoke Japan, Stark made no comment.

Richardson knew that the Fourteenth Naval District and the army detachment in Hawaii lacked patrol planes and other equipment needed to protect the fleet against a surprise Japanese attack. And he suspected that Stark was withholding crucial information.

On November 28 Richardson wrote to Stark again, and this time he forced the issue:

> I feel that the Fleet must operate on either of two assumptions, i.e., (a) that we are at peace and no security measures are required; or (b) that wartime measures of security must be carried out.

He pointed out that current security measures were peacetime measures, *taken for training purposes,* and he was changing that.

> Now, however . . . in view of your better information and position to evaluate the possibilities, I have come to the conclusion that I must operate on the basis of (b) above. I enclose a tentative draft of a directive which I plan to issue. . . . It is bound to result in the curtailment of badly needed basic training of new personnel.[140]

In short, he said he was curtailing training to put the fleet on alert.

That was unacceptable; the letter prompted Richardson's relief from command in January 1941. On replacing him with Kimmel, Stark told Richardson to show their correspondence to Kimmel. And he told Kimmel to give training first priority.[141] The correspondence carried a key lesson: Richardson had been relieved for declaring he was taking measures that violated orders to continue training. It reinforced the order Stark gave Kimmel on the priority of training. Whatever Kimmel understood from Richardson's relief, he obeyed orders about which he had grave reservations and he continued training up to the Japanese attack.

Perhaps Roosevelt learned from his trouble with Richardson; Kimmel was not given the glimpses Richardson got about underlying strategy. For the next year — up to the attack — almost all plane patrols and all operation of radar equipment in Hawaii were carried out for training purposes. And crews understood that their tour of duty in Hawaii was for training.

This account differs from the prevailing one — that Richardson was relieved because he "hurt the President's feelings" during their October confrontation.[142] Roosevelt, however, tolerated vehement argument from his subordinates remarkably well. He had been challenged by many; once, in a tirade Marshall delivered in a "cold fury."[143] And, as noted, MacArthur had confronted him in an insulting manner. When arguing with Roosevelt, Ickes often threatened to resign. Stimson and

Morgenthau were also outspoken when opposing Roosevelt's position. None of them was relieved, nor is there evidence that Roosevelt considered doing so or had lingering bad feelings toward them over being challenged.

This is not to say that Roosevelt lacked feelings. A year after a confrontation with Ickes, Roosevelt sent him an insulting note (see chapter 11). But Roosevelt followed it with a letter to soothe Ickes's feelings. Apparently he was angry with Richardson after their October confrontation. According to reporter Helen Lombard, Roosevelt then asked Knox, "What's the matter with [JO]? Has he become yellow?" But Roosevelt soon got over the incident, and Stark informed Richardson that he would continue as fleet commander for another year.[144]

Roosevelt's decision to relieve Richardson followed Richardson's letter informing Stark that, despite orders to the contrary, he was curtailing training in order to guard against an attack on the fleet. It was interference with Roosevelt's war strategy that was unacceptable.

The events Roosevelt anticipated in April 1940 took place. The German invasion of the Low Countries and France began on May 10, and Roosevelt then ordered the fleet to remain in Hawaii. Holland fell on May 14, followed by Belgium on May 28. And Italy invaded France on June 10. By July, when Richardson arrived in Washington, France had surrendered and Britain—expecting to be next on Hitler's invasion list—was in no position to deploy her fleet to protect her Pacific territories.

In his October confrontation with Richardson, Roosevelt touched on contingencies over which he and his cabinet would agonize in 1941. The key question in their planning then would be: if Japan attacked British, Dutch, or U.S. territories, which would enable Roosevelt to get a declaration of war against Japan? Early in 1941, the cabinet's judgment would be that only an attack on Hawaii or the fleet would move Congress to war. Late in the year, however, the cabinet's judgment would be that an attack on the Philippines or even on British territory alone would suffice. And behind the question of which attack would enable the United States to enter the war against Japan would be the question of which attack would enable her to enter the war against Germany. In view of the cabinet's coming deliberations, Roosevelt's answer to Richardson in October may have been the first indication, given outside Roosevelt's inner circle, of what would become the means of entering the war against Germany.

Richardson's suspicion that the United States would engage in provocative actions soon proved true, as Roosevelt began ordering units of the fleet on unannounced expeditions to various points west of Hawaii—expeditions recommended in McCollum's memo as likely to provoke Japan. To Stark, who questioned these expeditions and continued to oppose keeping the fleet in Hawaii, Roosevelt said:

> **just as soon as those ships come back from Australia and New Zealand, or perhaps a little before, I want to send more out. I just want to keep them popping up here and there, and keep the Japs guessing. I don't mind losing one or two cruisers, but do not take a chance on losing five or six.**[145]

Not announcing the expeditions—consistent with the idea of "popping up"—could have been intended to startle Japan's naval officers into an impulsive response. Fleet units were sent to Australia, New Zealand, Fiji, and Tahiti, all of which were far from Japan.[146] But one squadron was sent to Japan. When that move was planned in April 1941, Stark wrote to Kimmel:

> **Of course you can see what a striking force of the composition I gave you, and known to the Japs, would mean to them, in view of their unholy fear of bombing.**[147]

Evidently a carrier was to be included. The Japanese badly feared bombing because their buildings, largely constructed of wood and paper, made a bomb hit likely to start a fire that could spread across a city.

To "keep the Japs guessing" could have meant to deter them from an attack on British or Dutch territory. Early in 1941, Roosevelt proposed increasing the fleet in Manila as a warning to Japan, perhaps against a move into Malaya or the Dutch East Indies. This prompted a memo to him from Stark: "There is a chance that further moves against Japan will precipitate hostilities rather than prevent them."[148] To "keep the Japs guessing" could also have meant to provoke them into a "mistake." Evidently both possibilities were in Roosevelt's mind during his confrontation with Richardson. When he had ordered the fleet to remain in Hawaii, deterrence seems to have been his main purpose. By November 1941, provocation would be his main purpose.

CHAPTER 10
SECRET ALLIANCE AND UNDECLARED WAR

By the end of 1940, Roosevelt became convinced that supplying Great Britain would not be enough, and Stimson, Knox, Marshall, and Stark agreed with him that the United States must enter the European war. To defeat Hitler, an alliance with Great Britain seemed necessary, and Roosevelt had already begun to build one. In October he told the nation:

> Our course is clear. Our decision is made. We will continue to pile up our defense and our armaments. We will continue to help those who resist aggression and who now hold the aggressors far from our shores. Let no American question . . . the . . . danger from overseas. Why should we accept assurances that we are immune? . . . not long ago the same assurances were given [by Hitler] to the people of Holland and Belgium. It can no longer be disputed that forces of evil which are bent on conquest of the world will destroy whomever . . . they can destroy.[1]

He and Hull then made more speeches declaring that safeguarding the U.S. future required joining Great Britain in the fight against Germany.

The groundwork for an alliance had begun three years earlier. During World War I, the U.S. and British navies had carried out joint operations in the Far East. Japan's invasion of China in 1937 and Germany's preparation for war in Europe prompted U.S. and British leaders again to think about such operations. In December 1937 Japanese troops in China killed a British diplomat and seized British merchant ships and other property. London then proposed to Washington that British and U.S. warships make a joint appearance in the

Far East to deter Japan from further actions against them. London also proposed joint naval-staff talks to prepare for joint combat against Japan.[2] While the proposal was pending, on December 13, Japan attacked warships of both nations in China. British Ambassador Ronald Lindsay had a secret meeting with Roosevelt and Hull during the night of December 16, at which Lindsay renewed the proposal to send a joint naval force to the Far East.[3] In the words of Foreign Secretary Eden, "The President thought such an offer inadvisable and that it was more important for the British Government to keep their battleships to look after the situation in Europe."[4] Roosevelt did, however, accept the proposal to begin joint naval-staff talks, provided that they be kept secret. On January 10 he told Lindsay that he would have three cruisers visit Singapore shortly and he would advance the U.S. Fleet's annual trip to Hawaii for war games from May to February — both to deter further actions by Japan.[5] Neither action was taken, but consideration early in 1938 of sending the fleet to Hawaii is background for Roosevelt's 1940 decision to station it there.

For the joint naval talks, Roosevelt designated Royal Ingersoll to represent the United States.[6] Ingersoll arrived in London January 1, 1938 and said (in Eden's words):

> **The time had now come in the opinion of the President and Admiral Leahy [Chief of Naval Operations] to carry matters a stage further by exchanging information in order to co-ordinate our plans more closely. . . . [Ingersoll proposed] purely technical arrangements . . . if our two fleets were to cooperate in the Pacific, such as codes. All these preparations could be made in advance.[7]**

Admiral Ingersoll added that Roosevelt wanted a military agreement like the one President Wilson had made with Britain in 1916 — a year before the United States entered World War I — for joint naval operations.

Ingersoll's instructions included planning a joint blockade of Japan. Roosevelt said, "The occasion of the blockade would have to be the next grave outrage by the Japanese."[8] After his London talks, Ingersoll reported:

> **Discussion was held on the subject of a distant blockade [against Japan] or quarantine. No definite understanding was reached but . . . it is believed the British are prepared to cover the line from Singapore via Southern Philippines at least as far eastward as the New Hebrides and that the United States**

could cover to the eastward via Fiji, Samoa, Hawaii and the United States.[9]

With the public and Congress strongly opposed to an alliance with Great Britain, Ingersoll's report minimized the agreements made and was kept secret.

In a follow-up agreement made in July 1939, weeks before the European war began, U.S. representatives gave a vague assurance: if war broke out in Europe, the United States would assume some responsibility for defending British territories in the Pacific.[10] Presumably relying on this agreement, Britain withdrew most of her troops from her Pacific territories.

Ingersoll went again to London very briefly in January 1940 to advance the agreement further. He later testified that he returned with no agreement — with nothing more than a "Record of Conversations." But an agreement had been made, with recorded and unrecorded provisions.[11]

After Germany invaded the Low Countries and France in May, Churchill began pressing Roosevelt for resumption of the staff talks. As noted in the last chapter, U.S. war planning with Canada had already begun. In July 1940 Marshall and Stark urged U.S. use of sea and air bases in eastern Canada and Newfoundland. (Near Canada, Newfoundland was a British dominion, and British agreement was necessary. Newfoundland became a Canadian province after the war.) By an agreement in August 1940, the United States sent coast artillery and anti-aircraft guns to Newfoundland and, the following January, also sent troops.[12]

The agreement to send U.S. troops to Newfoundland constituted the first tangible secret alliance. It could not long remain a secret, because troops in Newfoundland obviously knew they were there, and they were noticeable to Newfoundlanders. Under the agreement, the United States and Canada also made plans for joint operations near Greenland and Iceland — not part of North America, but considered vital to Britain's survival. Roosevelt soon made the alliance with Canada public. However, when rumors of the unfolding one with Great Britain spread, along with strong objection to it, he vehemently denied them. Nonetheless the alliance with Britain also was not much of a secret.

In August 1940 Roosevelt agreed to resume joint staff talks, and Adm. Robert Ghormley and Generals George Strong and Delos Emmons went to England, joining army and navy officers already working on further agreements. Strong and Emmons returned to Washington in September, but Ghormley stayed and, along with army attaché Gen. Raymond Lee, continued planning joint military operations.[13] With their British counterparts, they agreed to standardize warplane and tank design so that models could be used by crews of both nations, and to station American military "observers" in England. By the end of 1940, even mid-level military officers in Washington were discussing the U.S. alliance with Britain, along with imminent U.S. entry into the European war.[14] By the above and subsequent agreements, in May 1941 U.S. military personnel served in British combat operations, and the British shared secret new weapons with the United States.[15]

In October 1940 Roosevelt told Admiral Richardson to delegate officers for exploratory talks with British and Dutch officers to coordinate naval operations in the Pacific.[16] Then Stark told Admiral Hart to designate his chief of staff, Capt. William Purnell, to represent Hart in the talks, which took place in Singapore that month and in November. While no record of an agreement has been found, Stark wrote to Hart in November:

> One thing (and this is for your ears alone) you can depend upon is that we would support you by sending a naval reinforcement to you at Soerabaja or Singapore.[17]

Purnell evidently made a report, for Stark referred to it in a December letter to Hart.[18] A third meeting took place that month between U.S. and Dutch officers at Batavia in the Dutch East Indies. And at a follow-up meeting in April it was agreed that, in case of war, Hart would remove his fleet from the Philippines.

Soerabaja was in the Dutch East Indies; Singapore, in British Malaya. Stark's letter implied an agreement for the U.S. Navy to use Dutch and British bases. Similar agreements for joint use of other bases followed. War Plan Rainbow-3 was based partly on the talks, and its stated premise was that U.S. participation in an alliance was necessary to defeat Germany.[19]

After rumors of the talks surfaced, U.S. officers participating in them were told to emphasize to their British counterparts that they were not authorized to make commitments. U.S. staff memos emphasized that the "conversations" resulted in no commitments — an emphasis for the record, although many scholars later accepted it as true. An official army history of joint staff talks with Canadian and British officers establishes that binding military agreements were made and implemented long before Pearl Harbor.[20]

The agreements covered actions against German ships. In November 1940 U.S. warships blockaded German merchant and war ships in Mexican ports. Some stayed in port, where the United States later seized them. Others tried to leave and, when stopped by U.S. ships, were scuttled by their own crews to prevent capture.[21]

Churchill's desperate pleading for a commitment from the U.S. and the success of the joint staff talks moved Roosevelt to offer him a strong assurance. In January 1941 he sent to London his personal representative, Harry Hopkins, who told Churchill:

> The President is determined that we shall win the war together. Make no mistake about it. He has sent me here to tell you that at all costs and by all means he will carry you through, no matter what happens to him—there is nothing he will not do.[22]

Then Hopkins suggested that the United States would probably enter the war fully after an incident with Japan.

Perhaps Hopkins saw that his vague words had had little effect — that Churchill did not take them to be different from Roosevelt's earlier general assurances. Hopkins then restated Roosevelt's commitment in Biblical words:

> Whither thou goest, I will go;
> and where thou lodgest, I will lodge:
> thy people shall be my people, and thy God my God.[23]

And he added, "Even to the end." According to Churchill's companion, "the words seemed like a rope thrown to a dying man," and Churchill wept.[24]

In the Bible, Ruth gave the above pledge to Naomi, her mother-in-law, who was bereaved and desperate. They were of different peoples and worshipped different gods. This pledge to the death, often used in connection with marriage, was apt. White House insider Robert Sherwood called the commitment then made a "common-law marriage," meaning an "alliance" not officially recorded.[25] Herbert Feis of the State Department wrote, "We walked out with Britain but would not admit an engagement . . . At each step it was repeated that no promise was being given."[26]

What Roosevelt would do and when he would do it was still unclear. Feeling he needed more than a general commitment, Churchill would keep trying to pin Roosevelt down on entering the war openly, but get no recorded specific commitment until December 1, 1941. In a memo of February 1941 to his naval leaders, Churchill wrote, "The first thing is to get the United States into the war. We can then settle how to fight it afterwards."[27] He would keep urging that the United States enter the war fully — the sooner, the better. And throughout 1941,

Roosevelt moved closer and closer to entering the war fully. But he held off about whether he would do so openly unless the United States herself was attacked.

While Hopkins was in England, Stark wrote to Ghormley:

> We may not be able to get the directive [from Roosevelt for the planning sessions] right now because of the political dynamite in it . . . but that should not deter us from going ahead on our own . . . I should ask the President to let me send you our study . . . but, in line with the *no commitment* idea, it should not appear that the President has seen it.[28]

The "study" was a memo on war strategy newly prepared by Stark for Roosevelt. Endorsed by Roosevelt, Stimson, and Knox, it became the basis for Plan Dog which, in turn, became the basis for subsequent U.S. war plans.[29] Agreements that came out of the staff talks included pooling intelligence, combining weapons development, testing military equipment jointly, arranging cooperation between the FBI and British counter-intelligence and counter-sabotage agents, and the military operations described below.[30]

The decision to go forward with these planning sessions had been made by Roosevelt in October 1940, but Stark would testify that he (Stark) made the decision in January 1941, and "on my own initiative . . . in early 1941, we started [conversations in Washington] with the British. When I asked them to come over initially I did not ask the President's permission or Colonel Knox."[31] Stark added that he "later informed the President that he was going forward with it, and the President was noncommittal."

Stark's statements denied Roosevelt's responsibility for the staff talks and the agreements made. In words that would become popular during Ronald Reagan's administration, they "provided deniability" to the president. According to an official army history, however, Roosevelt had authorized the talks by December 1940.[32]

Although the public had shifted to support Roosevelt in aiding Britain and even to consider entering the European war, many of his opponents were more suspicious of him and angrier than before. That same December, British Ambassador Lothian died. His successor as British Ambassador, Edward Wood (Lord Halifax), at dinner with Republican congressmen in January 1941, was told by one of them, "I would like you to know that everyone of us . . . thinks President Roosevelt is as dangerous a dictator as Hitler or Mussolini and that he is taking this country to hell as fast as he can."[33]

That January a larger group of U.S. and British officers began to meet in Washington. Stark defined the group's purposes as: to determine the best methods for joint warfare, "should the United States decide to resort to war"; to coordinate military action; and to agree on "areas of responsibility, major lines of strategy . . . strength of the forces . . . and . . . command arrangements."[34] Roosevelt changed "decide to resort to war" to "be compelled to resort to war."

The British officers, designated for the record as technical advisers to the British Purchasing Mission in Washington, wore civilian clothes as part of the deception. Sherwood later commented:

> It is an ironic fact that . . . no great damage would have been done had the details of these plans fallen into the hands of the Germans and the Japanese; whereas, had they fallen into the hands of Congress and the press, American preparation for war might have been well nigh wrecked and ruined.[35]

And Roosevelt confided to British agent William Stephenson, "I cannot bring a divided nation into war . . . I am going to be sure, very sure, that if the United States publicly enters the war, it will enter united."[36]

In February 1941, U.S., British, and Dutch officers met at Singapore. Hart's representative,

> Captain Purnell . . . was authorized to agree to tentative methods of command . . . and operations, either jointly or separately, and to exchange intelligence.[37]

"Methods of command" was not explained but, when combined with "operations . . . jointly," it meant that sometimes U.S. forces would serve under British or Dutch command, and vice versa.[38] This meaning was spelled out in agreements that followed and in U.S. war plans based on the agreements, which became standing orders for some U.S. forces.

In March, U.S. and British military staffs produced the first fully recorded agreement — ABC-1 (American-British Conversations #1). It provided "Plans for the Military operations of the Associated Powers," which began:

> (a) Since Germany is the predominant member of the Axis Powers, the Atlantic and European area is considered to be the decisive theatre. The principal United States Military effort will be exerted in that theatre, and *operations of United States forces in other theatres will be conducted in such a*

manner as to facilitate that effort.
(b) Owing to the threat to the sea communications of the United Kingdom, the principal task of the United States naval forces in the Atlantic will be protection of shipping of the Associated Powers.[39] (Italics added.)

The phrase italicized here defined U.S. strategy from then on. It is the key to understanding administration decisions that remain puzzling without giving priority to the war in Europe: weakening the Pacific Fleet to strengthen the Atlantic Fleet; neglecting defenses in Hawaii while strengthening them in the Philippines; and, when the outbreak of war in the Pacific was known to be days away, not having forces in Hawaii and the Philippines go on full alert.

Immediately the Joint Army-Navy Board ordered Rainbow-5 to be prepared on the basis of ABC-1. In April Stark notified his fleet commanders that Rainbow-5 was in preparation and sent them a copy of ABC-1, commenting:

The basic idea of the United States-British plan is that the United States will draw forces from the Pacific Fleet to reinforce the Atlantic Fleet, and that the British will, if necessary, transfer naval forces to the Far East in an attempt to hold the Japanese north of the Malay Barrier.[40]

On May 15 the Joint Army-Navy Board approved ABC-1 and Rainbow-5. Officially promulgated in the summer of 1941, this last of the Rainbow plans governed operations in the months before Pearl Harbor. It said agreements had been reached between the United States and the United Kingdom about war operations and specified that, "When units of both Powers cooperate tactically, command will be exercised by that officer of either Power who is senior in rank."[41]

In April U.S., Dutch, and British officers produced agreement ADB, which specified:

The United States will undertake . . . strategic direction of its own and British Forces in the Pacific area. . . . it is recommended that the British Commander-in-Chief, China Station, should exercise . . . direction over all naval forces, excluding those employed solely on local defense, or operating under the Commander-in-Chief, United States Asiatic Fleet.[42]

And it recommended "the immediate establishment at Singapore of a combined staff." By December 1941, the secret alliance included Australia, New Zealand, and India.

The agreements had clauses restricting U.S. participation in military operations. For example, ABC-1 said it applied to the United States, "should the United States be compelled to resort to war."[43] And Rainbow-5 and War Plan 46 carried similar restrictive clauses (e.g., "Upon entering the war, the United States will . . ."[44]). In addition, some of the agreements carried notations that Roosevelt had not approved them.[45] The impression conveyed by the restrictive clauses and notations was that the United States was not at war, and therefore was not a participant in any military operations specified. At a future time, she might enter the war; then she was to participate.

The clauses and notations may best be understood as for the record. In April Turner wrote to British Admiral Victor Danckwerts:

> The Chief of Naval Operations has instructed me to convey to you his view that . . . provisions . . . of ABC-1 ought to apply to major changes in the dispositions of the forces of the United States and the United Kingdom, even in advance of the time that the United States may enter the war.[46]

And Knox confirmed that parts of ABC-1 were already operative.

As Rainbow-5 said, the United States and Great Britain had entered into a military agreement. ABC-1 had been approved by Stimson and Knox, with Roosevelt's knowledge. In a memo to Roosevelt, Marshall and Stark would cite ABC-1 as governing U.S. strategy.[47] And on November 25, Stark would draw to Kimmel's attention that ABC-1 governed his operations.[48]

After Pearl Harbor, administration representatives countered allegations that the United States had entered an alliance with Great Britain beforehand by citing the restrictive clauses and notations. Scholars also stressed the clauses and notations in arguing that the agreements made in 1941 were not binding on the United States. For example:

> The fact is that these reports [of joint staff agreements] without exception contained provisos which made their proposals inoperative and of no effect unless and until the United States should enter the war. This differentiated them absolutely from "commitments to war." They were no more than plans to concert military activities *if* the United States went to war . . . *if* and *when* the United States should be attacked.[49]

But despite the clauses and notations, the United States treated the agreements as binding and carried them out. For example, ABC-1, agreed to at the end of March, provided for patrolling the North Atlantic, escorting British transports crossing it, and destroying enemy warships that might attack them. As noted below, in April Roosevelt ordered the navy to carry out those operations.

Despite notations that Roosevelt had not approved most of the agreements, he had approved them — some as presented to him, others with changes. According to an army memo about ABC-1 and Rainbow-5:

> The President on June 7, 1941 returned the subject papers without approval. In explanation of the President's failure to approve or disapprove the plans, his Military Aide, Major General E. M. Watson stated . . . :
> The President has familiarized himself with the two papers, but since . . . ABC-1 had not been approved by the British Government, he would not approve the report at this time; neither would he now give approval to . . . Rainbow No. 5, which is based upon the report ABC-1. However, in case of war the papers would be returned to the President for his approval.[50]

And Stark testified:

> I do know the President, except officially, approved of [ABC-1], although it shows he was not willing to do it officially until we got into the war.[51]

Stark also said ABC-1 was the basic war plan for both the army and navy by autumn 1941.[52]

According to an official U.S. Army history, the joint planning sessions marked the end of independent policy, as U.S. military operations became part of a publicly unacknowledged alliance with Great Britain.[53] ABC-1 provided for coordinated military action — including combat. And, as described below, starting in May 1941, U.S. forces accordingly engaged in coordinated military operations — including combat.

By April, British, Dutch, and U.S. military officers were assigned to each other's vessels and bases. Officially called "observers," they cooperated in military intelligence activities and in operating the vessels, and, by May, in combat operations against the German navy.

When Germany had invaded Denmark in April 1940, Britain had occupied the Danish territory Iceland to prevent Germans from doing so. In enemy hands, Iceland would be an ideal base for raiders attacking British shipping. During the following winter, the joint staff talks in Washington anticipated U.S. occupation of Iceland to free British forces for action elsewhere (as agreed to in ABC-1). Once U.S. troops arrived in Iceland, their presence could not be kept secret, and a worried Stark wrote in June 1941 that politically "there is so much potential dynamite in this order," and "I realize that this is practically an act of war."[54] On the other hand, the occupation could be helpful indirectly, as Stark wrote to Kimmel in July. After U.S. troops arrived there:

> The Iceland situation may produce an "incident" . . . Whether or not we will get an "incident" because of the protection we are giving Iceland . . . I do not know. Only Hitler can answer.[55]

During July Marshall ordered MacArthur to make arrangements with British and Dutch authorities for his warplanes to use their airports in anticipated operations against Japan. While those arrangements remained secret in the United States, rumors of them reached Japan. In September Ambassador Grew cabled Roosevelt, "The Japanese . . . see the United States and Great Britain steadily drawing closer in their measures of mutual defense with the American acquisition of naval bases in British possessions in the Atlantic . . . and even rumors of our eventual use of Singapore."[56]

Easier to hide than U.S. troops in foreign territories were joint operations on the sea or in the air. In November 1941 Admiral King, commanding the Atlantic Fleet, ordered a U.S. naval group deployed between Iceland and Greenland. As King later described it:

> In the event that the *Tirpitz* and other German heavy ships attempted to break into the North Atlantic, these [U.S.] battleships and cruisers were to . . . [hunt] them down under the orders of the British Commander in Chief.[57]

During 1940 Roosevelt had largely won his political battle to arm Britain, but making supplies effectively available to her was still a major problem in 1941, mostly because German submarines were sinking British merchant ships in large numbers. Protecting British shipping was vital because Britain imported by sea half her food, most of her raw materials and arms, and all her oil. In January 1941 Roosevelt told the press:

> Obviously, when a nation convoys ships . . . through a hostile zone . . . there is apt to be some shooting . . . and shooting comes awfully close to war. . . . It might almost *compel* shooting to start.[58]

He denied any intention to order convoying, but secretly had already decided on it in December and issued orders for U.S. warships to escort British merchant ships, commenting, "Convoys mean shooting and shooting means war" and "we fought an undeclared naval war with the French in the Caribbean."[59]

Convoying was considered an act of war, as Knox acknowledged during hearings on the Lend-Lease bill.[60] Administration representatives assured Congress that convoying would not be used in Lend-Lease. Unconvinced, Congress amended the bill to say that it did not make convoying legal. While Lend-Lease was under consideration, administration representative Jesse Jones testified on different bill, "We're in the war; at least we're nearly in the war; we're preparing for it."[61] Because of the expected political repercussions of his words, he asked that they be deleted from the *Congressional Record,* which was done.

In April Knox prepared a speech referring to naval operations in the Atlantic as "acts of war," and included "we are now at war with the Axis powers." Roosevelt deleted those words.[62]

"Patrolling," "escorting," and "convoying" were overlapping terms, sometimes used interchangeably. "Patrolling" did not imply shooting, but could easily lead to it. "Escorting" and "convoying" implied shooting at attackers of merchant vessels under protection. "Convoying" also implied shooting at nearby warships that had not made an attack — shooting first. If escorting and convoying included orders to fire before being fired on, they were obviously acts of war. And they did include such orders months before Pearl Harbor.

Meanwhile, to undercut opposition if convoying was discovered, Roosevelt gave it the official name "Neutrality Patrol." Admiral King told his staff, "We are preparing for — and are now close to . . . active operations" that are commonly called war.[63] Some navy officers called the prevailing state "belligerent neutrality," and officers participating in convoying quipped that they were "waging neutrality."[64] The combat operations were not much of a secret in the navy.

Preparations for escorting took King until April 1941. Adm. Arthur Bristol was put in command of an escort task force, operating from the British base Argentia in Newfoundland. According to his operations officer:

> Bristol said that the President had decided to establish a special force for protection of shipping in the Atlantic, and that certain ships and aircraft would be allocated to the force. Because of still-existing popular aversion to U.S. involvement in the war, the innocuous title of "Support Force" was assigned.

Admiral Bristol would be responsible to the President, not to the navy's Atlantic command—a most unusual arrangement.[65]

On completion of escort missions, records of them were destroyed.[66] And according to a semi-official navy history:

Although this service was essentially a belligerent one, Admiral King's operation plans of July had to be so cautiously worded that commanders of United States ships and planes were not sure what they were expected to do if a German [surface] raider, submarine or aircraft was encountered . . . to shoot first and let the Navy explain, or only fire if fired upon.[67]

In August, Bristol's force was increased by eight Canadian destroyers and twenty Canadian corvettes, with Canadian crews, serving under his command.[68]

In June Senator Burton Wheeler introduced a resolution for the Senate's Naval Affairs Committee to investigate charges that U.S. warships were escorting British merchant ships and attacking German submarines. Roosevelt then announced escorting, without saying it was already being done.[69]

When the Atlantic Fleet began convoying British shipping in April, Roosevelt wrote to Churchill:

We will want in great secrecy notification of movement of convoys so our patrol units can seek out any ships or planes of aggressor nations operating west of the new line of the security zone. We will immediately make public to you position of aggressor ships or planes when located in our patrol area.[70]

On receiving positions of German and Italian raiders from the U.S. Navy, the British navy proceeded to attack them.

There is an indication that the British were also aided militarily — perhaps as early as February 1941 — by receiving U.S. intelligence about targets in Germany for their bombing runs. Referring to this and other measures, Assistant State Secretary Breckinridge Long wrote in his diary, "We have *ipso facto* passed out of the sphere of neutrality. We are certainly no longer neutral."[71]

Some German, Italian, and Danish merchant ships in the Atlantic, when threatened by British warships, had fled to U.S. ports. Others had entered them for commercial purposes. In March Roosevelt ordered all those ships seized, ostensibly to prevent sabotage by their crews to U.S. ports. The ships were held in "protective custody" until turned over to Great Britain. In addition Roosevelt persuaded South and Central American nations to seize German, Italian, and Danish merchant ships in their ports. In all, Britain gained two million tons of merchant shipping from the seizures — about what she lost each year to German raiders. Roosevelt also had U.S. shipyards repair British warships, had U.S. air bases provide training to British pilots, sent pilot trainers to England, sent civilian and military technicians to repair warplanes in England, and had U.S. troops occupy Greenland.[72] (The military technicians wore civilian clothes.)

During the months that preceded Pearl Harbor, Congress and the public had some awareness that the United States was at war, insofar as some naval actions were announced publicly while others were not well-kept secrets. Stark later testified:

> we had orders to shoot any German or Italian [warship] on the high seas to the westward of the twenty-sixth meridian and . . . they in turn were attacking us and . . . as regards being in war, we were in the position of having command of Canadian [war] vessels or they might have of ours, or . . . [of] British vessels . . . or a British officer might have of ours.[73]

West of the twenty-sixth meridian meant most of the North Atlantic Ocean; it included the seas around Greenland, Iceland, and off the coast of Africa. As Stark commented on naval action in the Atlantic:

> Technically . . . we were not at war because war had not been declared, but actually it was war against any German craft that came inside that area.[74]

By not officially declaring these operations to be "war," Roosevelt managed to avoid a confrontation with Congress. With the noninterventionist movement dying, confrontation had become easier to avoid. In May two influential newspapers, the *St. Louis Post-Dispatch* and the *Detroit Free Press*, gave up their noninterventionist positions and advocated U.S. entry into the war.[75]

In the common view, the United States entered the war on December 7, 1941 because it was forced on her by the Japanese attack. In superficial terms, that is true. The attacks on that day were powerful determinants of what followed. But the explanation is too simple to account for why and how Pearl Harbor happened. Since 1942 controversy over whether the administration was surprised by the Pearl

Fighter planes: Japanese *Zero* (above) and U.S. *Wildcat,* both in use in 1941. By a U.S. stereotype, the Japanese were considered incapable of producing modern military aircraft. Consequently officials in Washington believed that even a surprise attack on Pearl Harbor could be fought off with little loss. According to a U.S. naval historian, however, a *Wildcat* was no match for a *Zero. See* Chapter 1. *Donald M. Goldstein Papers at the University of Pittsburgh.*

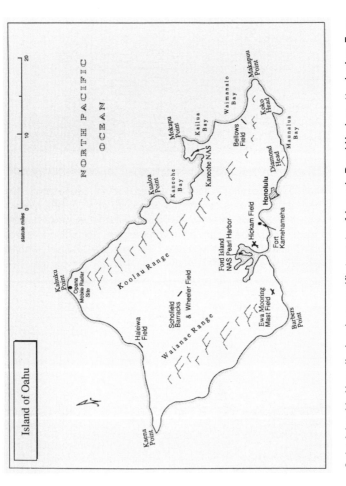

Oahu Island in Hawaii, showing specific targets of Japan's Pearl Harbor attack plan. From intercepted Japanese messages and from double agent Dusan Popov, U.S. intelligence knew these installations were targets, but withheld that from Short and Kimmel. See Chapter 3. *Donald M. Goldstein Papers at the University of Pittsburgh.*

2-12-41. Bespreking op Navy Dept. men wijst mij op de kaart de plaats van 2 Japanse carriers uit Japan vertrokken met Oostelijke koers.

Zaterdag 6-12-41.

Te 1400 naar Navy Dept.; het departement is gesloten behalve de afdeling O.N.I.; waar ook nachtwacht zal worden gedaan. Allen aanwezig op O.N.I. spreek Director Adm. Wilkinson, Capt. Mac Colium, Ltcdr. Kramer. Krijg nadere gegevens omtrent Japanse eskaderbewegingen in Zuid Chinese zee, Golf v. Siam. Men wijst mij - op mijn verzoek - de plaats aan van de 2 carriers (zie 2-12-41) bew. Honolulu.

Diary of Capt. Johan Ranneft. Dutch naval attaché in Washington, in 1941. According to these excerpts, U.S. Naval Intelligence officers showed Ranneft their tracking of Japan's fleet en route to Pearl Harbor. John Toland published the excerpts in his book *Infamy*, but historian John Costello discounted them by impugning Toland's character and claiming his translation was erroneous. See Chapter 3. *From Institute for Maritime History, The Hague, Netherlands; used by permission.*

Adm. Patrick Bellinger (above) and Gen. Frederick Martin, commanders of Navy and Army air wings in Hawaii. They repeatedly and dramatically warned Washington that lack of equipment—mainly patrol planes—was an invitation to disaster. Their warnings and others' resulted in no action. *See* Chapter 6. *Donald M. Goldstein Papers at the University of Pittsburgh.*

Adm. Claude Bloch, commander of the 14th Naval District, with headquarters in Hawaii. Bloch (not Kimmel or Short) was responsible for long-range aerial patrol all around Hawaii, to detect an approaching Japanese naval force. After the Pearl Harbor attack, he testified, "I did my utmost to implement my responsibility by demanding patrol planes . . . but I never had any; I never had one." See Chapter 6. *Donald M. Goldstein Papers at the University of Pittsburgh.*

Adm. James Richardson, commander of the U.S. Fleet, was alarmed that stationing it at Pearl Harbor made it vulnerable to a Japanese attack. After a heated confrontation with Pres. Roosevelt, Richardson concluded the Fleet was being used as a lure for a Japanese attack. When Richardson later violated orders by preparing to put the Fleet on alert, Roosevelt relieved him. *See* Chapter 9. *Donald M. Goldstein Papers at the University of Pittsburgh.*

USS *Isabel*. On December 2, 1941, President Roosevelt ordered the *Isabel* and two other small ships on an ostensible intelligence operation, into the path of a Japanese fleet moving to attack British and Dutch territories. The *Isabel*'s officers and their commander, Adm. Thomas Hart, believed the operation had a hidden purpose—to be sunk, providing justification for Congress to declare was on Japan. See Chapter 14. U.S. Naval Institute; used by permission.

Gen. George Marshall riding his horse near home in 1941, as he did almost daily. Early on the morning of December 7, 1941, Col. Rufus Bratton failed to reach Marshall with intelligence indicating Japan would attack the United States a few hours later. Marshall explained he was riding his horse, which prevented Bratton from reaching him. After other delays, Marshall sent a warning to Gen. Walter Short in Hawaii, which reached him after the attack. But Maj. Eugene Harrison said, "Whoever said he was riding horses lied, because I saw and I talked to him at that time," and other Army and Navy officers confirmed that Marshall was not riding. *See* Chapter 14. *From Gen. George C. Marshall Foundation; used by permission.*

Harbor attack has distracted attention from the unfolding U.S. war strategy and combat operations described above.

Before Pearl Harbor, a state of declared war already existed between Japan's allies (Germany and Italy) and U.S. allies (Britain, the British Commonwealth, the Dutch government in exile, and the Soviet Union). Opponents of Roosevelt said he led the nation into war with Germany by "the back door" — meaning by Japan's attack on Pearl Harbor. That criticism and the defense of Roosevelt it prompted put a piece of history into a distorted framework, which has endured. Roosevelt had already led the United States into war with Germany in the spring of 1941 — into a shooting war on a small scale. From then on, he gradually increased U.S. military participation. Japan's attack on December 7 enabled him to increase it further and to obtain a war declaration. Pearl Harbor is more fully accounted for as the end of a long chain of events, with the U.S. contribution reflecting a strategy formulated after France fell. The distinction between undeclared and declared war was important in administration dealings with Congress and in how far Roosevelt could go in ordering military action. But he had been ordering naval action since January 1941. After Pearl Harbor, Roosevelt was only able to make a small increase in warfare against Germany. It was one of many gradual increases until U.S. troops landed in Italy and then in France.

Early in 1941 the primary purpose of U.S. naval operations in the Atlantic was protecting British shipping; provoking Germany was secondary. By autumn — with British merchant and war fleets strengthened and with German forces heavily occupied in the Soviet Union — Britain was less vulnerable. Protection of her shipping fell in priority and provoking an incident, enabling the United States to go from undeclared war to declared war, rose in priority.

Most of the measures against Germany described in this chapter were considered acts of war by tradition, and were so considered by Roosevelt and his advisers. According to an official U.S. Navy history: "The furnishing of aid, whether logistical or military, to an ally or a potential ally is one of the oldest forms of cooperation between allies."[76] In the eyes of Roosevelt and his advisers, the measures taken early in 1941 justified a German declaration of war on the United States — a declaration that did not come, to their disappointment. In August Stark wrote to Hart, "We are starting considerable operations between North America and Iceland and the Good Lord knows if the Germans want an excuse for war, they have plenty."[77] Roosevelt told his ambassador to France, William Bullitt, that U.S. entry into war against Germany was certain but must wait for an "incident," which he was "confident that the Germans would give us."[78] But an incident sufficient to move Congress to war also did not come.

Meanwhile, in speech after speech Roosevelt hinted about U.S. entry into the war. In May he declared:

> I have said on many occasions that the United States is mustering its men and resources . . . to repel attack. . . . But we must be realistic when we use the word "attack"; we have to relate it to the lightning speed of modern warfare. Some people seem to think we are not attacked until bombs actually drop on [the United States]. . . . But they are simply shutting their eyes to the lessons we must learn from the facts of every nation that the Nazis have conquered. The attack on Czechoslovakia began with the conquest of Austria. The attack on Norway began with the occupation of Denmark . . . it would be suicide to wait until they are in our front yard.[79]

In a draft of the speech, Roosevelt had included:

> I am now ready to announce what is probably no secret to some foreign nations, that certain units of the American Navy have been recently transferred from the Pacific to the Atlantic . . . [and] will . . . perform duties now essential.[80]

On Hull's urging, he left that out. The "duties now essential" already included combat, as naval officers knew and as the public was gradually learning.

The suggestion of a war commitment was still clearer in a September speech:

> The forward march of Hitlerism can be stopped—and it will be stopped and very simply and very bluntly—*we are pledged* to put our own oar into the destruction of Hitlerism.[81] (Italics added.)

The pledge was to Great Britain, members of the British Commonwealth, and the Dutch government in exile.

In April 1941 Roosevelt designated shipping lanes between the United States and Britain as a U.S. "security zone." Then he designated a still larger part of the Atlantic as a "Neutrality Zone" and as "our defensive waters," placing it under U.S. protection under the Monroe Doctrine. (President James Monroe had established the doctrine in 1823 to prevent European aggression against South and Central American nations.) By summer Roosevelt had increased the zone to include half of the ocean between the United States and Europe — 80 percent of that ocean, by another estimate.[82] He ordered the navy to protect it, and in September 1941 threatened openly:

> **From now on, if German or Italian vessels of war enter the waters, the protection of which is necessary for American defense, they do so at their own peril.[83]**

This became known as his "shoot-on-sight" speech. But the U.S. destroyer *Niblack* had initiated an attack on what her captain took to be a German submarine as early as April.[84]

In May Roosevelt ordered an especially provocative operation. British intelligence had learned that the newly completed German battleship *Bismarck* (considered the most powerful in the world) and cruiser *Prinz Eugen* were ready to sortie from the port of Gdynia in conquered Poland. British Admiral John Tovey commanded a naval group assigned to destroy major German warships before they reached the Atlantic and joined in attacking British shipping. Churchill and Tovey gave priority to sinking the *Bismarck*.

The *Bismark* and the *Prinz Eugen* left Gdynia on May 18, and their movement north was quickly learned by British intelligence. But British planes sent to find them failed to, and on May 22 Churchill appealed to Roosevelt for help, saying, "Should we fail to catch them going out, your Navy should surely be able to mark them down for us. . . . Give us the news and we will finish the job."[85] Churchill dramatized his appeal by saying, if the *Bismarck* and *Prinz Eugen* reached the Atlantic, "they would alter the whole course of the war."[86] Roosevelt responded by sending navy patrol bombers and coast guard cutters stationed in Newfoundland toward Iceland to join the hunt.[87]

Meanwhile, without knowing the German ships' location, Tovey made a guess and sent a squadron to intercept them. It included the battleship *Hood*, the largest in the world and the pride of Britain's navy. Launched in 1920, she was still among the world's fastest and most heavily armed. Her weakness was the thinness of her armor. The British squadron ran into the German ships between Iceland and Greenland.

On May 24, in her first combat, the *Bismarck* sank the *Hood*, and only three among the latter's crew of fourteen hundred survived. Having suffered damage to her fuel tank and taken water into her fuel, the *Bismarck* continued into the Atlantic, circling south toward the port of Brest in German-occupied France for repairs. To conserve her uncontaminated fuel, the *Bismarck* steamed slowly when out of sight of her pursuers. As a result they found and lost her a few times.

During the evening on May 25, the U.S. Coast Guard cutter *Modoc* sighted the *Bismarck* briefly and radioed her location to the British. (The *Modoc* was part of the "Greenland Survey Expedition, itself a euphemism for a patrol to discourage a German attack [on Greenland] and occupation.") Based on the report, the *Bismarck* was spotted the next morning by a patrol bomber supplied to Britain under Lend-Lease, *piloted by a U.S. Navy officer with a mixed U.S. and British crew.*[88] The British then sank the *Bismark.*

U.S. participation in the search had a purpose in addition to sinking German warships, at least in Churchill's eyes. When the *Bismarck* had headed south for Brest, the *Prinz Eugen* had headed west. After sinking the *Bismarck*, Churchill focused on sinking the *Prinz Eugen*, and again asked Roosevelt for help in finding her. He explained in a secret memo to Admiral Dudley Pound, head of the British navy:

> **For First Lord and First Sea Lord [Pound] alone. In a locked box. The bringing into action of the *Prinz Eugen* and the search for her raise questions of the highest importance. It is most desirable that the United States Navy should play a part in this. It would be far better, for instance, that she should be located by a United States ship, as this might tempt her to fire upon that ship, thus providing the incident for which the United States government would be so thankful.**
>
> **Pray let this matter be considered from this point of view, apart from the ordinary naval aspect. If we can only create a situation where the *Prinz Eugen* is being shadowed by an American vessel, we shall have gone a long way to solve the largest problem.**[89]

In November Roosevelt ordered a navy task force to join in trying to sink the German battleships *Admiral Scheer* and *Tirpitz.*[90] The idea was that, while Germany could ignore the U.S. Navy sinking a submarine, she would have to declare war if it sank a battleship.

Serious clashes with Germany did not materialize because Hitler had ordered his navy to avoid them. When U.S. warships fired on German ones, Hitler's admirals pleaded for authority at least to shoot back. He put them off, explaining that he wanted to postpone war with the United States, and incidents must be avoided. And if an incident occurred, the captain of the German ship had to write an official report putting responsibility on the U.S. ship at which he had fired.

Incidents occurred nonetheless, because when under water submarine crews could not identify the nationalities of foreign ships on the surface. And the British navy's use of destroyers and cutters from

the United States added to German submarine crews' difficulty in identifying warships. In June a German submarine sank the U.S. merchant
ship *Robin Moor*. Germany apologized, saying the crew mistook her
for a British vessel. Almost everyone aboard the *Robin Moor* survived,
and the United States hardly reacted when Roosevelt denounced Germany as having deliberately sunk her.[91]

Roosevelt then froze Germany's assets in the United States, ordered her consular staffs to leave, and declared in another speech:

> Adolf Hitler never considered the domination of Europe as an
> end itself. European conquest was but a step toward ultimate
> goals in all other continents . . . unless the advance of Hitlerism
> is forcibly checked now, the Western Hemisphere will be within
> range of the Nazi weapons of destruction.[92]

Soon after, a German submarine fired torpedoes at the U.S. destroyer *Greer*, missing her. Roosevelt then made a fighting speech:

> I tell you the blunt fact that the German submarine fired first
> upon this American destroyer without warning. . . . We have
> sought no shooting war with Hitler. We do not seek it now.
> But neither do we want peace so much, that we are willing to
> pay for it by permitting him to attack our naval and merchant
> ships while they are on legitimate business [the *Greer* was
> carrying U.S. mail]. This incident is not isolated, but is part of
> a general plan. . . . It is the Nazi design to abolish freedom of
> the seas, and to acquire absolute control and domination of
> those seas for themselves. . . . The aggression is not ours.
> Ours is solely defense. . . . In the waters which we deem nec-
> essary for our defense, American naval vessels and Ameri-
> can planes will no longer wait until Axis . . . raiders . . . strike
> their deadly blow—first.[93]

As Roosevelt knew, the "blunt fact" was misleading, for the navy
had briefed him before his speech. Near Iceland, the *Greer* had been
alerted to the German submarine's position by a British plane. For
hours the *Greer* had trailed the submarine, reporting her position to
British planes, which attacked her repeatedly. Then the submarine fired
torpedoes at the *Greer*.[94]

Roosevelt's speech helped arouse public anger against Germany,
but nearly backfired in Congress. Some details of the *Greer* incident
came out, prompting calls for Senate and navy investigations. The
Senate called for the *Greer*'s log, but the navy did not provide it.[95]

Roosevelt stopped using the incident in calling for war, and his opponents dropped demands for investigations.

In October the U.S. destroyer *Kearny* was attacked while escorting British merchant ships. She was part of a U.S. destroyer group deployed near Iceland to reinforce Canadian warships engaged in escorting. When submarines attacked a convoy, the *Kearny* fired on them, and was then torpedoed, suffering heavy damage and loss of eleven lives.[96] Roosevelt took ten days preparing a speech, and then declared:

> All we Americans have cleared our decks and taken our battle stations. . . . We have wished to avoid shooting. But the shooting has started. And *history will record who fired the first shot.* In the long run, however, all that will matter is who fired the last shot. America has been attacked. . . . Our determination not to take it lying down has been expressed in orders to the American Navy to shoot on sight. Those orders stand.[97] (Italics added.)

The speech was a call to war. But the public, Congress, and Hitler largely ignored it.

Establishing a record in which the enemy fired the first shot was a theme that ran through Roosevelt's tactics. He touched on it in his *Greer* and *Kearny* speeches, and it would be a requirement in cabinet and other strategy meetings during that autumn.

In September Roosevelt also made a radio address about German plans for taking over the western hemisphere, citing as proof unspecified German documents in his possession. In an October speech he went further:

> Hitler has often protested that his plans for conquest do not extend across the Atlantic Ocean. I have in my possession a secret map, made in Germany by Hitler's government . . . [which has] ruthlessly obliterated all the existing boundary lines . . . [and] divided South America into five vassal states, bringing the whole continent under their domination. . . . [it] includes the Republic of Panama and our great life-line—the Panama Canal. This map makes clear the Nazi design . . . against the United States as well. . . .
>
> Your government has in its possession another document . . . [of] Hitler's government . . . a plan to abolish all existing religions—Catholic, Protestant, Mohammedan, Hindu, Buddhist and Jewish alike. . . . The cross and all other symbols of religion are to be forbidden. The clergy are to be forever liquidated.[98]

When reporters asked to see the map, Roosevelt refused, saying notes on it might reveal the source from which it had been obtained. The source was British counter-intelligence, which had forged it for use in bringing the United States into the European war. (That Hitler had designs on the western hemisphere and intentions to abolish religions was true.) Whether Roosevelt knew at the time that the map was a forgery is unclear. In any case, his speeches did not have the desired effect.

After failure of his *Greer* and *Kearny* speeches, Roosevelt gave up using attacks on U.S. ships in calls for war. After failure of his speeches about German plots to take over the western hemisphere and abolish religions, Roosevelt gave up those topics as well. At the end of October, the German navy sank the U.S. destroyer *Reuben James*, with all lives lost, and torpedoed the navy tanker *Salinas*. Roosevelt said little, perhaps having lost hope that an incident in the Atlantic would move the nation to war.

Meanwhile he had begun shifting his strategy to the Pacific. He may have contrasted the public's relative indifference over the sinking of U.S. ships in the Atlantic with the spontaneous anger and talk of war when Japan had attacked the U.S. gunboats *Panay* and *Tutuila*. He seems to have concluded — correctly, as it turned out — that Japan would be easier to provoke into a major attack on the United States than Germany would be. Ingersoll later testified that by autumn 1941:

> The undeclared war in the Atlantic had been going on for some time. We were virtually at war with Germany. . . . We felt that [declared] war would be precipitated in the Pacific and that we would only become involved in [declared] war in the Atlantic as the result of war in the Pacific.[99]

While seeking an incident in the Atlantic during 1941, Roosevelt made public statements that his naval deployments were to protect a U.S. "security zone," a "Neutrality Zone," and "our defensive waters," and to deter German aggression. He made similar statements to subordinates about protecting against and deterring Japanese aggression by stationing the U.S. Fleet in Hawaii, about keeping it there, and about sending fleet units to places nearer to Japan. Richardson, Stark, and Kimmel pointed out to him that the fleet was not strong enough to act as a deterrent against Japan — that, because of its weakness, its presence in Hawaii invited an attack. They lectured Roosevelt, as if doubting that he understood the difference between a deterrent force and a provocative force.

From a military viewpoint, the conceptual difference between deterrence and provocation is simple. A force powerful enough to be intimidating tends to deter. A weak force invites attack. Roosevelt had served as assistant secretary of the navy and studied naval history. The idea that he failed to distinguish between deterrence and provocation — and continued to make this error after the difference was pointed out to him repeatedly — is unreasonable. On the contrary, he himself pointed out the difference in 1940 to Ambassador Bullitt. After Germany's invasion of France, Bullitt urged Roosevelt to deter an expected Italian invasion of France by moving warships into the Mediterranean, and Roosevelt replied that "the presence of an American fleet at this time in the Mediterranean would result in very serious risks . . . unless any fleet sent were sufficiently large to be effective, the impression created would be the reverse of that desired."[100]

"Deterrence" and "provocation" are opposites; nonetheless, a strategy may combine them. A leader may decide that an enemy attack at some indefinite future time is the worst thing that can happen. The leader may then take action likely to deter the attack or to bring it on immediately — without being sure which will happen — on the basis that either is better than waiting without knowing when the attack will come. Such a decision may reflect a temporary state of readiness or an expectation that prolonged waiting is likely to erode troop morale or otherwise work to the enemy's advantage. Roosevelt saw U.S. interests in both deterring and provoking a Japanese attack. He may have taken measures without resolving whether they were more likely to deter or provoke.

Keeping the fleet in Hawaii from May 1940 on was a crucial decision. Keeping it there during autumn 1941, after warnings of Japan's plan to attack it there came in, was also a crucial decision. For the undeclared war in the Atlantic, there is ample evidence of Roosevelt's provocative intention. For his decision to keep the fleet in Hawaii, direct evidence of such an intention is lacking. However, a group of actions Roosevelt took in July 1941 and afterward support the possibility that he did it to provoke. These actions would eventually move Japan to attack the United States.

CHAPTER 11

COUNTDOWN IN WASHINGTON: THE JULY TURNING POINT

Until 1941 the priority of defeating Hitler required avoiding war with Japan. But a crucial development in the European war that year moved Roosevelt to risk war with Japan in order to prevent a German victory.

Early in 1940 members of Congress proposed embargoes on Japan, but Hull opposed them because they might provoke rather than deter her.[1] When France fell, Churchill proposed a full U.S. embargo on Japan. Hull responded that an embargo would risk war when the United States was unprepared for it, and Roosevelt agreed.[2] In September Roosevelt announced a "moral embargo," accompanied by an unannounced compulsory embargo on steel and scrap iron. He then made the compulsory embargo public and added to it petroleum products (not gasoline), weapons, ammunition, and other metals. By the winter of 1940–41 Roosevelt added to the list almost weekly.[3] He described the additions as punishments, mainly for Japan's actions in China, and said they were imposed to discourage their continuation. There is no evidence that Roosevelt meant them to provoke Japan or — with the exception of the scrap iron embargo — considered that they might have that effect. The growing list was limited to items not crucial to her economy or the continuation of her war in China.

In January 1941 the Joint Planning Committee of the Army-Navy Joint Board (Col. Joseph McNarney and Admiral Turner) advised:

> **With respect to Germany and Italy, it appears reasonably certain that neither will initiate hostilities with the United States,**

until they have succeeded in inflicting a major reverse on Great Britain. . . . With respect to Japan, hostilities prior to United States entry into the European war or the defeat of Britain may depend upon . . . steps taken by the United States to oppose Japanese aggression. If these steps seriously threaten her economic welfare or military adventures, there can be no assurance that Japan will not suddenly attack United States armed forces.

It listed steps likely to provoke a Japanese attack on the United States:

1. Strongly reinforce our Asiatic Fleet or the Philippine garrison.
2. Start fortifying Guam.
3. Impose additional important sanctions.
4. Greatly increase our material . . . aid to China.
5. A definite indication that an alliance with the British or Dutch had been consummated.
6. Our opposition to a Japanese attack on British or Dutch territory.[4]

U.S. policy was still to avoid war with Japan. If this policy changed, the steps could become means of provoking Japan to attack the United States.

U.S. leaders often thought about an oil embargo, considering it the heaviest of sanctions short of war. Roosevelt had first been advised to order one after Japan's invasion of China in 1937. He was advised to again and again up to 1941. Analysis of an oil embargo's likely effects was mainly the responsibility of the State Department. Hull and Welles consistently opposed one because it risked war. Ambassador Grew was on closest terms with Japan's leaders and best informed on their thinking. He opposed an oil embargo vigorously in 1939, 1940, and 1941, warning that "it would be hazardous to base our national policy on the belief, held in certain quarters, that our economic pressure will not drive Japan to war."[5]

Roosevelt agreed that some embargoes were too risky, and did not consider an oil embargo seriously. During the summer of 1940, his son Elliott urged an embargo on scrap iron, and he replied:

If we were suddenly to stop our sales of scrap iron to Japan, she would be within her rights in considering [it] an unfriendly act, that we were choking off and starving her commercially. Even more, she'd be entitled to consider such . . . sufficient cause to break off diplomatic relations with us. I'll go even further. *If she thought we were sufficiently unprepared . . . she might even use it as an excuse to declare war.*[6] (Italics added.)

The president added that the navy and army were unprepared at the time. Nonetheless he proceeded to embargo scrap iron and steel to Japan that September.

That same September Eleanor Roosevelt urged an oil embargo and he replied:

if we forbid oil shipments to Japan, Japan . . . may be driven by actual necessity to a descent on the Dutch East Indies . . . we all regard such action on our part as an encouragement to the spread of war in the Far East.[7]

And just before Roosevelt embargoed oil, Stark wrote to Admiral Hart about the possibility that Japan would invade Borneo, "I doubt that this will be done in the near future, *unless* we embargo oil shipments to them."[8]

The oil embargo of July 1941 was a sudden reversal of policy. At the end of May, Roosevelt made Interior Secretary Harold Ickes Petroleum Coordinator, with responsibility for conserving oil. In June Ickes stopped a shipment of oil to Japan, but Roosevelt countermanded his order. Ickes argued, citing not only the need to conserve oil, but also the adverse effect on morale of selling oil to Japan while Americans were suffering from gasoline shortages.[9] Then on June 23—with the argument between them unresolved—Ickes proposed an oil embargo, commenting:

There might develop from the embargoing of oil to Japan such a situation as would make it not only possible but easy to get into the war in an effective way. And if we should thus indirectly be brought in, we would avoid the criticism that we had gone in as an ally of communistic Russia . . . It may be difficult to get into this war the right way, but if we do not do it now, we will be, when our turn comes, without an ally anywhere in this world.[10]

Roosevelt replied, "Please let me know if this would continue to be your judgment if this were to tip the delicate scales and cause Japan to attack Russia or to attack the Dutch East Indies."[11] And he replied further with another letter, telling Ickes that foreign policy was "delicate," "peculiarly confidential," and not his business.[12] According to Ickes, this was "the most peremptory and ungracious communication that I have ever received from him."[13]

Ickes offered to resign, as he had done over earlier disagreements, but Roosevelt ignored his offer. Then on July 1, Roosevelt wrote to Ickes that he was not angry with him and that he had not been at all. To this mollification, Roosevelt added:

> I think it will interest you to know that the Japs are having a real drag-down and knock-out fight among themselves, and have been for the past week—trying to decide which way they are going to jump—attack Russia, attack the South Seas . . . or . . . sit on the fence and be more friendly with us. No one knows what the decision will be.[14]

The comment was based on intelligence, which was accurate. On that day Japan's cabinet presented to an Imperial Conference a proposal to attack the Soviet Union, South Sea nations, or the United States (see following).

Roosevelt's anger at Ickes and subsequent attempts to mollify him probably reflected Roosevelt's own conflict about measures against Japan. The expected consequences of such measures troubled him greatly, and the need to consider them was coming to a head. A cabinet meeting on July 18 resulted in a consensus for an oil embargo against Japan, but Roosevelt said that "to cut off oil altogether at this time would probably precipitate an outbreak of war."[15] He had already limited oil to Japan by granting no more export licenses after March. And the army and navy still opposed an oil embargo. In addition, on July 21 Ambassador Nomura visited Welles to warn him that an oil embargo would risk war. But in July, Japan had five million gallons of gasoline on order from the United States; she was not feeling a pinch yet.

When Roosevelt came to his decision to embargo oil, he apparently did so without consulting the army. The question is: what prompted Roosevelt's reversal, thereby risking war with Japan? According to the administration, the oil embargo was to deter Japan from completing her take-over of Indochina — plans of which United States knew in advance.[16] There are, however, reasons to question this explanation. When originally informed a year earlier that Japan might take over Indochina, Roosevelt had said Indochina was unimportant. In herself, Indochina counted for little in Washington.[17] As a potential staging ground for Japan to attack the Burma Road — threatening China's supply lifeline — or to open a new front in the invasion of China,

Indochina was very important to China. But China herself was never of high importance to Roosevelt.

Indochina was also a potential staging ground for invasions of Thailand, the Dutch East Indies, and Malaya. Thailand was not of strategic importance to Washington. The Dutch East Indies, however, did count heavily and, by alliance with the Dutch government in exile, the United States had undertaken limited obligations to defend this large territory, very rich in oil. But Roosevelt and most of his advisers believed an oil embargo would not deter Japan from invading the Dutch East Indies; rather, it would lead directly to such an invasion. Malaya also counted heavily, and the United States had also undertaken limited obligations to defend this mineral-rich British territory.

As Roosevelt remarked to Japan's Ambassador Nomura when informing him of the oil embargo, it was already too late to deter Japan's take-over of Indochina because it was virtually complete![18] In 1940 Roosevelt's cabinet discussed one of the embargoes as a deterrent to Japan's take-over of Indochina, which had already begun. Treasury Secretary Morgenthau's comment then — even more apt in July 1941 — was, "the time to put pressure on Japan was before she went into Indo-China and not after and I think it's too late and . . . the Japanese and the rest of the dictators are just going to laugh at us."[19] Japan's leaders did not laugh at the oil embargo; grimly they authorized preparations for war against the United States.

If action is taken too late for its stated purpose, that purpose does not explain it. In addition, given the priority of defeating Hitler, the official explanation failed to identify a purpose important enough to risk war with Japan. Deterring completion of Japan's take-over of Indochina was an insufficient reason to accept the consequences of the oil embargo.

A second way to understand the embargo is to infer that, with provocation to war failing in the Atlantic, Roosevelt turned to pressing it in the Pacific. That is, in provoking Japan into a "mistake," he went from fleet movements to measures better calculated to move her to war. This idea is supported by the belief held by Roosevelt, the State Department, the Navy Department, and the War Department that an oil embargo would have that effect. As noted earlier, Roosevelt was considering measures to provoke a Japanese mistake — an attack on the United States that might get him a war declaration — since October 1940. The measures he took against Japan after that were small. None, in itself, was considered likely to have that effect. By contrast, the oil embargo was a major blow to Japan, considered highly likely to provoke her to war against the United States. The question remains: why did Roosevelt do in July 1941 what he angrily refused to do in June?

When he reconsidered an oil embargo in July, Roosevelt requested an analysis by the navy. Its War Plans Division prepared one, endorsed by Stark, which concluded:

> It is generally believed that shutting off the American supply of petroleum will lead to an invasion of the Netherlands East Indies. . . . [It] will have an immediate severe psychological reaction in Japan against the United States. It is almost certain to intensify the determination . . . to continue their present course. Furthermore, it seems certain that, if Japan should take military measures against the British and Dutch, she would also include military action against the Philippines, which would immediately involve us in a Pacific war. . . .
>
> *Recommendation.*—That Japan not be embargoed at this time.[20]

A memo by G-2 chief Miles on July 25 noted Japan's "deplorable" economic condition and added, "The United States is now in a position to wreck completely the economic structure of the Japanese Empire."[21] And Stark testified, "When you throttle a nation's economic life she has got to do something . . . particularly with regard to oil."[22] And when Roosevelt decided to order the embargo, Stark informed his Pacific commanders, warning them to anticipate a Japanese attack in response.[23]

Objections to the embargo by Roosevelt's military experts are emphasized to show what advice he received and what his thinking included as he came to his decision. The strong opposition in the State and Navy Departments and the risk to which it exposed U.S. forces in the Pacific suggest that Roosevelt had a crucial reason for ordering the embargo. And the abruptness with which he reversed his position suggests the reason was new.

A third way to understand the decision is by searching its context for a vital reason not mentioned by the administration. When Roosevelt ordered the oil embargo, he also took three other measures affecting Japan: freezing her assets in the United States, breaking off diplomatic talks with her, and arming the Philippines. (These will be called "associated measures.") The four measures were taken a few days apart and seem to reflect a single policy decision. That inference is supported by their effects on Japan: each of them moved Japan's leaders toward the conclusion that diplomacy would not work and that, to continue her conquest of China, war with the United States probably could not be avoided. On learning of these four measures, Foreign Minister Toyoda Teijiro informed Ambassador Grew that

Japan might respond by making war on the United States.[24] Comments by Roosevelt and his advisers about the measures mark July as the end of "babying" or "appeasing" Japan—the beginning of a tough policy toward her. Such a policy change is compatible with a deterrent purpose as well as a provocative one.

The freeze has often been lumped with the embargo, even though it was said to serve a different purpose. For the embargo has generally been described as deterrent; the freeze, as punitive and provocative. Japan was expected to retaliate by freezing U.S. assets, which she did. The breaking off of talks has been described as a provocation, and with good reason, as will be seen. In contrast, arming the Philippines has been described as a deterrent and a measure to defend that territory.

The Philippines lie alongside sea routes from Japan and Taiwan to Malaya and the Dutch East Indies. A powerful U.S. military force in the Philippines would, therefore, expose a Japanese naval force approaching those targets to a flank attack. In that way, arming the Philippines could have served as a deterrent to Japanese moves against Malaya and the Dutch East Indies, as well as against the Philippines themselves. Admiral Turner later testified that he did not believe arming the Philippines would deter Japan from attacking them.[25] As matters developed, he was right; arming the Philippines turned out to be a provocation. It did not discourage Japan's moves against Malaya and the Dutch East Indies; it did move her to add the Philippines to her targets.

Possible purposes for arming the Philippines were defending them, deterring a Japanese move south, enabling the United States to bomb Japan, and provoking Japan. The decision could have been intended to implement any combination of them. Defense of the Philippines against a Japanese invasion had been proposed during the previous three decades and consistently rejected as not in U.S. interests. Evidence of a new consideration for reversing that policy in July 1941 is lacking. By contrast, deterrence was a new consideration, becoming more important as Japan was known to be approaching a move in Southeast Asia.

Requests from President Quezon to arm his country, prompted by his concern for her vulnerability, and from Gen. George Grunert, commander of the army's Philippine Department are on record. In 1940, "Grunert peppered the War Department with requisitions for new weapons and equipment and warnings that the United States could not depend on the readiness of MacArthur's [Filipino] Commonwealth forces" to defend the islands.[26] Growing tension between the United States and Japan also raised concerns within the War and

Navy Departments about Philippine vulnerability. Members of those departments made proposals, which are also on record, to arm the Philippines for their defense. Apparently Roosevelt did not consider the requests or proposals seriously, and feasibility studies were not done. The reason was probably the one Stimson gave in his diary in August 1940, when rejecting one such proposal:

> A proposition to double the number of the Philippine Scouts . . . was presented to me. . . . I think it is no time to raise *that particular pawn* which lies within reach of Japan. We already have about 5,000 white troops and 6,000 Philippine Scouts out there to fall into the hands of Japan if she chooses to attack the Islands, and I don't think there is any reason for adding to them. The forces, even if augmented, would be far too small to make any difference.[27] (Italics added.)

The "white troops" were U.S. soldiers; the "Scouts" were Filipinos in the U.S. force. The obvious meaning of "make any difference" was to make a successful defense possible. Another meaning is suggested by "pawn," taken from the game of chess — a war game in which a pawn may be moved to a position that risks its capture. The capture is then turned to the advantage of the player who moved the pawn. Such a move is carefully planned, tempting the opponent to make a mistake. The pawn is sacrificed to win the war. If Stimson so intended the phrase, he was not necessarily rejecting the tactic, but may have been questioning only that this was the time for it.

In November 1940 Marshall rejected Grunert's most recent proposal on the grounds that arming the Philippines would not contribute significantly to a successful defense, but "might result in involving us in action in that theater which we are not prepared to sustain."[28] Rather than deterring a Japanese invasion, it might provoke one.

Probably an unrecorded proposal in February 1941 to increase naval forces in the Philippines was what prompted Stark to advise Roosevelt:

> Sending a small force would probably be no deterrent to Japan and would not increase Japanese difficulties in advancing southward. I feel we would be exposing our force without compensating results. There is a chance that further moves against Japan will precipitate hostilities rather than prevent them. We want to give Japan no excuse for coming in in case we are forced into hostilities with Germany whom we all consider our major problem.

> The Pacific Fleet is now weaker . . . than the Japanese Navy. [But] . . . it remains a constant serious threat to Japan's flank. If any considerable division is sent to Manila it might prove an invitation to Japan to attack.[29]

Stark's mention of "Japan . . . advancing southward" showed anticipation in February of Japan's future moves against the Dutch East Indies and Malaya. It touched on a strategic question, at which Stimson may have hinted in using the word "pawn" and which would, logically, require urgent consideration in the summer. Were the Philippines to be armed sufficiently to deter a Japanese invasion of Malaya and the Dutch East Indies, sufficiently for defense against an invasion of the Philippines, or only enough to invite an attack on them?

On June 20, 1941, in reply to an inquiry from MacArthur, Marshall told him the War Department had no intention to arm the Philippines nor to give him a command there, unless a crisis arose in the Pacific.[30] No crisis arose there by the end of June, but a new proposal to arm the Philippines was made and approved in July. A major crisis had arisen, however, in Europe.

There is no record of who initiated the proposal at the end of June to arm the Philippines. Perhaps the idea came from Roosevelt or a cabinet member, or from an adviser outside the War or Navy Departments. (Proposals from within those departments were routinely recorded.) An official army history noted the irregularity of the project in that *it was adopted without consultation in the War Department*.[31]

In setting the decision to arm the Philippines against this background, how the arming was carried out suggests a subtle purpose. The buildup was an army operation, and an official army history described it as a series of blunders, as if the War Department was unaware of or failed to grasp the risks involved.[32] But that was not the case. Details of the buildup received much attention in the War Department, and at least four generals understood that it invited a Japanese attack.

Marshall informed MacArthur in July that he would be restored to active duty and take command of the Philippine department. MacArthur was optimistic about the buildup, telling people he was confident of defeating a Japanese invasion. His chief of staff, Gen. Richard Sutherland, considered the assignment — within the time left before an expected Japanese attack on the United States in October — an "insurmountable task."[33] Time was not the only limitation; according to Labor Secretary Frances Perkins, Stimson later said the administration's plan was still to abandon the Philippines.[34]

Marshall encouraged MacArthur's optimism about a successful

defense of the Philippines, despite the slowness of the buildup there. But even by December, it was woefully inadequate for its stated purpose. Gen. Jonathan Wainwright, commanding a Philippine army, wrote that his troops "were doomed before they started to fight" because they "were no more prepared than a child is prepared to fight a cruel and seasoned pugilist."[35]

Having no record on which to base an explanation for the decision in July to arm the Philippines, army historians came up with a minor reason. Until July the army could not supply long-range bombers for the Philippines without taking them from other bases. But the new Flying Fortress had just gone into mass production, which would soon make planes available.[36] The shortage of planes, however, had not been given as a reason for rejecting earlier proposals to arm the Philippines. And the availability of the Flying Fortress was not a sufficient reason to justify the grave risks in the decision. Their availability, however, gave the Philippines an important military capability — to bomb distant Japanese targets: staging areas and even Japan's home islands.

The army historians suggested:

> By developing this threat, the United States might be able to force the Japanese to either accept . . . [Philippine] neutrality . . . freeing American and British forces for operations against Germany, or *to open hostilities* before American forces should become heavily engaged across the Atlantic.[37] (Italics added.)

If Roosevelt was concerned about the risks in provoking Japan by arming the Philippines, he apparently did not say so. And he was not the only one who seemed unconcerned. In September nine Flying Fortresses arrived in the Philippines. In November, thirty-five arrived, constituting a serious threat to Japan.

Newly assigned to command the Army Air Corps there, Gen. Lewis Brereton noted that its new bombers lacked protection by an adequate force of fighter planes; therefore they were easy targets for a Japanese preemptive strike. He was troubled enough to express his apprehension to Air Corps Chief Arnold, pointing out that, in the circumstances, the new bombers there invited a Japanese attack. Arnold replied that he was aware of the danger.[38] Unsatisfied, Brereton went to Marshall, saying (as Brereton recalled):

> if the situation in the Far East was critical . . . the presence of strong and unprotected bombardment units might easily be a decisive factor to incite an aggressive enemy to air attack.

> The enemy would have everything to gain by neutralizing our bomber force before the arrival of units necessary for their protection.[39]

Marshall replied that the hazards involved were recognized. Marshall's staff member, Gen. Joseph Green, also warned him that the Flying Fortresses sent to the Philippines invited an attack on them.[40]

Fighter planes already in the Philippines were mostly obsolete, and newly arrived ones (P-40s) had serious operational defects. A fighter pilot there wrote home in November:

> They say that we are getting the latest equipment, but we who are here flying it know that it is no good. Our planes—the latest P-40s—are not good enough to fight with! . . . [W]e are doomed at the start.[41]

Even more than defective planes, what doomed troops in the Philippines were orders from Washington that prevented preemptive bombing of Taiwan or interception of Japanese planes approaching the Philippines.[42] Early in December, troops detected Japanese planes by radar and sighted them visually offshore and even overhead. Pursuant to MacArthur's orders, they did no more than observe the planes. On December 5 Brereton's chief of staff asked for authority to intercept them, and MacArthur's chief of staff give him new orders: they could not be intercepted while offshore, but only when over Philippine land.[43]

On December 7 the Japanese attacked by air, destroying Brereton's bombers. The Philippine buildup proved to have no value in deterring invasions of Malaya, the Dutch East Indies, or the Philippines, or in defending the Philippines themselves. But it did serve another purpose—one considered vital to British and U.S. security.

If—as it appears from the absence of records—Roosevelt made the decision to arm the Philippines without staff work, then there was no feasibility study. And if so, there was no basis for deciding how many troops, planes, and so on were needed in the Philippines. (A study of how many planes were needed for defense was done *after* the decision.) Even though the proposal was under consideration for several weeks, Roosevelt adopted it without knowing how much arming was needed for deterrence or defense. If, however, the purpose was provocation, then such staff work was unnecessary. Provocation required only the presence of a visible force large enough to impress Japan's leaders that their territory or operations were endangered. The only force there by mid-November (and by December 7) large enough to threaten Japan was the new bombers. The size of a force large enough to be perceived as a threat by Japan could be estimated without feasibility studies. Brereton, Arnold, Marshall, and Green understood that the Philippine buildup invited an attack; so also should other army leaders have understood that.

In addition, what followed the decision to arm the Philippines supports the possibility of a provocative purpose. After ordering the oil embargo and associated measures, Roosevelt and his advisers expected a Japanese attack on U.S. territory — perhaps immediately, more likely within a few months. From intercepted Japanese diplomatic messages, they soon learned that Japan planned such an attack in mid-October. If forces in the Philippines were to serve as a deterrent or to make a successful defense of the islands possible, the arming had to be done by October. But it was not organized to be completed that soon. Instead of rushing troops and equipment there, Washington sent them out at a slow pace, planning for completion possibly by December, more likely by March or April 1942. According to an official army history, "The month of April 1942 was commonly accepted as the critical date and most plans were based on that date."[44]

Troops and equipment began to arrive in mid-August at a rate described by army historians as "a trickle."[45] A schedule for their arrival, given by Marshall to Stark in September, showed the slow pace was to continue.[46] According to Marshall's authorized biographer, "the leaders in Washington and Manila seemed to forget how quickly time was running out and how many months were still needed to prepare an adequate Philippine defense."[47] But army leaders in both cities discussed with concern the slow pace and the resultant danger to the Philippines.

During the same month, Marshall informed MacArthur that the Philippine buildup had been given the highest priority. This was misleading; the European war continued to have highest priority. Probably Marshall's statement helped convince MacArthur that the administration intended an effective — rather than token — defense of the Philippines and that he would be able to accomplish it. He wrote to Marshall:

> I wish to express my personal appreciation for the splendid support that you and the entire War Department have given me. . . . With such backing the development of a completely adequate defense force will be rapid.[48]

This was wishful thinking; the buildup fell far short of MacArthur's expectations. When December came, many of MacArthur's pilots were still flying obsolete planes. His new planes were incompletely equipped and not yet broken in, and his pilots were still receiving training on them.

Men and equipment arrived in the Philippines surreptitiously at night. Nonetheless the arming was rather obvious and Stimson even made a public announcement about it![49] A War Department memo to Stimson on October 8 about the buildup of the Philippine air force emphasized that its new offensive power should be made clearly visible to Japan for the purpose of intimidation.[50] (It also discussed whether Japan was likely to invade Siberia, a possibility which the memo's authors considered a crippling blow to the Allies' chances in the European war.)

In discussions of arming the Philippines, there is no record of considering provocation as its purpose, but there is data from which it may be inferred. Japan was disturbed by the arming and asked the United States to stop it, offering to negotiate neutrality for the Philippines.[51] Philippine neutrality was badly needed by the Filipinos and considered necessary by officers in the War and Navy Departments to save the islands from a Japanese invasion. The administration, however, did not use Japan's concern as a bargaining chip to implement neutrality, deterrence, or any other purpose. Washington ignored Japan's request and offer, and the arming of the Philippines continued, but only at a trickle. It was not until December that troops and equipment began arriving in large numbers.

In short, it was soon evident that arming the Philippines was proceeding much too slowly for it to deter Japan's expected moves in October or to provide the capability for a successful defense by then. Both the War Department and Stark noted this. Nonetheless, the operation continued under these conditions. To conclude, the oil embargo and Philippine buildup were unsuited to their stated purposes of deterrence and defense.

If the oil embargo and Philippine buildup were intended to provoke Japan, a remaining question is, what prompted an abrupt reversal of policy in July? Historian Waldo Heinrichs suggested that U.S. dealings with Japan during the summer of 1941, including the oil embargo, were shaped by the need to save the Soviet Union—a need which "became the centerpiece of [Roosevelt's] world strategy."[52] Much data supports this unique idea.

Although tension with the United States grew markedly after the September 1940 moral embargo, Japanese leaders considered peace with her necessary for pursuing conquest in Asia. But by July 1941, the cabinet was considering a highly controversial policy that included war with the United States as a real possibility. On July 2 an Imperial

Conference adopted the policy. Its main action points were to continue establishing dominance over East Asia and to make Japan's position secure by winning the campaign in China, by advancing "into the Southern Regions," and by settling "the Soviet Question." And it projected a more aggressive policy toward the United States and Great Britain:

> *In case the diplomatic negotiations break down* [with the United States], preparations for a war with England and America will also be carried forward. . . . In carrying out the plans [to occupy Indochina and Thailand] we will not be deterred by the possibility of being involved in a war with England and America. . . . Our attitude with reference to the German-Soviet War will be based on the spirit of the Tri-Partite Pact. However, we will not enter the conflict for some time but will steadily proceed with military preparations against the Soviet and decide our final attitude independently. . . . *In case the German-Soviet War should develop to our advantage,* we will make use of our military strength, settle the Soviet question and guarantee the safety of our northern borders . . . all plans . . . will be carried out in such a way as to place no serious obstacles in the path of our basic military preparations for a war with England and America. . . . We will immediately turn our attention to placing the nation on a war basis and will take special measures to strengthen the defenses of the nation.[53] (Italics added.)

The "Southern Regions" were undefined, although the policy statement went on to mention Indochina and Thailand. The cabinet was considering invasions of Malaya and the Dutch East Indies, and probably they were included in this designation as well. Settling the "Soviet question" meant destroying Soviet ability to threaten Japan's position, for which Germany's June invasion of the Soviet Union had given Japan an exceptional opportunity. And before the Imperial Conference met on July 2, the army had begun concentrating troops in Manchuria to invade Siberia.[54]

Tokyo sent a summary of the Imperial Conference's decision to its diplomats in Moscow, Berlin, and Rome, intercepted by the United States, which included:

> As regards the Russo-German war, although the spirit of the Three-Power Axis shall be maintained, every preparation shall be made at the present and the situation shall be dealt with

> in our own way. In the meantime diplomatic negotiations shall
> be carried on with extreme care. Although every means avail-
> able shall be resorted to in order to prevent the United States
> from joining the war . . . Japan shall decide when and how
> force will be employed.[55]

As discussed in Japanese policy deliberations, this meant Japan would prepare for war against the Soviet Union and the United States, but would fight only one of them. If peace with the United States were negotiated, she would invade the Soviet Union.

According to Japan's Prime Minister Konoe Fumimaro, when Germany invaded the Soviet Union, Japan's "cabinet was now forced to concentrate its entire attention" on whether to join the invasion. And Ambassador Grew noted that the question prompted "almost continual cabinet meetings, conferences among high military and naval officers and conferences with the Emperor."[56] Foreign Minister Matsuoka Yosuke did not wait for the cabinet to decide; impulsively he bypassed it, seeking Emperor Hirohito's approval for invading Siberia. Hirohito refused, but Matsuoka persisted in urging to others an invasion of Siberia.[57]

The Imperial Conference had unanimously adopted, with Hirohito's approval, the proposal to prepare for war with the United States, Great Britain, and the Soviet Union. But the cabinet remained divided over it, as were military leaders and advisers in the palace. Germany had pressed Japan to join her against the Soviet Union by invading Siberia, and continued the pressure into autumn.[58] To consider doing so, Japan's cabinet had called Liaison Conferences — meetings of part of the cabinet with army and navy chiefs — on June 25, 26, 27, and 28. (Liaison Conferences had taken over formulating foreign policy.) At those conferences, Matsuoka strongly urged invading Siberia, army chiefs hesitantly favored it, and navy chiefs opposed it. In arguing for it, Matsuoka said, "If we attack the Soviets quickly, the United States won't come in. . . . the United States cannot help Soviet Russia; for one thing, she does not like the Soviet Union." On the other hand, he said, if Japan attacked southern lands, the United States would come into the war.[59] Until forced out of the cabinet in July, Matsuoka would continue pushing an invasion of Siberia.[60]

The Liaison Conferences decided to complete the occupation of Indochina in preparation for invading southern lands, while they held off on a decision about invading Siberia.[61] Matsuoka tried in vain to reverse the decision.

Roosevelt's July 1 letter to Ickes indicated he already had information that Japan was considering an invasion of Siberia. More and more such information came to Washington. On July 3 ONI reported:

> SUBJECT: Possibility of Early Aggressive Action by Japan.
> 1. The Commandant of the [New York] Naval District reports
> that a reliable informant close to Japanese industrial inter-
> ests has stated that those interests expect Japan to make an
> aggressive move against Russia on July 20th.[62]

A July 4 report from Germany read:

> I now learn that since the outbreak of the Russo-German con-
> flict complete agreement has been reached which calls for
> early action against Vladivostok by Japan.[63]

Vladivostok was the Soviet Union's main Siberian port, through which
she was receiving most of the military aid sent by the United States.
And Chiang Kai-shek reported on July 8:

> From the most reliable sources originating from Japan it is
> learned that a secret agreement has been concluded and
> signed between Germany, Italy and Japan on the 6th of July,
> covering . . . Japanese undertaking to advance southward and
> against Siberia. Please communicate the news to the Presi-
> dent immediately.[64]

And information of Japanese troop movements toward Siberia plus
supporting intelligence continued to come in.[65]

Foreign Minister Toyoda (Matsuoka's successor) confirmed
Japan's plans to invade Siberia in an intercepted Japanese diplomatic
message on July 31:

> Needless to say, the Russo-German war has given us an ex-
> cellent opportunity to settle the northern question, and it is a
> fact that we are proceeding with our preparations to take
> advantage of this occasion.[66]

The vital importance to Japan of diplomatic talks with the United
States — as emphasized in the decisions of the Imperial Conference —
was known in Washington. It was after learning of Japan's decision to
go to war with the United States if the talks "break down" that
Roosevelt decided to break them off.

As noted below, Roosevelt believed effective Soviet resistance to
Hitler's invasion provided the main hope of crushing Germany. But

he expected a Japanese invasion of Siberia to result in a Soviet collapse. That made saving the Soviet Union Roosevelt's highest immediate priority. As intelligence accumulated detailing Japan's plan to invade Siberia and as Japan implemented the plan by moving troops to the Siberian border, Roosevelt reversed his position against an oil embargo and took other measures expected to provoke Japan to attack the United States instead of the Soviet Union.

Even if Roosevelt had hoped the oil embargo would deter Japan from moves in Southeast Asia, that possibility was undercut by the provocative measures accompanying it and by provocative statements. On being informed of the embargo, Ambassador Nomura was alarmed and went to the State Department. He told Welles that he hoped the July measures would not mean any "further deterioration in the relations of our two countries." Welles said the United States had been very patient with Japan, implying her patience was at an end. Nomura urged some "compromise solution," to which Welles replied that there was not the "slightest ground for any compromise solution." Nomura asked if Roosevelt would meet with Japan's military attaché, and Welles said that was unlikely.[67]

The embargo did not deter Japanese moves to the south. Diplomatic messages and other intelligence showed that Japan was proceeding with her planned moves against Thailand, Malaya, and the Dutch East Indies. Because many of Roosevelt's advisers had opposed the embargo strongly, its seemingly counterproductive outcome should, logically, have moved them to point this out and urge reconsideration. And Japan's representatives pleaded for the United States to withdraw or reduce the embargo, to resume the diplomatic talks, and to stop arming the Philippines. Yet there is no indication that any of Roosevelt's advisers suggested he reconsider, nor that he did so. That Roosevelt failed to reconsider the embargo and was not urged to do so by trusted advisers supports the possibility that the measures were accomplishing their intended purpose — provoking Japan to war against the United States.

There seems to be no record of Roosevelt giving an explanation for going against advice on the embargo. Stark was second only to Hopkins in closeness to Roosevelt, but apparently was not taken into the president's confidence about the July policy reversal. He fruitlessly pressed Roosevelt about it, and wrote to a subordinate, "To some of my very pointed questions, which all of us would like to have answered, I get a smile or a 'Betty, please don't ask me that.'"[68]

Germany's invasion of the Soviet Union on June 22 was the largest military operation in history, with profound effects in London, Washington, and Tokyo. Roosevelt and Churchill had received intelligence well in advance that it was coming. According to Welles:

> Throughout the last months of 1940 evidence from reliable
> sources . . . [showed] a German attack upon the Soviet Union
> was imminent. In the first days of January, 1941, information
> proved beyond a shadow of a doubt that the German General
> Staff had agreed with Hitler that an attack suddenly be
> launched . . . the coming spring. The information was de-
> tailed.[69]

As a result of this intelligence Roosevelt began discussing with
Churchill how they would respond. And Roosevelt began to relax his
unofficial embargo on the Soviet Union and to supply her with war
materiel. Then, when Congress was debating the Lend-Lease act early
in 1941, Roosevelt defeated proposed amendments that would have
restricted aid to the Soviet Union.[70]

Nine days before the invasion, the U.S. ambassador to Britain,
John Winant, was instructed to tell Churchill that when Germany invaded, if Britain announced an alliance with the Soviet Union,
Roosevelt would immediately support it.[71] Welles told British Ambassador Halifax that the United States and Great Britain must take into
account the possibility that Japan would join the invasion.[72] And
Churchill responded by cabling Roosevelt:

> a vast German onslaught on Russia [is] imminent . . . we shall,
> of course, give all encouragement and any help we can spare
> to the Russians, following the principle that Hitler is the foe
> we have to beat. I do not expect any class political reactions
> here, and trust a German-Russian conflict will not cause you
> any embarrassment.[73]

On June 21 in the evening — hours before the invasion — Churchill told
Winant that Britain would go all out to aid the Soviet Union. And
Winant assured him the United States would do the same.[74]

On being wakened at 4:00 the next morning with news of the
invasion, Churchill said, "Tell the BBC I will broadcast at nine tonight."
In the broadcast he declared:

> The Nazi regime . . . is . . . all . . . appetite and racial domina-
> tion. It excels all forms of human wickedness . . . this cataract
> of horrors upon mankind . . . We are resolved to destroy Hitler
> and every vestige of the Nazi regime. From this nothing will
> turn us—nothing. We will never parley, we will never negotiate

with Hitler. . . . Any man or state who fights on against Nazism will have our aid . . . we shall give whatever help we can to Russia. . . . The Russian danger is . . . our danger, and the danger of the United States, just as the cause of any Russian fighting for his hearth and home is the cause of free men and free peoples in every corner of the globe.[75]

Roosevelt and Churchill had long opposed communism and been appalled by Soviet Premier Joseph Stalin's extreme domestic oppression, his takeover of the Baltic countries, and his invasion of Finland. But neither Roosevelt nor Churchill was doctrinaire, and they were fully agreed on the necessity of stopping Hitler. On becoming prime minister, Churchill had said, "I have only one aim in life, the defeat of Hitler, and this makes things very simple for me."[76] That exaggeration was a good indicator of his strategies and decisions to come.

As soon as the invasion began, Roosevelt's advisers came to him, voicing their sense of its importance. Stimson wrote, "For the past 30 hours I have done little but reflect on the German-Russian war and its effect on our immediate policy." He urged Roosevelt to ask Congress for a declaration of war against Germany. Hull immediately phoned Roosevelt to urge all-out aid to the Soviet Union. And Stark argued that "every day of delay in our getting into the war . . . [is] dangerous, and that much more delay might be fatal." According to a member of the State Department, the administration's reaction to the invasion was ruled by "one grim thought . . . that if Russia were defeated quickly and thoroughly, Great Britain, and soon the United States, would be faced with stronger and more confident assailants."[77] And Soviet Ambassador Constantin Oumansky went immediately to the State Department, asking that Japan be stopped from joining in the invasion. Roosevelt agreed with all of them, writing to his good friend, Admiral Leahy, "Now comes the Russian diversion. If it is more than just that, it will mean the liberation of Europe from Nazi domination. . . ."[78] This expressed Roosevelt's fervent hope that—unlike Germany's earlier victims, who had collapsed quickly—the Soviet Union might stop the invaders. Leaders across the globe similarly wondered if this invasion would succeed as easily as Germany's earlier ones. They considered the campaign in the Soviet Union likely to decide the outcome of World War II, and therefore the world's future.

Roosevelt believed he could not get a war declaration against Germany from Congress, especially if it appeared he was acting in behalf of the Soviet Union. But two days before the invasion, knowing it was about to begin, he had ordered a reduction in oil shipments to Japan.[79] And the next day, Hull had given Nomura the stiffest note since the diplomatic talks had begun, accompanying it with an undiplomatic, insulting oral statement. The note suggested there was no point in continuing the talks until the Japanese government provided a clear statement that it "is impelled by a desire to follow the ways of peace."[80] These obscure acts foreshadowed the oil embargo and break-off of the diplomatic talks. And according to a U.S. administration insider, the note and statement probably were taken by Japanese leaders to be "occasioned by Washington's knowledge that Germany was poised for an attack on Soviet Russia."[81]

Until the invasion of the Soviet Union, Britain had modestly restricted trade with Japan, careful not to provoke her. After the invasion, Churchill urged Roosevelt again to embargo oil. And this time he proposed that England join in the embargo, which she did, thereby risking a Japanese invasion of British territory that Churchill was unprepared to defend.[82]

Roosevelt had reason to expect more of a problem with his legislators and public in embracing the Soviet Union as an ally than Churchill did. He made no speech like Churchill's, limiting himself to a brief pro-Soviet comment to reporters. He did, however, have Welles make a speech like Churchill's, saying that "Hitler's armies are today the chief danger of the Americas" and "the defeat of Hitler's plan of world conquest" is the key issue, adding:

> In the opinion of this Government . . . any defense against Hitlerism, any rallying of the forces opposing Hitlerism . . . will hasten the eventual downfall of the present German leaders, and will therefore redound to . . . our own defense and security.[83]

Welles declared the United States would support the Soviet Union.

Roosevelt's acceptance of the Soviet Union as an ally and the help he extended to her were swifter and more open than his aid to France and Britain had been. Perhaps he had learned from France's fall after his hesitancy in helping her. His and Churchill's greatest immediate worry was that Stalin would surrender. And they feared a Japanese invasion of Siberia might move Stalin to do so.[84]

Roosevelt personally expedited supplies for the Soviet Union, despite the strong opposition which began immediately, not only from noninterventionists, but also from Catholics and other anti-Communists. Some members of Congress attacked Roosevelt for evilly aiding the Soviet Union, for she and communism were much feared and hated in the United States. Most Americans wished for a Soviet defeat or for the Soviets and Germans to destroy each other.

Shortly after the invasion, a quick defeat of the Soviet Union seemed imminent. As expected in Washington, Germany won battle after battle. Soviet armies fell back quickly, losing enormous numbers of soldiers by casualty, capture, and desertion, and losing much equipment. It appeared that by autumn — if they had not yet been beaten — the Soviets would be on the verge of collapse. By mid-July German armies, seemingly racing to victory, had advanced seven hundred miles, capturing territory equal in size to the United States east of the Mississippi River. Their success affected not only U.S. strategy, but also public opinion. A poll showed 72 percent believed that Hitler meant to conquer the world, and another showed the same percent wished for a Soviet victory.[85]

The U.S. Navy's War Plans Division predicted a Japanese invasion of Siberia in August. On July 3 Stark informed navy commanders:

> **The unmistakable deduction from numerous sources is that the Japanese Govt has determined on its future policy . . . [which] involves war in the near future. An advance against the British and Dutch cannot be ruled out. . . . The neutrality pact with Russia will be abrogated and a major military effort will be against their maritime provinces.[86]**

Stark sent more such messages to his Pacific commanders over the next few months, showing that a Japanese invasion of the Soviet Union was often on his mind.[87]

Stalin did not commit his troops fully to meet the German invasion. He held many in reserve for the defense of Moscow, which was soon in danger. And he deployed about 1.5 million in Siberia against a Japanese invasion. Both of these measures contributed to the rapid German advances.

Roosevelt's and Churchill's commitment to supply arms for the Soviet Union overrode their advisers' apprehension that what they sent would fall into advancing Germans' hands. Roosevelt allocated to the Soviet Union arms already designated for Great Britain, and Churchill agreed to it.[88] They feared not only Germany's military power to crush the Soviet Union quickly, but also that the Soviet people had limited determination to fight. Remembering Russia's surrender in World War I — premature and most unfortunate in the view of her Western allies — they dreaded an early Soviet surrender in World War II.

Immediately after the invasion, Churchill ordered his chiefs of staff to study the possibility of sending a small expedition to France to divert German forces from the Soviet Union.[89] His chiefs said Britain lacked the resources to do it. In July Stalin pleaded with Churchill to establish a front in France, and Churchill said he would, in order to bolster Stalin's determination to hold out. Britain intermittently planned a diversionary expedition, and in 1942 the United States joined in planning one. In August of that year a British force raided France, prompting Germany to transfer a division from the Soviet Union to France. In 1943, despite opposition from U.S. military leaders, U.S. troops invaded Italy. Soon after, Marshall told the House Military Affairs Committee that the campaign in Italy had already accomplished its purpose — to draw German troops out of the Soviet Union.[90]

Actually — like Britain's position in the summer and fall of 1940 — the Soviet Union's position in the summer and fall of 1941 was not as precarious as Churchill and Roosevelt thought. Evidence from Germany, available only after the war, showed that Hitler was not bent on a blitzkrieg, but rather that he slowed and hampered the campaign and specifically halted the advance on Moscow.[91] As previously noted, to carry out the Holocaust, Hitler needed the cover of a long war.

Not knowing this, Churchill and Roosevelt rushed to bolster Stalin's position not only by military aid and promises, but also by extraordinary measures. On July 4 Roosevelt had a personal message sent directly to Prime Minister Konoe, bypassing diplomatic protocol — an unprecedented intervention. It included:

> **We have information that Japan is starting military operations against the Soviets. We request assurance that this is contrary to fact.[92]**

It was followed up by a long message to Konoe, which included:

> **Should Japan enter upon a course of military aggression and conquest it stands to reason that such action would render illusory the cherished hope of the American Government . . . [for] peace in the Pacific Area. . . . It is the earnest hope of the United States that the reports of Japan's decision to enter upon hostilities against the Soviet Union are not based upon fact, and an assurance to that effect . . . would be deeply appreciated.[93]**

When Konoe tried to evade receiving the messages and responding to them, Ambassador Grew put pressure on him to respond, emphasizing their importance.[94]

On July 7 the United States received an answer from Matsuoka that Japan had not considered invading the Soviet Union. Knowing this to be false, the administration was hardly assured.[95] The State

Department followed up by telling Japan that the United States might be compelled *to respond in her own defense* to a Japanese invasion of the Soviet Union. This impressed Nomura, who informed Tokyo:

> **The United States has suddenly established very close relations with the Soviet Union . . . it is highly doubtful that the United States would merely watch from the sidelines if we should make any move to the north.**[96]

The U.S. messages and threat countered Matsuoka's position that, if Japan invaded the Soviet Union, the United States would take no action. Roosevelt's threat of war was by far the most aggressive U.S. action against Japan to this point. And most administration experts on Japan believed the threat would provoke her to attack the United States.

Early in September, to induce the United States to negotiate with her, Japan would offer to undertake no operation from Indochina — specifically to make no move in Southeast Asia. The United States would counter by asking if Japan would commit to making no move against the Soviet Union.[97]

These events emphasize Churchill and Roosevelt's greatest immediate concern when Churchill proposed the oil embargo and Roosevelt decided to order it. Given the priority of defeating Hitler, the fate of the Soviet Union made the fates of Indochina, Thailand, Malaya, and the Dutch East Indies secondary. The need to save the Soviet Union does provide a sufficient reason for Roosevelt's abrupt policy shift, despite strong opposition by the State Department and his military advisers to the embargo. And it provides a sufficient reason to risk war with Japan at the time.

If that was Roosevelt's purpose, the measures taken were a success. The embargo and associated measures and Roosevelt's threat influenced Japan's leaders to commit their nation to war against the United States. And when they did so, they dropped the plan of invading the Soviet Union. As a result, when Stalin learned from intelligence in October that Japan was not going to invade Siberia, he moved the troops there to the western front. Those fresh troops made a major contribution that winter to stopping the German advance. That the effects on Japan of the July measures and Roosevelt's threat were the intended ones is supported by Roosevelt's subsequent actions.

With early reports of Japan's response to the July measures just in, Roosevelt and Churchill completed preparations for their first summit meeting — the Atlantic Conference. Churchill had the impression that the meeting might advance secret military agreements made earlier in the year into an open treaty. He notified Common-wealth governments to be ready to ratify a treaty.

Churchill's preparations for the meeting were not fully secret. This upset Roosevelt, and he admonished Churchill. Roosevelt him-self shrouded the meeting in extraordinary secrecy and deception. Many of his advisers did not know he was meeting Churchill. And most of those who accompanied him to the meeting did not know its purpose. His surreptitiousness has been detailed in accounts of the conference. By one, he told people he was going on a fishing trip, and "bulletins" about fish he and his staff supposedly caught off Cape Cod were written in advance for release in Washington. And while he sailed on the cruiser *Augusta* to meet Churchill in Newfoundland, a double was reportedly seen on the president's yacht *Potomac* sailing to Cape Cod.[98]

Arriving at the conference on August 9, Roosevelt was angered to find that Churchill brought staff along to sit in on and record dis-cussions and agreements between himself and Roosevelt.[99] This, Roosevelt did not allow. His secrecy fed speculation that he made a secret alliance with Great Britain and a commitment to enter the Euro-pean war at the conference. In postwar years controversy grew over whether Roosevelt made such a commitment at the conference, and historians scrutinized its scant records and memoirs and recollections by people attending it for signs of one. Those efforts produced noth-ing definitive, perhaps because the commitment had already been made early in the year.

Churchill did press Roosevelt at the conference for a fuller, more specific commitment. By some accounts, Churchill's concern was ob-sessive. Afterward he reported to his cabinet:

> The President . . . said that he would wage war but not declare it, and that he would become more and more provocative. If the Germans did not like it they could attack. . . . Everything was to be done to force an incident.[100]

The July measures alarmed Australian leaders who feared that Japan might attack their nation. They pressed Churchill to demand a com-mitment from the United States. After the Atlantic Conference he told them:

> You should . . . be aware that the general impression derived . . . at the Atlantic meeting was that, although the United States could not make any satisfactory declaration on the point, there was no doubt that in practice we could count on United States

support if, as a result of Japanese aggression, we became involved in war with Japan.[101]

If known, such discussions were expected to have serious repercussions in the United States, and were a reason for secrecy at the conference.

The conference's most notable, straightforward achievement was the Atlantic Charter — a statement embodying Roosevelt and Churchill's vision of principles and a postwar structure to advance international peace and justice. It became the basis for the United Nations. The charter — made public shortly after the conference — did not require secrecy. Features of the charter that would help colonial nations gain independence were repugnant to Churchill, but he agreed, apparently because he considered getting the United States openly into the European war the first priority.

Roosevelt and Churchill were also occupied with immediate concerns about the Soviet Union and Japan. Some scholars concluded that they spent most of their time discussing these nations, but without connecting the two.[102] Little background on Churchill's thinking about Japan or the Soviet Union while preparing for the conference has come out. On Roosevelt's thinking, however, there is considerable data.

Roosevelt had given Harry Hopkins the job of finding out how desperate the Soviet Union's situation was. Hopkins had been Roosevelt's commerce secretary, but resigned in 1940 because of cancer, which often confined him to bed and occasionally to the hospital. A devoted aide to the president, he tenaciously continued working, even in the hospital. Roosevelt had invited him to live in the White House, and Hopkins had become his chief confidant and adviser, having more of an influence in the administration than when he held a cabinet post. His precarious health emphasizes the importance of what follows.

During the planning of the Atlantic Conference, Roosevelt sent Hopkins to London, where he was impressed by the extent to which Anglo-American planning depended on the outcome of the war in the Soviet Union. He then wrote to Roosevelt:

> I have the feeling that everything possible should be done to make the Russians maintain a permanent front. . . . If Stalin could in any way be influenced . . . [to do so] I think the stakes are so great it should be done.[103]

Hopkins then left for Moscow to ascertain the Soviet Union's situation. Before he left England, Churchill gave him a message for Stalin:

> Tell him, tell him. Tell him that Britain has but one ambition today, but one desire—to crush Hitler. Tell him that he can depend upon us.[104]

And Roosevelt gave Hopkins a written message for Stalin, which included:

> Mr. Hopkins is in Moscow at my request for discussions . . . on the vitally important question of how we can most expeditiously and effectively make available the assistance the United States can render to your country in its magnificent resistance to the treacherous aggression by Hitlerite Germany.[105]

Stalin told Hopkins that he badly needed war materiel, giving him a long list. He also assured Hopkins that the Soviet situation was much improved and that his armies were about to bring the invaders to a complete halt! As Hopkins reported to Roosevelt, Stalin had no basis for this wildly optimistic statement. In fact, the rapid German advance would continue and soon reach the outskirts of Moscow. Probably Stalin made the statement to assure Roosevelt that aid to the Soviet Union would not be wasted. The Soviet Union and Great Britain were both in urgent need of aid, and U.S. military leaders advised giving what was available to Britain. They expected that arms sent to the Soviet Union would not only be lost to the British, but also would fall into German hands as the Soviet Union fell.

During Hopkins's visit to Moscow he also met with Foreign Minister Vyacheslav Molotov and told him Roosevelt was deeply concerned that Japan would invade the Soviet Union. Hopkins suggested Roosevelt might take action if that happened. Apparently he asked Molotov how the United States might best help the Soviet Union, and according to Hopkins report, Molotov replied:

> the only thing he thought would keep Japan from making an aggressive move would be for the President to . . . [give] Japan . . . a "warning." While Mr. Molotov did not use the exact words, it was perfectly clear that the implication of his statement was that the warning would include a statement that the United States would come to the assistance of the Soviet Union in the event of its being attacked by Japan.[106]

The arduous trip to Moscow so weakened Hopkins that, on his return to England, he was thought to be dying. Nonetheless, he immediately went to the Atlantic Conference to participate in it and present his long report on the Soviet Union.

The conference began with ceremonial activities. Then Roosevelt and Churchill took up business with only Hopkins present. What they discussed apparently concerned the Soviet Union. Hopkins's first words to Roosevelt before the three met had urged all-out aid to the Soviets. When Churchill joined them, Roosevelt proposed to continue giving the Soviet Union priority in allocating military aid, and Churchill agreed. Churchill reported back to his War Cabinet that he pressed the necessity of keeping the Soviet Union in the war, and that Roosevelt assented.[107]

Later in the conference Churchill proposed a joint warning to Japan that new aggression might result in Great Britain and the United States attacking her. According to Welles, who was present during that discussion:

> The President expressed his enthusiastic approval of the proposal, since it entirely coincided with his own plans. He stated, however, that he would like to consider the precise text very fully in order to be certain that all the points *which he himself had already formulated*, and which he regarded as essential, were amply covered.[108] (Italics added.)

What Roosevelt had in mind, Welles did not say, but it may be inferred from the following.

Churchill then gave Roosevelt a draft for a U.S. warning:

> 1. Any further encroachment by Japan in the Southwestern Pacific would produce a situation in which the United States Government would be compelled to take counter measures even though these might lead to war between the United States and Japan.
>
> 2. If any third Power becomes the object of aggression by Japan in consequence of such counter measures or of their support of them, the President would have the intention to seek authority from Congress to give aid to such Power.[109]

The "Southwestern Pacific" contained Britain's dominions Australia and New Zealand and colonies Malaya and Borneo. By implication, that made the "third Power" Great Britain.

After the conference, Roosevelt discussed the draft with Hull and changed it. Churchill's words threatened consequences if Japan attacked in "the Southwestern Pacific," for which Roosevelt substituted "neighboring countries."[110] The lands of the southwest Pacific were more than a thousand miles from Japan. She had four neighboring countries: Korea and Manchuria, which she already possessed, and the independent nations China and the Soviet Union, sharing borders with both. She was already at war with China. By the change of words, the warning threatened Japan with serious consequences if she attacked the Soviet Union.

By Roosevelt's change, the warning was no longer what Churchill had proposed. It was what Molotov had asked for as the only thing that would save the Soviet Union. Churchill voiced no surprise over Roosevelt's change, which he evidently had reason to anticipate. According to Welles, at the Atlantic Conference, "There was . . . discussed the desirability of . . . possibly including in the warning to Japan a statement which would cover any aggressive steps by Japan against the Soviet Union."[111]

Finally, Roosevelt treated the warning as if it were the most urgent matter that came out of the Atlantic Conference. Before going home he had two telegrams sent to Hull, arranging for presentation of the warning to Nomura as soon as possible.[112] And he told Welles, who left the conference a day before Roosevelt, "to make all arrangements necessary so that he [Roosevelt] could see [Nomura] the moment after his return."[113]

When he gave Nomura the warning, Roosevelt read a long statement reviewing U.S. negotiations with Japan. When Roosevelt had left for the Atlantic Conference on August 8, Japan had asked again for resumption of negotiations. On his return, Japan asked once again. Roosevelt replied that Japan's move in Indochina had prompted the U.S. to break-off the talks. He ended by saying the United States would resume them "if the Japanese Government would be so good as to furnish a clearer statement . . . as to its present attitude and plans."[114] This was rather vague, but combined with the warning and his earlier threat, it seems to have been clear enough. The Japanese replied on August 26:

> **The Japanese Government is prepared to withdraw its troops from Indo-China. . . . Furthermore . . . the Japanese Government reaffirms herewith . . . that its present action in Indo-China is not a preparatory step for a military advance into neighboring countries [specifically Thailand, and] . . . in a word, the Japanese Government has no intention of using, without provocation, military force against *any neighboring nation*.[115] (Italics added.)**

Japan clarified the last sentence two days later: as long as the Soviet Union abided by the Soviet-Japanese neutrality treaty, Japan would not attack her. This was the assurance Roosevelt had been seeking. He then ordered the talks resumed.

By September Grew was gravely worried that Roosevelt did not realize Japan was likely to react to the July measures by going to war against the United States. He reemphasized the point to Roosevelt, adding, "*Facilis descensus Averno est*"[116] (Latin for "To fall into error is easy"). This was a sharp warning to Roosevelt against what Grew saw as the blunder of unintentionally provoking Japan. Stark had given this same warning earlier and in November Hull would do so as well. Grew believed war with Japan would be a tragedy, but his idea that Roosevelt still meant to avoid it was wishful thinking.

After the Atlantic Conference, most of Roosevelt's military advisers pleaded with him to delay war with Japan. He agreed with them about not prematurely provoking Japan further. That agreement, however, was secondary to the priority of saving the Soviet Union and Great Britain, and of defeating Germany. Keeping the Soviet Union in the war continued to stay in the forefront of U.S. planning. It was stressed in the Joint Army-Navy Board's strategic analysis of September 11, 1941:

> The maintenance of an active front in Russia offers by far the best opportunity for a successful land offensive against Germany, because only Russia possesses adequate manpower. . . . Predictions as to the result of the present conflict in Russia are premature. However, were the Soviet forces to be driven even beyond the Ural Mountains, and were they there to continue an organized resistance, there would always remain the hope of a final and complete defeat of Germany by land operations. The effective arming of Russian forces, both by the supply of munitions from the outside and by providing industrial capacity . . . would be one of the most important moves that could be made by the Associated Powers.[117]

Konoe's last major effort to avoid war with the United States was his proposal for a personal meeting with Roosevelt, which he urged repeatedly during September. When Roosevelt did not respond, Grew joined Konoe in urging the meeting as the last hope of avoiding war. With the proposal pending, Miles's assistant in G-2, Col. Hayes Kroner, wrote an analysis for Roosevelt and the War Department on October 2:

> a cessation of hostilities in China followed by the withdrawal of . . . Japanese divisions . . . and . . . aircraft therefrom would be highly detrimental to our interests . . . it seems imperative, for the present at least, to keep as much of the Japanese

Army as possible pinned down in China . . . *we must cease at once our attempts to bring about the withdrawal of Japanese armed forces from China* and must give to China whatever aid is possible in sustaining the Chinese power and will to continue. . . to . . . occupy the bulk of the Japanese Army. . . . *Any action which would liberate Japanese forces for action against Russia's rear in Siberia would be foolhardy.* . . . The initial feeling of revulsion over this apparent utilization of China as a cat's paw in our plan of strategy will be alleviated by an examination of the situation of the anti-Axis powers in the light of cold reason. Our objective is the destruction of Nazism . . . [As to Konoe's proposal] neither a conference of leaders, nor economic concessions at this time would be of any material advantage . . . unless a definite commitment to withdraw from the Axis were obtained from Japan prior to the conference. The immediate objective of the United States is to weaken Hitler in every way possible. A Japanese guarantee not to attack Russia in Siberia would free Russia, psychologically and militarily for stronger opposition to Hitler.[118] (Italics added.)

Miles reinforced the point in a memo to Marshall about negotiating with Japan:

a conference of leaders . . . would be of [no] material advantage . . . unless a definite commitment to withdraw from the Axis were obtained from Japan prior to the conference. . . . a definite condition . . . should be a complete withdrawal by Japan from the Axis and a guarantee, backed by substantial evidence of sincerity not to attack Russia in Siberia.[119]

Turner then suggested to Nomura that, for Roosevelt to meet with Konoe, Konoe must first agree not to invade Siberia. Turner emphasized the point (in Nomura's words, reporting their conversation to Tokyo): "What the United States wants is not just a pretense but a definite promise . . . [because] should an advance be made into Siberia, the President would be placed in a terrible predicament."[120] The last words were a reminder of Roosevelt's threat.

Saving the Soviet Union continued to be the most immediate U.S. concern. Meanwhile Japan was completing her preparations and assembling her fleets. In November she would be ready for war with the United States, but her decision to attack would wait for one more button to be pressed.

CHAPTER 12
COUNTDOWN IN TOKYO

Western condemnation of her expansion into China left many of Japan's leaders wary, seeing impending threats before there were any. They took Roosevelt's 1937 "quarantine" speech and his other criticism of her conquests as more than words long before he came near action. Having adopted from the Kwantung Army and other superpatriots a policy of expansion in vast East Asia, they anticipated an eventual war with Western nations—a war they would try to avoid, but which honor might require them to accept. Before Japan joined the Axis, many of her leaders believed that, until she might win new partners among Asian nations she conquered or dominated, she stood alone, nobly dedicated to a mission in which her worth and existence were staked. It was a mission they thought likely to fail, like noble missions of Japan's heroes from the past.

With government adoption of their policies, the superpatriots had fewer grounds for coups and assassinations. Attempted coups stopped and attempted assassinations became less frequent, although cabinet members and other leaders were still at risk. Because such violence waned and because of Prince Konoe's prestige and palace connections, his three administrations were relatively long lasting. During his first, the war with China began. It was during his last administration, which began in June 1940, that war with the United States turned from a possibility to a grave undertaking.

Except for problems with zealots and aggressive army leaders, Japanese administrations ruled more easily than U.S. administrations. Japan's parliament had lost some of the limited power and independence given to it by Emperor Meiji. It approved almost every measure presented, and initiated no major ones. Cabinet decisions leading to war with the United States followed a fairly simple course. Cautious

217

some times, bold at other times, administrations continued a course of expansion in Asia.

Japan's leaders saw Great Britain, the United States, and the Soviet Union as the main threats to expansion. To a few, an apocalyptic war with the West was inevitable. Most, however, believed Japan could continue her expansion only by avoiding war with Great Britain and the United States, while she might have to fight the Soviet Union.

The Japanese saw Britain and the United States as typical colonial powers, seeking territories in far away Asia and oppressing Asian peoples. Like France, Spain, Portugal, Holland, and Belgium, they established overseas empires, treating subject peoples as inferior. The Japanese thought they understood the threat posed by these nations. The Russian threat was more of an enigma.

Russia became interested in China later than other European nations did, and competed with Japan for influence in Manchuria. Her Soviet regime, however, allowed Japan to take over Manchuria. On the other hand, after Japan invaded China, the Soviet Union became the main provider of military aid to Chiang Kai-shek. Japan's leaders saw Great Britain and the United States as militaristic powers bent on dominating Japan. But they viewed the Soviet Union, with its spreading communism, as threatening to corrupt the traditions and vital essence on which their nation depended.

Many were convinced that Japan's existence would require eventually crushing the Soviet Union. But they had more immediate problems to confront—defeating China and ending Japan's reliance on Western nations for oil and other vital resources. In no hurry, they waited for an opportune time to attack the Soviet Union, until Germany's invasion provided it.

To the Japanese, Great Britain and France were powers roughly equal to Japan in size, population, and military potential. By contrast, the Soviet Union—like China—was a giant, potentially overwhelming in her power, but rendered temporarily weak by internal conditions. Military leaders considered the Soviet Union and the United States to be the most awesome threats, and going to war against both at the same time to be suicidal.

The fall of France and its consequences removed Britain from the Pacific scene as a serious obstacle to Japanese expansion, leaving the United States as the sole Western power with whom Japanese leaders tried to deal, and they did so mainly by accommodation. In their decision-making, they included Great Britain and the Dutch East Indies as potential enemy nations linked with the United States. A decision to attack one meant attacking all three. But it was the United States and her probable responses to Japan's moves on which leaders focused. At times of strong U.S. opposition, they offered to back down in China and even asked the United States to mediate a truce and settlement there.

During the 1930s, a third of Japan's foreign trade was with the United States, who supplied three-fourths of her imported war materiel. The U.S. announcement in 1938 that she was ending her trade treaty with Japan, and the "moral embargo" of 1940, alarmed Japanese leaders. Their greatest worry was an oil embargo, and by the end of 1940 they anticipated that, if it came, they would go to war against the United States.

The "moral embargo" may have strengthened the position of pro-Germans in the government. After it was imposed the cabinet finalized a decision to join Germany and Italy in the Axis Pact—a highly controversial decision in Japan. But the cabinet also pleaded with Ambassador Grew to help resolve differences with the United States over trade and over China. The U.S. reply was that negotiation could begin only after Japan agreed to certain principles. Renewed Japanese requests to negotiate were refused with the same demand.

How far Japan might go in negotiating was limited by pressure from patriotic societies and some military leaders, to whom even a single backward step seemed like treason. Her war minister, General Tojo Hideki, opposed yielding parts of China or removing troops from there. An exceptionally forceful person, influential in the army, he was in a position to bring down Konoe's cabinet by resigning. How much Japan might have compromised is a subject only for speculation because the United States did not negotiate. The Japanese cabinet discussed concessions and offered some, but never had to commit itself to compromises because the United States did not offer or agree to any.

To most Japanese leaders, giving up Manchuria or Korea was out of the question. But there is no indication that U.S. leaders considered asking Japan to give them up. Beyond maintaining possession of these two terrritories, it was important to many Japanese army leaders and to some outside the army that Japan retain control of China's northern provinces adjoining Manchuria and Korea by keeping troops there or keeping Chinese warlords allied with Japan in power. After the U.S. measures against Japan in July 1941, the cabinet's goals in negotiating were to resume unlimited trade with the United States, to continue Japan's expansion in East Asia, and to retain conquered areas of China. Japan's actions in the months leading to Pearl Harbor are largely accounted for by these goals.

Admiral Yamamoto Isoroku was strongly opposed to war with the United States and Great Britain. He saw a slim chance of success only if the U.S. Fleet could be crippled at the outset.[1] In December 1940 he turned to devising the Pearl Harbor attack plan that would be used a year later. His main idea was that incapacitating the U.S. Fleet would enable Japan to seize Southeast Asia, with its enormous mineral resources. That would put Japan in a position either to fight a long war with the United States or to win reasonable terms in a negotiated peace.[2]

In January 1941 Yamamoto described his strategy to Navy Minister Oikawa Koshiro, adding that Japan might be "favored by God's blessing" if the troops taking part were "firmly determined to devote themselves to their task even at the sacrifice of their lives." He ended with, "I sincerely desire to be appointed Commander in Chief of the air fleet to attack Pearl Harbor so that I may personally command that attack force . . . [and] be able to devote myself exclusively to my last duty to our country."[3] His idea was that planes would leave their carriers so far from Pearl Harbor that they could not return — that all the pilots, including Yamamoto, would give their lives. (Later he was persuaded to drop that idea.)

Meanwhile, in December 1940, frustrated by rejection of their pleas to negotiate with the United States, Japan's cabinet had tried to bypass the U.S. State Department through the intercession of two U.S. missionary priests. Bishop James Walsh and Father James Drought agreed, for the sake of peace, to put Japan's position to their friend, Postmaster General Frank Walker. He then interceded with Roosevelt, who agreed to diplomatic talks.[4] And to aid her chances, Japan sent a new ambassador to Washington, Admiral Nomura. Although he had had prior diplomatic experience, his main assets for this assignment were probably his positive attitude toward the United States, his acquaintance with U.S. officials, and his intense personal commitment to peace between the two nations.

As a result of the priests' intervention, Nomura and Hull began in March the fifty talks that would continue until December. They were fruitless because, as Hull later put it:

> The Government had made it clear to the Japanese from the outset that our conversations must remain on an exploratory basis until we could determine whether there existed a basis for negotiations. That point was never reached.[5]

After the talks began, Hull gave Nomura a list of principles to which Japan must agree before negotiations could begin:

> I. Respect for the territorial integrity and sovereignty of each and all nations.
> 2. Support for the principle of non-interference in the internal

affairs of other countries.

   3. Support for the principle of equality, including equality of commercial opportunity.

   4. Non-disturbance of the *status quo* in the Pacific except . . . by peaceful means.[6]

Agreement to the first two required Japan to give up her conquests in China before learning what she might gain in return — to give them up for the opportunity to negotiate.

Nomura tried to get negotiations started by stating Japan's respect for the principles and, in this, Japanese leaders were insincere. Their view was that the United States also held territories acquired by conquest, but only Japan was being asked to give hers up. As a Tokyo newspaper put it, "Japan in no wise has interfered with America's sphere of influence . . . whereas the United States has leaped across an ocean to intrude into affairs in the Far East."[7] And when Japan stated her agreement to the principles and even offered to give up her conquests in China, Hull and Roosevelt still did not agree to negotiate. The statement of principles seems to have been for the record.

Books have analyzed at length the points and proposals made by both sides in the Hull-Nomura talks. In my judgment, the merits of the positions taken are unimportant here because the situation — as perceived in Tokyo and Washington — developed into one of irreconcilable differences. What made them irreconcilable was not objective reality. The Japanese believed it was their destiny to build an empire and dominate East Asia. To even consider giving up their dream and their conquests was to be expected no more than for the United States to consider giving up Hawaii and returning the vast southwest to Mexico. In addition, the habitual Japanese response to intimidation — fierce resistance — was so ingrained that they were in a poor position to balance material consequences.

Hull was a moralist who saw his job largely as preventing war; probably he believed in the four principles as ideals. Others in the U.S. administration believed Japan should be made to adhere to the principles, with force if necessary. But to Roosevelt and his military advisers, the principles and Japan's violation of them were hardly a sufficient reason for war.

With the invasion of the Soviet Union in June 1941, and with German pressure on Japan to join it, Liaison Conferences turned to that issue. The proponent at the conferences of invading Siberia was Foreign Minister Matsuoka, who pressed for immediate action, arousing concern that he was being rash. An admirer of Hitler, Matsuoka has been described as impulsive and hostile to the point of madness.[8]

In pushing his proposal, he bullied fellow cabinet members. At the June 26 conference, he said, "I would like a decision to attack the Soviet Union."[9] The army's chief of staff, General Sugiyama Hajime, said no. Matsuoka then went beyond the propriety usually observed, demanding, "are you going to accept my views or aren't you?"[10] Sugiyama changed the subject. While military leaders did want to attack the Soviet Union, they opposed doing so when war with the United States might be in prospect.

At the June 28 conference, Matsuoka pressed his demand again, and was rebuffed by all military leaders present. The more he was frustrated, the more grandiose he became. At the June 30 conference, he referred to himself as a great man, declaring, "I have never made a mistake in predicting what would happen."[11] But he won no one to his position, and a decision was made to propose at the July 2 Imperial Conference the policy described in the last chapter: a definite invasion of southern territories and preparation for possible wars with the United States, Great Britain, and the Soviet Union.

On June 21, the day before Germany invaded the Soviet Union, Hull had responded to Japan's latest proposal for negotiation with the stiffest note since the talks began. In addition he told Nomura that although Nomura wanted peace, "some Japanese leaders in influential official positions" were pro-Hitler. Therefore:

> **So long as such leaders maintain this attitude in their official positions and apparently seek to influence public opinion in Japan in the direction indicated, is it not illusory to expect that adoption of a proposal such as the one under consideration offers a basis for achieving substantial results?[12]**

Matsuoka took the words — correctly — as an attack on him, and urged a hostile response and an end to the diplomatic talks. But other leaders delayed a response to Hull's note out of determination to be diplomatic and avoid a break. At the July 11 Liaison Conference, Matsuoka again urged not only sharply rejecting Hull's note, but also breaking off the diplomatic talks. Despite the conference's refusal of these proposals, Matsuoka took independent action and sent a hostile note to the United States.[13]

Konoe had been increasingly troubled by Matsuoka's hostility toward the United States. After Matsuoka's hostile note, Tojo pressed Konoe to oust him from the cabinet, and army and navy leaders supported his ouster to avoid jeopardizing negotiation with the United States.[14] Choosing a nonconfrontational method, Konoe resigned. Then, when asked to form a new cabinet, he renamed all his ministers except Matsuoka, replacing him with Toyoda.

Although Hull had suggested that no progress in the talks could occur as long as Matsuoka remained the foreign minister, his ouster did not change the U.S. position. Although Hull had complained to Nomura about Matsuoka being Hitlerian, Hull had not considered Matsuoka a major factor in Japanese policy.[15]

Some scholars explained the talks' failure by problems of communication. John Toland's thesis was that basic cultural differences, not grasped by either side, rendered the diplomats incapable of fully understanding each other on key matters.[16] Others cited Nomura's poor English (Hull spoke no Japanese) as contributing to a crucial failure of communication. Nomura, however, was aware of errors in translation and corrected them. He did hamper communication by not reporting to Tokyo some discouraging statements by Hull, Welles, and Roosevelt. His purpose was to extend Tokyo's deadline for an agreement, in hopes of preventing war with the United States. In sum, while misunderstandings did develop, so did clarifications. In the long run, culture and language problems were irrelevant. Leaders in both nations developed rather accurate pictures of each other's needs and plans from diplomatic contacts and from intelligence.

The oil embargo and Roosevelt's other July 1941 measures turned the worst fears of Japan's leaders — rational and irrational — into a nightmare. Fatalistically, they began implementing the decision for war. A tentative decision, it had been made without a feasibility study or up-to-date plans. Turning it into action was difficult also because most of Japan's leaders — including military officers — believed war with the United States would probably end in disaster. They did not usually say this, because the samurai spirit called on them to predict victory and offer the sacrifice of their lives for it. But they saw the United States as vastly more powerful militarily than Japan.

From an outsider's viewpoint, Japan's situation was hardly desperate, but her leaders did experience it so. Prince Higashikuni Naruhiko, Hirohito, and Konoe had not been reared in the samurai code. (Higashikuni was Hirohito's uncle and an army leader.) Unmystical modernists who had adopted Western rationalism as their model, they rejected many Japanese traditions in private. Nonetheless, in the end, they too accepted the inevitability of war with the United States. Perhaps they went along with the believers out of awareness that — as in any nation — Japan's life was organized around her beliefs, and that to go against them would demoralize the nation.

In August Konoe made a new proposal to break the diplomatic deadlock — a personal meeting between him and Roosevelt. Army leaders opposed it as likely to be fruitless and to delay a decision to start war with the United States. Tojo presented their view to the cabinet, but then he agreed with the majority, making adoption of Konoe's proposal unanimous. Hirohito approved it and the proposal was sent to Hull.

The United States did not respond and, at the end of August, Konoe renewed his proposal, accompanying it with a statement:

> Regarding the principles and directives set forth by the American Government . . . the Japanese Government wishes to state that it considers that these principles and the practical application thereof, in the friendliest manner possible, are the prime requisites of a true peace.[17]

And he proposed to start negotiations by offering to withdraw Japanese troops from Indochina on the conclusion of peace with China, by agreeing to no new aggression, and specifically by promising that Japan would not invade the Soviet Union.

Even though Konoe stated his agreement to the principles that the United States insisted on as a prerequisite for starting negotiations, his proposal was rejected with the comment that he must first agree to the principles![18] On the basis of data presented in the last chapter and below, Roosevelt probably had already decided on war with Japan, and Konoe's statements made no difference.

After this rebuff, Japan's cabinet met with the military chiefs of staff, and Admiral Nagano Osami advised:

> With each day we will get weaker and weaker, until finally we will not be able to stand on our feet. Although I feel sure we have a chance to win a war right now, I'm afraid this chance will vanish with the passage of time.[19]

The United States was arming the Philippines and had increased arms production greatly. The U.S. program of warship construction was far larger than Japan's. And since the embargo, Japan's oil stockpile was dwindling. These changes were eroding Japan's military advantage.

Sugiyama proposed October 10 as a deadline for progress in diplomatic efforts. The cabinet then asked him and the navy's chief to estimate Japan's chances in a war with the United States. Sugiyama had little military basis for an estimate. The only up-to-date army plans were for war with the Soviet Union. Probably his answer came from what he thought his duty as a warrior required; he predicted victory.[20]

Like the army's plans for war with the United States, the navy's had been for a hypothetical war — not for one in prospect. And recently its staff work had been devoted to projected campaigns in the South Seas. Its most up-to-date plan for war with the United States was Yamamoto's, still under development. The navy's general staff had not yet reviewed it. On the basis of staff work he had reviewed, Nagano predicted defeat.[21]

The cabinet then affirmed the July decision for war with the United States, adopted October 10 as the deadline for diplomatic efforts, and requested an Imperial Conference to act on its decision. The navy reviewed Yamamoto's plan and accepted it conditionally, authorizing a fuller study of its potential, including more war games. Games were then conducted at the Naval War College, using an enormous model of Pearl Harbor with warships at anchor.[22] In the exercise, Japan lost two aircraft carriers in the attack. (In the actual attack, not one was even damaged.) The results were judged encouraging enough for the navy and army to adopt the plan. Yamamoto then worked to improve it by additional paper games at the college and by simulated attacks carried out at Japanese ports.

Meanwhile Konoe informed Hirohito of the cabinet's decision, prompting a series of interventions by the emperor. A pacifist, Hirohito had chosen the name Showa (Enlightened Peace) for himself and his reign. Despite his modern, Western inclinations, including an interest in foreign affairs, he had usually accepted the traditional restraint by which emperors stayed out of politics. (His grandfather, Meiji, had been extraordinarily involved in politics; his father had reverted to tradition and not been involved at all.)

In 1931 and 1933, Hirohito had intervened briefly to curb military moves in Manchuria, but failed. And he had intervened ineffectually again in 1938 to prevent a move against the Soviet Union. The move had resulted in brief, indecisive warfare on the border between Manchuria and Siberia. But mostly he had watched passively, with growing alarm, the conquest of Manchuria and war against China. And at the Imperial Conference of July 1941, Hirohito had listened in silence to the conditional decision for war with the United States. His silence ended on reading a proposal to implement that decision, which was to be presented to an Imperial Conference on September 6:

1. Determined not to be deterred by the possibility of being involved in a war with America (and England and Holland), in order to secure our national existence, we will proceed with war preparations so that they be completed approximately toward the end of October.

2. At the same time, we will endeavor by every possible diplomatic means to have our demands agreed to by America and England . . .

3. If by the early part of October there is no reasonable hope of having our demands agreed to in the diplomatic negotiations . . . we will immediately make up our minds to get ready for war against America (and England and Holland).[23]

The cabinet had added a comment:

Although America's defeat is judged utterly impossible, it is not inconceivable that a shift in American public opinion due to our victories in Southeast Asia or to England's surrender might bring the war to an end.[24]

According to Konoe, Hirohito "pointed out that the proposal placed war preparations first and diplomatic relations second." This, he said, would seem to give precedence to war over diplomacy.[25] Konoe argued against his interpretation, but Hirohito was dissatisfied and summoned Sugiyama and Nagano. To Sugiyama he made the same point about war having precedence, and Sugiyama also said that was not so.[26]

Still dissatisfied, Hirohito asked Sugiyama to estimate the outcome of war with the United States. Sugiyama said he believed the United States would be beaten in three months! As Konoe describe the confrontation, Hirohito then commented that Sugiyama "had been Minister of War at the time of the outbreak of the China Incident, and that he had then informed the Throne that the incident would be disposed of in about one month. He pointed out that, despite the General's assurance, the incident was not yet concluded after four long years of fighting."[27]

Hirohito spoke in polite words and a soft tone. It was against tradition to criticize advisers openly or speak harshly to them. Instead, emperors indicated dissatisfaction by asking questions and by allusions—occasionally by reading poems. Under his polite words and tone, however, Hirohito had rebuked Sugiyama sharply.

Sugiyama began a long explanation about conditions in China that hindered completion of the campaign there. Hirohito interrupted and raised his voice "in great anger."[28] This was extraordinary and conveyed that Sugiyama should rethink his position and find a more realistic one. Sugiyama was humiliated and did not answer Hirohito's follow-up question about the basis for his forecast of a three-month victory over the United States.[29]

At this point Nagano intervened, addressing Hirohito's key question, which Konoe and Sugiyama had evaded. Nagano said that the proposed policy did give precedence to war, but the time for desperate action was at hand. That meant pursuing diplomacy fully, but only for a short time.[30] Hirohito then asked Sugiyama and Nagano if they would give diplomacy precedence during that time, and they said yes.

Still troubled, Hirohito resolved to take action the next day at the Imperial Conference. He meant to point out the folly of war with the United States and to indicate his wishes by asking sharp questions. His chief adviser at court, Marquis Kido Koichi, cautioned that open intervention in a political decision jeopardized the emperor's position as above politics. Instead, Kido arranged for Hara Yoshimichi to ask Hirohito's questions.[31]

As President of the Privy Council, Hara spoke for the emperor. By having people speak for him—by avoiding the appearance of involvement in controversy—an emperor's position as a divine figure with a ceremonial role was maintained. At the Imperial Conference, Hara raised and received answers to military questions. Despite his belief to the contrary, Nagano joined Sugiyama in forecasting victory over the United States. Then Hara asked whether war or diplomacy was to take precedence, and Navy Minister Oikawa said that diplomacy was to. Sugiyama and Nagano did not answer.[32] Hara pressed Sugiyama on this point, but he remained silent. Then Hara said he was satisfied that the chiefs of staff were in agreement with him and that he had no more questions. (This was probably Hara's tactful way of suggesting the emperor wished diplomacy to take precedence.)

But Hirohito rose and asked, "Why don't you answer?" When the chiefs of staff still kept silent, he said, "I am sorry the Supreme Command has nothing to say."[33] From an emperor, this was an extreme rebuke. Hirohito then read a poem by Meiji:

> I believe that every sea, to every other,
> Is bound together as a brother.
> Why is it now, the seas must rise
> To strike each other with angry cries?[34]

His point was clear to the conference, and the ensuing silence probably reflected awe and embarrassment. But Hirohito insisted on a response, saying, "I make it a rule to read this poem from time to time to remind me of Emperor Meiji's love of peace. How do you feel about all this?"[35]

Nagano rose and said:

> Representing the Supreme Command, I express our deep
> regret for not replying to His Majesty's request. . . . I think
> exactly the same as President Hara. . . . Since President Hara
> said he understood my intentions, I didn't feel there was any
> need to emphasize the point.[36]

Sugiyama then rose and said:

> It was exactly the same with me. I was about to rise from my
> seat to answer President Hara's question when Navy Minister
> Oikawa answered it for me. However I am overawed to hear
> His Majesty tell us directly that His Majesty regrets our silence.
> Allow me to assume that His Majesty feels we should make
> every effort to accomplish our goals by diplomatic means. I
> also gather His Majesty suspects that the Supreme Command
> may be giving first consideration to war, not diplomacy.[37]

Hirohito had spoken decisively. From then on Japan's leaders supported diplomacy as the first priority. Army leaders grumbled at lack of progress in the talks, but did cooperate with diplomatic efforts. Since Tojo was a dominant member of the cabinet and Hirohito was still unsure of his devotion to diplomacy, Higashikuni told Tojo the next day:

> America knows how inept Japan is diplomatically, so she'll
> make moves to abuse you inch by inch until you start a fight.
> But if you lose your temper and start a war you will surely be
> defeated, because America has great strength. So you must
> bear anything and not play into her hands.[38]

Tojo assured Higashikuni unequivocally that he would support diplomacy, and did so in letter and spirit.

By "abuse," Higashikuni may have had in mind that Hull often scolded Nomura and had been particularly insulting in his statement of June 21, which had provoked Matsuoka to impulsive action. And only three days before Higashikuni spoke to Tojo, Hull had rejected Japan's latest proposal for negotiation, saying:

> The Secretary of State has no reason to doubt that many of
> Japan's leaders share the viewpoint of the Ambassador
> [Nomura] and his associates and support them in pressing
> forward to the attainment of our high purposes. Unfortunately,

however, among the powerful leaders of Japan are some who have committed themselves to follow the path of Nazi Germany and its policy of aggression. These people can think of no other possible understanding with America than that they must join on Hitler's side. . . . Well authenticated reports to this effect have been flowing to this Government from many different countries. . . . The tone of many recent unnecessary declarations by Japanese [spokesmen] concerning Japan's plans and promises under the Tri-Partite Pact unmistakably reveal this attitude. As long as those occupying responsible positions keep up this attitude and persist in directing Japan's public opinion in this direction, any hopes for the acceptance of the proposals now under consideration or the attainment of practical results from these discussions are inevitably doomed to disillusionment.[39]

What Hull meant by "well-authenticated reports" is unknown; none were found in State Department files. Who he meant by spokesmen and "those occupying responsible positions" is also unknown. As Hull had been informed, besides Matsuoka, pro-Germans at lower levels had been ousted from the administration. Japan's press was making fierce statements against the United States — as happens in most nations under the circumstances — but aggression in a foreign press was no factor in U.S. policy.

Higashikuni seems to have understood how Hull's insults were provoking Japanese leaders toward war. Perhaps he also understood that Roosevelt was in no position to go to war against Japan unless Japan made the first move. His words were prophetic. Unfortunately for Japan, his rationality played little part in her planning.

Konoe had been impressed by Hirohito's extraordinary intervention at the Imperial Conference. As soon as the conference adopted the proposed policy with the October deadline, he arranged a private meeting with Grew. Konoe again stated his agreement to Hull's principles — this time going beyond vague generalities to specify his willingness to adhere to each of the four. And he pressed for a meeting with Roosevelt as soon as possible; later might be too late.[40] As Konoe recalled it:

I stressed the fact that the present cabinet, including the army and navy representatives, was unified in its wish for a successful conclusion of negotiations, and moreover that the present cabinet was the only one capable of carrying it through. I also made a most significant statement . . . that should we miss this one opportunity, another might not arise.[41]

Grew took Konoe at his word and was moved strongly. Alarmed by the trend toward war, Grew had already cabled Roosevelt that administration "objectives will not be reached by insisting . . . during the preliminary conversations that Japan provide the sort of clear-cut, specific commitments which appear in any final treaty."[42] And about Konoe's proposal for a meeting with Roosevelt, he cabled Hull:

> the ambassador [Grew] urges. . . with all the force at his command, for the sake of avoiding the obviously growing possibility of an utterly futile war between Japan and the United States, that this Japanese proposal not be turned aside without very prayerful consideration. Not only is the proposal unprecedented in Japanese history . . . [but it] has the approval of the emperor.[43]

Later, aware that Hull had not responded favorably, Grew again went around him, writing directly to Roosevelt:

> [I am] in close touch with Prince Konoye who in the face of bitter antagonism from extremist and pro-Axis elements in the country is courageously working for an improvement in Japan's relations with the United States . . . he no doubt now sees the handwriting on the wall and realizes that Japan has nothing to hope for from the Tripartite Pact and must shift her orientation if she is to avoid disaster. . . . I am convinced that he now means business and will go as far as possible, without incurring open rebellion in Japan, to reach a reasonable understanding with us. . . . It seems to me highly unlikely that this chance will come again.[44]

The problem, however, was not with Hull; it was Roosevelt who would not agree to a meeting.

Meanwhile Japan's cabinet developed two more proposals for negotiation with the United States—variations on earlier proposals with more specific detail. On September 22 Foreign Minister Toyoda proposed terms for ending the war with China.[45] And on September 28 Japan presented a long document that started with principles to be agreed to at the outset and went on to provide details of matters to be worked out in accord with the principles. The proposals had no effect on the U.S. position.

The October deadline was fast approaching, with no diplomatic progress. On October 5 Tojo called army leaders in for a discussion, which ended with agreement that, "There is no possibility to settle the matter by diplomatic negotiations. We must therefore petition the Emperor to hold an imperial conference and decide upon war."[46] Delaying what may have seemed unavoidable, Konoe convened a meeting of cabinet members with Sugiyama and Nagano, whom he asked for an extension of the deadline. They agreed, but only to October 15.[47]

Feeling hopeless, Konoe visited the palace to tell Kido he could not fulfill Hirohito's wishes and had to resign. Kido scolded Konoe and sent him back to persevere with peace efforts.[48] Konoe then called a meeting of the War Council—the part of the cabinet that dealt specifically with war decisions—for October 12. Just before it met, he received a note from the chief of the Naval Affairs Bureau:

> The Navy does not want the Japanese-American negotiations stopped and wishes to avoid war if at all possible. But we cannot see our way to expressing this openly at the meeting.[49]

Konoe showed the note to Tojo, who became angry. At the meeting, Tojo demanded that Navy Minister Oikawa state the navy's position openly. Oikawa then said:

> We are now at the crossroads—war or peace. If we are to continue with diplomacy, we must give up war preparations and go in completely for talks—to negotiate for months and then suddenly change our tack won't do. . . . The Navy is willing to leave the decision entirely up to the Prime Minister.[50]

This gem of ambiguity—typical of Japanese in delicate situations—suggested that the navy favored continued negotiation, inasmuch as Konoe was known to favor it. The refusal by navy leaders to state their position openly seems to have reflected a sense of obligation to adhere to the Imperial Conference's decision of September 6.

Another obstacle to reaching a decision was Hirohito's insistence that no decision for war be taken unless the army and navy were truly agreed on a favorable outcome. Speaking for the navy's general staff on September 6, Nagano had stated his agreement with Sugiyama that war with the United States was winnable. Despite that statement, the navy's belief to the contrary was not much of a secret. But it was ignored until October 12, when navy leaders drew it to Konoe's attention. Since the navy was the only government branch in a position to make an expert judgment about the outcome of a naval war, leaving its judgment out of the decision-making process was folly. Nonetheless, except for Tojo, the War Council still did not confront the problem.

Even army leaders, despite being seriously troubled about lack of progress in the diplomatic talks with the United States, allowed them to continue.

On October 13 Konoe went to the palace to report the impasse. The next day he held a round of individual talks with Tojo and other cabinet members, but arrived at no resolution. On the contrary, Tojo's position hardened and he told Konoe that further discussion was pointless because they were not going to agree. (This was in contrast to other cabinet members and advisers to Hirohito in the palace who talked endlessly during crises without taking action.) Tojo then sent Konoe a note:

> According to what we have been able to discover lately, it looks as if the Navy does not wish to have war. . . . If there were any clear statements to me from the Navy Minister, then I too would have to reconsider matters. . . . If the Navy can not make up its mind, the [decision of the Imperial] conference on September 6th in the presence of the Emperor will have been fundamentally overturned. Hence this would mean that . . . the Premier, the Ministers of War and the Navy and the President of the Supreme Command all did not sufficiently perform their responsibilities as advisers to the throne. Hence I believe that there is no other way but that at this time we all resign, declare insolvent everything that has happened up to now, and reconsider our plans once more.[51]

Konoe immediately agreed, probably in relief. Tojo's note, which prompted the end of Konoe's third administration, has been described as a power grab with the purpose of leading Japan into war against the United States. It is true that Tojo was the cabinet member who most favored going to war. Nonetheless, the argument in his note was correct about the folly of making a decision for war without the navy's agreement. And events that followed showed that Tojo was not yet committed to war.

Tojo's note went on to say that revising the Imperial Conference's decision would risk trouble from militants in the army. He suggested that, in the circumstances, the only one capable of controlling the army while leading the nation was Higashikuni, and urged Konoe to propose him as the next prime minister.[52]

Konoe agreed and visited Hirohito the next day, saying the cabinet was resigning and recommending Higashikuni as his successor. Hirohito and Kido decided against the recommendation, turning instead to Tojo, whom they considered exceptionally suited to control the army if the conference decision of September were to be undone. They were correct in judging that Tojo was well qualified to control it and that he would work devotedly for peace with the United States if so instructed.[53] Hirohito named Tojo and enjoined him to "go back to blank paper" — to rethink Japan's situation completely.[54] He told Tojo to do all he could to avoid war with the United States.

Tojo played a key role in Japan's entry into war with the United States. Perhaps his intolerance of delay came from his samurai father. But despite his mysticism and his reputation in the West and among some Japanese as a war lover, he was the most realistic of government leaders in judging events from July to December and in confronting hard choices. It was he who had taken the initiative to force Matsuoka out of Konoe's cabinet for sending a hostile message to the United States. And it was he who kept urging the cabinet to face the fact that the United States was stalling in the diplomatic talks. In October his response to Konoe's proposal for continuing the diplomatic talks had been:

> ought we not to determine here whether or not there is any possibility of bringing the negotiations to fruition? To carry on negotiations for which there is no possibility of fruition, and in the end to let slip the time for fighting, would be a matter of the greatest consequence.[55]

Urging that Konoe make a decision without further delay, Tojo had added:

> There are times when we must have the courage to do extraordinary things—like jumping, with eyes closed, off the veranda of the Kiomizu Temple![56]

Many people attempted suicide by jumping from the temple, which was on a hill overlooking a ravine. Tojo's metaphor suggested that an act risking one's probable or even certain death was sometimes the best choice. At his war crime trial, he would say, "To adopt a policy of patience . . . was tantamount to self-annihilation of our nation. Rather than await extinction, it was better to face death."[57] In June, urging an invasion of the Soviet Union, Matsuoka had said in the same vein, "We must either shed our blood or embark on diplomacy. And it's better to shed our blood."[58] Also similar was Yamamoto's offer to lead personally a suicide attack on Pearl Harbor. The basic idea was that self-sacrifice was the only way to save Japan.

Although extreme, their thinking was echoed by moderate leaders.

One was Higashikuni, who strongly opposed war with the United States. Nonetheless, after the war, he said:

> Japan entered the war with a tragic determination and in desperate self-abandonment [realizing that if she lost] there will be nothing to regret because she is doomed to collapse even without war.[59]

Although he also opposed war with the United States, Nagano advised Hirohito (in Konoe's words) that:

> Japan was like a patient suffering from a serious illness . . . so critical that the question of whether or not to operate had to be determined without delay . . . without an operation there was danger of a gradual decline. An operation, while it might be extremely dangerous, would still offer some hope of saving his life.[60]

Later he said:

> The government has decided that if there is no war, the fate of the nation is sealed. Even if there is war, the country may be ruined. Nevertheless, a nation that does not fight in this plight has lost its spirit and is already doomed.[61]

On December 1, after adoption of the order to launch Japan's attack, Tojo said:

> Should Japan submit to [U.S.] demands . . . Japan's existence itself would be endangered. . . . I am convinced that the whole nation, presenting a united front and laying down their lives . . . will surely deliver us from the present national crisis.[62]

He did not mean that the whole nation must sacrifice itself, but that only large-scale suicide would save her.

The cabinet Tojo chose was called a "war cabinet" by writers who believed its purpose was war. But it was truly a peace-oriented cabinet. For the key position of foreign minister, Tojo chose Togo Shigenori, known to be unusually pro-American. He and Tojo's choice for Finance Minister, Kaya Okinori, initially declined to serve because of Tojo's militant record. Tojo then convinced them of his determination to work for peace and that Togo would have his full support in diplomatic efforts. Then Tojo and Kaya agreed to serve.[63] It is worth noting that, during the next seven weeks until the end of diplomatic efforts, the army not only made no trouble, but also cooperated with the cabinet.

Tojo immediately appealed for an extension of the October deadline. The army agreed to November 30 as the date by which a decision for war must be made if diplomacy failed. On this basis, the cabinet set November 25 as the new deadline for negotiation.

Army leaders still grumbled over stalling by the United States. They were convinced that, if the final decision was for war, delay was on the side of the United States. But they had no real problem with the extension itself because Admiral Yamamoto had not yet completed his preparations. The October 10 deadline had been chosen with the expectation that he would need until then to prepare the Pearl Harbor attack. His preparations, however, were taking longer, and the cabinet now expected them to be completed in mid-November. That left a narrow period of opportunity between when Japan would be ready to attack and when the United States was expected to be armed sufficiently to withstand an attack.

During this critical period, the foreign ministry sent another diplomat, Kurusu Saburo, to aid Nomura. He and Nomura tried very hard to reach an agreement in their talks with Hull and Roosevelt, as well as with Stark and anyone else in the United States government whom they knew. Nomura also tried by sending encouraging reports to Tokyo.[64] Those reports had no realistic basis and led to inferences that Nomura misunderstood what Hull was saying. A more likely explanation, consistent with the full record of Nomura's actions in Washington, his dispatches to Togo, and Togo's dispatches to him, is that Nomura's reports of favorable responses by Hull and Roosevelt were intended to keep the Japanese cabinet from acting on its November 25 deadline — to win as much time as possible for negotiation. If this was his intent, he succeeded, but only briefly, as the cabinet extended the deadline to November 29.

When it sent Kurusu to aid Nomura, the cabinet formulated two final proposals, approved by an Imperial Conference on November 5, with Hirohito observing in silence. Called Proposal A and Proposal B, they were to be presented with a request for quick responses by the United States. From intercepted diplomatic messages, U.S. leaders had the texts in advance, enabling them to make prompt responses if they chose to, but they did not.

Proposal A, presented on November 11, was similar to earlier proposals, but contained more specific details. It included offers of equal trade rights in China and of a phased removal of Japanese troops from there and from Indochina.[65] Following up on it, Nomura asked to meet with Roosevelt, and did so on November 15. (On the same day Japan's task force was ordered to assemble in Hitokappu Bay before departing to attack Pearl Harbor.) Nomura pleaded with Roosevelt to accept the proposal, and Roosevelt replied that, before he would consider it, Japan must start removing troops from China and Indochina.[66]

Meanwhile Nomura pleaded for Japan's cabinet to be patient "for one or two months."[67] Togo answered that the latest deadline was unalterable, "therefore do not allow the United States to sidetrack us and delay the negotiations any further."[68] He instructed Nomura that, after Kurusu's arrival, they should present Proposal B.

On November 18 Nomura and Kurusu tactfully felt out Hull on Proposal B, which provided for a truce and return to conditions as of July 1. Hull asked, if the United States accepted it, would the diplomatic talks continue? Yes, answered Nomura. As if tentatively accepting Proposal B—which he had not yet officially seen—Hull said he would submit it favorably to the British and Dutch.[69] (They had joined in the oil embargo and would have to agree for it to be lifted.) According to a subordinate of Hull, as soon as Nomura and Kurusu left, Hull began eagerly to present the proposal to the British and then to the Chinese, Australians, and Dutch.[70]

Hull and Roosevelt had known the text of Proposal B for two weeks before Nomura formally presented it on November 20, and they had welcomed it enthusiastically. Despite Togo's statement that the November 29 deadline was unalterable, Proposal B did allow for considerable delay. It is remarkable that Japan's military leaders—perceiving as they did that the United States was stalling, and preoccupied as they were with concern that Japan's military advantage was slipping away—approved the proposal. Japanese and U.S. officials called it a stopgap measure for peace, a truce, and a modus vivendi. It read:

1. Both the Government of Japan and the United States undertake not to make any armed advancement into any of the regions in the South-eastern Asia and the Pacific area excepting the part of French Indo-China where the Japanese troops are stationed at present.

2. The Japanese Government undertakes to withdraw its troops now stationed in French Indo-China upon either the restoration of peace between Japan and China or the establishment of an equitable peace in the Pacific area. In the meantime the Government of Japan declares that it is prepared to remove its troops now stationed in the southern part of French Indo-China to the northern part of the said territory upon the conclusion of the present arrangement which shall be embodied in the final agreement.

3. The Government of Japan and the United States shall cooperate with a view to securing the acquisition of those goods and commodities which the two countries need in the Netherlands East Indies.

4. The Government of Japan and the United States mutually undertake to restore their commercial relations to those prevailing prior to the freezing of the assets. The Government of the United States shall supply Japan a required quantity of oil.

5. The Government of the United States undertakes to refrain from such measures and actions as will be prejudicial to the endeavors for the restoration of general peace between Japan and China.[71]

In brief, Japan proposed that, after restoring conditions as they were before the oil embargo, negotiation proceed toward complete removal of Japanese troops from Indochina and toward peace between Japan and China.

If the United States accepted the proposal, negotiation of specifics was to follow. How long the negotiation might take was unspecified. In that respect, Proposal B allowed for an indefinite suspension of Japan's attack plan and thus involved a heavy risk for Japan. If the United States accepted it and the negotiations then failed, the United States would gain time to complete arming the Philippines and other bases in the Pacific. Japan would then be starting a war from a most disadvantageous position. Japan's leaders were offering to give up her advantage for an opportunity to negotiate.

Marshall and Stark saw Proposal B as highly advantageous to the United States (see chapter 13). It provided time badly needed to arm for the coming war in the Pacific. In the circumstances, the puzzling thing was Roosevelt's decision to reject it, knowing as he did that doing so would bring on Japan's attack before the buildup was completed. He and his advisers had seen a series of intercepted messages to that effect. On October 1 Foreign Minister Toyoda had cabled his embassy in Washington:

Time is now the utmost important element. Whether [negotiation with the United States] materializes or not has a direct and important bearing on peace.[72]

Three weeks later Togo had cabled Nomura:

let it be known to the United States by indirection that our country is not in a position to spend much more time discussing this matter.[73]

The next day Wakasugi Kaname, Nomura's assistant, had told Welles that Japan's "circumstances . . . do not permit prolonging these conversations any longer."[74] On November 2 Togo had cabled Nomura:

> **we expect to reach a final decision . . . on . . . the 5th . . . This will be our Government's last effort to improve diplomatic relations. The situation is very grave.**[75]

Togo's reading of intercepted U.S. diplomatic messages contributed to his giving up hope. (Japan's cryptographers had broken U.S. and British diplomatic codes.[76]) Earlier Togo had believed Hull was sincerely pursuing negotiation, but the messages sharply disillusioned him.

When on November 27 Japan's leaders realized Proposal B had been rejected, her fleets were already en route to their targets, but with orders to remain ready to return in case of a last-minute diplomatic resolution. On December 1 the final decision for war was proposed at an Imperial Conference. Tojo summarized the diplomatic efforts of recent weeks and their failure, concluding:

> **Under the circumstances, our Empire has no alternative but to begin war against the United States, Great Britain, and the Netherlands in order to resolve the present crisis and assure survival. We have been engaged in the China Incident for more than four years and now we are going to get involved in a great war. We are indeed dismayed that we have caused His Majesty to worry.**[77]

He expressed hopes for success. Then Togo and Nagano spoke in the same vein, and Tojo's last words were:

> **our Empire stands at the threshold of glory or oblivion. We tremble with fear in the presence of His Majesty. We subjects are keenly aware of the great responsibility we must assume from this point on . . . to repay our obligations to him . . . to achieve our war aims and set His Majesty's mind at ease.**[78]

Speaking for the emperor, Hara gave approval. Hirohito remained silent, nodding in agreement. The proposal was adopted.

CHAPTER 13
COUNTDOWN IN WASHINGTON: THE NOVEMBER TURNING POINT

November began with Tokyo and Washington following policies adopted despite grave dangers. At a Joint Army-Navy Board meeting on November 3, Marshall and Stark said, in view of the time needed to build up MacArthur's forces, the priority of the Atlantic-European theater required avoiding a flare up in the Pacific at least until mid-December. Marshall proposed that, instead of taking a tough position toward Japan, the United States make minor concessions in order to gain time. The Board agreed, noting that:

> **The United States Army Air Forces in the Philippines will have reached their projected strength by February or March 1942. The potency of this threat will have then increased to a point where it might well be a deciding factor in deterring Japan in operations in the area south and west of the Philippines.**[1]

The Board meeting ended in unanimous opposition, as it had before, to "the issuance of an ultimatum to Japan" and urged an agreement with her "to tide the situation over for the next several months." Noting that, "At the present time the United States Fleet in the Pacific is inferior to the Japanese Fleet," it emphasized that provoking Japan at this time invited an attack on the Pacific Fleet. In addition it proposed, "that Japan should be warned against movement into Siberia."

Roosevelt and Hull had been telling Japanese diplomats that, before the United States would negotiate, Japan must agree to remove her troops from China. On November 4 Japan offered to do so if peace with China was agreed to, and asked that Roosevelt help bring it about.

Togo then offered to remove most Japanese troops in China and to temporarily transfer the rest to northern China and Hainan Island.[2] Japanese leaders haggled among themselves about details, including how long it might take for the last Japanese troops to leave China, which suggests the offer was serious. In any case, it had no effect on the U.S. position.

Roosevelt received the joint board's recommendation on November 5. The next day he told Stimson, "He was trying to think of something which would give us further time . . . [and] suggested he might propose a truce . . . for 6 months." As an inducement for Japan to accept it, he might offer a small reduction of the oil embargo.[3] While working on details of a proposal, Roosevelt continued to get reminders from his military advisers on the necessity of delaying war with Japan.

But he also had something else in mind. According to Stimson, at a cabinet meeting on November 7, Roosevelt raised the possibility that Japan would attack British Malaya or the Dutch East Indies. He asked, if the United States then attacked Japan, would the people support him? The cabinet unanimously said yes.[4] Apparently Roosevelt was not convinced. According to Attorney General Francis Biddle, Roosevelt said he hoped for an "incident" in the Pacific to bring the United States into the European war.[5] What he may have had in mind is suggested by an extraordinary measure Marshall took eight days later.

Knowing that Japan was about to propose a temporary modus vivendi, on November 15 Marshall called in seven reporters for a secret briefing. He said that, if they were unwilling to keep what he was about to tell them secret, they could leave. The briefing, he said, was to aid their interpretation of current and forthcoming events so that what they wrote would not upset a crucial U.S. military strategy. Then he made the following points (paraphrased and numbered here for reference):

1. The United States was on the brink of war with Japan.
2. The U.S. military position was highly favorable for it.
3. The buildup in the Philippines had been kept secret from Japan.
4. It was far more powerful than the Japanese thought.
5. It was for an offensive war against Japan, although the Japanese thought it was to defend the Philippines.
6. In case of war, "Flying Fortresses will be dispatched immediately to set the paper cities of Japan on fire."
7. This information was going to be leaked by the White House or the State Department.[6]

Marshall showed them a map that identified Japanese targets for U.S. bombers. He went on with other details, including that the Philippine buildup was not yet complete and that war with Japan needed to be delayed until December 15.

Then he warned them again, "Nothing that I am telling you today is publishable, even in hinted form." And a third time, "None of this is for publication."[7]

No background information for Marshall's briefing has come to light. What military strategy the reporters were to avoid upsetting was unstated. Marshall said the administration leak would be limited to Japanese government leaders. If Japan's public found out, her government would be unable to restrain Japan from going to war. Thus only by a carefully controlled leak could U.S. strategy be implemented. By what Marshall said, the projected government leak seemed designed to deter Japan from aggression against the United States until the buildup was complete. As with earlier measures, the key question is whether the leak was to serve as a deterrent or provocation.

Further complicating Marshall's briefing is that, while statement 1 was true, 2, 3, 4, and 5 were false. The Philippine buildup was hardly secret, and reporters were in a position to discover how weak the Philippine forces were. Statements 6 and 7 were not borne out; no orders for MacArthur's Air Corps to bomb Japanese cities were issued and the administration made no leak. Perhaps more to the point, the simplest way to prevent a leak by reporters is not to give them information they can leak. Lacking background data for this briefing, one can only consider possibilities.

Giving reporters secret information "not for publication" in order for them to publish hints of it is an old practice. None of the seven published Marshall's information. But Charles Hurd of the *New York Times*, evidently gave the information to his colleague there, Arthur Krock. On November 19 Krock published an article based on Marshall's briefing, which included:

> **The President and Secretary of State . . . may already . . . have [told] the Japanese . . . that our ability to "defend" the Philippines includes ability to attack any Far Eastern power. . . . The changed condition, reversing all our military plans . . . is the consequence of two developments . . . the naval alliance with Great Britain . . . [and] the coming of age of aircraft in battle. . . . A strong concentration in the Philippines of heavy American bombers, held superior in most respects to the Japanese . . . And prepared air positions in Alaska, making possible a pincer attack by air on Japan. These developments . . . carried**

> out secretly, have put the United States in a very strong position in the Far Pacific . . . there are enough bombing planes . . . to drop bombs on Japan, land in Siberia, refuel, and rebomb . . . on a return trip to Manila. . . . [T]he United States Fleet in the Pacific . . . in conjunction with the British Fleet . . . create a naval force outnumbering the Japanese.[8]

An accompanying map showed Japan surrounded by air bases in Manila, Guam, Alaska, and the Soviet cities of Nikolaievsk and Vladivostok.

Whether Krock's story had any effect on Japan is unknown. It did seriously disturb Hull and his assistant secretary of state, Breckinridge Long, who noted in his diary:

> It is obvious that it played into the hands of the war party in Japan. . . . It had every indication of being . . . provocative. Certainly it is not in the province of the War Department to get into that field of policy—during such negotiations.[9]

The story was an obstacle to negotiating and to delaying the outbreak of war with Japan. And it gave Japan a strong reason to attack the Philippines.

When Roosevelt began drafting a modus, the State Department also began drafting one. Japan's proposal, Roosevelt's draft, and the State Department's draft differed in details but, from the U.S. viewpoint, most of the differences were unimportant. A modus was to be used for delay, not for reaching a settlement. One State Department draft, however, included the point that Japan must agree not to attack the Soviet Union.[10] More reports of Japanese preparations to invade Siberia had come in during autumn, prolonging administration worries that Japan might still do it.

On November 18 Nomura broached the idea of a modus to Hull, prompting his most favorable response since the talks began. On the same day, British intelligence predicted that failure of the talks would result in Japan attacking U.S. and British territories, and not attacking the Soviet Union.[11]

On November 19 an intercepted a message to Nomura included:

> please present our B proposal . . . no further concession can be made. If the U.S. consent to this cannot be secured the negotiations will have to be broken off.[12]

The translation was marked as completed November 20.

On the twentieth Nomura gave Japan's modus to Hull, who began immediately to implement it by arranging for consultations with Ambassadors Hu Shih of China, Halifax of Britain, Alexander Loudon of Holland, and Minister Richard Casey of Australia. On November 22 Hull showed them Japan's modus and a State Department one, which he proposed to use as a counteroffer. According to his memo of the meeting, there was general agreement to go with the U.S. version, except that Hu was "somewhat disturbed, as he always is when any question concerning China arises not entirely to his way of thinking. . . . He did not show serious concern."[13]

Then Hull told Nomura and Kurusu that the British, Dutch, and Chinese favored relaxing economic sanctions against Japan, provided that she showed peaceful intentions.[14] He added that Japan could expect a formal reply to her proposal within two days. Meanwhile the United States intercepted a message from Togo to Nomura:

> if within the next three or four days you can finish your conversations with the Americans; if the [modus] signing can be completed by the 29th . . . we have decided to wait until that date. This time we mean it, that the deadline absolutely cannot be changed. After that things are automatically going to happen. Please . . . work harder than you ever have before.[15]

The State Department made changes in its modus and Hull presented what became the final draft to Stark and Gerow (representing Marshall) on November 24. They approved it.[16] Then Roosevelt cabled Churchill that the United States was going to present the changed modus to Japan, together with an offer to ease the embargo. He added that he was asking the British, Australians, and Dutch to ease their embargoes also.[17]

On the same day Hull presented the final draft to the ambassadors. Hu objected to the clause that Japan was to keep twenty-five thousand troops in Indochina during the interval of the modus, and proposed reducing the number to five thousand. Hull explained again that the modus vivendi's sole purpose was delaying an outbreak of war for three months; therefore, details did not matter. According to his memo, "They seemed to be very much gratified."[18] But by the session's end Hull realized that—except for Loudon—the ambassadors were giving their own opinions, without having received instructions from their governments. Further consideration was put off while they got instructions.

Chiang Kai-shek then protested vigorously, asking T. V. Soong, his brother-in-law and personal representative in Washington, to intervene with Stimson. Chiang also sent telegrams to members of Roosevelt's cabinet, to congressional leaders, and to Churchill, appealing for their support against the modus. He included a warning: if the modus were agreed to, China's morale might break and her resistance to Japan collapse, with dire consequences for Great Britain and the United States.[19]

When Hull phoned Roosevelt early in the morning of November 25 about Chiang's protest, both considered it an overreaction based on a misconception of what a modus vivendi was. They thought an explanation would satisfy Chiang, and Roosevelt said he would see Hu and Soong himself, and "I will quiet them down."[20]

Roosevelt's confidence in his ability to reassure Chiang was probably based on a prior episode. By the end of August, Chiang had become optimistic about China's military situation. On September 4 Hu had called on Hull to inquire about developments in the U.S. diplomatic talks with Japan. Hull had told him there was nothing new, and his memo of the conversation included:

> The Ambassador made it rather clear that China did not desire any peace at this time. . . . Japan was showing signs of weakening . . . and . . . within a reasonable time she would be obliged to abandon any aggressive military activities and to seek peace.[21]

Alarmed by reports that the United States and Japan might come to an agreement, Chiang had then sent a protest. Hull had responded with assurances to Chiang, who had accepted them, and Hu had apologized for Chiang's protest, suggesting it was an unfortunate lapse of his trust in Roosevelt.

On November 25 Stimson wrote in his diary that Soong brought him Chiang's protest of the modus. According to Stimson, Chiang was troubled "because it involves giving to the Japanese the small modicum of oil for civilian use during the interval of the truce of the three months."[22] Hull later characterized what Japan was to get from the modus as "only chicken feed in the shape of some cotton, oil and a few other commodities in very limited quantities."[23]

That same morning Roosevelt met with his "inner cabinet" (Hull, Stimson, and Knox). Despite Chiang's protest, they decided to respond to Japan's modus the next day by offering the State Department's last draft.[24] By Stimson's account, "Hull showed us the proposal for a three-month's truce which he was going to lay before the Japanese. . . . It adequately safeguarded all our interests."[25]

That evening Hu called on Hull to present Chiang's protest

formally, explaining that Chiang "was not so well acquainted with the situation, hence his reported opposition to our *modus vivendi*."[26] Hull then gave Hu lengthy assurances and argued that the modus was in China's interest. He stressed that "the limited amount of more or less inferior oil products that we might let Japan have during [the three months] would not to any appreciable extent" help her in her war with China.[27] According to Hull, Hu was sure he could give Chiang a "fuller explanation" to relieve his fears. Hu also told a member of Hull's staff that Chiang's protest came from misunderstanding the modus. And Hu later wrote, "Both the Generalissimo [Chiang] and the [Chinese] Foreign Minister were reassured by the sympathetic and helpful spirit underlying these conversations."[28]

Hull's memo of his conversation with Hu implies that no decision to drop the modus had been made. Or, if Roosevelt had made it by then, Hull did not yet know that. But there is evidence that before Hull met with Hu, Roosevelt began to reconsider presenting the modus.

What happened next is harder to follow, but the need to deal with Chiang's protest vanished when the decision to present the State Department modus was reversed. In accounts later given by the administration, the first indication of a change came early the next morning—the twenty-sixth—just hours before Hull was to present the State Department's modus to Nomura. Not yet having replied to Soong, Stimson phoned Hull for guidance about what to say. But Hull told him that "he had about made up his mind not to give [the modus] to the Japanese but to kick the whole thing over—to tell them that he has no other proposition at all."[29]

Hull's words about making up his mind were taken by writers to mean the decision was his. "Kick the whole thing over" was taken to mean he was angry with the Japanese and therefore leaning toward dropping the modus and making no response to Japan's proposal. From these words, scholars explained dropping the modus as a decision made by Hull because he was old, "tired," and moralistic.[30] In his *Memoirs*, Hull later wrote that he himself made the decision.[31] His testimony and memos in the congressional committee record show both strong endorsement of and opposition to the modus. His strongest testimony opposing it was:

> **The Japanese proposal of November 20 . . . was of so preposterous a character that no responsible American official could ever have dreamed of accepting it.**[32]

Whether the United States might have accepted Japan's modus or not, it did offer a means of delaying Japan's attack. And Hull had told Halifax that the idea was "attractive enough to warrant its being tried at least."[33] And Hull's other testimony and memos fully contradicted his statement that Japan's modus could not be accepted. For example:

> our policy was not to say "No" to the Japanese . . . it was to grab at every straw in sight, in an effort to keep up the conversations and give time to our armies and navies here, and among our future Allies, to make further preparation. . . . So this modus vivendi was given every possible consideration. . . . On November 21, 22, 23, 24, and 25 we made a desperate effort to get something worked out that might stay the . . . Japanese armies and navies for a few days or a few weeks. . . . I was making every possible effort to get some delay.[34]

Hull's mention of time needed by "our future Allies" touched on a key point. The British, Australians, and Dutch had grave interests at stake and had agreed to the planned modus. For it to be dropped without consulting them — without even informing them — was most extraordinary. Such a unilateral action might be taken in an emergency so immediate as not to permit consultation. But the administration's account included no such emergency — no new development that required instant reversal of the plan just agreed to by the ambassadors.

The administration account implied that Hull had authority to reverse the decision. It implied that Hull — on his own — countermanded a decision made the day before by Roosevelt and his "inner cabinet." The suggestion that so crucial a decision resulted from Hull's pique or other transient emotional reaction — although widely accepted — is unreasonable. Although especially moralistic, Hull was a responsible professional, loyal to Roosevelt and devoted to carrying out his policies.[35] And Roosevelt was described by biographers as "his own Secretary of State."[36] He set foreign policy and personally controlled diplomacy.

Furthermore Hull's strong support for the modus is documented, and there is evidence that the decision was Roosevelt's. For two of his earlier decisions over which he had reason to expect severe criticism — to station the fleet in Hawaii and to carry out joint war planning with Great Britain — Roosevelt had arranged for Richardson and Stark to take public responsibility.

The decision to drop the modus was made suddenly, without consideration by the cabinet, the "inner cabinet," or the War Council. And there is no record of consultation with or notice to U.S. allies about it. On the contrary, British and Dutch officials thought the State Department's modus had been presented.[37] The Australians had been particularly apprehensive that Japan might attack them before a U.S. commitment to a joint defense. On learning the modus had been dropped, they asked that the decision be reconsidered and proposed to mediate between the United States and Japan. In recording the Australian plea, Hull wrote:

> I really gave the matter no serious attention except to tell [the Australian Minister] that the diplomatic stage was over and that nothing would come of a move of that kind. I interrupted him to make this conclusive comment before the Minister could make a detailed statement.[38]

Nonetheless, Australia kept pressing for reconsideration up to December 2.

As it dropped the modus, the administration presented instead a ten-point proposal on November 26 that aroused much controversy in later years. Critics of the administration called it an insult and an ultimatum to Japan, and some of Roosevelt's advisers agreed.[39] Other advisers and supporters of the administration called it a genuine proposal to negotiate peace. Formally, the proposal was no ultimatum; it contained no deadline or threat. But the words in it are less important than what the administration expected the proposal's effects would be—the end of the talks and the launching of Japan's attack on the United States.[40]

Besides the ten-point proposal, Hull gave Nomura and Kurusu a long written statement about U.S. principles governing negotiation with Japan.[41] It and the proposal were immediately released to the press, suggesting that both served to establish a record in anticipation of the war now expected within days.

After reading the proposal, Nomura and Kurusu protested vigorously. According to Hull's notes:

> [Kurusu] suggested that his Government would be likely to throw up its hands at our proposal . . . The Japanese clearly indicated . . . their feeling that we had reached an end. They asked whether we were not interested in a modus vivendi; whether any other arrangement was not possible and whether they could see the President.[42]

And according to Nomura:

> In view of our negotiations all along, we were both dumbfounded and said we could not even cooperate to the extent

of reporting this to Tokyo. We argued back furiously, but Hull remained solid as a rock.[43]

On November 29 — the Japanese deadline — Tokyo cabled Nomura to make a final effort for U.S. reconsideration of a modus.[44] Presumably Nomura did so; the next day Hull told him that Japan had been furthering Hitlerism, and,

> In view of the fact that Japan is acting in the manner described above, there is *absolutely no way of bringing about a settlement* . . . Disruptions in Japanese-U.S. relations [are] exceedingly unfortunate . . . There shall be nothing constructive about a Japanese-U.S. war . . . nothing other than destructive . . . However, with the existence of the above described conditions . . . the Secretary of State and the President are placed in an exceedingly difficult position.[45] (Italics added.)

Another intercepted message from Tokyo confirmed what Roosevelt, his advisers, and Nomura and Kurusu expected:

> the United States has presented this humiliating proposal. This was quite unexpected and extremely regrettable. The Imperial Government can by no means use it as a basis for negotiations. Therefore . . . in two or three days, the negotiations will be de facto ruptured. This is inevitable. However I do not wish you to give the impression that the negotiations are broken off. Merely say to them that you are awaiting instructions.[46]

And an intercepted message from Tokyo to Berlin said:

> The conversations . . . between Tokyo and Washington now stand broken . . . lately England and the United States have taken a provocative attitude . . . war may suddenly break out.[47]

Confirmation of the proposal's expected effect and Nomura's last effort led to no reconsideration. The effect was evidently what the administration intended or at least accepted. And with preparations for war against Japan far short of completion, the decision to present the ten-point proposal instead of the modus put U.S. Pacific forces in extreme danger — the danger of the destruction suffered on December 7. Therefore the decision to substitute the proposal for the modus was probably made for the strongest of reasons.

Documents show it was not the Japanese with whom Hull was exasperated; it was the Chinese. He considered Chiang's reaction to the modus immature and was angry that Chiang went around him in objecting to it—that he "sent numerous hysterical cable messages to different cabinet officers and high officials in the Government . . . intruding into a delicate and serious situation with no real idea of what the facts are."[48] As Hull saw it, he had given Hu repeated, detailed explanations of the purpose behind the modus, but the Chinese persisted in misunderstanding it.

On the morning of November 26, minutes after talking to Hull, Stimson phoned Roosevelt and mentioned intelligence, which he had sent to Roosevelt the day before, of a Japanese fleet movement from Shanghai toward Indochina. To his surprise,

> [Roosevelt] fairly blew up—jumped into the air, so to speak, and said he hadn't seen it and that *that changed the whole situation* because it was evidence of bad faith on the part of the Japanese that while they were negotiating for an entire truce . . . they should be sending this expedition down there to Indo-China.[49] (Italics added.)

Stimson's mention of Japan's fleet move, combined with Roosevelt's complaint of Japanese bad faith, suggested that Roosevelt reversed his decision about the modus because of outrage.

Before that Japanese fleet left Shanghai, however, U.S. and British intelligence learned it was assembling there for action in Southeast Asia. On about November 1, advance units had begun sailing and had been sighted heading south by the British in Hong Kong, by a nearby shipmaster, and by other sources, and reported to Washington. And the British had informed Washington on the twenty-first that the main part of the fleet had departed, moving south.[50] The Japanese had done little to keep that fleet's activities secret, and Stimson's phone call told Roosevelt nothing new. If Roosevelt had believed the Japanese were acting in good faith until then, a sense of betrayal would have been logical. But he had not believed it. And their good faith was irrelevant to the intended use of the modus, which was only to stall Japan.

When Stimson telephoned him, Roosevelt presumably did not know Hull had just told Stimson that the modus would be dropped. Perhaps Roosevelt had not yet arrived at an explanation for Stimson and Knox about dropping it. They had only yesterday approved presenting the State Department's final modus; Roosevelt owed them an explanation. Stimson's call may inadvertently have suggested one, and Roosevelt may have tried it out on the spur of the moment. In any case, he later provided a more judicious-sounding and more plausible explanation for the reversal, which became the official one, widely accepted: the modus was dropped because of Chinese and British opposition.[51]

On being informed of the State Department's final modus, Churchill had told Foreign Secretary Anthony Eden that he approved it.[52] Then, on receiving Chiang's appeal, Churchill had cabled Roosevelt:

> we certainly do not want an additional war. There is only one point that disquiets us. What about Chiang Kai-shek? Is he not having a very thin diet? Our anxiety is about China. If they collapse, our joint danger would enormously increase.[53]

The cable reached the White House at 1 a.m. on the twenty-sixth.

Insofar as the campaign in China tied down Japanese armies, a Chinese collapse would have increased Japan's resources for attacking British, Dutch, Soviet, or U.S. territories. But Chiang had tried to move Churchill and Roosevelt with the prospect of a Chinese collapse before. On November 2 he had sent them long telegrams, which included:

> Intelligence shows that the Japanese are determined upon an attack against Yunnan [province of China] from Indo-China in order to take [the city of] Kunming and to cut China's [supply line] and encircle her armies. And [if that attack succeeds] the morale of the Chinese army and the Chinese people will be shaken to its foundation. . . . For the first time in this long war a real collapse of resistance would be possible. . . . China has reached the most critical phase of her resistance.[54]

Chiang had gone on to cite dangers to Great Britain, the United States, and the Dutch East Indies that would result.

His plea for British and U.S. action had fallen on deaf ears then. Indeed, since the summer of 1940 Chiang had been emphasizing his pleas for U.S. support with dire warnings, but Chiang's subordinates had undercut him. For example, in October 1940 his military attaché in London had told the U.S. military attaché, "We will never give in and we will win a war which is doing the Chinese good because it is welding them into a nation."[55] Churchill's comment on Chiang's November 2 plea had been, "I could do little more than pass this to President Roosevelt."[56] He and Roosevelt had not taken Chiang's protests seriously then, nor had Roosevelt on November 25.

As noted, by autumn 1941 Chiang was optimistic about victory over Japan.[57] In view of his earlier protest when Japan and the United

States seemed near an agreement, his optimism may have contributed to his protests of November 25, especially if he thought he might win better terms from victory than from a truce mediated by Roosevelt.

Churchill's ambiguous cable was the basis for conclusions that he opposed the modus. It can be read in different ways, and Hull described it as "lukewarm support" for the modus. On hearing that the modus had been dropped, Halifax went to Welles, who wrote a memo of their conversation.

> The British Ambassador called to see me this morning urgently . . . [and] said that Secretary Hull had called him . . . last night to inform him of the [ten-point proposal] which he had handed to the Japanese envoys . . . [Halifax asked] the reasons which prompted this sudden change . . .
>
> I said that Secretary Hull had requested me to say to the Ambassador that one of the reasons . . . was the half-hearted support given by the British Government to the [modus] . . . and the raising of repeated questions by the British Government . . .
>
> Lord Halifax said he could not understand this in as much as he had communicated to Secretary Hull the full support of the British government.
>
> To that I replied that the message sent by Mr. Churchill . . . could hardly be regarded as "full support", but on the contrary, a very grave questioning . . .
>
> Lord Halifax said that this message had been intended *merely to express the objections on the part of the Chinese Government*.[58] (Italics added.)

Halifax's words suggest that Churchill's message was for the record, to show he had not ignored Chiang's plea. Churchill himself later both asserted and denied opposing the modus.[59]

Whichever may be true, Churchill's cable falls short of justifying an abrupt, extremely risky reversal of U.S. policy. Probably his most relevant statement on the modus was in a letter to Anthony Eden two days before the decision to drop it:

> Our major interest is: no further [Japanese] encroachments and no war . . . The United States will not throw over the Chinese cause, and we may safely follow them in this. *We could not of course agree to an arrangement whereby Japan was free to attack Russia*.[60] (Italics added.)

An additional point about China's opposition to the modus is that it specified two clauses as objectionable — the number of Japanese troops in Indochina and the supplying of oil to Japan. There was no known obstacle to changing the clauses. The relatively small number of Japanese troops in Indochina had little bearing on Japan defeating China or invading Malaya and the Dutch East Indies. Also limited was Japan's need for a tiny fraction of the oil she was consuming. Still further, the United States could have agreed to supply the oil and then not sent it, thereby delaying Japan's attack. Intercepted diplomatic instructions indicated Japan would hold off on war with the United States if a modus was signed by November 29. And instructions from Tokyo did not stipulate when terms of the modus had to be implemented. In any case, Japan was given no opportunity to consider a modus that satisfied China's objections.

Substitution of the ten-point proposal for the modus was so abrupt that Roosevelt's advisers were not consulted — not even those who had approved the modus on November 25. Stimson learned of it when he phoned Hull about another matter. Marshall and Stark said they did not know until after presentation of the ten-point proposal to Japan. Most of Roosevelt's advisers were still strongly in favor of the modus, and some continued to urge its use after it was dropped.

Another version of how the modus was dropped came from Landreth Harrison, a member of Hull's staff, who said that before Stimson's phone call to Hull on the 26th:

> [Hull] was summoned by private telephone to the White House. . . . The Secretary was gone only 15 minutes or so and came back in a very agitated frame of mind. He said something like this: "Those men over there do not believe me when I tell them the Japanese will attack us. You cannot give an ultimatum to a powerful and proud people and not expect them to resist violently."[61]

By "over there," he meant the White House. Hopkins lived there; he and Roosevelt were its only men with a role in foreign policy. Presumably they were "those men."

Hull's final version in his *Memoirs* was that he spontaneously decided to reject the modus, and, on his own, went to the White House early in the morning of the twenty-sixth with a memo, which concluded:

> In view of the opposition of the Chinese Government and either the half-hearted support or the actual opposition of the British, the Netherlands, and the Australian Governments, and

in view of the wide publicity of the opposition and of the additional opposition that will naturally follow *through utter lack of an understanding of the vast importance . . . of the modus vivendi, without in any way departing from my views about the wisdom of this step . . .* I desire very earnestly to recommend [dropping the modus and presenting instead the ten-point proposal].[62] (Italics added.)

Hull added, "The President promptly agreed," but gave no explanation of Roosevelt's instant policy reversal.[63] (Actually the Dutch and Australians had supported the modus strongly.)

To accept Hull's account requires also accepting that Hull gave up a position he had embraced vigorously—and still embraced—as vital to U.S. interests, and that he did so on the basis of considerations he had already rejected with contempt. Despite saying the decision to drop the modus was his own, Hull was angry about it. He voiced his bitterness to Harrison and Halifax, saying (in Halifax's words), "His careful efforts to postpone the row had been blown out of the water by the intervention of many people who didn't understand how delicate the balance was."[64] He also expressed his bitterness to Stanley Hornbeck of his staff. To console Hull over the modus being dropped, Hornbeck told him Japan probably would have rejected it anyway, and in time Hull would look on taking a tough position with Japan (the ten-point proposal) "with great satisfaction." Hull responded:

We differ so entirely . . . that I must in writing offer my dissent. It is no answer to the question of whether [the modus] is sound and desirable at this most critical period to say that it probably would not have been accepted by Japan in any event. If that sort of demagoguery stuff would be wrung into this sort of undertaking, then there could never be any settlement between countries except at the point of a sword.[65]

Hull was still seething. Probably it was his anger at "those men" in the White House that he vented on Hornbeck. Most important, Hull's final account provides no sufficient reason for Roosevelt to have accepted the risk of military disaster.

To summarize, writers have explained the dropping of the modus by reasons that do not hold up. Some reasons were irrelevant and minor—Hull's moral rigidity, age, and pique. Others were false—Hull's opposition to the modus along with the assumption that he had authority to make the decision to drop it. And reasons that were relevant and true—Chiang's protest and Churchill's equivocal cable—were insufficient to make the consequences of dropping the modus acceptable. If the decision to reverse the policy of delaying war with Japan was not based on the reasons given, what prompted it?

There are indications that Roosevelt's thinking began to change on the twenty-fifth, shortly after the "inner cabinet" meeting at which the decision to present the modus was adopted. He then met for fifty minutes with William Donovan, the chief of his new intelligence agency, but no record of the meeting is available.[66] A reasonable inference is that Donovan gave him new intelligence. It could have been that Japan was going to attack Pearl Harbor; Donovan's agent, Edgar Mowrer, had just arrived in Washington with that information (see chapter 3). Another possibility is that Donovan gave Roosevelt alarming news about the Soviet Union — news mentioned in a military intelligence summary issued that day:

> *General Anders, Commander-in-Chief of Polish forces in Russia*, is reported to have expressed doubt of Moscow's ability to hold out and Russian officials in general are reported for the first time indicating worry over the situation.[67]

As noted in chapter 11, grave concern in July about the Soviet Union's ability to hold out had prompted high-risk measures, including a reversal of policy toward Japan. The prospect on November 25 of a Soviet collapse could again have provided a reason for a high-risk measure to save the Soviet Union.

At noon on the twenty-fifth, Roosevelt met with his War Council (Stimson, Knox, Hull, Marshall, and Stark) for an hour and a half, during which he took the discussion in an unexpected direction. Stimson's diary note (see below) of the meeting is supported by the recollections of Hull, Marshall, and Stark. According to his diary, Stimson, Knox, and Hull expected the meeting to be about the European war and they prepared accordingly. Instead, Roosevelt began by saying Japan might attack the United States within days. The problem, he said, was how to "maneuver" her to attack, without heavy U.S. losses. According to Stark, Roosevelt gave the War Council no basis for expecting Japan's attack within days. According to David Bergamini, the basis was a memo by Bratton about Japan's coming attack.[68] (No such memo has come to light.) Mowrer's information could have been the basis. Still another possibility was specific intelligence, which had just come in, that a Japanese attack fleet was en route to Hawaii.

Stimson did not mention an answer to the question of how to "maneuver" Japan. But Marshall's and Stark's testimony (see the following) on the meeting supports the conclusion that the decision to drop the modus and present the ten-point proposal became the answer.

The English historian John Costello searched for an unknown event on November 25 or 26 to account for the policy reversal. In Halifax's diary he found that, on November 25 in the evening, Halifax received instructions to tell Hull to hold off on presenting the modus "until Winston had sent a message to the President."[69] The diary of Oliver Harvey of Britain's foreign office supports Halifax on this.[70] Hours later, the "thin-diet" cable arrived. Costello, however, did not consider it decisive. (Halifax's conversation with Welles supports Costello's judgment of Churchill's message.) Costello inferred that Churchill sent a second message to Roosevelt at about the same time, which influenced him to abandon the policy of delay, but he found no second message. (Costello died shortly after writing this.) Another researcher also reported that Churchill sent a second message, but the British government has sealed its contents until 2060.[71]

Still another researcher reported a telephone call from Churchill to Roosevelt two hours after the thin-diet note. Germany had established on Holland's coast a station to intercept government telephone calls between London and Washington. By September 1941 German intelligence had broken the scrambler code used in the calls and was decoding them regularly during a period including November 1941.[72] These facts are not in question. Gregory Douglas's find was a transcript, supposedly made by the German station in Holland, of a call from Churchill to Roosevelt at 3:15 a.m. on November 26, Washington time. Churchill's part of the conversation included:

> **matters of a most vital import have transpired . . . I have in my hands, reports from our agents in Japan as well as the most specific intelligence in the form of the highest level Japanese naval messages. . . . A powerful Japanese task force . . . has sailed yesterday . . . moving across the northern Pacific . . . their goal is the fleet in Hawaii. At Pearl Harbor . . . The actual date given is the eighth of December. That's a Monday.**[73]

According to the document, Roosevelt said he believed what Churchill told him and would act accordingly. Douglas commented that the source of Churchill's intelligence probably gave the attack date in Tokyo time, and Churchill probably failed to adjust it to Sunday, December 7, London and Washington time.

I have been unable to verify the document's authenticity. A German official told me it is a fake, but also wrote that he had no basis for calling it a fake.[74] The document has not been definitively discredited or validated, and the dramatic question remains: Was such a phone call made?

For historical purposes, a better question is: Did British or U.S. intelligence have information at that time of a Japanese fleet sailing toward Hawaii? As documented in chapter 3, both did, and the information included Japanese naval messages. Two were:

> **The task force, keeping its movement strictly secret . . . shall advance into Hawaiian waters, and . . . attack the main force of the United States Fleet.**

> **The task force . . . shall leave Hitokappu Bay on the morning of 26th November and advance to 42° N. 170° E. on the afternoon of 3 December and speedily complete refueling.[75]**

The refueling position is most of the way from Hitokappu to Hawaii. U.S. intelligence workers intercepted the messages on November 25, but evidence that they were decoded in time is lacking.

That Churchill conveyed such information to Roosevelt was supported by William Casey of U.S. intelligence, later director of the CIA. He wrote (without identifying his source), "The British had sent word that a Japanese fleet was steaming east toward Hawaii."[76] That British intelligence had obtained such information between November 25 and December 5 and informed the United States was confirmed by a secretary of William Stephenson (Britain's agent in the United States), by Victor Cavendish-Bentinck (chief of British intelligence), by the chief of British intelligence in Singapore, and by Murton Seymour (president of Canada's Aeronautical Association).[77] And Marshall told the Army Pearl Harbor Board that the November 27 war warning "was based on something that came in on the 26th."[78] He was not asked what it was.

Asked by the naval court if he had received intelligence on November 26 about Japan attacking the United States, Stark said, "No, I don't recall that."[79] The court also asked Stark's assistant, Adm. Roscoe Schuirmann, if ONI received on the twenty-sixth "specific evidence" of Japan's intention, and noted, "The witness stated that to answer the question would involve the disclosure of information detrimental to the public interest and that he claimed his privilege against revealing state secrets."[80] The court did not press him to answer.

The ten-point proposal presented on November 26 was based on a draft written by a member of Morgenthau's staff six months earlier. According to Morgenthau's diary entry of November 27, the draft "had been prepared some time ago in case the United States was ready to break off with Japan."[81] To break off the talks when Japan would respond by attacking the Soviet Union, Thailand, the Dutch East Indies, or Malaya, without attacking the United States, could prove disastrous if Congress did not then declare war against Japan. To break them off when she would respond by attacking the United States was expected to get Congress to declare war on Japan. The crucial needs were to save the Soviet Union and have Japan attack in circumstances that would move Congress to declare war on Germany.

Japan had been seeking a commitment from Germany to join her in a war against the United States. On November 13 Donovan had brought Roosevelt intelligence that Germany would do so. On the sixteenth Korean agent Haan Kilsoo informed the State Department of this as well.[82] And their intelligence was confirmed by Japanese diplomatic intercepts. In view of Roosevelt's priorities, that knowledge, combined with information of a fleet moving to attack Pearl Harbor, could have sufficed for submitting the ten-point proposal instead of the modus. According to an official army history, "In the Pacific, the United States wanted to avoid war with Japan unless Japan attacked American territory or vital areas in and around the East Indies."[83] If that was Roosevelt's view, it was timely to rupture the talks before Japan changed her plans.

On receiving the ten-point proposal, Japan ordered the task force to carry out its attack on Pearl Harbor. Initial U. S., British, and Dutch losses in the Pacific were heavy. (Racist underestimation of Japan's military power had led the administration to minimize the destruction even of a surprise attack and, as noted in the afterword, two chance events increased the carnage.) Congress declared war on Japan and — after Hitler declared war on the United States — on Germany and Italy as well. And Germany was defeated. The steps, forming a causal chain, were anticipated in the strategy of Roosevelt and his advisers.

Some of Roosevelt's words at the War Council meeting on November 25 raised so much controversy that they have been quoted over and over. According to Stimson:

> the President, instead of bringing up the [European war], brought up entirely the relations with the Japanese. He brought up the event that we were likely to be attacked perhaps next *Monday*, for the Japanese are notorious for making an attack without warning, and the question was what we should do. *The question was how we should maneuver them into the position of firing the first shot without allowing too much danger to ourselves.* It was a difficult proposition.[84] (Italics added.)

Based on intelligence projections since 1932, a Sunday was most likely for a Japanese attack; a Monday was unlikely. Perhaps Roosevelt made the same mistake that Douglas imputed to Churchill. The other italics mark the inflammatory sentence. Controversy over it, generating much heat with little light, distracted attention from Stimson's glimpse of U.S. war strategy.

According to a scholar, Stimson's "language was hurried and elliptic." According to two others, Stimson made an "infelicitous and hurried choice of words"; he could not possibly have meant what he wrote.[85] But they and others who discounted the diary entry got no support from Stimson himself. In his congressional testimony four years later, Stimson stood by his words, repeated them, and expanded on them in a carefully prepared statement:

> One problem troubled us very much. If you know your enemy is going to strike you, it is not usually wise to wait until he gets the jump on you by taking the initiative. In spite of the risk involved, however, in letting Japan fire the first shot, we realized that in order to have the full support of the American people it was desirable to make sure the Japanese be the ones to do this. . . . We discussed . . . the basis on which this country's position could be most clearly explained to our own people and to the world.[86]

And Stark, who was present at the meeting, stressed the difficulty of getting a war declaration from Congress without Japan's attack on Pearl Harbor.[87] He testified that he did not remember the discussion of maneuvering Japan, but noted that Stimson's words were clear:

> if you take the language baldly, just what it says, that it was trying to get them to shoot at us . . . that we should not commit the first overt act, and I heard Marshall's testimony yesterday when he said he thought that this was to keep the record clear . . . maybe that was it.[88]

Marshall testified about what "maneuver" meant:

> I am assuming that is the diplomatic procedure. . . . So far as the war plan goes, *the concern was whether or not the final alert should be given.* . . . I take it [this] was a discussion of the diplomatic procedure involved, having in mind that it was the accepted thought in all of our minds at the time, that if

> we were forced to take offensive action . . . that it would be a
> most serious matter as to its interpretation by the American
> people, whether we would have a united nation, or whether
> we would have a divided nation in getting into a world conflict
> . . . the expression [Stimson] is using relates to what would be
> the diplomatic procedure we would follow, so we would not
> find ourselves . . . initiating a fight.[89] (Italics added.)

Marshall then repeated what maneuvering Japan meant, leaving no question about what he understood had been at stake in November 1941:

> it was the accepted thought in all of our minds at that time,
> that if we were forced to take offensive action . . . it would be
> a most serious matter as to its interpretation by the Ameri-
> can people, whether we would have a united nation, or . . . a
> divided nation in getting into a world conflict.[90]

He also suggested that consideration of maneuvering Japan was not new; it "had been talked about back and forth through so many combinations."[91]

Marshall's words, "the concern was whether or not the final alert should be given," bear strongly on the most troubling question of all about Pearl Harbor. With war expected in days, the War Council was considering whether to have the Pacific commands go on full alert or not.

In itself, a full alert could be considered a warlike or hostile act, and it would authorize the Pacific commanders to intercept approaching Japanese ships and planes before they reached Hawaii or other U.S. territories. The orders sent fell short of a full alert and misled MacArthur, Short, and Kimmel about the imminence of war.

As of November 26 in the morning, the commanders in Hawaii were to get no additional warning. Marshall testified that before he left Washington on that day, he and Stark

> agreed, at a joint board meeting, on the necessity for dis-
> patching a further warning to Commanders on the Japanese
> front, particularly to the Philippines, and . . . we there dis-
> cussed the draft of such a message.[92]

By the instructions Marshall and Stark gave their staffs, "particularly to the Philippines" meant only to the Philippines.

Roosevelt had instructed Marshall and Stark to send warnings only to MacArthur and Hart. Marshall gave Gerow a draft of a warning for MacArthur to be sent in Marshall's absence. He left no draft or instruction for a warning to Short *as matters stood*. He did leave a draft for a warning to Short, to be sent *only if the talks with Japan were formally broken off*. (They were not broken off formally until December 7.) Short and Kimmel got warnings on November 27 because Stimson, after seeing drafts that warned only MacArthur and Hart, insisted on it. As Stimson noted, for him to intervene in the drafting "was unusual, since I do not believe it is advisable for the Secretary of War to meddle with military matters."[93]

In describing the War Council meeting of November 26, no implication of wrongdoing is intended here. Under the prevailing circumstances — Hitler's plan to conquer the world, exterminate peoples, and destroy Western civilization, plus the devastating losses being suffered by the Soviet Union, and the apprehension that she might collapse — Roosevelt's strategy was reasonable. War strategy always involves sacrifice. In attempting to deal with these threats, Roosevelt was fulfilling his duties as president, and more. He was shouldering the heavy responsibility of stopping Hitler — a responsibility Chamberlain, Daladier, and many others had evaded. And the strain on him was great.

Hitler's plan to conquer and enslave most of the world was hardly a secret. It included — in his own words — a return to "barbarism," in which hundreds of millions of children, generation after generation, were to be denied an education, rendering them suitable for their lot as German slaves. Churchill's statement — that the alternative to defeating Hitler was to enter a "Dark Age" — was no exaggeration. Western civilization was at stake, literally.

Also not much of a secret was Hitler's intention to eliminate from the world people with "Jewish blood," including people with "one drop of Jewish blood." The number he had in mind is unknown; from estimates of his scientists, it may have been over fifty million. Neither was his intention to eliminate other ethnic groups, Jehovah's Witnesses, homosexuals, and disabled people, much of a secret. The largest group among them — Slavs — numbered in the hundreds of millions.[94] The slaughter he planned was the most extensive in history by far.

By November 1941 Hitler's plan was well under way. His slaughter of innocent (noncombatant) men, women, and children was approaching three million, and his death camps — which would claim another six million before Germany's defeat put a stop to them — were under construction, with one already operating. These details were not fully known in the United States, but they were partly known — enough to confirm that Hitler was carrying out the Holocaust he had repeatedly threatened. Churchill called it "a crime without a name."[95]

Despite Hitler's boastful public forecasts of the slaughter to come, few people had taken him seriously. The enormity of Hitler's destructiveness later contributed to generations of Holocaust denial and still does. Churchill, too, was slow to see the threat. But by 1940 he saw it as clearly as Roosevelt did and turned with ruthless dedication to defeating Hitler. The two of them, together with Stalin, saved much of the world.

These observations suggest the burden with which Roosevelt struggled in 1941. According to Stark, it was "about as difficult a situation as ever confronted any man anywhere in public life."[96] What he accomplished ensures his place in history, despite criticism of the means he used.

Could he have done it by other means? Such questions — despite their strong appeal — "are unhistorical and in essence irrelevant."[97] They invite speculation about a hypothetical situation. The historical fact is: Roosevelt had a plan to defeat Hitler, and it was the only plan operative in the United States. Stimson, Knox, Ickes, and Morgenthau urged him to take the United States openly into war against Germany by forthright, vigorous leadership — to take her kicking and screaming, if necessary. Their urging never won serious consideration because Roosevelt believed a forthright approach would fail. Because he did not try it, we cannot know if it would have succeeded. History can only try to describe what Roosevelt did and why he did it.

Four months earlier, by the oil embargo and associated measures, Roosevelt acted to prevent the Soviet Union's immediate defeat and Germany's eventual victory. His action put U.S. forces in the Pacific at high risk. Then he waited and waited, resisting pressure from Churchill and from members of his own cabinet to take precipitous measures, until he had assurance that risks taken in the Pacific would enable him to bring his nation fully and undividedly into the war against Germany.

CHAPTER 14
AWAITING THE BLOW

After presenting the ten-point proposal to Japan, the administration alerted people. Roosevelt had a message sent to Churchill: "Japanese negotiations off. Sources expect action within two weeks."[1] The Navy Department informed its representatives in London that the talks had been broken off and military action was expected, and ordered its forces to give "full cooperation" to British and Dutch forces.[2] Hoover told the head of the FBI in Hawaii that negotiations with Japan were breaking down and to be on the alert.[3] Hull told Halifax, "The matter will now go to the Army and Navy." He also hinted to Grew, who wrote in his diary that he (Grew) told a Japanese friend that, "everything was over and that I would soon be leaving Japan."[4]

Nonetheless, Roosevelt and his principal subordinates gave outsiders the impression that there was no emergency. Marshall left Washington for a day and a half to observe army maneuvers in North Carolina, during which time he was "unavailable." It was a task he could have delegated. And Roosevelt left for a four-day Thanksgiving trip, which he announced to the press. (His trip was shortened by an emergency call from Hull, reacting to the news that Tojo had made a warlike speech.) And after Marshall and Roosevelt returned, they and Stark seemed to follow a leisurely routine — movies, theater, dinner parties, quiet evenings at home, and much horseback riding by Marshall. During those activities they were often unavailable, or seemed to be. (During this interval, lower-level officers worked extra-long shifts and many offices were staffed around the clock.) Despite expecting Japan to attack the United States within days, despite intelligence that the attack would fall on Pearl Harbor, "Roosevelt seemed to view the crisis almost as if it were unreal, and might at any moment evaporate."[5] This behavior gave members of the congressional committee and scholars an impression of negligence at the top.

The emphasis here is on "seemed," for there is ample evidence that, while they appeared to be at leisure, Roosevelt, Marshall, and Stark were dealing actively with the crisis. Stark testified that he "talked very frequently with the President. I think you will be surprised to know how much, how minutely he was following every detail," and that during the days before Pearl Harbor, Roosevelt "was intensely interested in every move [of the Japanese navy] at that time, as we all were."[6] And Marshall was in daily consultation about the Pacific situation with Stark, Stimson, Knox, and Hull. The seemingly leisurely, business-as-usual routines of Roosevelt, Marshall, and Stark may have given the impression to Japanese spies and observers in Washington that U.S. leaders were unprepared for war.

After the ten-point proposal reached Tokyo, Nomura received instructions to mislead officials in Washington by acting as if the diplomatic talks were to continue.[7] The United States intercepted and decoded Japanese messages saying so on November 28 and December 1. Presumably top officials in Washington knew of those instructions. Perhaps an illusion of business as usual was designed to play along with Nomura's deception. Perhaps for the same reason, Roosevelt told the press on December 2, "The United States is at peace with Japan and perfectly friendly, too."[8]

At that time Britain was considering an arrangement with Japan, in case of war between them, for an exchange of nationals in each other's territories. Informed of this, State Department officers considered the advisability of seeking such an arrangement for the benefit of Americans in Japan, and concluded:

> As the making of such an approach would be interpreted as a definite indication that *this Government expects war between Japan and United States*, the Secretary may wish to speak to the President.[9] (Italics added.)

The United States sought no such arrangement. Evidently a sign of expecting war was to be avoided.

The possibility that Roosevelt was setting out bait is supported by an extraordinary dispatch, described below, which he himself wrote. It ordered three small ships to sail into the path of the Japanese fleet moving south from Shanghai, with the expectation that the ships would be sunk.

Hart had learned by September 1941 that he was not to defend the Philippines, and had moved the surface warships of his Asiatic Fleet to the south, out of harm's way. In October, informing Stark, he had brought them back to Manila, to join MacArthur in defending against a Japanese attack. On November 20, Stark again ordered Hart to move the ships out of harm's way, and he did.[10] After the war, Hart said what he understood from his November 27 dispatch was "quite simple. We were told that we were to await the blow, in dispositions such as to minimize the danger from it."[11] Specific orders to Kimmel after November 27 also put parts of his fleet — including his carriers, the most valuable part — out of harm's way (see chapter 6).

After a flurry of dispatches to the Pacific commands on November 27 and 28, top officials in Washington awaited an attack. In London the wait was more anxious. Churchill expected Japanese attacks on Malaya and Hong Kong, but had only token forces to meet them and — until December 1 — no specific assurance of when the United States would come fully into the war. His military chiefs advised him:

> From the military point of view it would pay us to attack those convoys at sea, but our present political instructions preclude us from doing this. *Unless we are absolutely assured that an attack delivered in these circumstances would have the armed support of the United States*, we ought not to make the first move.[12] (Italics added.)

By "those convoys," they meant the Japanese fleet moving south. A worker in British intelligence noted that Churchill phoned "at all hours of the day and night" for the latest information on where Japan's attack forces were headed.[13]

The Australian government pressed London to forestall an invasion of Thailand or the Dutch East Indies by making a preemptive strike against the Japanese fleet moving south. Churchill told Halifax to ask Roosevelt for an assurance that the United States would join Britain if she took such action. Halifax did so on December 1, and reported back that Roosevelt said (in Halifax's words):

> any of these hypothetical actions [could] be a prelude to some further action and threat to our common interests against which we ought to react together at once . . . in the case of any direct attack on [British territory] or the Dutch, we should obviously all be in it together . . . we could certainly count on their support, although it might take a short time . . . a few days, to get things into political shape here.[14]

By getting "things into political shape," Roosevelt probably meant going to Congress for a war declaration. He had already begun preparing a speech to Congress for that purpose in case Japan invaded the Dutch East Indies or Malaya without attacking U.S. territory. Halifax wrote in his diary, "I feel pretty clear that if we get into war with Japan we can count on the United States."[15]

Perhaps thinking he had not been clear enough, on December 4 Roosevelt told Halifax that he meant openly to enter the war. On December 5 Roosevelt told him the commitment applied in case of a Japanese attack on Malaya, the Dutch East Indies, or Thailand.[16] London then informed Australia:

> we have now received an assurance from the United States. If we find it necessary to forestall a Japanese landing in Kra Isthmus . . . [and] If the Japanese attack the Netherlands East Indies and we go at once to support the latter . . . [and] If the Japanese attack us . . . we have accordingly instructed the Commander in Chief, Far East that he should take action . . . if (a) He has good information that a Japanese expedition is advancing with the apparent intention of landing on Kra Isthmus, or (b) The Japanese violate any other part of Thailand . . . [or] the Japanese attack . . . the Netherlands East Indies.[17]

Apparently London also informed Malaya and the Dutch East Indies. And Churchill cabled General Claude Auchinleck in Egypt, "This is an immense relief as I had long dreaded being at war with Japan without or before the United States."[18] And Britain firmed up her commitment to aid the Dutch East Indies in case of a Japanese attack.

On December 6 Halifax asked Roosevelt specifically if he would agree to a British preemptive strike against the Japanese fleet approaching the Kra Isthmus. The isthmus was part of Thailand, bordering on Malaya. Roosevelt agreed vaguely, adding, "If we saw Japanese transports steaming . . . across the Gulf of Thailand we should obviously attack them since they must be going for Thailand or Malaya."[19] Roosevelt's agreement to Halifax's request gave Churchill the option — by attacking the Japanese fleet — of involving the United States in war with Japan. It approved preemptive action by the British, while similar or even less aggressive action remained forbidden to Short, Kimmel, MacArthur, and Hart.

Churchill did not have time to exercise the option. To be certain he understood exactly what Roosevelt had agreed to, on December 7 Churchill drafted a cable to Halifax:

> 1. From your recent telegrams we understand we can rely on armed support of the United States if we become involved in hostilities with Japan in the following circumstances:

(a) Japanese invasion of Malaya or Netherlands East Indies.

(b) Action on our part in the Kra Isthmus to forestall or repel Japanese landing in that Isthmus . . .

2. We read your telegram . . . of December 6 . . . as meaning that in President Roosevelt's view we should be justified in attacking at sea any Japanese expedition sailing in direction of Thailand or Malaya.[20]

Before he sent the cable, Japan launched her attacks.

Japan's fleet heading south was tracked easily, while her fleet heading east, toward Pearl Harbor, was harder to locate. U.S. officials expected an attack on U.S. territory, but without certainty about where it would fall or even that it would happen.

On December 1 Tokyo cabled diplomatic officers in Washington and London to destroy codes and other documents, and on December 2 sent another such cable.[21] The United States intercepted both. On December 2 Roosevelt told a subordinate that he expected to be at war with Japan within a few days. On December 4 Knox told a subordinate the same.[22]

According to some scholars, no one in Washington realized that crucial intelligence was being withheld from Short and Kimmel. That was untrue. Even before war became imminent, intelligence officers were troubled that Kimmel and Short were not receiving needed information. In October the outgoing director of ONI, Capt. Alan Kirk, and his subordinate, Capt. Howard Bode, proposed sending to Kimmel the "bomb-plot" messages, indicating that Pearl Harbor was a likely Japanese target.[23] The new director, Adm. Theodore Wilkinson, did not act on the proposal. (From what follows, Stark probably stopped Wilkinson.) Safford made the same proposal and his director, Noyes, rejected it.[24]

By December Safford and McCollum were seriously concerned about intelligence being withheld from Kimmel. On December 1 McCollum drafted a three-page summary of intelligence and showed it to Wilkinson, Ingersoll, Turner, and Stark. He testified that, after pointing out to them that it indicated imminent war with Japan,

[I] requested information as to whether or not the fleets in the Pacific had been adequately alerted. I was given a categorical assurance by both Admiral Stark and Admiral Turner that dispatches fully alerting the fleets and placing them on a war basis had been sent.[25]

Safford testified that on December 3 he phoned McCollum, drew recent intercepted Japanese diplomatic messages to his attention, and asked, "Are you people in Naval Intelligence doing anything to get a warning out to the Pacific Fleet?" And McCollum answered, "*We* are doing everything that *we* can to get the news out to the Fleet."[26] On December 4 McCollum prepared a summary of recent intelligence for Kimmel and Bloch, indicating a Japanese attack was imminent.[27] Wilkinson endorsed it and presented it to Noyes, who rejected it, saying, "I think it an insult to the intelligence of the Commander-in-Chief," meaning Kimmel.[28] Although Noyes was senior to him, Wilkinson insisted, "I do not agree with you. Admiral Kimmel is a very busy man and may not see the picture as clearly as you and I do . . . I am going to send it if I can get it released by the front office."[29] Perhaps the reference to Kimmel being busy was a polite way of saying that Kimmel had not received the intelligence, as both Wilkinson and Noyes knew. The "front office" meant Stark. The proposed dispatch was not sent.

Still troubled early in the morning of December 6 that Kimmel had not been adequately alerted, Safford drafted a message to him, "In view of the imminence of war destroy all [code documents] on Wake Island."[30] He testified that he brought it to Noyes's assistant, Capt. Joseph Redman, who rejected it. Safford then went to Noyes, who said, "What do you mean by using such language as that?"[31] They argued about whether war was about to break out or not, and then Noyes rewrote Safford's draft to read:

> In view of the international situation and the exposed position of our outlying Pacific islands you may authorize destruction by them of secret and confidential documents now or under later conditions of greater emergency.[32]

The "outlying Pacific islands" did not include Hawaii. Noyes sent it by deferred priority, by which it would be delivered on Monday, December 8.

On December 3 Col. Otis Sadtler had seen an intercepted Japanese order for diplomatic officers to destroy code machines, codes, and other documents. Then Noyes told him that a winds execute had come in. Sadtler drafted a dispatch for the army's Pacific commands: "Reliable information indicates war with Japan in very near future. Take every precaution to prevent a repetition of Port Arthur. Notify Navy."[33] Miles supported sending the warning but, according to Sadtler, Gerow rejected it, saying, "I think they have had plenty of notification."[34] Dissatisfied, Sadtler went to Bedell Smith, who said he did not want to discuss the matter.[35]

In all, Bratton, Sadtler, Miles, Safford, McCollum, Kirk, Bode,

Wilkinson, Turner, and later Noyes, urged sending warnings to the Pacific commands, especially to Hawaii. Bratton testified:

> [I] never received a definite prohibition on [sending warnings] but every time that I tried to send a message of this sort, and the Navy found out about it, the Chief of Naval operations would call up the Chief of Staff on the telephone and object most vociferously and emphatically. He in turn would call [Miles] and object strenuously, and by the time it got to me . . . it was disapproval expressed in no uncertain terms . . . And I in each case would be instructed not to do it again.[36]

Marshall testified that the policy restricting dispatches was that "they must not send anything that would produce an operational reaction . . . for attack or defense."[37]

The need to send warnings continued to worry Bratton. He testified further:

> I felt the Japanese were showing unusual interest in the port at Honolulu, and discussed this matter with my opposite numbers in the Navy on several occasions . . . and I was assured of this—when the emergency arises the fleet is not going to be there. . . . Nobody in [navy or army intelligence in Washington] knew that any major element of the fleet was in Pearl Harbor on Sunday morning on the 7th of December. We all thought they had gone to sea.[38]

The port at Honolulu was Pearl Harbor. And pursuant to orders from Washington, most of the fleet was at anchor. Under Kimmel's war plan, the fleet would put to sea only after war broke out or after receipt of orders to put the plan into operation. Until then — as Washington understood — it was to hold itself in readiness for action.

Thus to mid-level army and navy officers, intelligence received from October to early December called urgently for warnings to the Hawaiian commands. Their superiors, however, rejected their pleas to send warnings.

In the midst of intelligence officers' efforts to get warnings sent to Hawaii, Roosevelt tried an additional provocation — his "three-small-vessels" order, which scholars have largely ignored. Stark sent it to Hart on December 2:

> President directs that the following be done as soon as possible and within two days if possible after receipt this

despatch. Charter 3 small vessels to form a "defensive information patrol". Minimum requirements to establish identity
as U.S. men-of-war are command by a naval officer and to
mount a small gun and 1 machine gun would suffice. Filipino
crews may be employed with a minimum number naval ratings to accomplish purpose which is to observe and report by
radio Japanese movements in west China sea and Gulf of
Siam. One vessel to be stationed between Hainan and Hue
one vessel off the Indo-China Coast between Camranh Bay
and Cape St. Jacques and one vessel off Pointe de Camau.
Use of Isabel authorized by president as one of the three but
not other naval vessels. Report measures taken to carry out
president's views. At same time inform me as to what reconnaissance measures are being regularly performed at sea by
both army and navy whether by air surface vessels or submarines and your opinion as to the effectiveness of these latter
measures.[39]

"Naval ratings" meant warrant officers. The *Isabel* was a long-obso-
lete warship, converted for Admiral Hart's use as a yacht. The two
other vessels chosen by Hart for the mission had been commercial
boats. None of the three was suited for military use.

Context and staff work for the order are lacking. By navy procedures, orders were rarely given in such detail. It was taken for
granted that fleet commanders knew how to carry out ordinary commands. And Hart received even more detailed instructions about
the mission — instructions not found in dispatches to him or in other
records.

Logically, a reply to the last sentence in the dispatch should have
preceded the decision to order the mission. If Hart was already carrying out effective reconnaissance — tracking the Japanese fleet moving
south — the mission was unnecessary for its stated purpose. And Hart
was in fact doing so, as the Navy Department knew.[40] He had begun
aerial reconnaissance of that fleet on November 25, and received an
order to continue it on November 30. And the Navy Department was
receiving the results of his reconnaissance. In response to the three-
small-vessels order, Hart immediately informed Stark of that, but the
order remained in effect.[41] In addition, Washington was receiving information on that Japanese fleet from the British, whose aircraft were
tracking it well. The purpose stated in the dispatch did not account for
the order. One writer explained it away by the speculation that
Roosevelt's "rather irritating busybodyism" caused it, but he was not
a busybody.[42]

According to Lt. Kemp Tolley, assigned to command one of the three vessels, Hart told him on December 4:

> Arm her with one cannon of some kind, one machine gun, and provision her for a two-week cruise, get a crew on board and be ready to sail in 24 hours. . . . The rules do not apply in this case! [We have] been directed to give you the highest priority on your verbal request, *without paper work of any kind.* Of this you can be absolutely assured; the President himself has personally ordered it . (Italics added.)

Tolley's vessel, the *Lanikai*, came equipped with a homemade transmitter whose range was short.[43] The transmitter was inadequate for radioing back information he might acquire near Indochina. Nonetheless, Tolley was not told to replace it. (Even without an adequate transmitter, Tolley was unable to get the *Lanikai* ready to sail before Japan attacked.)

Only one of the three, the *Isabel*, was ready in time. According to her commander, Lt. John Payne, Hart told him

> to proceed on a special reconnaissance mission off the coast of Indo-China . . . Utmost secrecy was to be observed, actual orders were to be given verbally, memorized and recited to the Admiral. No one was to know the actual mission of the *Isabel* except the Admiral and myself until we were at sea, then the executive officer was to be taken into confidence. *A fake operational despatch* . . . was transmitted, ordering *Isabel* to search . . . for a lost Navy PBY plane. . . . Additional orders . . . were *to fight the ship* as necessary and *to destroy it rather than let it fall into enemy hands.* The ship was to remain white.[44] (Italics added.)

The color white made the *Isabel* easy to spot for the Japanese. As to the fake dispatch, governments routinely provide cover stories for secret operations.

Most extraordinary was the order for Payne to sink his own ship. On hearing Hart's instructions, Payne thought the *Isabel*'s mission was to produce an incident to get the United States into war.[45]

To state the obvious, none of the three vessels was equipped to put up a fight against Japanese warships or planes, and none was fast enough to flee from them. Nor did they have anything on board worth preserving from Japanese capture, except the *Isabel*, which had a navy transmitter, presumably with a code device. But if the *Isabel* ran into trouble, the transmitter alone could have been blown up or thrown overboard. That left Payne's order to sink the *Isabel* puzzling.

After the war Hart wrote that the three-small-vessels order caused him "consternation" because "as a war measure the project was very ill-advised." It involved risk to personnel and vessels without the prospect of providing "useful" reconnaissance; the vessels would have "no chance to . . . see anything of value."[46] According to Tolley, Hart told him that, if the congressional committee had asked him different questions about the order, he would have told them what he knew and "then the fat would have been in the fire."[47] But Hart did not explain the comment. Hart also told Tolley, "Yes, you were bait."[48]

Tolley, who later became an admiral, devoted years to discovering what purpose — other than reconnaissance — the three-small-vessels order might have had. He found that some navy personnel involved would not talk about it. He and Hart concluded that the vessels' mission was to be sunk by Japan, providing the United States with an incident to justify war.[49]

The *Isabel* discovered nothing new, and was recalled to Manila shortly before December 7. According to Adm. Edwin Layton, the *Isabel* had been spotted and buzzed by Japanese planes. "When it was clear that the Japanese were not going to take the bait and attack, Hart recalled her."[50] And Lt. Marion Buass, Payne's executive officer, concluded, "The true nature of our mission was to . . . result in an incident in which the ship would probably be sunk."[51] If any of the three vessels had been sunk by the Japanese or by her own crew, Roosevelt would have been in a position to declare that Japan had sunk a U.S. warship engaged in a peaceful rescue mission.

Ingersoll had dispatched the order. Questioned closely by the congressional committee about why he wanted the three vessels sent out, he said:

> **The reason we wanted them there is because it says in the beginning of the dispatch the "President directs that the following be done as soon as possible." That was our reason for doing it. Admiral Stark was told by the President to do it.[52]**

Asked if the navy had a need for reconnaissance by the three vessels, Ingersoll said, "Admiral Hart was already conducting reconnaissance of that coast by planes from Manila . . . I am sure Admiral Stark would not have done this unless he had been told." He also testified, "We were getting sufficient information from Admiral Hart by the searches which his planes were making."[53] Answers to more questions in this vein made Ingersoll's position clear: the order served no intelligence purpose.

The committee's questions then turned to whether the order could have served to provoke an incident, and Ingersoll said yes. Even if one of the vessels were only fired on, "It would have been an incident on which we could have declared war."[54] Comparing use of the three vessels to use of planes for tracking Japan's fleet, he said, "the chance of an overt incident occurring in the case of a plane search are very much less than that of a small ship trying to trail a force."[55]

Why the use of Filipino crews was specified remains unexplained. A possibility is that they were considered more expendable than U.S. crews.

When the order was written, Japan's attack was expected within days. And according to intelligence, her attack would include U.S. territory. Why, then, might Roosevelt have needed an additional incident? Because no record, scrap of conversation, or other direct evidence of his thinking about the order has come to light, one can only list possibilities. Perhaps Roosevelt's order reflected uncertainty about Japanese plans—specifically his worry that, without an attack on the United States, Congress would not declare war. The three-small-vessels order may have been inexpensive insurance that Japan would provide an incident.

Another possibility is that the order was an eleventh-hour effort to save Hawaii and the Philippines. If one of the vessels had been sunk, enabling Roosevelt to enter the war openly, the Hawaiian and Philippine commands could have been placed on full alert. And Kimmel could have ordered his ships out of Pearl Harbor.

By the time the *Isabel* was recalled, Washington had strong evidence that Japan was about to strike Pearl Harbor. Labor Secretary Frances Perkins described an aborted cabinet conversation on December 5 in which Knox was extremely agitated and suddenly blurted out:

> "Well, you know, Mr. President, we know where the Japanese fleet is." The President looked up and looked around and then asked Knox to tell us. "Well . . . we have very secret information that mustn't go outside this room that the Japanese fleet is out. They're out of harbor. They're out at sea." The President interrupted Knox and kept him from going much further. Then he [Roosevelt] said . . . "We haven't got anything like perfect information as to their apparent destination. The question is in the minds of the Navy and in my mind whether the fleet is going south."

Knox then said, "Every indication is that they are going south."[56]

Perhaps Knox had been about to say that when Roosevelt stopped him. But the location of the Japanese fleet moving south had been known for weeks, along with the fact that it contained no aircraft carriers. That it was moving south was no secret. The crucial question was: where were Japan's carriers? In mid-November, naval intelligence had lost track of Japanese fleet units that were not moving south (including the carriers), assumed they were still where they had been (in home waters), and tried especially hard to locate the carriers.

From what Knox's aide Beatty later revealed, Knox was probably in a position at the cabinet meeting to say that Japan's carriers were moving east, toward Hawaii. Since December 1 naval intelligence had been reporting daily that "a large part of the Japanese fleet was apparently at sea with its whereabouts not known," and it included carriers.[57] According to Beatty, just before Knox's dramatic statement to the cabinet, in an intelligence briefing based on intercepted Japanese radio messages, Wilkinson had told Knox that naval intelligence had located Japan's aircraft carriers.[58]

The navy had long expected Japan to use carriers for an attack on Pearl Harbor. That emphasizes the importance of Wilkinson's December 5 briefing. If what Beatty remembered years later is accurate—and Ranneft's, Ogg's, and Hosner's evidence confirms it—naval intelligence had indeed located the carriers, which were then near Hawaii. That was a vital secret.

As noted, vigilance in Washington seemed to decrease after November 26. It reached what seemed its lowest point on Saturday, December 6. That morning the White House press secretary told reporters they had no "need for pads and pencils or even minds," because the president was taking the day off. Roosevelt had no appointments scheduled that day or the next, and was devoting his time to catching up on paperwork—letters, memos, and reports. And he advised the nation that it was a good time for Christmas shopping.[59]

Roosevelt, however, had appointments with several people, and not all their names were recorded in his calendar or the White House visitors log.[60] Despite the expectation of War, Navy, and State Department staff that Japan's attack on the United States would fall within a day, the press secretary's announcement, which received wide publicity, gave a false impression of no emergency.

At 7:20 a.m. on that day, U.S. intelligence intercepted message #901—known as the pilot message—from Togo to Nomura, and completed its translation at 2 p.m.:

> 1. The Government has deliberated deeply on the American proposal of the 26th of November and as a result we have drawn up a memorandum for the United States contained in

my separate message #902 (in English).

2. This separate message is a very long one. I will send it in fourteen parts and I imagine you will receive it tomorrow . . . The situation is very delicate, and when you receive it I want you to please keep it secret for the time being.

3. Concerning the time of presenting this memorandum to the United States, I will wire you in a separate message. However I want you to . . . make every preparation to present it to the Americans just as soon as you receive instructions.[61]

By sending the next message (#902) in English, Tokyo ensured against delay by its Washington staff in translating it.

Intelligence workers took the pilot message — correctly — to mean that Japan's reply to the ten-point proposal would follow and that, probably on Sunday, Nomura was to inform Hull that the talks were broken off. And the time he did so might coincide with a Japanese declaration of war or attack on the United States.[62] A member of the army's Signal Intelligence Service later wrote, "Shortly after midday on Saturday, December 6, 1941 . . . [we] knew that war was as certain as death" and "it was known in our agency that Japan would surely attack us in the early afternoon of the following day . . . Not an iota of doubt."[63] (Early afternoon in Washington was early morning in Hawaii.)

The importance of message #901 was obscured by administration efforts to prove that it was not delivered to key officers until the next day. It should have been delivered as soon as possible to the president, the war, navy, and state secretaries, and several army and navy officers. Couriers carried intercepts to them in locked pouches. But as intelligence officers processed #901, #902 began to come in. Foretold by message #901, #902 was expected to be most important. Thinking they would soon have #902 to deliver along with #901, army and navy intelligence workers held up delivering #901 while they worked on #902.[64] An intelligence office that had closed was reopened in the evening, and workers who had gone home — including one who was sick — were recalled to duty. Some cryptographers worked through the night on message #902 and a message that followed it.

Message #902 was a long rehashing of Japan's good intentions and efforts during the diplomatic talks, and of bad intentions and acts of the United States. It was for the record. Therefore delaying delivery of the pilot message while waiting for the rest of the long message proved counterproductive.

By evening thirteen parts of #902 had come in, but further waiting did not produce the fourteenth. Bratton was responsible for deliveries to Hull and War Department personnel; Kramer, for deliveries to the president and Navy Department personnel. According to Bratton and Kramer, they rushed out at 9 p.m., carrying the pouches to the people on their lists.

Bratton testified to the army board and Kramer to the naval court that they delivered the messages that evening to all recipients who could be found – to most people on their lists.[65] The administration then mounted an effort (see chapter 5) to discredit Bratton's testimony and to have him change it. Some people on his list, to whom he claimed to have made deliveries, said not only that they did not receive the messages, but also that they had been unavailable to receive them. The administration's point was that key officials did not receive the messages before 8:30 the next morning – a delay of about eighteen hours. The implication was that Bratton's negligence caused a crucial delay in sending warnings to Hawaii.

That was untrue and a red herring. Whether Bratton and Kramer made or attempted all the deliveries during Saturday evening is unimportant here, because it is undisputed that they made some of them. And there is evidence that Marshall was informed of the pilot message on Saturday afternoon. Miles testified:

> **[I] had every reason to believe that General Marshall did receive [on Saturday] this message. I heard his testimony this morning. I think he is mistaken in saying he did not receive that message on the afternoon of the 6th.[66]**

If Miles was right, what Marshall received then was probably a gist. Miles also said:

> **it was in the Saturday afternoon locked pouch . . . and . . . it did go to General Marshall. He does not remember seeing it.[67]**

And Undersecretary of State Adolf Berle noted that the message reached the State Department at 7:30 that evening, where Hull saw it.

At 9:30 p.m. Kramer arrived at the White House and gave the pilot and thirteen-part messages to Lt. Lester Schulz, saying, "the President should see [them] as quickly as possible."[68] Schulz brought them in to Roosevelt, who was talking to Hopkins. Schulz noted Roosevelt's calm, unhurried manner as he read them and talked to Hopkins about them, commenting, "This means war." He also noted that the president appeared to be expecting the intelligence and that neither Roosevelt nor Hopkins mentioned warnings to the Pacific commands.[69]

Hopkins commented that it was "too bad" Japan would have the advantage of striking the first blow – that we could not strike first and prevent being taken by surprise — and Roosevelt said, "No, we can't do that. We are a democracy and a peaceful people. But we have a good record."[70] Schulz testified, "The impression that I got was that we could not make the first overt move. We would have to wait until it came."[71] And according to a biographer of Marshall, "we have a good record" meant "the United States would have clean hands, leaving the isolationists without effective argument against American intervention on the side of the British and Dutch."[72]

According to Schulz, Roosevelt and Hopkins continued talking, and then Roosevelt tried to phone Stark at home and was told he was at the theater. Roosevelt said he would not have Stark paged at the theater, for that might cause "undue alarm" to the public; he would speak to him later.[73] It is worth noting Roosevelt's appearance of unconcern. Stark had given his servant the theater's phone number, and given the theater usher his seat number so that he could be reached if something urgent came up. That was normal procedure in the circumstances, but Roosevelt chose not to use it.

The only action Roosevelt is officially known to have taken after reading the messages was sending a letter to Hirohito. It had the form of a last-minute plea for peace, and has been described so by scholars. He sent it by a slow conveyance, and it reached Hirohito after the Pearl Harbor attack began. Even if it had it reached him in time, the message contained no offer by Roosevelt — nothing to justify reconsideration of war by Japan's leaders. And as David Bergamini pointed out, the opening sentences distorted history in a way offensive to the Japanese.[74] It began: "Almost a century ago the President of the United States addressed to the Emperor of Japan a message extending an offer of friendship of the people of the United States to the people of Japan. The offer was accepted."[75] The "offer" to which Roosevelt referred had been extended at the point of naval cannons, along with the threat to destroy Tokyo if it were refused. And it had been accepted because of that threat.

As he sent the letter to Hirohito, Roosevelt quipped to White House guests, "The son of man has just sent his final message to the Son of God."[76] If the word "final" is taken literally, it suggests Roosevelt expected no reply, probably because he did expect war immediately. The next day, an hour before news of the attack came in, Roosevelt read a copy of the letter with satisfaction to Chinese Ambassador Hu, commenting, "That will be fine for the record." Hu told a reporter that Roosevelt said he was certain Japan would attack the United States before Tuesday morning.[77]

Even if only one person on Bratton's and Kramer's lists received the pilot message, that should have sufficed for others to be informed of the emergency and for them to take immediate action. It is established that Roosevelt, Hopkins, Bratton, Kramer, McCollum, Noyes, Turner, and Knox understood the message to mean a Japanese attack on the United States was about to occur. Furthermore, when hand delivery of crucial intelligence was delayed, procedure called for its gist to be conveyed immediately, either orally or in writing. Notations of when Japanese diplomatic intercepts were ready for delivery in locked pouches was the time when polished translations were complete. Gists and rough translations of urgent messages were conveyed before translations were complete. And there is no indication that the procedure failed during December 6; on the contrary, testimony from several administration officials supports that normal procedure was followed.

Noyes testified about the December 6 messages:

> I was either informed [orally] or saw the rough originals . . . and I particularly instructed Kramer to be sure that the Secretary of State got his copies promptly, although it was the Army responsibility [to handle deliveries to Hull] . . . I saw enough of it to get a sense of it before I left [the office on Saturday evening] between 7 and 8.[78]

Similarly, Ingersoll and Wilkinson testified that, before they left their offices that afternoon or evening, they saw the pilot message (probably in rough form).[79] And Bratton said he informed Marshall orally of the pilot message on Saturday afternoon.[80] Representative Frank Keefe of the congressional committee said, "There is evidence before the committee that the pilot message was delivered to certain people around about 3 o'clock" on Saturday afternoon.[81]

Marshall testified that he did not see the pilot message until Sunday morning. Asked why his staff did not give it to him on Saturday, Marshall said, "I did not look into it at all until . . . about two days ago." He gave no explanation, but implied that the message lacked sufficient importance.[82] When pressed on the question, he still gave no explanation. Pressed again, his final answer was, "The fact of the matter is it was not brought to my attention."[83]

Other high officials also explained not sending warnings to the Hawaiian commands by their subordinates' failure to bring intelligence of the coming attack to their attention. As in Marshall's case, they seemed unconcerned about their subordinates "lapses." They did not look into the "lapses"; apparently they did not replace or even reprimand their subordinates.

It is worth emphasizing that Bratton and Miles said unequivocally that the pilot message was given to Marshall on Saturday.

According to Bratton, he informed Marshall of it in the afternoon and urged him to send a war alert. But Marshall refused and left the office, saying he was going home and "did not want to be disturbed."[84]

After trying to phone Stark and being told he was at the theater, Roosevelt reportedly did nothing else in reaction to the pilot message. His inaction makes no sense in relation to the apparent necessity to warn the Pacific commands of an imminent attack. It did, however, fit with giving Japan the impression that Washington was not expecting an attack—that Japan's deception was working. According to White House records, Roosevelt did not phone Stark again that evening, nor did he phone Marshall or anyone else, nor did he receive any calls. Instead, he retired early. And Stark testified repeatedly that he did not talk to Roosevelt that evening.

At the end of the congressional committee hearings, however, Stark recanted his testimony in which he denied speaking to Roosevelt Saturday evening. He then testified that they had spoken by phone in the late evening, but *discussed nothing of importance.*[85] The implication was that Roosevelt made no mention of the pilot message. Why the call was missing from White House telephone logs remains unexplained. After the hearings ended, Stark wrote to the committee chairman, correcting his testimony still again:

> **Krick further stated that when I came downstairs after the phone call I said . . . the situation with Japan was very serious.**[86]

Capt. Harold Krick was a friend of Stark's. He and his wife had spent Saturday evening with Stark and his wife. Krick had pointed out to Stark that his testimony was untrue, prompting Stark's recantation.

Stark's final testimony was that he still did not recall his phone conversation with Roosevelt. In place of his specific recollection, he offered a reconstruction of what was probably said, based on his and Roosevelt's thinking at the time. The key part of Stark's statement was:

> **I can only assume that when the President phoned me that he mentioned this note that we had received from the Japanese, that he did not, certainly did not, impress me that it was anything that required action; I took none. I am rather certain that he gave me no directive.**[87]

Inasmuch as other administration officials testified that they immediately understood the pilot message to mean that a Japanese attack on the United States was likely the next day, Stark's testimony was puzzling. The pilot message called for reviewing dispositions of forces in the Pacific and of their readiness for an outbreak of war. Not to have reviewed their readiness would have been gross negligence. There is, however, obscure evidence that the review was at least begun.

After the pilot message was decoded, Stimson and Knox requested information on the dispositions of naval forces in the Pacific — mostly on Kimmel's forces.[88] (Marshall similarly requested material bearing mostly on the situation in the Philippines.) As indicated below, it is possible that some of the information collected was reviewed at a meeting in the White House Saturday night. What is known is that in the evening, Stimson had a call for the information placed to Stark's watch officer, Cato Glover, who wrote in his log:

> At 2000 Major E.L. Harrison, aide to the Secretary of War, telephoned that the Secretary of War desired the following information by 0900 Sunday 7 December. Compilation of men-of-war in the Far East. British, American, Dutch, Russian. Also compilation of American men-of-war in Pacific Fleet, with locations, and a list of American men-of-war in the Atlantic without locations . . . [Knox] directed that the information be delivered prior to 1000 Sunday.[89]

Glover apparently consulted Knox, Ingersoll, and perhaps Stark before complying with Harrison's request.[90]

Stark had testified many times that he had no memory of his activities after leaving the office that evening, which was before Harrison phoned Glover, and that whatever he had done involved no official business. In questioning Stark, the congressional committee suggested Glover consulted him before 8:00 p.m. Stark's response was to disagree about the time and to offer testimony about it. No one paid attention, and he interrupted to offer it again and again.[91] Committee members were apparently absorbed in other aspects of Stimson's intervention, and Stark did not give the testimony he offered. He did, however, insist that the watch officer consulted him after 8:00 p.m.

At this point in the congressional hearings, Stark was saying that he might have gone to the theater on Saturday evening. If he had been at the theater (as was later established), his statement implied that the watch officer consulted him after he returned — during the night.

From what was eventually determined about Stark's activities Saturday evening, he left his office at about 6:30 p.m. and drove home, where he found the Kricks. Stark dined with his wife and the Kricks in the Starks' home and all four then went to the theater for a performance at 8:00 or 8:30 p.m.[92] Up to this time, Stark received no phone call, and none came to him at the theater.

After the theater, the Starks and Kricks returned to the Starks' home, where Admiral Stark was told the White House had called during his absence. Stark excused himself, went upstairs, and phoned Roosevelt, who discussed the intercepted Japanese messages with him. Five or ten minutes later Stark rejoined the others, saying (in Krick's words), "that conditions in the Pacific were serious . . . that conditions with Japan were in a critical state."[93] According to Krick, Stark seemed quite undisturbed. The Kricks left about fifteen minutes later, at 11:30 p.m. By Krick's and Stark's testimony, Glover did not phone before that. According to Glover, he reached Stark about Stimson's request after midnight.[94]

The committee asked Stark why Glover needed to consult Knox, Ingersoll, and Stark before supplying the data Stimson wanted, and received no answer. Early that evening, Knox had learned of the intercepts and on his own (or perhaps in consultation with Stimson) had decided to hold a top-level meeting to discuss them. Knox was reachable by phone during the evening. If he had approved Stimson's request, there would have been no need for Glover to phone Stark after midnight. The lateness of Glover's call suggests it required immediate attention. From what follows, it may be that in talking to Knox, Glover heard of a meeting at the White House that night, and called Stark to inform him so that he could attend it.

Logically, the disaster of Pearl Harbor and accusations of administration responsibility for it should have fixed events of December 6 in the minds of leading officers. Marshall was concerned enough to have his staff write detailed recollections of their activities around the Pearl Harbor attack, which included December 6.[95] The result was a book-length set of memoirs which he kept. His testimony that he had no idea where he had been that Saturday evening aroused skepticism. Pressed, Marshall insisted, "I don't know where I was. I never thought of it until this instant."[96] Of leaders in Washington, Marshall was most scrutinized and criticized for unhurried performance of duty in the days before the attack.

More than others, he seemed to be following a routine adopted during more peaceful times: riding his horse before or after his work days and on Sunday mornings, not answering his home phone after dinner, and retiring early. Details of Marshall's activities created the impression that he was unavailable at those times. But while riding, he took the same path daily so his orderly could find him quickly if he were needed.[97] The orderly also had instructions, if calls after dinner were urgent, to call Marshall to the phone. And his military staff was instructed to phone—and, if necessary, to have him awakened—if urgent matters came up. The appearance of Marshall's unavailability was misleading.

The committee questioned Marshall and Stark very closely about their activities Saturday night. Behind some of the questions was a rumor, which had come to the committee's attention, of a top-level meeting at the White House that night. While claiming he remembered nothing of his activities that evening, and in contrast to other vague answers, Marshall said he was "certain" and "absolutely certain" that Roosevelt had not contacted him.[98]

Stark also said he was "absolutely certain" that Roosevelt had not contacted him.[99] He was then asked if he had received a phone message from Knox that night, and answered, "I am certain that I heard nothing that Knox said that night."[100] The phrasing of his answer was odd, suggesting that something related to the question might have happened. Stark gave another odd denial to a related question:

> In view of the fact that the Chief of Staff cannot remember where he was on that night is it possible that you and he could have been together?
> Stark: I think we had no such conspiracy at that time, sir.[101]

Thirty years later James Stahlman, an old friend of Knox, wrote:

> [Knox] told me that the following had sat for a considerable portion of the night of December 6, anticipating a Japanese strike somewhere: FDR, Hopkins, Stimson, Marshall, Knox, with John McCrea and Frank Beatty.[102]

Stahlman also wrote:

> The Colonel [Knox] told me that he, Stimson, Marshall, Betty Stark and Harry Hopkins had spent most of the night before [the Pearl Harbor attack] at the White House with FDR, all waiting for what they knew was coming after those intercepts.[103]

McCrea was Stark's assistant. Stahlman added that McCrea "confirmed that he had been with Stark, et al, at the White House."

The only mention of what passed at the White House, according to Stahlman, is that the group talked about ensuring that Japan fire the first shot. Possibly a decision to warn Kimmel was made, Knox left, and the decision was then reconsidered. According to the congressional committee's counsel, Beatty and Capt. John Dillon (another aide to Knox) said Knox himself wrote a warning to Kimmel that was not sent.[104] If so, the decision to withhold information and warnings from Kimmel and Short, made in the spring, was reconsidered, but left in place.

Stahlman's account helps explain otherwise puzzling events of December 6: the apparent inaction after receipt of the pilot message (especially the apparent failure to consider sending warnings to the Pacific commanders); Marshall's and Stark's memory lapses; and Stimson's and Knox's actions. It also helps explain Marshall's and Stark's seemingly bizarre actions on Sunday morning, after being told that Japan was likely to launch her attack in a few hours.

Still another unrecorded meeting may have taken place at the White House on Saturday evening. According to Dutch naval attaché Ranneft, Dutch Ambassador Loudon visited Roosevelt at about 10 p.m., and Roosevelt told him that he anticipated a Japanese attack on Monday.[105]

While no record has been found of a warning sent Saturday night, Hart, in the Philippines, reportedly did receive one and shared it with MacArthur's staff.[106] According to Brereton, on December 7 (December 6 Washington time), Purnell of Hart's staff told him, "It was only a question of days or perhaps hours until the shooting started."[107] MacArthur's chief of staff, Gen. Richard Sutherland, told Brereton the same.[108]

The fourteenth part of Japan's long message came in at midnight (or at 3:10 a.m., by another account). After concluding Japan's version of what transpired in the failed talks, it ended with:

> **The Japanese Government regrets to have to notify hereby the American Government that in view of the attitude of the American Government it cannot but consider that it is impossible to reach an agreement through further negotiations.[109]**

Intelligence workers took it to mean that, when presented to Hull, it would constitute notice that Japan was declaring war on the United States. It was followed at 3 a.m. or 4:37 a.m. by another intercepted message from Tokyo:

> **Re my #902. Will the Ambassador please submit to the United States Government (if possible to the Secretary of State) our reply to the United States at 1:00 p. m. on the 7th, your time.[110]**

Intelligence workers understood these instructions to mean that Japan would probably begin a surprise attack on the United States then. They noted that 1 p.m. in Washington was 7:30 a.m. in Hawaii — shortly after dawn — the most likely time for a surprise air attack.[111]

These messages were so strikingly important as to require that high officials be notified instantly. Marshall testified:

> When I [read] the 1 o'clock message . . . to my mind . . . action was needed as quickly as it could be managed, and I proceeded on that basis.[112]

Marshall's staff, however, contradicted him.

Kramer had been up part of the night delivering Saturday's messages. He was up early on Sunday delivering part fourteen and the 1 p.m. messages. Stark was in his office by 8:30 a.m., discussing the pilot and thirteen-part messages with Wilkinson and McCollum. At 9:00 a.m. Kramer arrived with the new ones. He said that he pointed out to them the significance of 1 p.m. being 7:30 a.m. in Hawaii.[113] And according to McCollum's testimony:

> the possible significance of the time of delivery was pointed out to all hands . . . that 1 p. m. Washington time would mean about 8 o'clock in the morning Honolulu time.[114]

Four hours remained until Pearl Harbor might be hit. McCollum said that he, Wilkinson, and Kramer advised Stark to send a warning to Kimmel, and Stark said, "No, I don't think any further warning is necessary."[115] Wilkinson then said, "Why don't you pick up the telephone and call Kimmel?" Stark picked up the phone as if to do so, but said, "I think I will call the President."[116] Later McCollum wrote:

> Admiral Stark understood right away, and he didn't seem to be much perturbed. Captain Wilkinson asked again, it was almost monotonous, whether the Pacific Fleet had been alerted. Admiral Stark said, yes, they had.[117]

The repeated questioning implies that Wilkinson and McCollum were not satisfied by Stark's answer. They were right not to believe that Kimmel had been alerted. But posing questions and making suggestions was as far as they went in pressing the head of the navy.

On phoning the White House, Stark was told Roosevelt was not taking calls. (By one account, Roosevelt was being treated for a sinus attack; by another, working on his stamp collection.) Stark did not tell whoever answered that the call was urgent enough for Roosevelt to be called immediately to the phone. After hanging up, Stark did nothing about the messages even though—according to McCollum—at 11 a.m., we asked again whether the Pacific Fleet had been warned, and I believe Captain Wilkinson suggested to Admiral Stark that he pick up the telephone and call Admiral Kimmel.[118]

And Noyes came in and added his urging.[119]

Meanwhile part fourteen of Japan's message was brought to Roosevelt at 10:00 a.m. According to the officer who gave it to him, Roosevelt took it calmly, saying, "It looks like the Japanese are going to break off the negotiations."[120] There is no indication that he spoke to anyone about it.

Bratton also was up early trying to inform Marshall about part fourteen and the 1 p.m. message, but Marshall was not in his office. At 9:00 a.m. Bratton phoned Marshall's home, and his orderly said Marshall was riding his horse. Bratton said he told the orderly:

Get assistance. Find General Marshall, ask him—tell him—who I am and tell him to go to the nearest telephone, that it is vitally important that I communicate with him at the earliest possible moment![121]

The orderly agreed to search for Marshall and convey the message. By one account, he searched along Marshall's riding trail, but failed to find him. By another, he did not try.[122] Marshall gave no explanation of his orderly's apparent failure to reach him for an hour and a half.

At 10:30 a.m. Marshall returned Bratton's call and stopped him from rushing to Marshall's home with the intercepts. Instead he said he would leave home and meet Bratton at the office.[123] That was a seven-minute trip, but it appeared to take Marshall almost an hour.

The riding story apparently was fabricated. That Sunday morning there was a flurry of action in the War Department, and evidently Marshall was part of it. According to Col. John Deane of Marshall's staff, during the period when Marshall returned Bratton's call—seemingly from home—he was in the War Department having "a series of conferences with staff officers from G-2 and the War Plans Division." According to Stimson's assistant, Maj. Eugene Harrison, "whoever said [Marshall] was out riding horses lied, because I saw and talked to him at that time." And reportedly navy personnel also saw Marshall during the time he and his orderly said he was riding.[124]

At 11:30 a.m. Marshall was in his office. Miles entered and found him reading the pilot and thirteen-part messages. Bratton then entered and said in effect, "General, I have a very important message here which I think you should see at once."[125] His effort to interrupt Marshall's time-consuming reading failed, according to Marshall, because "nobody could talk to me while I was reading it."[126] Among the above-mentioned memoirs done at Marshall's request, Miles's included:

> I found you alone in your office at about 11:25 a.m. We were joined by Colonel Bratton, who brought in the Japanese reply and the directive that [it] be given . . . at 1:00 p.m. that day. You then read *aloud* the Japanese reply, which was of considerable length. You then asked what Bratton and I thought should be done about it, or what it signified. We said that we believed . . . that some military action would be undertaken by the Japanese at [1 p.m.] . . . I urged that the Philippines, Hawaii [and other commands] be informed immediately . . . to be on the alert. You then picked up the telephone and got Admiral Stark . . . you put down the telephone and said that Admiral Stark did not think any further warnings necessary. . . . Colonel Bratton and I nevertheless urged that warnings be sent. You then wrote out the warning message. There was some discussion as to whether the Philippines should be included or not. . . . You again got Admiral Stark on the telephone and read the message to him . . . General Gerow and Col. Bundy arrived. You asked us in succession, beginning with me, what we thought the Japanese reply and timing meant. [All answered it meant a Japanese attack, and warnings should be sent.] There was a little discussion here as to whether [the warning Marshall wrote by hand] should go to General Gerow's office for typing first.[127] (Italics added.)

After writing the memoir, Miles also wrote a "Memorandum for the record" which included:

> *On the morning of December 7, 1941,* having received certain information that morning that the Japanese negotiations would definitely be broken at 1 p.m. that afternoon, and being convinced that this might well be timed with a planned Japanese attack somewhere, I went to the Chief of Staff's office and urged him to send a warning message to the overseas departments. While I was there General Gerow, Col. Bratton . . . and Col. Bundy came in. They fully concurred in the necessity for such a message.[128]

And Gerow's memo of the session included:

> about 11:30 a.m. . . . . General Marshall called me to his office. General Miles and Colonel Bratton were present. General Marshall referred to the fact that the Japanese Ambassador had been directed to deliver a note to the State Department at 1 p.m. . . . . He felt that the delivery of the note at an exact . . . time might have great significance.[129]

Thus, with a Japanese attack expected in ninety minutes — with time vital for warning the Pacific commands — Marshall took the extra time involved in reading the fourteen-part message out loud. Then he asked his staff what the 1 p.m. message meant. Then he called in more people. And after Gerow and Bundy arrived, he asked Miles and Bratton a second time what the message meant.

A key question is, why did Stark and Marshall resist urging by their staffs to send warnings and to send them immediately? Marshall's explanation before the naval court for his delay was:

> I read [the fourteen-part message] through, naturally carefully, and some parts of it *several times* to get the full significance of it. As I finished it I found . . . the 1:00 p.m. . . . . I spent quite a long time reading [the fourteen-part] thing. It is quite a remarkable document. Therefore I lost quite a lot of time reading that.[130] (Italics added.)

Similarly inadequate was his explanation to the army board. After giving the same description of his protracted reading of the fourteen-part message, he added:

> we didn't know what "one o'clock" meant . . . We still did not know what "one o'clock" meant . . . we had at that time no knowledge of just what "one o'clock" meant.[131]

But no one else present at the meeting expressed doubt about what 1 p.m. meant.

In summary, to mid-level and some high-level army and navy officers, the pilot and one o'clock messages called for immediate warnings to the Hawaiian commands, but not to Marshall and Stark.

If Bratton's and Miles's evidence is valid, Marshall knew about the pilot message the day before he read it and the fourteen-part message aloud in front of his staff. If so, on Sunday morning, he performed an elaborate, time-consuming act, which delayed sending a warning.

The main point buried in these details is that for the commands at Pearl Harbor and the Philippines to go on combat alert would have violated an overriding administration strategy.

Military procedure called for emergency dispatches to be sent by a variety of means simultaneously, to ensure both delivery and speed. The fastest means was to phone Short. Questioned sharply for not phoning him, Marshall gave two explanations. One was that safeguarding the secret of having broken Japan's diplomatic codes required a more secure conveyance than the telephone, because his dispatch included information obtained from diplomatic messages. It did contain such information, but it need not have. All he had to say was, "Go on combat alert." Alternatively, Marshall could have given Short a false source for the order — for example, "Chinese intelligence warns of a Japanese attack on U.S. territory. Go on full alert." (Great Britain routinely hid having broken German codes by giving false sources in dispatches to field commanders, as by citing an imaginary intelligence agent "Boniface.") Marshall, by choosing to send the warning by a secure conveyance, delayed the warning further. And by not classifying it "urgent," he delayed it still further.[132]

Marshall's other explanation for the delay seems more accurate. If Short went on combat alert, he would have violated the requirement that Japan commit the first overt act. Marshall testified that, "the Japanese would have grasped at most any straw to bring to . . . our public . . . that we were committing an act that forced action on their part."[133]

Lastly, the dispatch Marshall sent was hardly worth sending:

Japanese are presenting at one pm eastern standard time what amounts to an ultimatum also they are under orders to destroy their code machine immediately. Just what significance the hour set may have we do not know but be on the alert accordingly. Inform naval authorities of this communication.[134]

Asked if the dispatch was an alert, Marshall testified, "It was not a command message" except that it meant for Short to be alert.[135] And telling Short "what significance the hour set may have we do not know" was misleading. Given the history of dispatches ordering Short to take measures against sabotage, and of his going on alert against sabotage in response to the November 27 dispatch, if Short had received the December 7 dispatch before the attack, a reasonable expectation was that he would take additional measures against sabotage.

Meanwhile U.S. intelligence intercepted another Japanese diplomatic message: "Relations with the following countries are not in accordance with expectation: England, United States."[136] On the basis of earlier intercepts, intelligence officials interpreted it to mean Japan was about to attack Great Britain and the United States. According to a naval intelligence note, "the above . . . [was] furnished the *President* and other high officials at 1100 (EST) on December 7, 1941."[137] There is no indication that it prompted any action.

The simplest point is that, after the 1:00 p.m. message was brought to Stark's and Marshall's attention, there was still time to send warnings. But they delayed until too late. Their actions painted a consistent picture of delaying a warning to Pearl Harbor until too late.

What most disturbs people today is the idea that Roosevelt and other high officials expected the attack and did not warn Kimmel and Short—that they permitted the disaster. The idea strikes many as a betrayal of trust—as so Machiavellian and so repugnant that it is unthinkable. In the preface, I argued that people tend to put the history of their own country in an unrealistic, idealistic framework. Across the world, rulers have long permitted or ordered sacrifice of their own people and resources for military purposes. The practice has been common enough to define what is expected of rulers.

Despite the disasters suffered by the United States and Great Britain from Japan's attacks, some in both nations welcomed the news. Churchill wrote of receiving news about the Pearl Harbor attack:

> to have the United States at our side was to me the greatest joy . . . I knew the United States was in the war, up to the neck and in to the death. So we had won after all! . . . England would live . . . I went to bed and slept the sleep of the saved and thankful.[138]

He also wrote, "It was a blessing that Japan attacked the United States and thus brought America wholeheartedly into the war."[139]

Averell Harriman, U.S. Minister to England, and John Winant, U.S. Ambassador there, shared Churchill's view. On his own and Winant's reaction to news of the attack and destruction of the fleet, Harriman wrote:

> We all knew the grim future that it held, but at least there was a future now. We both had realized that the British could not win the war alone. On the Russian front there was still a question whether the Red Army would hold out. At least we could see a prospect of winning.[140]

According to Eleanor Roosevelt, after news of the Pearl Harbor attack, she "thought that in spite of his anxiety Franklin was . . . more serene than he had appeared in a long time."[141] In 1944 she said, "December 7th . . . to us . . . was far from the shock it proved to the country . . . We had expected something of the sort for a long time."[142]

Other associates also noted Franklin Roosevelt's serenity. (It ended several hours later when accusations against him over the disaster began.) Hopkins provided an explanation:

> I recall talking to the President many times in the past year, and it always disturbed him because he really thought that the tactics of the Japanese would be to avoid conflict with us; that they would not attack either the Philippines or Hawaii, but would move on Thailand, French Indo-China . . . China . . . the Malay Straits . . . Russia . . . This would have left the President with the very difficult problem of protecting our interests . . . Hence his great relief at the method that Japan used . . . In spite of the disaster at Pearl Harbour . . . it completely solidified the American people.[143]

Hopkins also noted that, after news of the Pearl Harbor attack, Roosevelt called in his War Council, and:

> The conference met in not too tense an atmosphere because . . . all of us believed that . . . the enemy was Hitler and that he could never be defeated without force of arms; that sooner or later we were bound to be in the war and that Japan had given us an opportunity.[144]

On hearing of the attack, Edgar Mowrer, a U.S. secret agent and friend of Knox's, who had brought a warning of it to Washington in November, was troubled, thinking, "Why had the President . . . Knox and Stimson and Hull . . . not known and taken the necessary precautions?" On reflection he wrote, "Nothing but *a direct attack could have brought the United States into the War!*"[145] An intelligence officer made the point in the most practical, Machiavellian terms: the destruction at Pearl Harbor "was a pretty cheap price to pay for unifying the country."[146] Reversing its position, the *Chicago Tribune* endorsed the war, as did many noninterventionists. A highly respected one, Senator Arthur Vandenberg, wrote, "That day ended isolationism for any realist."[147] And the America First Committee voted to disband.[148] Except for Nazis and a few other passionate enemies of Roosevelt, noninterventionists kept quiet or criticized him only in moderation. For to oppose the war now meant to risk being branded a subversive or traitor. The attack did solve Roosevelt's most urgent problem.

Although his plan worked, a gap remains. Roosevelt's main military strategy called for U.S. armed forces to be thrown into the Atlantic-European theater. Only after defeating Germany and Italy would they turn to defeating Japan. But the attacks on Pearl Harbor and other Pacific territories, in themselves, justified going to war only against Japan. Roosevelt had considered with his advisers whether an attack by Japan would suffice for a congressional declaration of war against Germany and Italy. Some of them thought so, but he seems to have been unconvinced. On December 8 he did not ask Congress for a war declaration against Germany and Italy. And without it, he could not have carried out the war plan. In short, after the Pearl Harbor attack he still had no way of openly going to war against Germany.

He had, however, received intelligence weeks earlier that, after Japan attacked, Germany would declare war on the United States, and he may have relied on it. After the attack he told his cabinet, "We have reason to believe that the Germans have told the Japanese that if Japan declares war they will too."[149] On the other hand, Hitler was known to be unreliable about honoring commitments; the intelligence that Germany would declare war on the United States did not provide full assurance.

Two obscure events help fill the gap. Although Japan and China had been at war since 1937, neither had declared war on the other. On December 8, 1941 Chiang declared war on Japan—and on Germany and Italy![150] No background is known for this declaration and, in itself, it served no Chinese interest. Ravaged by the Japanese invaders, China needed no more enemies. Given China's dependence on the United States, such a declaration without Roosevelt's agreement seems unlikely. Possibly Chiang's declaration against Germany was designed to provoke Hitler—a bit of insurance for Hitler to fulfill his commitment to declare war on the United States, completing the solution to Roosevelt's problem.

On that same December 8, Japan had not yet attacked the Dutch East Indies. Nonetheless, that territory declared war on Japan and on Germany.[151] Unlike China, she had no substantial army—no real defense—and when Japan then attacked, the Dutch East Indies were quickly overrun and suffered heavily. Dutch people in Holland were already conquered and helpless in the hands of their German masters. Given Hitler's record of vengefulness, the declaration of war against Germany also put them at risk. The declaration against Japan and Germany, in itself, served no Dutch interest. Again, background for the declaration is unknown. Perhaps it was done to provoke Hitler. The simultaneous declarations of war on Germany by the Chinese and Dutch suggest a prior agreement.

Hart's understanding of what Washington wanted was for him "to await the blow" while taking measures to minimize harm from it. His understanding provides a framework by which otherwise puzzling actions make sense: top officials acting as if no attack was coming, sending no warning to Short and Kimmel after the pilot message came in, and delaying until too late a warning to them after the 1:00 p.m. message came in. Waiting for Japan to strike the first blow was the tactic by which the United States openly entered the war to defeat Hitler and save much of the world.

When Roosevelt took office, his nation's most pressing problem was the Great Depression, and he devoted himself to solving it, even though he was an internationalist at heart. His greatest ambition was to prevent aggression across the world but, at first, all he did was staff the State Department and diplomatic service with like-minded people. In 1933 he was the only leader of a major nation to grasp Hitler's destructive inclinations, to take them seriously, and to lay plans for stopping him. The threat that Roosevelt confronted was graver than the one Lincoln confronted.

Over the years, Japan's aggression in Manchuria and China, Italy's in Ethiopia, and Germany's in Europe moved Roosevelt in halting steps to intervention. Developments in Europe during 1940 and 1941 resulted in the strategy and concrete measures that led to Pearl Harbor. Because of strident domestic opposition to his moves against Hitler, because of his penchant for deception, and because he distrusted the American people and Congress, he posed as a peacemaker, and left only limited records of his war plans. His plans are, however, clear enough in records of the State, War, and Navy Departments.

Because of the attacks on his administration that began on December 7, 1941 and of the need to unify the nation for an enormous war, he took a position on December 8 that hid what he and his chief advisers had planned. He especially hid that they had known of Japan's coming attack on Pearl Harbor.

As warnings of the coming attack came to light after the war, most scholars explained the failure to warn Kimmel and Short by assuming that Roosevelt's subordinates had made a series of blunders. Roosevelt's defense demeaned himself and his subordinates. It hid their anticipation of Japan's likely moves in 1941. And it denied their outstanding foresight in anticipating Hitler's moves and the plans they made and carried out to stop him. A couple of scholars have speculated that, if Roosevelt had lived through the war, he would have cleared the record and those victimized by it. We will never know. As he left the record, it diminished his efforts to prevent destruction of civilization and to advance the painfully slow civilizing process.

HISTORY AND THE UNTHINKABLE

All hidden things the endless flowing years
Bring forth, and bury that which all men know. . . .
And none may say "It cannot happen here."

—Sophocles

Horror about the Holocaust fostered massive denial; even to-day, some people passionately insist it did not happen and advance complex technical proofs that it could not possibly have happened. The denial moved philosopher Karl Jaspers to write:

> That which has happened is a warning . . . It must be continu-ally remembered. It was possible to happen, and it remains possible for it to happen again at any minute. Only in knowl-edge can it be prevented.[1]

Within the next few decades, additional holocausts happened in Cam-bodia, Rwanda, Yugoslavia, and elsewhere.

Pearl Harbor provides a less urgent lesson. The disaster there needs to be remembered, not for anything about Japanese treachery or U.S. blunders. Its main lessons are about sacrifice, deception, and political considerations as common features of military planning.

Events are poorly explained by making assumptions that crucial acts by competent, conscientious leaders were capricious, careless, or neg-ligent. And U.S. leaders who figured in the Pearl Harbor disaster were highly competent and conscientious. Major historical events are better understood on the basis of strong trends and established policies. To step back from the details, the disaster of Pearl Harbor resulted from the colli-sion of an overriding Japanese policy with an overriding U.S. policy. Those policies make sense of decisions made and measures taken in Tokyo and Washington during the second half of 1941. Without assigning a determining role to the policies, the decisions and measures make little sense.

Herbert Feis, a scholar who served in Roosevelt's administration, later wrote:

> **Of all the accusations made, the most shocking to me is that Roosevelt and his chief advisers deliberately left the Pacific Fleet and base at Pearl Harbor exposed as a lure to bring about a direct Japanese attack upon us.[2]**

He rejected the idea because of "the sense of duty and regard for human life of President Roosevelt and his chief advisers" and because to believe it "is to believe that [they] were given to deep deception." Others rejected the idea more vehemently.

After Roosevelt stationed the fleet at Pearl Harbor, Commander McCollum wrote a memo for him, recommending its use as a lure. Roosevelt implemented the recommendation. Admiral Richardson concluded that administration use of the fleet endangered it gravely, and he argued the point over and over with his superiors. When he took measures to protect his fleet, Roosevelt relieved him. Stark then kept Kimmel uninformed of Japan's plans to attack it at Pearl Harbor. And Marshall kept Short uninformed of them.

To most Americans, manipulating one's nation into war is something done by foreign tyrants — not our own leaders. Since 1942 U.S. history has been distorted by the idea that presidents simply do not do what Roosevelt's enemies said he did.

That Roosevelt and his advisers had a high sense of duty and regard for human life is true. In my judgment, it was higher than in many administrations. But that is irrelevant here. Throughout history, rulers have deceptively ordered sacrifice in making war. Across the world government acts considered unthinkable — in the sense of repugnant — have happened over and over. The idea that certain acts are unthinkable — and therefore could not have happened — reflects how repugnant people find them. Rulers with a high sense of duty and regard for life, as well as other rulers, have deceptively ordered sacrifice, and U.S. history is no exception to the use of lures.

On becoming president in 1845, James Polk told his cabinet that California would be annexed. (His predecessors had offered to buy California, but Mexico had refused to sell.) To his consul in California, Polk suggested fomenting a revolution and promised U.S. support for residents who rose against Mexico. A tiny uprising under Capt. John Fremont had no effect on California's status. Polk then sent an army to the Rio Grande.[3]

History books describe that area as U.S. territory, Texas territory, or land in dispute between the United States and Mexico. The area was, however, recognized by a U.S. treaty as within Mexico's borders. As Polk expected, Mexico attacked the army, slaughtering a troop.

On sending the army, Polk wrote, in advance, a request to Congress for a declaration of war based on the incident he expected. After it happened, he submitted his request, claiming that Mexican troops "had passed the boundary of the United States . . . invaded our territory and shed American blood upon American soil. . . . War exists notwithstanding all our efforts to avoid it."[4] But Polk, not Mexico, had sought the war. Congress then declared war on Mexico, and by an easy victory, Polk acquired the southwest for his nation.

Before the incident, Congress had opposed war with Mexico. If known at the time, Polk's manipulation could have provided strong ammunition to his opponents. After it became known, however, Polk's stature among historians grew. He is now viewed as an exceptional president because he knew clearly what he meant to accomplish in office and carried it out effectively.

On becoming president in 1861, Abraham Lincoln's highest priority was preserving the Union. To end the secession, he was willing to guarantee federal noninterference with slavery. He therefore pushed a constitutional amendment for noninterference through Congress, and three states quickly ratified it, but the secession continued. Lincoln was also willing—if necessary for preserving the Union—to fight a war. But he found his nation—and his own cabinet—against such a war. Even radical abolitionists opposed it.

The Confederacy had taken over most federal installations in its states—installations surrendered on request by their administrators. Of those remaining in federal hands, Fort Sumter in South Carolina was exposed to attack and running out of supplies. Lincoln asked his cabinet's advice on whether to supply the fort. With one exception, they opposed it because doing it risked war. Lincoln then sent the supplies, prompting an attack on the fort, which became the incident he used to start the Civil War.[5]

If known at the time, Lincoln's deliberate exposure of the fort might have caused serious political repercussions. Later historical accounts that imputed to him the intention of fostering an incident for war in order to preserve the Union have created little stir. His towering place in history is undamaged by them and he, too, is viewed as a president with a clear idea of his mission, effective in carrying it out.

In 1898, while he was considering war with Spain, William McKinley sent the battleship *Maine* into Havana harbor, which was

Spanish territory. She exploded and sank, with the loss of 260 sailors — most of her crew. The explosion's cause was unknown. Nonetheless, Assistant Navy Secretary Theodore Roosevelt declared, "The *Maine* was sunk by an act of dirty treachery on the part of the Spaniards."[6] "Remember the *Maine!*" became a battle cry as the incident was used to arouse the public for war.[7]

Aware of her military weakness, Spain's government had made conciliatory responses to insults and complied substantially with increasing U.S. demands. The United States coerced Spain into the war, which followed weeks after the *Maine* exploded. By an easy victory, the United States won control in the Caribbean and acquired the Philippines and Hawaii.

Polk, Lincoln, and McKinley confronted dilemmas between what they considered important U.S. interests and popular opposition to war. Lincoln's problem was extreme; for years, conflict over slavery had been tearing the nation apart. As Lincoln saw it, the secession and the likelihood of further splitting threatened the nation's existence. "However, there was one way out," according to historian Richard Hofstadter, "the Confederates themselves might bring matters to a head by attacking Sumter. . . . It was precisely such an attack that Lincoln's strategy brought about."[8] Hofstadter added that "the Japanese attack on Pearl Harbor did for [Roosevelt] what the Confederate attack on Fort Sumter had done for Lincoln."[9]

Even when Roosevelt's actions prior to Pearl Harbor are placed in the context of history, troubling questions remain. The most disturbing is: If Roosevelt did know an attack on Pearl Harbor was coming, why did he not allow an adequate warning to be sent to Short and Kimmel? Lacking direct evidence of his thinking, further inferences will be offered.

Washington had received more than enough intelligence by November 25 to make clear that the fleet at Pearl Harbor was a likely target. Still more came in between November 26 and December 7. The intelligence was withheld from Short and Kimmel, while they were told Japan was expected to attack other U.S. territories, not Hawaii. These are simple facts. Why Washington withheld the intelligence is complex.

If Roosevelt wanted Short and Kimmel to await an attack passively, while limiting the damage from it, why not tell them that? Or, why not order the Pacific Fleet out of Hawaii? Pacific commanders did get hints of what Washington wanted. Hart, commanding the Asiatic Fleet, got the most hints, understood what was wanted, and acted accordingly, saving most of his ships. MacArthur also received hints, but was confused. He failed to take action, and consequently lost his air corps. Short and Kimmel got the fewest hints and did not understand what was expected of them.

Intercepted Japanese espionage messages suggested to U.S. intelligence that Japan would carry out her planned attack only if the defenders were unprepared for it and if a large part of the Pacific Fleet—including capital ships—was in harbor. Short and Kimmel could have been instructed to go on alert against an air attack, while disguising the alert from observers. But Japanese agents in Hawaii might have seen through the deception, jeopardizing crucial administration strategy. And such an order would have been evidence that Roosevelt anticipated the attack on Pearl Harbor. It could have provided the strongest ammunition for his enemies—grounds for impeachment proceedings. An alternative was to deceive Short and Kimmel, mainly by withholding crucial information from them.

Deception is as old as the history of war. According to the classic work *The Art of War* by Sun-tzu, "All warfare is based on deception."[10] It is, of course, practiced on enemies, but deception is also used on subordinates. A common example is a suicide attack. In order to have troops carry it out, officers may hide the attack's hopelessness from them. They may even mislead troops to believe it will succeed.

A case in point involves MacArthur's defense of the Philippines. Despite public statements by U.S. leaders to the contrary, the Philippines had little value in itself to the administration. Despite vague assurances, protection of the islands against a Japanese invasion had never been a U.S. priority. Despite reconsideration from time to time, that policy remained in force. MacArthur's intelligence chief, General Willoughby later wrote:

> [In] the spring of 1941, secret British-American diplomatic understandings had relegated the Philippines to a secondary theater—a potential doom in the event of war with Japan. This was not known by MacArthur.[11]

In 1940 Navy Secretary Knox told a reporter, "As long as those [Philippine] territories fly the American flag, the Navy is ready to defend them."[12] But the navy had not been ready, and military planners had omitted defense of the Philippines from war plans. The decision in July 1941 to arm the Philippines seemed to change this policy, but did not. Washington's plan was still to abandon the Philippines after a limited defense.

MacArthur had assumed responsibility to defend the Philippines successfully—an impossible task in the circumstances. He failed to grasp what was essential among conflicting data. During the weeks before Japan's invasion, he alternated between two illusions: Japan would not attack the Philippines; and, if she did, he would defend it successfully. On December 4 he told his chief of staff, "They [Washington] are going to give us everything we have asked for."[13] A reporter who saw him that day said, "He looked completely sure of himself. He looked like a man who couldn't lose."[14] The next day he told British Admiral Tom Philips that the Philippine islands were secure because Japan could not mount an air attack on them.[15] But he got little of the reinforcement for which he had asked. (More realistically, one of MacArthur's air commanders told his pilots to write out their wills and deposit them in squadron safes, adding, "You are not necessarily a suicide squadron, but you are Goddamn near it!"[16]) Unprepared mentally for the coming attack, MacArthur failed to take effective action.

Many Americans were misled about administration intentions in the Philippines, including at least one cabinet member. Frances Perkins later described a cabinet meeting on December 5, 1941. After discussion of possible Japanese targets, Stimson said:

> "The plan for the Philippines is absolutely letter perfect. The Philippines are indefensible. We have always known it . . ." As Stimson had explained, the plan was to abandon them. I had thus learned with horror from the Secretary of War that the U.S. Army had never expected to defend the islands.[17]

On the morning of December 8 (December 7, Washington time), after learning of the attack on Pearl Harbor — after knowing war with Japan had begun — General Brereton repeatedly urged MacArthur to authorize a preemptive strike against airfields in Taiwan, from which bombers were expected to attack the Philippines. MacArthur delayed and delayed.[18] During the hours remaining before Japan's invasion, he apparently clung to his belief that Japan would not invade the Philippines, and continued to do so even after small-scale attacks on the Philippines began.

Washington's deception of MacArthur continued after the attack began. Marshall informed him that he would be sent all possible aid, but it was not sent.[19] MacArthur pleaded with Marshall to rush equipment and troops to the Philippines. He tried to convince Washington that defense of the Philippines was more important than war in the Atlantic-European theater. His pleas were most unrealistic, but Marshall encouraged him, for the administration wanted the hopeless defense of the Philippines prolonged. On December 13 MacArthur radioed Marshall, "Every resource of the Allies should be converged here immediately. The Philippine theatre is the locus of victory or defeat and I urge a strategic review of the entire situation lest a fatal mistake be made."[20] He pleaded for reinforcement again on December 14.

Despite a decision in Washington to send only enough aid to delay surrender of the Philippines, Marshall radioed MacArthur on December 15:

> Your messages of December thirteenth and fourteenth have been studied by the president. The strategic importance of the Philippines is fully recognized and there has been and will be no wavering in the determination to support you . . . as recommended in yours of December fourteenth bomber and pursuit reinforcements are to be rushed to you.[21]

Later the same day Roosevelt met with Stimson, Knox, Marshall, and Stark, and renewed the policy of minimal support for MacArthur.[22] He was not to get the planes, but Washington withheld that from him.

On January 3, 1942, General Gerow completed an army analysis and recommended "operations for the relief of the Philippines not be undertaken."[23] On the same day Marshall radioed MacArthur:

> There is keen appreciation here of your situation. The president and prime minister [Churchill], Colonel Stimson and Colonel Knox, the British chiefs of staff and our corresponding officials have been surveying every possibility looking toward the development of strength in the Far East so as to break the enemy's hold on the Philippines.[24]

The message went on about supplies intended for MacArthur, who then told his commanders, "Help is on the way from the United States, thousands of troops and hundred of planes are being dispatched . . . It is imperative that our troops hold until these reinforcements arrive."[25] The troops and planes were not being dispatched.

Days later MacArthur was told by a newly arrived officer that plans in Washington had not included an effective defense of the Philippines.[26] MacArthur then said, "Never before in history has so gallant an army been 'written off' so callously."[27] Gen. Courtney Whitney, who later served under MacArthur, wrote, "The administration subjected him and his men to one of the cruelest deceptions of the war. Not only were no large reinforcements sent to the Philippines . . . the administration *never intended to send them and concealed the fact*."[28]

Asked by the congressional committee if the War Department should transmit "very important information" to commanders in the field, Marshall answered, "Not necessarily."[29] Apparently shocked, the questioner pressed Marshall, and he equivocated. The questioner then asked specifically if Kimmel and Short should have been informed about the bomb-plot messages — the intelligence obtained by the committee indicating a likely air attack on Pearl Harbor — and Marshall answered, "I am not at all certain as to that, sir."[30] Later he testified:

> when we put out any operation *almost invariably* we are involved in restricting the knowledge of the operation to a very few people. We have to do that *practically every time*. That is always an embarrassment to the officers that are carrying out the operation. . . . It would be a simpler thing . . . if everyone knew exactly what was planned, but *in almost all* . . . *cases* it is not a practical procedure or else you will certainly leak information.[31] (Italics added.)

Withholding information fosters mistaken beliefs — beliefs on which subordinates may act. That possibility calls for consideration when making a decision to withhold critical information. A leader who makes such a decision assumes — logically, at least — responsibility for the consequences of mistaken beliefs that result. The Army Pearl Harbor Board emphasized:

> Under the circumstances where . . . information cannot be disclosed . . . to . . . field commanders, it is incumbent upon the War Department then to assume responsibility for *specific directions* to the theatre commanders. . . . Short got neither form of assistance from the War Department.[32] (Italics added.)

Such responsibility is ordinarily necessary for the success of military operations. My impression, however, is that when withholding of information contributes to military disasters, leaders usually do not acknowledge their responsibility. Their subordinates take the blame.

Intelligence Chief Miles testified to the congressional committee that U.S. military leaders believed Japan would carry out the Pearl Harbor attack if — and only if — they found "that fortress and that fleet unprepared to meet the attack."[33] Representative Bayard Clark then questioned Miles:

> Clark: Do you mean unprepared or unalerted?
> Miles: I mean both, sir.
> Clark: Well, cannot a command be prepared even if it is unalerted?
> Miles: Not if they were unalerted, sir . . . Are you speaking, sir,

of the military weapons and the means available or of the
personnel that handle those things? No gun will go off unless
the man pulls the trigger, and if the man who is supposed to
pull the trigger is not prepared to pull the trigger then that
gun is unprepared.[34]

Miles's point was that, whether or not troops in Hawaii expected an
air attack was crucial. If they did not expect it, they would fail to meet
it effectively. And only if they appeared not to expect it, would Japan
carry it out.

Japanese agents repeatedly informed Tokyo that army and navy
forces in Hawaii were unprepared—specifically, that barrage balloons
were not in use, air reconnaissance was not being conducted, ships in
harbor lacked antitorpedo nets, and troops were still following a peacetime routine of shore leaves on weekends. Officers in Washington read
those reports.

According to Marshall and Stark, in phrasing the November 27
dispatches to Short and Kimmel, a major question was whether or not
to issue a final alert. None of the dispatches sent to them were final
alerts. There is evidence that during the night of December 6 after the
pilot message came in, a final alert was considered at a White House
meeting, and Knox drafted one to Kimmel, but it was not sent. The
next morning—Sunday, December 7—Marshall's and Stark's staffs
pressed them repeatedly to issue a final alert. Stark refused and
Marshall delayed. And the warning Marshall then sent—even if it had
arrived in time—was still not a final alert.

As a result, the army and navy in Hawaii were unprepared for
the attack. During Saturday, December 6, and the hours of Sunday
before the attack, ship crews were partly ashore. Warships were
bunched closely in the harbor, limiting crews' range of vision in aim-
ing antiaircraft guns and their ability to fire at attacking planes without hitting ships moored next to them. Army antiaircraft guns were
not manned, nor did they have shells at hand. Army fighter planes
were not ready to take off, and pilots were not at hand to fly them. No
barrage balloons were up and no preparations to send them up had
been made. And only rather limited patrols around Hawaii were being carried out.

In theory Kimmel and Short could have gone on a disguised alert
for an air attack. Navy crews could have gone ashore openly and then
slipped back on board and hidden below deck. Instead of being in
barracks or in town, army pilots could have hidden in hangars near
their planes. Shells could have been hidden near antiaircraft guns, and
crews dressed as civilians could have been near the guns.

Such measures were, however, likely to be self-defeating. Japanese spies known to be observing Pearl Harbor could have noticed these activities and reported them to Tokyo. And with thousands of sailors and soldiers involved in the deception, discovery of the strategy after the attack — with disastrous political repercussions — was to be expected. Instead of risking failure of the first-strike policy, failure to deceive Japan, and political disaster at home, officials in Washington could have made a decision not to warn the Hawaiian commands, thereby insuring that, to Japanese spies in Hawaii, U.S. forces would appear unprepared. The data presented, the inferences drawn from it, and the possibilities listed may be all we will ever have on the most disturbing question about Pearl Harbor.

In the Pearl Harbor attack, the United States lost twenty-four hundred troops along with a quarter of her fleet. Many military leaders and Knox, Hull, and Roosevelt had underestimated the harm Japan could do, even by a surprise attack. And U.S. losses were much increased by two unlikely events. A Japanese bomb penetrated the battleship *Arizona*'s armor at an odd angle, reaching her magazine and causing her to explode. And the torpedoed battleship *Oklahoma* capsized. The explosion of the *Arizona* and capsizing of the *Oklahoma* resulted in the drowning of sixteen hundred sailors.

Although far greater than expected, the loss of life at Pearl Harbor was far less than the sacrifice in the Philippines, where about forty-five thousand troops were killed, wounded, and captured, and a million or more civilians were killed. And it was less than sacrifices in other parts of the war and less than sacrifices in other wars.

Whether intentionally or not, Roosevelt exposed the fleet to a Japanese attack by stationing it in Hawaii. Then he intentionally used naval units as lures by ordering them on various expeditions in the Pacific. Withholding key information from Kimmel and Short increased the fleet's exposure greatly and it was most glaringly increased by not sending a warning on December 6, 1941.

Despite the history of war, the idea that Roosevelt withheld warnings from Kimmel and Short for the purpose of getting the United States openly into the European war is still unthinkable to many people, but to fewer and fewer as the years pass. As has happened over time with other unthinkable acts, the repugnance aroused by the idea of using the Pacific Fleet as a lure will probably continue to fade. Polk's exposure of an army, Lincoln's exposure of a fort, and McKinley's exposure of a battleship are more or less accepted. In the Philippines, Midway, Wake, Guam, Samoa, and in other outlying islands, U.S. forces were exposed to Japanese attack, and that is also more or less accepted.

The Pearl Harbor disaster was different from losses of the Philippines and other Pacific islands because it shattered America's confidence, arousing massive fear, a crisis of trust in the nation's leaders, and an outcry for scapegoats. The nation seized on the administration's explanation of betrayal by Japan and by Kimmel and Short, and the disaster unified the nation to fight World War II with the slogan "Remember Pearl Harbor!" The explanation became a major national myth, which has substantially withstood the unearthing of secret alliances, war strategies, and warnings received in Washington.

NOTES

ABBREVIATIONS

FRUS   Department of State, *Papers Relating to the Foreign Relations of the United States, Japan 1931–1941.*

NA-FDR   National Archives, Franklin Roosevelt Library, Hyde Park, NY.

NA-MD   National Archives, College Park, MD, in which RG means Record Group, RIP means Radio Intelligence Publications, and SRH means Special Research History.

PHA   Joint Congressional Committee on the Investigation of the Pearl Harbor Attack, *Pearl Harbor Attack*. Referenced by volume and page number.

PREFACE

1. *PHA* 11:5433.
2. Costello, *Days of Infamy*, 355; Prange, *Pearl Harbor*, 62, 64.
3. Lewin, *Other Ultra*, 50.
4. Brandenburg, "Otto Bismarck," 669, 661.
5. Burns, *Roosevelt: Lion and Fox*, vii, 472.
6. Andrew and Gordievsky, *KGB*, 287–89.

CHAPTER 1: BIRTH OF A MYTH

1. Prange, *At Dawn We Slept*, 582.
2. Aster, "Guilty Men," 235.
3. While they preferred to be called "noninterventionists," those who favored intervention called them "isolationists"—a pejorative term implying that they were selfish and shortsighted. Many noninterventionists wanted war with Japan, however, and were not really advocates of an isolated or pacifist position.
4. Mintz, *Revisionism and Pearl Harbor*, 10.
5. Garlinski, *Enigma War*, 121.
6. Prados, *Combined Fleet Decoded*, 33–34; Young, "Racial Attitudes," 178, 180; Whitcomb, *Escape from Corregidor*, 12, 16; Wilford, *Pearl Harbor Redefined*, 114; *PHA* 14:1355.
7. Hough, *Mountbatten*, after page 276; Wohlstetter, *Pearl Harbor*, 337; Falk, *Seventy Days to Singapore*, 29.
8. Hoehling, *Week Before Pearl Harbour*, 127; *PHA* 6:2751, 14:1064; H. Russell, *Pearl Harbor Story*, 156.
9. Weintraub, *Long Day's Journey*, 104–5; Falk, *Seventy Days to Singapore*, 9–10, 44, 55–58; Gray, *Operation Pacific*, 19–20.
10. Collier, *Road to Pearl Harbor*, 216.
11. Weintraub, *Long Day's Journey*, 105.

12. Lowe, *Origins of Pacific War*, 277.
13. Ibid., 280.
14. Ibid.
15. Herzstein, *Roosevelt and Hitler*, 177–78.
16. *PHA* 40:441.
17. Goodwin, *No Ordinary Time*, 292–93.
18. Connally, *My Name*, 248–49.
19. McJimsey, *Harry Hopkins*, 209; Welles, *Time for Decision*, 295–96.
20. Falk, *Seventy Days to Singapore*, 9, 10, 44; Collier, *Road to Pearl Harbor*, 214–15.
21. Burns, *Roosevelt: Soldier of Freedom*, 165–67.
22. Badsey, *Pearl Harbor*, 13–14; *PHA* 2:875–77; Grenfell, *Main Fleet to Singapore*, 107; Dorwart, *Conflict of Duty*, 128.
23. Sherwood, *Roosevelt and Hopkins*, 437; Beard, *Roosevelt and War*, 211.
24. Beard, *Roosevelt and War*, 211–12.
25. Ibid., 210.
26. H. Russell, *Pearl Harbor Story*, 133.
27. *PHA* 4:1708.
28. *PHA* 35:652–53. See also *PHA* 20:4528–36; R. Lee, *London Observer*, 453; C. Lee, *They Call It Pacific*, 1–3.
29. *PHA* 2:434, 11:5421.
30. *PHA* 2:434.
31. *PHA* 7:3295.
32. Gannon, *Pearl Harbor Betrayed*, 17–18.
33. *Congressional Record* 104:8147.
34. *PHA* 39:299, 319.
35. Farley, *Jim Farley's Story*, 345.
36. Hull, *Memoirs of Cordell Hull*, 987.

CHAPTER 2:
ESTABLISHING THE MYTH

1. Prange, *At Dawn We Slept*, 584.
2. *PHA* 5:2338; 8:3815, 3823.
3. Prange, *At Dawn We Slept*, 586.
4. *PHA* 7:3360; Beatty, "Background of Secret Report," 1263.
5. *PHA* 5:2338, 2344.
6. See chap. 14.
7. Layton, *And I Was There*, 335; Prange, *At Dawn We Slept*, 588.
8. See chap. 14.
9. *PHA* 8:3824; Beatty, "Background of Secret Report," 1264.
10. Prange, *At Dawn We Slept*, 588–89.
11. Ibid., 594.
12. Ibid., 595.
13. *PHA* 22:1; Costello, *Days of Infamy*, 253.
14. See chaps. 6 and 14.
15. Toland, *Infamy*, 1st ed., 30, 188; Costello, *Days of Infamy*, 253.
16. Toland, *Infamy*, 1st ed., 30, 32, 33, 36, 321.
17. *PHA* 23:1075–76.
18. See chap. 5.
19. Layton, *And I Was There*, 352.
20. *PHA* 5:2229, 2236.
21. Beck, *MacArthur and Wainwright*, 13; Rovere and Schlesinger, *MacArthur Controversy*, 49; Arnold, *Global Mission*, 271–72.
22. Whitcomb, *Escape from Corregidor*, 20–23.
23. Morison, *Two-Ocean War*, 77; Bartsch, *December 8, 1941*, 423.
24. Dolan, *Philippines*, 41.
25. Kenney, *MacArthur I Know*, 79; Hersey, *Men in Bataan*, i, 3–6.
26. Tolley, *Cruise of the Lanikai*, 26.
27. Ibid., 36; Bartsch, *December 8, 1941*, 190; *PHA* 12:182.
28. Watson, *Chief of Staff*, 451; Bartsch, *December 8, 1941*, 190.
29. Hunt, *Untold Story*, 151–52.
30. Iriye, *Across the Pacific*, 107.
31. Watson, *Chief of Staff*, 414–15; Wheeler, *Prelude to Pearl Harbor*, 5, 12ff., 79ff., 190–91; Pelz, *Race to Pearl Harbor*, 198; E. Miller, *War Plan Orange*, 55–61.
32. Wheeler, *Prelude to Pearl Harbor*, 87.
33. Rovere and Schlesinger, *MacArthur Controversy*, 44.
34. Ibid.
35. Dolan, *Philippines*, 39.
36. Quezon, *Good Fight*, 153–54.
37. Morton, *Fall of the Philippines*, 11.
38. Beck, *MacArthur and Wainwright*, 1. See also Muggah, *MacArthur Story*, 40.

39. Quezon, *Good Fight*, 178–80.
40. See chaps. 9, 11, and 13.
41. *FRUS*, 549–50.
42. Quezon, *Good Fight*, 185.
43. Hunt, *Untold Story*, 252.
44. Abaya, *Betrayal in the Philippines*, 22.
45. Ibid., 24–25.
46. Prange, *At Dawn We Slept*, 593–95.
47. *PHA* 39:19–21.

CHAPTER 3: WARNINGS OF THE PEARL HARBOR ATTACK

1. *PHA* 7:3278.
2. *PHA* 4:1754. See also *PHA* 2:818–19, 32:562.
3. *PHA* 12:254ff.; Documents of November 20, 1941, November 28, 1941, and December 1, 1941, RG 38, folders 58 and 62, NA-MD.
4. Morison, *Rising Sun*, 141.
5. Rauch, *Roosevelt*, 433.
6. *PHA* 2:898.
7. Layton, *And I Was There*, 93, 206; Haslach, *Nishi no Kaze, Hare*, 172ff.; Hinsley, *British Intelligence*, 53; Myron Smith, *Pearl Harbor*, 57; Rusbridger and Nave, *Betrayal at Pearl Harbor*, 147, 174–76.
8. *PHA* 4:1727, 1794; *PHA* 9:4562; *PHA* 27:55; Wohlstetter, *Pearl Harbor*, 281, 314.
9. *PHA* 4:1795; *PHA* 32:179; Aldrich, *Intelligence and the War*, 95; Alsop and Braden, *Sub Rosa*, 14; Leahy, *I Was There*, 15–18; Long, *War Diary*, 63; Murphy, *Diplomat Among Warriors*, 70; Dorwart, "Roosevelt-Astor Espionage Ring," 311–14; Corson, *Armies of Ignorance*, 94.
10. Andrew, *President's Eyes*, 83, 92; *PHA* 27:55–56.
11. *PHA* 9:4370; 27:56; 31:3217ff.
12. Brown, *Last Hero*, 159–65, 170–73; Aldrich, *Intelligence and the War*, 101; Andrew, *President's Eyes*, 85; Persico, *Roosevelt's Secret War*, 111; Casey, *Secret War Against Hitler*, 7.
13. *PHA* 8:3561; *PHA* 3:1124.
14. Wohlstetter, *Pearl Harbor*, 1.
15. Ibid., 387.
16. *PHA* 2:784, 789, 817; 8:3383; 29:2355; 36:13–14. See also chap. 14.
17. Wohlstetter, *Pearl Harbor*, 392. See also p. 56.
18. *PHA* 39:77. See also *PHA* 4:1963.
19. Farago, *Broken Seal*, 124; *PHA* 4:1962–63.
20. Farago, *Broken Seal*, 127.
21. *PHA* 2:821–22, 866–67; *PHA* 3:1218; E. Miller, *War Plan Orange*, 14, 16.
22. Pogue, *Marshall: Ordeal and Hope*, 172.
23. *PHA* 5:2136; Potter, *Yamamoto*, 69–70.
24. *PHA* 4:1986; 5:2213; 9:4235; 26:273; 32:605.
25. *PHA* 34:57. See also *PHA* 2:819, 837–38, 921; Watson, *Chief of Staff*, 99, 467, 500.
26. *PHA* 34:18.
27. Gannon, *Pearl Harbor Betrayed*, 38.
28. Prange, *At Dawn We Slept*, 16ff., 28–30; Goldstein and Dillon, *Pearl Harbor Papers*, 147; *PHA* 13:707.
29. *PHA* 14:1042; Van Der Rhoer, *Deadly Magic*, 57; Grew, *Ten Years in Japan*, 368.
30. Toland, *Infamy*, 1st ed., 261.
31. *PHA* 31:3217.
32. Popov, *Spy/Counter-Spy*, 148, 155ff., 169; Persico, *Roosevelt's Secret War*, 139.
33. Montagu, *Beyond Top Secret*, 74–75; West, *Thread of Deceit*, 75ff.; Gentry, *J. Edgar Hoover*, 269–73; Riebling, *Wedge*, 19–30, 472–76.
34. Stevenson, *Man Called Intrepid*, 258–60; FBI "Memorandum[s] for Mr. Ladd," October 20, 1941, October 31, 1941, and November 8, 1941.
35. Farago, *Burn After Reading*, 173; Meissner, *Man with Three Faces*, 218.
36. Toland, *Infamy*, 1st ed., 260–61; R. Thompson, *Time for War*, 309, 370–71.
37. *PHA* 30:2861; RG 59, reel 6, NA-MD.
38. Toland, *Infamy*, 2nd ed., 349–50; Costello, *Days of Infamy*, 356–57.
39. Gannon, *Pearl Harbor Betrayed*, 182–83; Prange, *Pearl Harbor*, 53–54.

40. Weintraub, *Long Day's Journey*, 670; Gannon, *Pearl Harbor Betrayed*, 182–83; Prange, *Pearl Harbor*, 53–54.

41. Willey, *Pearl Harbor*, 344–45.

42. Goldstein and Dillon, *Pearl Harbor Papers*, viii. See also Willey, *Pearl Harbor*, 349.

43. Goldstein and Dillon, *Pearl Harbor Papers*, 225, 243.

44. Hoehling, *Week before Pearl Harbour*, 59; *PHA* 4:1879–80; 8:3395; 9:3949, 4169–70; 36:303–4.

45. *PHA* 37:1084–87.

46. *PHA* 33:850.

47. Layton, *And I Was There*, 283–84.

48. Albright, *Pearl Harbor*, 98; Farago, *Broken Seal*, 230–32.

49. *PHA* 2:795; Farago, *Broken Seal*, 230.

50. *PHA* 2:888; 12:1–316, see especially 261–63.

51. *PHA* 9:4381. See also *PHA* 16:2290; Whitehead, *FBI Story*, 344.

52. *PHA* 12:269.

53. Ibid.

54. Stinnett, *Day of Deceit*, 109, 113.

55. *PHA* 2:877.

56. "Pre-Pearl Harbor Despatches," RG 406, SRH 460:1, NA-MD; Parker, *Pearl Harbor Revisited*, 53.

57. Wilford, *Pearl Harbor Redefined*, 20.

58. *PHA* 4:1755.

59. *PHA* 10:4774; 18:3335–36; 36:48; Beatty, "Background of Secret Report," 1261; Lewin, *American Magic*, 87, 89ff.

60. Fitzgibbon, *Secret Intelligence*, 255. See also Costello, *Days of Infamy*, 321. In addition, a Dutch intelligence unit penetrated Japanese naval codes and reportedly warned Washington of the coming Pearl Harbor attack (Layton, *And I Was There*, 206; Haslach, *Nishi no Kaze, Hare*, 172ff).

61. Casey, *Secret War Against Hitler*, 7.

62. *PHA* 2:462, 464.

63. *PHA* 2:497; Furer, *Administration of Navy*, 87.

64. *PHA* 2:448; 26:300.

65. Churchill, *Grand Alliance*, 598.

66. Aldrich, *Intelligence and the War*, 385–86.

67. "Pre-Pearl Harbor Despatches," RG 406, SRH 460:16–17, NA-MD. See also *PHA* 23:683.

68. Parker, *Pearl Harbor Revisited*, 63.

69. *PHA* 35:69. See also *PHA* 17:2675.

70. Rusbridger and Nave, *Betrayal at Pearl Harbor*, 154. See also 146; Costello, *Days of Infamy*, 320.

71. Toland, *Infamy*, 1st ed., 283.

72. Ibid., after 272.

73. Ibid., after 272, 298.

74. Costello in Layton, *And I Was There*, 506–7; Costello, *Days of Infamy*, 355.

75. Costello, *Days of Infamy*, 423.

76. Toland, Papers, box 122, NA-FDR.

77. Toland, *Infamy*, 2nd ed., 296, 332.

78. Stinnett, *Day of Deceit*, 189–90; Toland, Papers, box 122, reel 1, side 1, NA-FDR.

79. Brown, *C*, 383, 385.

80. Mowrer, *Triumph and Turmoil*, 325, 327.

81. Dies, "Assassination," 33.

82. Thorpe, *East Wind, Rain*, 51.

83. Toland, *Infamy*, 1st ed., 290, 317–18.

84. *PHA* 32:906.

85. *PHA* 39:36.

86. R. Thompson, *Time for War*, xiii.

87. Wilford, *Pearl Harbor Redefined*, 75; Mosley, *Marshall*, 166. For other vague, scanty reports, see *PHA* 9:4216; *PHA* 10:4802, 4904–5; *PHA* 32:632; *PHA* 34:171; Landis and Gunn, *Deceit at Pearl Harbor*, 37–38; Prange, *Target Tokyo*, 409–10; Layton, *And I Was There*, 207; Tolley, *Cruise of the Lanikai*, 301.

88. Toland, *Infamy*, 1st ed., 317; Stinnett, *Day of Deceit*, 196–97.

89. *PHA* 14:1044.

90. Ibid.

91. Clausen and Lee, *Pearl Harbor*, 81.

92. Layton, *And I Was There*, 117.

93. Clausen and Lee, *Pearl Harbor*, 45–46; Prange, *At Dawn We Slept*, 119.

94. Andrew, *President's Eyes*, 109; Prange, *At Dawn We Slept*, 119; *PHA* 11:5475–76; 34:1.

95. McCurry, "Newsman Claims," 1, 4; Piper, "Aide Says," 16.

96. Ketchum, *Recollections of Colonel*

Retread, 30; Toland, *Infamy*, 2nd ed., 342–43.

97. Borquist, "Advance Warning?" 21. See also *PHA* 30:2481.

CHAPTER 4: CHALLENGES TO THE MYTH

1. Prange, *At Dawn We Slept*, 6, 11, 670.
2. *PHA* 8:3602, 3857–58; 29:2373; Kimmel, *Admiral Kimmel's Story*, 130.
3. Kimmel, *Admiral Kimmel's Story*, 158; Leutze, *Different Kind of Victory*, 293–94.
4. Melosi, *Shadow of Pearl Harbor*, 63.
5. C. Beard, *Roosevelt and War*, 280–81.
6. *PHA* 3:1130–33.
7. Cray, *General of the Army*, 479–80.
8. Cray, *General of the Army*, 480; R. Smith, *Thomas E. Dewey*, 426–30.
9. Prange, *At Dawn We Slept*, 645; Melosi, *Shadow of Pearl Harbor*, 79.
10. Melosi, *Shadow of Pearl Harbor*, 80.
11. Prange, *At Dawn We Slept*, 652–53.
12. Cray, *General of the Army*, 481.
13. Pogue, *Marshall: Ordeal and Hope*, 430.
14. Prange, *At Dawn We Slept*, 656.
15. Ibid.; Toland, *Infamy*, 2nd ed., 133.
16. Bartlett, *Cover-Up*, 78.
17. *PHA* 9:4319.
18. Clausen and Lee, *Pearl Harbor*, 2, 28–29, 204–5, 225ff., 278–79, passim.
19. *PHA* 9:4428.
20. *PHA* 9:4319.
21. Kimmel, *Admiral Kimmel's Story*, 160–61.
22. *PHA* 39:330–32.
23. Gannon, *Pearl Harbor Betrayed*, 281; Kimmel, *Admiral Kimmel's Story*, 161; Buell, *Admiral Ernest J. King*, 353; King and Whitehill, *Fleet Admiral King*, 633.
24. *PHA* 39:330.
25. *PHA* 39:331.
26. Prange, *At Dawn We Slept*, 615.
27. Layton, *And I Was There*, 351–52.
28. Prange, *At Dawn We Slept*, 659.
29. Ibid., 659–60

30. Ibid., 658.
31. Ibid., 663, 666.

CHAPTER 5: SECRECY AND COVER-UP

1. Friedrich, *Pathology of Politics*, passim.
2. *PHA* 4:1623–24; 8:3565–70, 3882–84; Spector, *Listening to the Enemy*, 9ff., 63ff., 156, passim; Layton, *And I Was There*, 100. See also *PHA* 32:21, 53–54, 103–4, 119–20; H. Russell, *Pearl Harbor Story*, 37; Melosi, *Shadow of Pearl Harbor*, 125; Hoehling, *Week Before Pearl Harbour*, 156; Toland, *Infamy*, 1st ed., 152; Greaves, "Pearl Harbor Investigations," 450. On State Department alteration and destruction of documents, see Costello, *Days of Infamy*, 384; Schuler and Moore, *Pearl Harbor Cover-Up*, 146ff., 180, 200, 216, 241, 243–69; Layton, *And I Was There*, 194, 543.
3. *PHA* 27:72.
4. *PHA* 8:3571.
5. *PHA* 10:4739.
6. *PHA* 3:1330, 1332; 4:1623–24; 9:4502; 10:4645; 11:5493–94, 5498; 27:19–24, 26; 29:2375, 2412–36, 4502; 32:21, 53–54; H. Russell, *Pearl Harbor Story*, 37ff., 98–99; Prange, *At Dawn We Slept*, 627; Wohlstetter, *Pearl Harbor*, 119–20.
7. Kimmel, *Admiral Kimmel's Story*, 124.
8. *PHA* 29:2413.
9. *PHA* 3:1330; 2:800.
10. *PHA* 27:77ff; H. Russell, *Pearl Harbor Story*, 98–99.
11. McCollum, Oral History, 401; Clausen and Lee, *Pearl Harbor*, 36. See also *PHA* 3:1198–99; 7:3278; Layton, *And I Was There*, 100; Stinnett, *Day of Deceit*, 207–8.
12. *PHA* 1:8.
13. Ibid., 6.
14. Ibid., 6.
15. Ibid., 8.
16. Ibid., 9.
17. *PHA* 8:3883.

18. Ibid., 3884.
19. Warnings from Korean agent Haan Kilsoo. See chap. 3.
20. Warnings from Dusan Popov and raids on German agents in the United States. See chap. 3.
21. *PHA* 1:15.
22. H. Russell, *Pearl Harbor Story*, 37ff., 98–99.
23. *PHA* 39:221, 228, 230.
24. See chap. 14.
25. Estimate in chap. 3.
26. Schuler and Moore, *Pearl Harbor Cover-Up*, 216.
27. Stinnett, *Day of Deceit*, 256; McCollum, Oral History, 401.
28. Stimson File, RG 170, NA-MD.
29. *PHA* 32:120, see also 103–4, 119, 121, 130–31.
30. *PHA* 32:194, passim.
31. McCollum, Oral History, 401.
32. *PHA* 35:5.
33. *PHA* 10:4616.
34. *PHA* 35:116. See also Clausen and Lee, *Pearl Harbor*, 49, 171ff.; 4:1661–62; *PHA* 9:4315, 4326–27; 10:4608ff.
35. *PHA* 10:4648.
36. Clausen and Lee, *Pearl Harbor*, 49. Clausen added, "I wore the pouch into the office of the person I was interviewing. If an individual appeared reluctant to talk . . . I would open up my shirt, unbuckle the pouch, and pull out the specific Magic document I wanted to ask questions about . . . people I interviewed flinched visibly . . . one by one they changed . . . the stories they had previously told under oath." Such passages do not specify whether it was the pouch or the document that frightened them. If it were the document alone, his mention of the pouch was irrelevant. But Clausen repeatedly emphasized the danger of the pouch in these descriptions. Most of the documents were intercepted Japanese diplomatic messages, and Clausen did not explain why they should have frightened

people he interviewed. He could have removed the documents from his pouch before entering their offices, and they would not have seen the pouch. As in his description of the effect on Layton, he evidently relished the shock induced when he exposed the it.
38. Ibid., 35.
39. *PHA* 10:5021; 35:23, 25; Layton, *And I Was There*, 265; *PHA* 36:69ff.
40. Witnesses also differed on whether they had seen a winds execute before or after the Pearl Harbor attack. And some who said they had seen one before December 7 changed their stories to say they had seen it after that date. U.S. officers who said they had seen one or been informed authoritatively that one had come in before December 7 were Warrant Officer Ralph Briggs, Lt. Harold Bryant, Yeoman Robert Dowd, Col. Carlisle Dusenbury, Adm. Royal Ingersoll, Cdr. Alwin Kramer, Lt. Thomas Mackie, Col. Moses Pettigrew, Col. Otis Sadtler, Capt. Laurance Safford, and Adm. Richmond Turner. See RG 457, SRH 51, NA-MD; *PHA* 8:3792, 3888–90; 26:469; 29:2430; 33:853–54, 871, 876, 885–86; Prados, *Combined Fleet Decoded*, 214. Shortly after the war, U.S. officers in Japan questioned Japanese officials and reported that "all pertinent records were burned August 1945," and no winds execute was sent before December 7. See *PHA* 18:3308. Later evidence from Japan indicated one had been sent. Komatsu, *Origins of Pacific War*, 324. On British and Dutch interception of a winds execute, see Costello, *Days of Infamy*, 160–61, 348–49; Rusbridger and Nave, *Betrayal at Pearl Harbor*, 25, 147.
41. After interviews by Sonnett, Safford wrote, "Sonnett tried to persuade me that there had been no 'Winds Execute' Message, that my memory was playing tricks on me,

that I have confused the 'False Winds Message' with what I had been expecting, and that I ought to change my testimony." *PHA* 8:3606–9.

42. *PHA* 10:5021.

43. Costello, *Days of Infamy*, 347. A civilian member of Kramer's staff, Eunice Rice, said Kramer was "instructed on orders from above" to change his testimony that he had delivered a winds execute to Navy Department chiefs. Layton, *And I Was There*, 519; Costello, *Days of Infamy*, 307. Asked by the congressional committee if he had been coerced, Kramer vigorously said no. Details of his testimony indicate, however, that Sonnett did try to persuade him to reverse his prior testimony. *PHA* 9:4056ff., 4135.

44. *PHA* 33:853–76; 9:3933, 3934, 3936.

45. *PHA* 9:3932, 3936.

46. *PHA* 39:225. According to the Army Pearl Harbor Board, "The Navy now admits having received this 'winds' activating message about December 6, but the War Department files show no copy of such a message." *PHA* 3:1446.

47. *PHA* 33:905–6; 34:68; Prange, *At Dawn We Slept*, 458–59.

48. RG 457, SRH 51, NA-MD.

49. *PHA* 35:6.

50. *PHA* 10:4790. See also 4744–45.

51. Toland, *Infamy*, 1st ed., 203–4.

52. Ibid., 201–3.

53. Prange, *At Dawn We Slept*, 458; Baker, "FDR: Not Guilty," 59.

54. Layton, *And I Was There*, 519.

55. *PHA* 9:4015.

56. Clausen and Lee, *Pearl Harbor*, 171.

57. *PHA* 9:4515.

58. Costello, *Days of Infamy*, 207.

59. *PHA* 35:91; Pogue, *Marshall: Ordeal and Hope*, 431.

60. *PHA* 33:826.

61. *PHA* 11:5139, 5193–94.

62. Ibid., 5193–94; *PHA* 3:1110.

63. *PHA* 11:5232.

64. Ibid., 5549.

65. See chap. 14.

66. *PHA* 11:5343–44. See also 5153, 5157.

67. Theobald, *Final Secret*, 26.

68. Toland, *Infamy*, 1st ed., 170; Pogue, *Marshall: Ordeal and Hope*, 431, 483–84.

69. *PHA* 29:2409.

70. *PHA* 36:306.

71. Hewitt to Marshall, memo, July 5, 1945, Hewitt File, Naval Academy Library, Annapolis, MD.

72. *PHA* 34:77–92.

73. Ibid., 101–2.

74. Undated memo purportedly by Tansill of May 4, 1961, conversation, Kimmel Papers. Fellers related the conversation to Toland (*Infamy*, 1st ed., 321, 323). Toland referred to the original source as "an unnamed officer close to Marshall" and as "General V." According to Prange (*Pearl Harbor*, 263), Toland meant Gen. Carter Clarke.

75. Clausen and B. Lee, *Pearl Harbor*, 35–36.

76. *PHA* 3:1334–35.

77. Ibid., 1198–99, 1203.

CHAPTER 6: THE ACCUSED

1. *PHA* 11:5495–97.

2. *PHA* 7:3145–47, 3191–94; 18:3217–19; 19:3809.

3. *PHA* 14:1406 (date of dispatch given as November 7 in error).

4. *PHA* 23:1106; 29:2071–72, 2162–63; Dyer, *Amphibians Came to Conquer*, 2:1182.

5. *PHA* 2:828.

6. H. Russell, *Pearl Harbor Story*, 148–49. See also Furer, *Administration of Navy*, 99; Gannon, *Pearl Harbor Betrayed*, 301.

7. *PHA* 5:2180.

8. *PHA* 4:1647ff.

9. *PHA* 39:82.

10. *PHA* 14:1407.

11. *PHA* 4:1651–52; *PHA* 23:1112.

12. *PHA* 24:1389–90.

13. *PHA* 3:1063, 1077, 1119–20; Cray, *General of the Army*, 231.

14. *PHA* 3:1092–93. See also *PHA* 15:1635; Conn, Engelman, and Fairchild, *Guarding United States*, 163–64.

15. *PHA* 3:1077, 1120.

16. *PHA* 15:1437–38.

17. *PHA* 14:1019–21; 18:3231.

18. *PHA* 14:1031.

19. *PHA* 5:2318; 6:2627; *PHA* 32:610; 33:1301; Wohlstetter, *Pearl Harbor*, 257; Kimmel, *Admiral Kimmel's Story*, 36–37; Willoughby and Chamberlain, *MacArthur*, 23.

20. *PHA* 3:1290–91; 14:1328; 16:2213, 2215; 36:15.

21. *PHA* 23:1108.

22. *PHA* 33:1194, 1280–83. See also *PHA* 6:2507.

23. *PHA* 21:4597.

24. Hoehling, *Week before Pearl Harbour*, 32.

25. *PHA* 27:92; 16:2448.

26. Prange, *At Dawn We Slept*, 291.

27. *PHA* 6:2507.

28. *PHA* 32:236; 21:4593.

29. Prange, *At Dawn We Slept*, 403; Watson, *Chief of Staff*, 474; *PHA* 21:4467, 4469.

30. Prange, *At Dawn We Slept*, 410; *PHA* 32:287.

31. *PHA* 2:831; 3:1082ff.; 26:467.

32. *PHA* 2:870.

33. Conorton, "The Role of Radio Intelligence in the American-Japanese Naval War," vii, RG 38, box 46, NA-MD.

34. Stinnett, *Day of Deceit*, 23, 316. See also Hinsley, *British Intelligence*, 53.

35. *PHA* 24:1422.

36. *PHA* 2:831; 3:1083ff.; 5:2141; 26:467; 27:292–93.

37. *PHA* 3:1116; 4:2034–35; 5:2141. The estimate of one direction rests on the above estimate of 250 planes for reconnaissance all around Hawaii.

38. Moore, *December 8, 1941*, 5.

39. *PHA* 32:49; Dyer, *Amphibians Came to Conquer*, 2:1182.

40. *PHA* 16:2325–26.

41. *PHA* 1:273.

42. Ibid., 257; *PHA* 16:2144.

43. *PHA* 2:830. On the drafting of the dispatch, see *PHA* 4:1952; 21:4608–9;23:1106–7; 29:2162–63; Pogue, *Marshall: Ordeal and Hope*, 207–10; Mosley, *Marshall*, 163–69. Marshall's biographers filled gaps in data with interpretive assumptions—Pogue's "dust in the eyes" (210) and Mosley's "bungling" (168)—without evidence that errors were made. But among the drafters, Gerow, Stimson, and Stark testified that restrictions and vagueness in the November 27 dispatches were due to established policy and instructions from Roosevelt.

44. Prange, *At Dawn We Slept*, 403, 729, 869.

45. *PHA* 17:2870–74; 35:209.

46. Clarke, *Pearl Harbor Ghosts*, 56–63, 234–35; 6:2682–96; 27:124–25; 39:43ff; and see especially *PHA* 35:249.

47. Layton, *And I Was There*, 148.

48. *PHA* 35:188–91.

49. Hoehling, *Week before Pearl Harbour*, 66; *PHA* 28:1538.

50. Pogue, *Marshall: Ordeal and Hope*, 172. See also *PHA* 3:1534; 15:1602–12.

51. *PHA* 3:1177.

52. Ibid.; *PHA* 15:1625, 1630; 27:33.

53. *PHA* 2:829.

54. *PHA* 35:228–39.

55. Ibid., 15.

56. Ibid., 228–39.

57. Ibid., 240.

58. *PHA* 16:2155; 1:327.

59. *PHA* 3:1026.

60. *PHA* 23:1106.

61. *PHA* 3:1097–99; 29:2189–90; Pogue, *Marshall; Ordeal and Hope*, 210.

62. *PHA* 3:1097–99; 29:2189–90.

63. *PHA* 3:1424.

64. Pogue, *Marshall: Ordeal and Hope*, 210.

65. *PHA* 3:1097.

66. Mosley, *Marshall*, 168.

67. *PHA* 16:2275.

68. *PHA* 32:27.

69. *PHA* 4:1952–53.

70. Ibid., 1958.

71. *PHA* 37:840ff.; 6:2822; 33:1177, 1360–61.

72. *PHA* 33:1178.

73. *PHA* 4:1916, 1950.

74. Ibid., 1916; *PHA* 5:2375.

75. *PHA* 4:1916.

76. *PHA* 5:2152. See also *PHA* 4:1805.

77. *PHA* 32:151; 26:265.

78. *PHA* 33:1284–91, 1360.

79. Prange, *At Dawn We Slept*, 413.

80. Parker, *Pearl Harbor Revisited*, 29; Miller, *War Plan Orange*, 310–11.

81. Wellborn, "Fog of War," 95.

82. *PHA* 32:144. See also *PHA* 4:1952.

83. MacArthur, *Reminiscences*, 113.

84. Furer, *Administration of Navy*, 99.

85. *PHA* 11:5424. See also *PHA* 39:85.

86. *PHA* 15:1602–4, 1609.

87. M. Smith, *Emperor's Codes*, 108.

88. *PHA* 16:2229.

89. Layton, *And I Was There*, 142–43; *PHA* 4:1728–30, 1739, 1833ff., 1914, 1926ff.

90. *PHA* 33:1208.

91. *PHA* 10:4845–46.

92. *PHA* 2:791–94, 812–13; 4:1737–38, 1830, 1839–40, 1853; 33:897.

93. *PHA* 2:791.

94. Layton, *And I Was There*, 91.

95. Ibid., 123–24, 239–40.

96. *PHA* 3:1510, 1512, 1533.

97. *PHA* 27:34; Furer, *Administration of Navy*, 99.

98. Layton, *And I Was There*, 91; Gannon, *Pearl Harbor Betrayed*, 103; *PHA* 16:2238; 32:100.

99. *PHA* 16:2238.

100. *PHA* 6:2540–41; 33:692; Prange, *At Dawn We Slept*, 138–39.

101. *PHA* 16:2181–82.

102. *PHA* 15:1606; 3:1071–73; 7:3084; 31:3140ff.

103. *PHA* 15:1607; 39:58.

104. *PHA* 7:3155–56; 29:2207; 39:110–11.

105. *PHA* 22:220–23.

106. Kimmel, *Admiral Kimmel's Story*, 118–21.

107. *PHA* 1:327; 6:2519, 2524; 9:4296; 16:2232–33; 18:2970–77, 3020–3107; 32:191; 39:44–45, 58, 116–18; Layton, *And I Was There*, 214.

CHAPTER 7: ORIGINS OF WAR BETWEEN JAPAN AND THE UNITED STATES

1. Martinez, *Troublesome Border*, 10, 12–14.

2. LaFeber, *Clash*, 10ff.

3. Beasley, *Modern History of Japan*, 46ff.; Reischauer, *Japan*, 110ff.; LaFeber, *Clash*, 13ff.

4. Asahi, *Pacific Rivals*, 45–46.

5. Neu, *Troubled Encounter*, 8ff.

6. Asahi, *Pacific Rivals*, 43, 45–46; B. Chamberlain, *Japanese Things*, 488–89.

7. Anesaki, *Art, Life, and Nature*, 139ff.; Hearn, *Japan*, 343; Norman, *Japan's Emergence*, 12.

8. Sansom, *Japan*, 417ff., 449ff; Reischauer, *Japan*, 86ff.; Jansen, *Japan and Its World*, 16–17.

9. Sansom, *Japan*, 452–53.

10. Leonard, *Early Japan*, 28; Trewartha, *Japan*, 10; W. Browne and Dole, *New America and Far East*, 34; Durant, *Our Oriental Heritage*, 830–31.

11. Dürckheim, *Japanese Cult of Tranquility*.

12. Leonard, *Early Japan*, 29.

13. Morris, *Nobility of Failure*, passim.

14. Ibid.; Leonard, *Early Japan*, 57.

15. Leonard, *Early Japan*, 61–62; Lamont-Brown, *Kamikaze*, 34.

16. Leonard, *Early Japan*, 62–63; Lamont-Brown, *Kamikaze*, 34–35.

17. Storry, *History of Modern Japan*, 91.

18. Preble, *Opening of Japan*, 138.

19. Feis, *Road to Pearl Harbor*, v.

20. Hearn, *Japan*, 175; Chamberlain, *Japanese Things*, 415–17.

21. Neu, *Troubled Encounter*, 13–14; Reischauer, *Japan*, 115–16.

22. LaFeber, *Clash*, 28–29; Beasley, *Modern History of Japan*, 84–85.

23. Reischauer, *Japan*, 117ff.; Norman, *Japan's Emergence*, 7ff.; Harootunian, *Toward Restoration*, 410.

24. Byas, *Government by Assassination,* v, vi; LaFeber, *Clash,* 34–35.
25. Iriye, *Across the Pacific,* 65.
26. LaFeber, *Clash,* 48–51; Beasley, *Modern History of Japan,* 155ff.
27. LaFeber, *Clash,* 51.
28. Wray, "Japanese-American Relations," 3.
29. Asahi, *Pacific Rivals,* 54, 60.
30. Albright, *Pearl Harbor,* 35.
31. Asahi, *Pacific Rivals,* 54; Neu, *Troubled Encounter,* 41–42: LaFeber, *Clash,* 78.
32. Hofstadter, Miller, and Aaron, *United States,* 616ff.
33. Reischauer, *Japan,* 155–56.
34. Neumann, *Genesis of Pearl Harbor,* 5; Asahi, *Pacific Rivals,* 72.
35. Hunt, *Untold Story,* 177–78: Neu, *Troubled Encounter,* 2.
36. Neu, *Troubled Encounter,* 48ff.; Iriye, *Across the Pacific,* 134–35, 140.
37. Haight, "Roosevelt and Naval Quarantine," 208, 214; Storry, *History of Modern Japan,* 204.
38. Feis, *Road to Pearl Harbor,* 6–7; Brownlow, *Accused,* 23, 31.
39. Freidel, *Franklin D. Roosevelt,* 379–80.

CHAPTER 8:
JAPAN'S MOVES TO
DOMINATE EAST ASIA

1. Beasley, *Modern History of Japan,* 9–13; Morris, *Nobility of Failure,* 248; Badsey, *Pearl Harbor,* 12.
2. Morris, *Nobility of Failure,* 260.
3. Ryusaku, de Bary, and Keene, *Sources of Japanese Tradition,* 2:147–49; Morris, *Nobility of Failure,* 272–75.
4. Sato, *Legends of the Samurai,* 3ff.; Morris, *Nobility of Failure,* 360; Coleman, "Losing Glorious," 52.
5. Morris, *Nobility of Failure,* 219–20, 269, 275.
6. Ibid., 22–23.
7. Ibid., 14ff.
8. Ryusaku, de Bary, and Keene, *Sources of Japanese Tradition,* 2:114.
9. Ibid., 254, 259; Shiroyama, *War Criminal,* 8; Norman, "Genyosha," 355–67.

10. Storry, *Double Patriots,* 10ff.
11. Beasley, *Modern History of Japan,* 200–1.
12. Storry, *Double Patriots,* 54ff.; Chamberlain, *Japanese Things,* 89–90.
13. Morris, *Shining Prince,* 121–25, 194–95; Singer, *Mirror, Sword and Jewel,* 49–53.
14. Morris, *Nobility of Failure,* 276–334.
15. Shiroyama, *War Criminal,* 103, 122–23.
16. Byas, *Government by Assassination,* passim; Tolischus, *Tokyo Record,* 226–27.
17. Kido, *Diary of Marquis Kido,* passim.
18. Ibid.
19. Ienaga, *Pacific War,* 10–12, 59ff.; E. Russell, *Knights of Bushido,* 5ff.; Storry, *Double Patriots,* 69ff.
20. Neu, *Troubled Encounter,* 132–33; Beasley, *Modern History of Japan,* 223.
21. Beasley, *Modern History of Japan,* 245ff.
22. LaFeber, *Clash,* 173.
23. Crowley, *Japan's Quest for Autonomy,* 4.
24. Beasley, *Modern History of Japan,* 246, 258ff.; Orchard, "Japanese Dilemma," 39ff.
25. Shiroyama, *War Criminal,* 168ff.; Offner, *American Appeasement,* 199–200.
26. Ryusaku, de Bary, and Keene, *Sources of Japanese Tradition,* 2:288–89.
27. Jansen, *Japan and Its World,* 82–83.
28. Feis, *Road to Pearl Harbor,* 64.
29. Chang, *Rape of Nanking,* passim.

CHAPTER 9: ROOSEVELT'S
TENTATIVE MOVES
AGAINST GERMANY

1. Kinsella, *Leadership in Isolation,* 33ff., 174ff.; Freidel, *Franklin D. Roosevelt,* 178–79.
2. Brinkley, *Washington Goes to War,* 15; Offner, *American Appeasement,* 104; Heardon, *Roosevelt Confronts Hitler,* 54.
3. Stimson and Bundy, *On Active Service,* 374; Sherwood, *Papers of*

Hopkins, 162.

4. Feiling, *Life of Neville Chamberlain*, 254.

5. Ibid., 253. See also 354, 419, 424.

6. Kershaw, *Hitler: Nemesis*, 29; L. Thompson, *1940*, 158.

7. Churchill, *Great Contemporaries*.

8. Heardon, *Roosevelt Confronts Hitler*, 76; Haight, "Roosevelt and Naval Quarantine," 220; Gellman, *Secret Affairs*, 148–49.

9. Davis, *FDR: The War President*, 72.

10. Marks, *Wind Over Sand*, 9–12; Macleod, *Neville Chamberlain*, 177ff., 206.

11. Heardon, *Roosevelt Confronts Hitler*, 28; Rosenman, *Working with Roosevelt*, 181ff.

12. Heardon, *Roosevelt Confronts Hitler*, 31.

13. Sherwood, *Roosevelt and Hopkins*, 127.

14. Davis, *FDR: The War President*, 41–42.

15. Hofstadter, Miller, and Aaron, *United States*, 674.

16. Kinsella, *Leadership in Isolation*, 104–5.

17. Adamthwaite, *Making of War*, 133–34.

18. Kinsella, *Leadership in Isolation*, 115.

19. Eden, *Facing the Dictators*, 334.

20. Churchill, *Gathering Storm*, 263.

21. Freidel, *Franklin D. Roosevelt*, 271–22.

22. Divine, *Illusion of Neutrality*, 168–69; Freidel, *Franklin D. Roosevelt*, 270.

23. Freidel, *Franklin D. Roosevelt*, 272.

24. Ibid., 184, 263ff., 291.

25. Langer and Gleason, *Challenge to Isolation*, 24ff.; Rosenman, *Working with Roosevelt*, 165–66.

26. Bohlen, *Transformation of Policy*, 13; Rosenman, *Working with Roosevelt*, 164–65.

27. Brinkley, *Washington Goes to War*, 16–17.

28. Rosenman, *Working with Roosevelt*, 167.

29. *PHA* 1:305; Freidel, *Franklin D. Roosevelt*, 184, 261, 263, 291–92.

30. Haight, "Roosevelt and Naval Quarantine," 223.

31. Kinsella, *Leadership in Isolation*, 113.

32. Berle, *Navigating the Rapids*, 231–33.

33. Haight, *American Aid to France*, 70, 83, 115–16, 138, 168, 211–13.

34. Ibid., 70, 151ff., 204; Watson, *Chief of Staff*, 302ff.; Pogue, *Marshall: Ordeal and Hope*, 64ff.

35. D. Kennedy, *Freedom from Fear*, 421; Watson, *Chief of Staff*, 133, Haight, *American Aid to France*, 95.

36. R. Thompson, *Time for War*, 133–36.

37. Haight, *American Aid to France*, 98–99; D. Kennedy, *Freedom from Fear*, 421.

38. Sherwood, *Papers of Hopkins*, 126.

39. Ibid.

40. Haight, *American Aid to France*, 233.

41. Lazareff, *Deadline*, 185.

42. Ibid., 80–83.

43. Ibid., 184ff.

44. Amery, *Unforgiving Years*, 262–63, 317; Churchill, *Gathering Storm*, 274; Feiling, *Life of Neville Chamberlain*, 408ff.

45. Feiling, *Life of Neville Chamberlain*, 328.

46. Roberts, *House That Hitler Built*, 363.

47. Eden, *Facing the Dictators*, 514. See also Adamthwaite, *Making of War*, 67–82.

48. Eden, *Facing the Dictators*, 514, 645.

49. Adamthwaite, *Making of War*, 62.

50. Eden, *Facing the Dictators*, 412.

51. Feiling, *Life of Neville Chamberlain*, 367.

52. Macleod, *Neville Chamberlain*, 242.

53. Ibid.

54. Churchill, *Gathering Storm*, 306.

55. Adamthwaite, *Making of War*, 63. According to Thorne (*Approach of War*, 186), Chamberlain also believed that he alone could manage Mussolini.

56. Mosley, *On Borrowed Time*, 90, 91, 95.

57. Herzstein, *Roosevelt and Hitler*, 216; Mosley, *On Borrowed Time*, 88–89.

58. Feiling, *Life of Neville Chamberlain*, 375.

59. Mosley, *On Borrowed Time*, 88;

Churchill, *Gathering Storm*, 322–23; Thorne, *Approach of War*, 96ff.

60. Burns, *Roosevelt: Lion and Fox*, 387.
61. Wyman, *Paper Walls*, 73; Kinsella, *Leadership in Isolation*, 126; Brinkley, *Washington Goes to War*, 36.
62. Wyman, *Paper Walls*, 22; Herzstein, *Roosevelt and Hitler*, 233, 239.
63. Kershaw, *Hitler: Nemesis*, 61.
64. Gutman, *Witness to Genocide*, 174.
65. Burns, *Roosevelt: Lion and Fox*, 391; Amery, *Unforgiving Years*, 310.
66. *PHA* 5:2360; Kase, *Journey to the Missouri*, 42.
67. Leahy, *I Was There*, 4; Freidel, *Franklin D. Roosevelt*, 361, 365.
68. Bartsch, *December 8, 1941*, 50.
69. Feiling, *Life of Neville Chamberlain*, 419.
70. Pogue, *Marshall: Ordeal and Hope*, 127.
71. Divine, *Illusion of Neutrality*, 276.
72. R. Thompson, *Time for War*, 164.
73. Leigh, *Mobilizing Consent*, 30, 75.
74. Costello, *Days of Infamy*, 57.
75. Freidel, *Franklin D. Roosevelt*, 335.
76. Reynolds, *Creation of Alliance*, 114.
77. Amery, *Unforgiving Years*, 373.
78. Ibid., 375.
79. R. Thompson, *Time for War*, 219.
80. Dziuban, *Military Relations*, 3–4, 22–24, 53; Conn and Fairchild, *Framework of Hemispheric Defense*, 364–89.
81. R. Thompson, *Time for War*, 156–60.
82. Stacey, *Arms, Men and Governments*, 327.
83. Dziuban, *Military Relations*, 22–26, 53; Stacey, *Arms, Men and Governments*, 328–30.
84. Dziuban, *Military Relations*, 25.
85. Leutze, *Bargaining for Supremacy*, 74ff.; Conn and Fairchild, *Framework of Hemispheric Defense*, 53, 56, 371–72; Loewenheim, Langley, and Jones, *Roosevelt and Churchill*, 105–6, 108.
86. Cray, *General of the Army*, 159; Horne, *To Lose a Battle*, 571.
87. Divine, *Reluctant Belligerent*, 88.
88. Langer, *Our Vichy Gamble*, 28.
89. Ibid., 30–31.

90. James, *Churchill: Complete Speeches*, 6231.
91. Sanborn, *Design for War*, 170.
92. James, *Churchill: Complete Speeches*, 6238.
93. Haight, *American Aid to France*, 237.
94. Klingaman, *1941*, 6.
95. Baudot et al., *Encyclopedia of World War II*, 61–62; Sherwood, *Papers of Hopkins*, 150–51.
96. Victor, *Hitler*, 193ff.; Irving, *Hitler's War*, 298, 301ff.
97. Klingaman, *1941*, 13.
98. Simpson, *Admiral Harold R. Stark*, 41.
99. Ibid., 52–53; Leutze, *Bargaining for Supremacy*, 118.
100. Conn and Fairchild, *Framework of Hemispheric Defense*, 53, 56; Langer and Gleason, *Undeclared War*, 215–18.
101. Tully, *F.D.R., My Boss*, 244.
102. Dallek, *Roosevelt Diplomacy*, 2; Langer and Gleason, *Challenge to Isolation*, 770–73.
103. Ibid.
104. Ibid., 771.
105. Dallek, *Roosevelt Diplomacy*, 2.
106. Davis, *FDR: The War President*, 46–47, 49.
107. Ibid., 49; Bland, *Papers of Marshall*, 352–53.
108. See Afterword.
109. Weintraub, *Long Day's Journey*, 5–6.
110. Byrnes, *Speaking Frankly*, 12.
111. Brinkley, *Washington Goes to War*, 51; Berle, *Navigating the Rapids*, 364–67.
112. Conn and Fairchild, *Framework of Hemispheric Defense*, 101–2.
113. Watson, *Chief of Staff*, 325.
114. Slessor, *Central Blue*, 364; Conn and Fairchild, *Framework of Hemispheric Defense*, 103.
115. Schroeder, *Axis Alliance*, 14.
116. Pogue, *Marshall: Ordeal and Hope*, 127; Schroeder, *Axis Alliance*, 11.
117. Matloff and Snell, *Strategic Planning*, 15–16, 18.
118. Simpson, *Admiral Harold R. Stark*, 55.

119. *PHA* 14:933.
120. *PHA* 1:260.
121. *PHA* 36:20–21.
122. *PHA* 14:934.
123. *PHA* 1:292.
124. Ibid., 291.
125. *PHA* 14:940.
126. Ibid., 943.
127. Ibid.
128. *PHA* 16:2151.
129. *PHA* 14:946.
130. *PHA* 1:265ff., 342ff.
131. Ibid., 266; *PHA* 2:720–22.
132. Richardson, *Treadmill to Pearl Harbor*, 427; *PHA* 1:356–57.
133. Stinnett, *Day of Deceit*, 263–65.
134. Doyle, *Inside the Oval Office*, 34; Lash, *Roosevelt and Churchill*, 298.
135. Richardson, *Treadmill to Pearl Harbor*, 399; *PHA* 1:304–5, 318–19, 335.
136. *PHA* 14:963–69.
137. *PHA* 26:268.
138. *PHA* 14:969.
139. Ibid., 943–46.
140. *PHA* 1:273.
141. *PHA* 32:49. See also Dyer, *Amphibians Came to Conquer*, 2:1182.
142. Gellman, *Secret Affairs*, 41–52; Herzstein, *Roosevelt and Hitler*, 98. Kimmel also challenged Roosevelt with offensive words, and was not relieved. *PHA* 6:2716.
143. Cray, *General of the Army*, 154–55.
144. Lombard, *While They Fought*, 17; Dyer, *Amphibians Came to Conquer*, 1:44; *PHA* 1:322.
145. *PHA* 5:2414–15; Gannon, *Pearl Harbor Betrayed*, 78–80.
146. *PHA* 16:2158.
147. Ibid., 2164.
148. Ibid., 2151.

CHAPTER 10: SECRET ALLIANCE AND UNDECLARED WAR

1. F. Moore, *With Japan's Leaders*, 146.
2. Leutze, *Bargaining for Supremacy*, 18–26; Marder, *Old Friends, New Enemies*, 11; Watson, *Chief of Staff*, 92–93.
3. Marder, *Old Friends, New Enemies*, 73.
4. Eden, *Facing the Dictators*, 618.
5. Haight, "Roosevelt and Naval Quarantine," 215.
6. *PHA* 9:272–73; Reynolds, *Creation of Alliance*, 61.
7. Eden, *Facing the Dictators*, 619.
8. Haight, "Roosevelt and Naval Quarantine," 210.
9. Ibid., 217.
10. Leighton and Coakley, *Global Logistics and Strategy*, 53.
11. *PHA* 9:4273–76; *PHA* 3:1524; Kittredge, "U.S. British Cooperation," sec. A, 12ff.; Watson, *Chief of Staff*, 376ff.; Haight, "Roosevelt and Naval Quarantine," 217–18; Wilford, *Pearl Harbor Redefined*, 6, 14; Leutze, *Bargaining for Supremacy*, 30; Morton, "Germany First," 20ff.
12. W. Douglas, *Creation of Air Force*, 383; R. Thompson, *Time for War*, 101ff.
13. R. Lee, *London Observer*, 29ff.
14. Bartsch, *December 8, 1941*, 50; Rauch, *Roosevelt*, 314–15, 324.
15. *PHA* 5:2292; Watson, *Chief of Staff*, 381; Furer, *Administration of Navy*, 796–97; Sherwood, *Roosevelt and Hopkins*, 261.
16. R. Lee, *London Observer*, 281–82.
17. *PHA* 14:973.
18. Ibid., 984; Leutze, *Bargaining for Supremacy*, 294.
19. R. Thompson, *Time for War*, 280; Bartsch, *December 8, 1941*, 145–46.
20. Leighton and Coakley, *Global Strategy and Strategy*, 52ff. See also *PHA* 9:4242; 17:2462–63; 19:3457; 33:929, 954; Watson, *Chief of Staff*, 386; W. Douglas, *Creation of Air Force*, 383.
21. Abbazia, *Mr. Roosevelt's Navy*, 126–29; Heinrichs, *Threshold of War*, 48.
22. Fehrenbach, *F.D.R.'s Undeclared War*, 221; Sherwood, *Roosevelt and Hopkins*, 234–36.
23. C. Wilson, *Churchill*, 6.
24. Ibid.
25. Sherwood, *Roosevelt and Hopkins*, 270; Cray, *General of the Army*, 181;

Matloff and Snell, *Strategic Planning*, 30.

26. Feis, *Road to Pearl Harbor*, 125.
27. Marder, *Old Friends, New Enemies*, 196.
28. Abbazia, *Mr. Roosevelt's Navy*, 122.
29. Ibid., 120–21.
30. Leutze, *Bargaining for Supremacy*, 48; Leighton and Coakley, *Global Logistics and Strategy*, 37; Watson, *Chief of Staff*, 384; Furer, *Administration of Navy*, 796–97; Sherwood, *Papers of Hopkins*, 270–71; Stafford, *Roosevelt and Churchill*, 56.
31. *PHA* 5:2332–33.
32. Conn and Fairchild, *Framework of Hemispheric Defense*, 92; Leighton and Coakley, *Global Logistics and Strategy*, 52.
33. E. Wood, *Fullness of Days*, 248.
34. Davis, *FDR: The War President*, 77; R. Lee, *London Observer*, 32–33; Slessor, *Central Blue*, 320.
35. Sherwood, *Roosevelt and Hopkins*, 274.
36. Stevenson, *Man Called Intrepid*, 159.
37. *PHA* 4:1929, 1932; 5:2388.
38. *PHA* 3:1525–26; 5:2292; 16:2210; R. Lee, *London Observer*, 143–44; Leutze, *Bargaining for Supremacy*, 258; Dunmore, *In Great Waters*, 94.
39. *PHA* 15:1485ff., see particularly 1491. "ABC" is also identified as meaning "American-British-Canadian" in histories.
40. *PHA* 17:2462.
41. *PHA* 18:2894, 2911; 16:2209–10.
42. *PHA* 15:1566.
43. *PHA* 3:993, 1224.
44. *PHA* 18:2911.
45. Quinlan, "United States Fleet," 168; *PHA* 3:994–95, 997, 1221; 9:4242; 15:1485; Feis, *Road to Pearl Harbor*, 168; Morton, "Germany First," 46.
46. *PHA* 19:3457.
47. *PHA* 16:2223.
48. Ibid.
49. Rauch, *Roosevelt*, 329, 331–38.
50. *PHA* 3:995.
51. *PHA* 5:2391.
52. *PHA* 3:1542–44.

53. Matloff and Snell, *Strategic Planning*, 30.
54. Sherwood, *Roosevelt and Hopkins*, 290.
55. *PHA* 16:2175.
56. *PHA* 2:642.
57. King and Whitehill, *Fleet Admiral King*, 345.
58. Freidel, *Franklin D. Roosevelt*, 369; Bland, *Papers of Marshall*, 392.
59. Collier, *Road to Pearl Harbor*, 25.
60. C. Beard, *Roosevelt and War*, 31.
61. Ibid., 21, 32.
62. Langer and Gleason, *Undeclared War*, 448.
63. Leutze, *Bargaining for Supremacy*, 44–45, passim; Abbazia, *Mr. Roosevelt's Navy*, 136.
64. Roscoe, *Destroyer Operations*, 27, 33; *PHA* 5:2292; 9:4249.
65. Carney, "Well-Kept Secret," 27; Morison, *Battle of the Atlantic*, 85–86; *PHA* 16:2162–63; Abbazia, *Mr. Roosevelt's Navy*, 142–45, 244–60.
66. Carney, "Well-Kept Secret," 28; Morison, *Battle of the Atlantic*, 98.
67. Ibid., 79; Roscoe, *Destroyer Operations*, 33.
68. Carney, "Well-Kept Secret," 28.
69. Langer and Gleason, *Undeclared War*, 539–40.
70. Abbazia, *Mr. Roosevelt's Navy*, 154–55.
71. Long, *War Diary*, 183, 185.
72. Heinrichs, *Threshold of War*, 48; Abbazia, *Mr. Roosevelt's Navy*, 153; Burns, *Roosevelt: Soldier of Freedom*, 86; Sherwood, *Roosevelt and Hopkins*, 258.
73. *PHA* 5:2292.
74. Ibid., 2310, 2296.
75. Collier, *Road to Pearl Harbor*, 97.
76. Furer, *Administration of Navy*, 668.
77. *PHA* 16:2518.
78. Colville, *Fringes of Power*, 346; Weintraub, *Long Day's Journey*, 96.
79. C. Beard, *Roosevelt and War*, 135–36.
80. Rosenman, *Working with Roosevelt*, 280.
81. *PHA* 5:2313.
82. Ibid., 2295; Gellman, *Secret Affairs*,

254; Gannon, *Pearl Harbor Betrayed*, 83; Heinrichs, *Threshold of War*, 46–47.

83. Rosenman, *Working with Roosevelt*, 293.
84. Watson, *Chief of Staff*, 383–84; Fairchild, "Decision to Land," 76; Roscoe, *Destroyer Operations*, 30.
85. L. Kennedy, *Pursuit*, 49.
86. Stevenson, *Man Called Intrepid*, 236.
87. The preceding and following account is based on L. Kennedy, *Pursuit*; Hough, *Mountbatten*, 100ff; Abbazia, *Mr. Roosevelt's Navy*, 184–89.
88. Stevenson, *Man Called Intrepid*, 235–44.
89. L. Kennedy, *Pursuit*, 222. During heavy German bombing of London in 1940, Churchill had sought to evacuate English children to the United States. English protests of safety measure as available only to the affluent led Churchill to delay it, saying Britain could not spare warships to convoy ships transporting the children. "Cryptically, Churchill, in answer to a question, mentioned that an offer of American ships to take the children out 'would immediately engage the most earnest attention of His Majesty's Government.'" No explanation of Churchill's comment has come to light. U.S. opposition to a measure (then moving through Congress) for such use of U.S. ships centered on the risk that, if Germany sank such a ship, it would inflame public opinion to enter the war against her. See Wyman, *Paper Walls*, 118–26, quote on 122. Given Churchill's priority of involving the United States in the war, that possibility might have interested him. Congress adopted the measure, but it was not carried out.
90. Gannon, *Pearl Harbor Betrayed*, 85; Abbazia, *Mr. Roosevelt's Navy*, 241.
91. Freidel, *Franklin D. Roosevelt*, 372.

92. Gellman, *Secret Affairs*, 255.
93. C. Beard, *Roosevelt and War*, 139–40; Langer and Gleason, *Undeclared War*, 744–45.
94. Abbazia, *Mr. Roosevelt's Navy*, 224–28.
95. *PHA* 16:2210.
96. Rosenman, *Working with Roosevelt*, 294–95; Roscoe, *Destroyer Operations*, 36–38.
97. C. Beard, *Roosevelt and War*, 143–44.
98. Andrew, *President's Eyes*, 102–3; R. Thompson, *Time for War*, after 210, 258ff.; Gellman, *Secret Affairs*, 260; Stafford, *Roosevelt and Churchill*, 75–78.
99. *PHA* 26:469–470.
100. Langer, *Our Vichy Gamble*, 15–16.

CHAPTER 11: COUNTDOWN IN WASHINGTON: THE JULY TURNING POINT

1. B. Smith, *Shadow Warriors*, 519.
2. Ibid.; Persico, *Roosevelt's Secret War*, 59–60.
3. Blum, *Years of Urgency*, 372–73; Morison, *Rising Sun*, 60; Gannon, *Pearl Harbor Betrayed*, 88.
4. Dyer, *Amphibians Came to Conquer*, 158.
5. B. Smith, *Shadow Warriors*, 510; Feis, *Road to Pearl Harbor*, 50; Langer and Gleason, *Undeclared War*, 653–54; *PHA* 16:2173; Grew, *Ten Years in Japan*, 470.
6. Elliott Roosevelt, *As He Saw It*, 11–12.
7. Rollins, *Roosevelt and Howe*, 257.
8. *PHA* 33:1352.
9. Ickes, *Lowering Clouds*, 529, 543–46.
10. Ibid., 557, 630; Ben-Zvi, *Illusion of Deterrence*, 21.
11. Ickes, *Lowering Clouds*, 558.
12. Ibid., 559.
13. Ibid., 560.
14. Ibid., 567.
15. Blum, *Years of Urgency*, 377; Anderson, *Standard-Vacuum Oil Company*, 174–75.
16. Burns, *Roosevelt: Soldier of Freedom*, 109.

17. Iriye, *Across the Pacific*, 108–12.
18. Feis, *Road to Pearl Harbor*, 233.
19. Divine, *Reluctant Belligerent*, 101.
20. *PHA* 5:2383; 21:4590; 26:267–68.
21. *PHA* 14:1345; 5:2380; 20:4032ff.; Morton, "Germany First," 190; Anderson, *Standard-Vacuum Oil Company*, 169.
22. *PHA* 5:2410–11.
23. *PHA* 24:1355.
24. Langer and Gleason, *Undeclared War*, 653–54.
25. *PHA* 4:2012.
26. Watson, *Chief of Staff*, 414, 417–19; Pogue, *Marshall: Ordeal and Hope*, 177–78; Bartsch, *December 8, 1941*, 24ff.
27. Stimson, Diaries, 102.
28. Pogue, *Marshall: Ordeal and Hope*, 178.
29. *PHA* 16:2151.
30. Matloff and Snell, *Strategic Planning*, 94.
31. Ibid., 67–68; Morton, *Fall of the Philippines*, 31; Watson, *Chief of Staff*, 434–38.
32. Watson, *Chief of Staff*, 425.
33. Costello, *Days of Infamy*, 60.
34. Perkins, "President Faces War," 115.
35. Wainwright, *General Wainwright's Story*, 16, 22.
36. Matloff and Snell, *Strategic Planning*, 69–70.
37. Ibid.
38. Bartsch, *December 8, 1941*, 144.
39. Brereton, *Brereton Diaries*, 6, 8; Pogue, *Marshall: Ordeal and Hope*, 187; *PHA* 32:526, 561.
40. Bartsch, *December 8, 1941*, 153–54.
41. Ibid., vi, 35–36; Edmonds, *Fought With What Had*, xi–xiv, 35–36. See also *PHA* 27:17.
42. Willoughby and J. Chamberlain, *MacArthur*, 25.
43. Bartsch, *Doomed at the Start*, 39.
44. Morton, *Fall of the Philippines*, 50.
45. Ibid., 36; Bland, *Papers of Marshall*, 599; Matloff and Snell, *Strategic Planning*, 70–71.
46. *PHA* 16:2211–12; Bland, *Papers of Marshall*, 605.
47. Pogue, *Marshall: Ordeal and Hope*, 187.
48. *PHA* 3:1161; Bland, *Papers of Marshall*, 368.
49. Watson, *Chief of Staff*, 446.
50. Ibid., 445.
51. *PHA* 20:3998; Schroeder, *Axis Alliance*, 55.
52. Heinrichs, *Threshold of War*, 92–117, 142, 163; Dawson, *Decision to Aid Russia*, 55, 290.
53. *PHA* 20:4018–19.
54. Langer and Gleason, *Undeclared War*, 655–56; Bergamini, *Japan's Imperial Conspiracy*, 819; *PHA* 31:3219–20.
55. *PHA* 12:2.
56. *PHA* 20:3993; Grew, *Ten Years in Japan*, 395, 401–2.
57. *PHA* 20:3993.
58. SRH 406:119, 121–22, NA-MD; *PHA* 18:2948, 2951.
59. Ike, *Japan's Decision for War*, 65.
60. Ibid., 68–70, 87.
61. Ibid., 60.
62. *PHA* 15:1852.
63. Morgenthau, *Morgenthau Diary*, 443.
64. *PHA* 19:3496.
65. R. Lee, *London Observer*, 308, 312ff.; Langer and Gleason, *Undeclared War*, 655–56.
66. *PHA* 12:9.
67. *FRUS*, 538–39.
68. *PHA* 16:2177.
69. Welles, *Time for Decision*, 170. Germany's invasion of the Soviet Union was joined by armies (in descending order of size) from Romania, Finland, Hungary, Italy, and Slovakia, plus divisions from Spain and Belgium. For simplicity, the invasion is called Hitler's and German here.
70. Dawson, *Decision to Aid Russia*, 22–23.
71. Ibid., 65.
72. Ibid., 62.
73. Churchill, *Grand Alliance*, 369.
74. Bernstein and Loewenheim, "Aid

to Russia," 100.

75. Churchill, *Grand Alliance*, 371–73.

76. Le Vien and Lord, *Winston Churchill*, 112.

77. Toland, *Infamy*, 1st ed., 255–56; Prange, *At Dawn We Slept*, 142; *PHA* 33:1354; Ickes, *Lowering Clouds*, 550; Feis, *Churchill, Roosevelt, Stalin*, 9–10.

78. Leahy, *I Was There*, 37–38, 40–41.

79. Langer and Gleason, *Undeclared War*, 634; Feis, *Road to Pearl Harbor*, 206.

80. *PHA* 20:4021; Ike, *Japan's Decision for War*, 93ff.

81. Langer and Gleason, *Undeclared War*, 634; Lowe, *Origins of Pacific War*, 464.

82. Feis, *Road to Pearl Harbor*, 227ff.; *PHA* 4:1945.

83. Gellman, *Secret Affairs*, 256; Hornbeck, *United States and Far East*, 48.

84. Dawson, *Decision to Aid Russia*, 138, 142–43, 156–60; Kinsella, *Leadership in Isolation*, 196ff.; Heinrichs, *Threshold of War*, 102ff., 140–41; C. Beard, *Roosevelt and War*, 413; Sherwood, *Roosevelt and Hopkins*, 306–7; Lash, *Roosevelt and Churchill*, 374ff.

85. Heinrichs, *Threshold of War*, 117.

86. *PHA* 14:1396.

87. Ibid., 1397; *PHA* 32:1231, 1236.

88. Lash, *Roosevelt and Churchill*, 361, 377, 386, 435ff.; Sherwood, *Roosevelt and Hopkins*, 306–7; Heinrichs, *Threshold of War*, 102–3.

89. Harvey, *War Diaries*, 20, 22, 29, 48, 56; Lash, *Roosevelt and Churchill*, 362; Gwyer, *Grand Strategy*, 94–95.

90. Baldwin, *Battles Lost and Won*, 162–63; Lombard, *While They Fought*, 146.

91. Victor, *Hitler*, 202ff.; Collier, *Road to Pearl Harbor*, 163–65, 182–84.

92. *PHA* 20:3993; Dawson, *Decision to Aid Russia*, 125; Butow, *John Doe Associates*, 218–19.

93. Grew, *Ten Years in Japan*, 399–400.

94. Ibid., 397.

95. Layton, *And I Was There*, 118.

96. *PHA* 12:14; Ike, *Japan's Decision for War*, 116.

97. Heinrichs, *Threshold of War*, 176.

98. Lash, *Roosevelt and Churchill*, 393; Persico, *Roosevelt's Secret War*, 121.

99. Lash, *Roosevelt and Churchill*, 393.

100. Marks, *Wind Over Sand*, 165.

101. Hasluck, *Government and People*, 530–31, 534, 539–40.

102. Harriman, *Special Envoy*, 72–74; Dawson, *Decision to Aid Russia*, 180–81; Elliott Roosevelt, *As He Saw It*, 22, 30, 33; C. Wilson, *Churchill*, 37.

103. *PHA* 20:4384.

104. Sherwood, *Roosevelt and Hopkins*, 321.

105. Ibid., 321–22.

106. Ibid., 332–33.

107. Kimball, *Forged in War*, 92, 110; T. Wilson, *First Summit*, 77, 80, 93, 100–2; Gilbert, *Winston S. Churchill*, 1260; *PHA* 5:2225; See also Gwyer, *Grand Strategy*, 146.

108. Welles, *Time for Decision*, 175; T. Wilson, *First Summit*, 82–85.

109. *PHA* 2:480.

110. Ibid., 488.

111. *PHA* 4:1787; Gwyer, *Grand Strategy*, 136; Churchill, *Grand Alliance*, 595.

112. *PHA* 2:483; 14:1254.

113. *PHA* 2:459.

114. Ibid., 775–77.

115. Langer and Gleason, *Undeclared War*, 700; *PHA* 20:4001–2.

116. Toland, *Rising Sun*, 104.

117. Sherwood, *Papers of Hopkins*, 421; Heinrichs, *Threshold of War*, 193.

118. *PHA* 14:1357–58.

119. Ibid., 1387.

120. *PHA* 33:1363.

CHAPTER 12: COUNTDOWN IN TOKYO

1. Agawa, *Reluctant Admiral*, passim; Farago, *Broken Seal*, 124–28.

2. Albright, *Pearl Harbor*, 43–53; Farago, *Broken Seal*, 130ff.; Wohlstetter, *Pearl Harbor*, 371–73.

3. Prange, *At Dawn We Slept*, 17.

4. Butow, *John Doe Associates*, 21; Bergamini, *Japan's Imperial Conspiracy*, 789ff.; Toland, *Rising Sun*, 67ff.
5. *PHA* 11:5375.
6. Feis, *Road to Pearl Harbor*, 178.
7. Wohlstetter, *Pearl Harbor*, 164.
8. Bergamini, *Japan's Imperial Conspiracy*, 799ff.; Feis, *Road to Pearl Harbor*, 202–3; Toland, *Rising Sun*, 77, passim.
9. Ike, *Japan's Decision for War*, 67; Toland, *Rising Sun*, 81.
10. Ike, *Japan's Decision for War*, 67.
11. Ibid., 72; Toland, *Rising Sun*, 81.
12. Ike, *Japan's Decision for War*, 103–4.
13. Kido, *Diary of Marquis Kido*, 291–92.
14. Butow, *Tojo*, 206, 212.
15. Lowe, "Britain's Assessment," 252–53.
16. Toland, *Rising Sun*, 133–35.
17. Ibid., 94.
18. Millis, *This is Pearl*, 142.
19. Toland, *Rising Sun*, 95.
20. Ibid., 97.
21. Deakin and Storry, *Case of Richard Sorge*, 234; Farago, *Broken Seal*, 113–14; Morton, "Japan's Decision for War," 101–2.
22. C. Browne, *Tojo*, 112.
23. *PHA* 20:4022.
24. Ienaga, *Pacific War*, 139.
25. *PHA* 20:4004.
26. Kido, *Diary of Marquis Kido*, 304; *PHA* 20:4004.
27. *PHA* 20:4004.
28. Ike, *Japan's Decision for War*, 133; *PHA* 20:4004; Mosley, *Hirohito*, 215.
29. *PHA* 20:4004.
30. Ibid., 4005.
31. Toland, *Rising Sun*, 98.
32. Ibid., 99.
33. Ibid.
34. Mosley, *Hirohito*, 220. Japanese verse does not rhyme, instead relying on syllable arrangement for poetic effect. I added rhyme to provide a poetic effect for Americans.
35. Toland, *Rising Sun*, 99.
36. Ibid.
37. Ibid.
38. Ibid., 103.
39. *PHA* 20:4021.
40. Morison, *Rising Sun*, 67–68.
41. *PHA* 20:4005.
42. Grew, *Ten Years in Japan*, 441.
43. Toland, *Rising Sun*, 93.
44. Ibid., 104.
45. Grew, *Ten Years in Japan*, 434–35.
46. Toland, *Rising Sun*, 108.
47. Ibid., 105.
48. Ibid.
49. Ibid., 109.
50. Ibid.
51. Butow, *Tojo*, 281; *PHA* 20:4010.
52. *PHA* 20:4010.
53. C. Browne, *Tojo*, 99.
54. Toland, *Rising Sun*, 118.
55. *PHA* 20:4009.
56. Toland, *Rising Sun*, 112.
57. R. Thompson, *Time for War*, 400.
58. Toland, *Rising Sun*, 80.
59. Morton, "Japan's Decision for War," 211.
60. *PHA* 20:4005.
61. Jansen, *Japan and Its World*, 90.
62. Langer and Gleason, *Undeclared War*, 910.
63. Ike, *Japan's Decision for War*, 185; Kase, *Journey to the Missouri*, 55–56.
64. *PHA* 12:150–51, 154.
65. Ibid., 94–95.
66. Ibid., 22, 45.
67. Ibid., 129.
68. Ibid., 138.
69. Ibid., 135.
70. *PHA* 14:1143–46.
71. *PHA* 12:96–97.
72. Ibid., 47–48.
73. Ibid., 81.
74. Ibid., 82.
75. Ibid., 90.
76. Reitman, "Japan Broke U.S. Code."
77. Lowe, *Origins of Pacific War*, 275.
78. Ibid.; Ike, *Japan's Decision for War*, 279–83.

CHAPTER 13: COUNTDOWN IN WASHINGTON: THE NOVEMBER TURNING POINT

1. *PHA* 14:1061–67.
2. Feis, *Road to Pearl Harbor*, 295.

3. *PHA* 11:5431.
4. Ibid., 5420.
5. Collier, *Road to Pearl Harbor*, 209.
6. Bland, *Papers of Marshall*, 676–80.
7. Ibid., 678, 679.
8. Krock, "Philippines as a Fortress," 10.
9. Long, *War Diary*, 224. See also Stimson, Diaries, 168.
10. *PHA* 14:1165.
11. *PHA* 16:2143; 31:3221.
12. *PHA* 12:155.
13. *PHA* 14:1122–23.
14. Ibid., 1144–46.
15. *PHA* 12:165. See also *PHA* 11:5397–98.
16. Ben-Zvi, *Illusion of Deterrence*, 69–70.
17. Freidel, *Franklin D. Roosevelt*, 399; *PHA* 14:1139–41.
18. Langer and Gleason, *Undeclared War*, 883. See also Hull, *Memoirs of Cordell Hull*, 1073.
19. *PHA* 2:774–75.
20. Lash, *Roosevelt and Churchill*, 471.
21. *PHA* 14:1347–48; 20:4085–87; Feis, *Road to Pearl Harbor*, 316; Langer and Gleason, *Undeclared War*, 712–13.
22. *PHA* 11:5435; 2:434.
23. *PHA* 2:434.
24. *PHA* 5:2315.
25. *PHA* 11:5433.
26. *PHA* 14:1167–74.
27. Ibid., 1167–69.
28. Ibid., 1198–2000.
29. *PHA* 11:5434.
30. Pogue, *Marshall: Ordeal and Hope*, 203, 207; Layton, *And I Was There*, 190–91; Utley, *Going to War*, 175, 178.
31. *PHA* 11:5371; Hull, *Memoirs of Cordell Hull*, 1081–82.
32. *PHA* 11:5371.
33. *PHA* 14:1162–63.
34. *PHA* 2:554.
35. Feis, *Road to Pearl Harbor*, 39.
36. Gellman, *Secret Affairs*, 11–19, 22, passim; Sherwood, *Papers of Hopkins*, 160; Grew, *Ten Years in Japan*, 109; Watson, *Chief of Staff*, 5.
37. Hasluck, *Government and People*,
551, 553, 555; *PHA* 14:1182–83.
38. *PHA* 11:5374; 19:3689; Hasluck, *Government and People*, 551–53.
39. *PHA* 2:968; 27:64; 31:166.
40. Beatty, "Another Version," 48; *PHA* 2:495–98, 500; 29:2082–83.
41. *PHA* 19:3661; Langer and Gleason, *Undeclared War*, 898.
42. *PHA* 4:1708.
43. *PHA* 11:5423, 5425; 34:110; Pogue, *Marshall: Ordeal and Hope*, 206–9; Mosley, *Marshall*, 163–69; Cray, *General of the Army*, 244.
44. *PHA* 12:199.
45. *PHA* 33:1379.
46. *PHA* 35:654.
47. *PHA* 34:136.
48. *PHA* 14:1168, 1195; 5:2326–27, 2329–30.
49. *PHA* 11:5422, 5434; Costello, *Days of Infamy*, 133–34.
50. *PHA* 5:2198; 31:3217; 35:50–51; 37:794–95.
51. Costello, *Days of Infamy*, 117–18.
52. Ibid., 119; Harvey, *War Diaries*, 40, 66, 69.
53. *PHA* 14:1300.
54. *PHA* 15:1476–77; Feis, *Road to Pearl Harbor*, 316; Loewenheim, Langley, and Jonas, *Roosevelt and Churchill*, 163–64.
55. R. Lee, *London Observer*, 80.
56. Churchill, *Grand Alliance*, 489.
57. *PHA* 20:4085–87; 33:1234.
58. *PHA* 14:1179–80.
59. Churchill, *Grand Alliance*, 596; Gilbert, *Winston S. Churchill*, 1260.
60. Churchill, *Grand Alliance*, 595.
61. Costello, *Days of Infamy*, 127, 386.
62. Hull, *Memoirs of Cordell Hull*, 1081–82.
63. Ibid., 1082.
64. Costello, *Days of Infamy*, 128; *PHA* 14:1194–97.
65. Costello, *Days of Infamy*, 127–28; Berle, *Navigating the Rapids*, 381; *PHA* 2:554–55; 4:1694.
66. Stinnett, *Day of Deceit*, 178.
67. *PHA* 20:4473. See also *PHA* 15:1825, 1848; Kimball, *Forged in War*, 112.
68. Bergamini, *Japan's Imperial Conspiracy*, 867. Langer and Gleason

also rejected Chiang's protest and Churchill's cable as sufficient reason to drop the modus, writing, "There must, therefore, have been something more behind the decision to abandon the project." *Undeclared War*, 890–91. Gleason had been an intelligence officer in Roosevelt's administration.

69. Costello, *Days of Infamy*, 119.
70. Harvey, *War Diaries*, 66; Beach, *Scapegoats*, 32.
71. Rusbridger and Nave, *Betrayal at Pearl Harbor*, 141.
72. Kahn, "Codebreaking," 143; *PHA* 3:1213; Stafford, *Roosevelt and Churchill*, 22.
73. G. Douglas, *Gestapo Chief*, 1:46–50.
74. Archivist Dr. Lenz (Bundesarchiv in Coblenz), letters to author, February 23, 1999; March 9, 1999; and March 24, 1999.
75. United States Strategic Bombing Survey, *Campaigns*, 50.
76. Casey, *Secret War Against Hitler*, 7.
77. Fitzgibbon, *Secret Intelligence*, 255; Rusbridger and Nave, *Betrayal at Pearl Harbor*, 154; Wilford, *Pearl Harbor Redefined*, 99; Stonehouse, "Pearl Harbor Conspiracy," 1–2.
78. *PHA* 27:27. See also 14:1366; 29:2351.
79. *PHA* 33:729.
80. Ibid., 732–33.
81. Blum, *Roosevelt and Morgenthau*, 417–18. Morgenthau's diary in NA-FDR is an enormous collection of memos, clippings, and so on, which he saw on a given day, and includes notes he made.
82. *PHA* 19:3506. See also chap. 14.
83. Conn and Fairchild, *Framework of Hemispheric Defense*, 153.
84. *PHA* 11:5433.
85. Langer and Gleason, *Undeclared War*, 886; Prange, *At Dawn We Slept*, 287, 372; Prange, *Pearl Harbor*, 206.
86. *PHA* 11:5421.
87. Ibid., 5226. And Stimson told the committee, "it was important . . . that we should not be placed in the position of firing the first shot, if this could be done without sacrificing our safety, but that Japan should appear in her true role as the real aggressor." *PHA* 11:5419.
88. *PHA* 11:5227, 5224, 5230.
89. Ibid., 5188.
90. Ibid. See also *PHA* 3:1173–74.
91. *PHA* 11:5194.
92. *PHA* 29:2402.
93. *PHA* 11:5425–26; 29:2162–64, 2402; Pogue, *Marshall: Ordeal and Hope*, 207–8; Cray, *General of the Army*, 242.
94. Victor, *Hitler*, 197, 241–42.
95. Le Vien and Lord, *Winston Churchill*, 118.
96. *PHA* 16:2164–65.
97. Lowe, *Origins of Pacific War*, 286; Slessor, *Central Blue*, 340.

CHAPTER 14:
AWAITING THE BLOW

1. Stevenson, *Man Called Intrepid*, 239; *PHA* 14:1186.
2. *PHA* 14:1196; Conorton, "The Role of Radio Intelligence in the American-Japanese Naval War," 17; Layton, *And I Was There*, 259; *PHA* 49:4216; Falk, *Seventy Days to Singapore*, 60.
3. *PHA* 35:43.
4. *PHA* 14:1184–85; 39:43.
5. Freidel, *Franklin D. Roosevelt*, 401.
6. *PHA* 11:5545–46.
7. *PHA* 12:195, 208.
8. Willey, *Pearl Harbor*, 79.
9. *PHA* 15:1743.
10. Parker, *Pearl Harbor Revisited*, 47.
11. Hoehling, *Week Before Pearl Harbour*, 160; *PHA* 10:4812–13. McCollum said, "It was realized that with a surprise attack coming . . . that we were going to take it on the chin. The problem actually was one for . . . Admiral Kimmel and Admiral Hart to hope that they could minimize the extent of the damages." McCollum, Oral History, 87.

12. Costello, *Days of Infamy*, 326.
13. Ibid., 327.
14. Layton, *And I Was There*, 240–41, 248, 252.
15. Costello, *Days of Infamy*, 140–45. See also Lowe, *Origins of Pacific War*, 270–71.
16. Esthus, *From Enmity to Alliance*, 215–18.
17. Robertson and McCarthy, *Australian War Strategy*, 279.
18. Weintraub, *Long Day's Journey*, 152.
19. Layton, *And I Was There*, 287.
20. Ibid., after 528.
21. *PHA* 9:4240; 3:1569–70.
22. Nelson, *Arsenal of Democracy*, 182–83; C. Beard, *Roosevelt and War*, 537.
23. Layton, *And I Was There*, 166.
24. Costello, *Days of Infamy*, 189.
25. *PHA* 8:3385, 3388–90, 3412; 32:880; McCollum, Oral History, 84.
26. *PHA* 29:2396.
27. *PHA* 8:3384–85.
28. *PHA* 4:1758, 1867–68; 33:774.
29. *PHA* 33:774.
30. *PHA* 29:2399.
31. Ibid.
32. Ibid.
33. *PHA* 10:4645–46.
34. *PHA* 29:2430.
35. *PHA* 10:4630, 4636–37.
36. *PHA* 29:2454.
37. *PHA* 3:1343–44; 4:1963, 2002; 29:2454.
38. *PHA* 9:4534.
39. *PHA* 14:1407.
40. *PHA* 9:4252; Costello, *Pacific War*, 642; Morton, *Fall of the Philippines*, 47.
41. Prange, *Pearl Harbor*, 45.
42. Tolley, *Cruise of the Lanikai*, 15.
43. Fleming, *New Dealer's War*, 13.
44. Tolley, *Cruise of the Lanikai*, 269.
45. Winslow, *Fleet the Gods Forgot*, 251.
46. Prange, *Pearl Harbor*, 49.
47. Ibid., 50.
48. Tolley, *Cruise of the Lanikai*, 279.
49. Ibid., 270.
50. Layton, *And I Was There*, 248.
51. Winslow, *Fleet the Gods Forgot*, 251.
52. *PHA* 9:4252.
53. Ibid., 4252–53; Tolley, *Cruise of the Lanikai*, 264.
54. *PHA* 9:4253–54.
55. Ibid., 4254.
56. Perkins, "President Faces War," 114; Toland, *Infamy*, 1st ed., 294–95.
57. *PHA* 4:1742, 1756, 1779, 1878, 1967, 2018; 36:233.
58. Beatty, "Another Version," 49.
59. Weintraub, *Long Day's Journey*, 34; Bridgeman, "Saturday December 6, 1941" 144–46.
60. Bridgeman, "Saturday December 6, 1941," 144–49, 167; Farago, *Broken Seal*, 343–47.
61. *PHA* 33:1380; 10:4926–30.
62. *PHA* 8:3556–57; 9:3983; 39:228.
63. Hurt, "Version of Japanese Problem," 3, 28.
64. *PHA* 9:4509, 4512–13; 10:4926–29.
65. *PHA* 2:945; 4:1761, 1763; 9:3988–94, 4027–28, 4509–13; 29:2419–23, 2455.
66. *PHA* 3:1366, 1555.
67. *PHA* 3:1555–56, Pogue, *Marshall: Ordeal and Hope*, 224.
68. Hoehling, *Week Before Pearl Harbour*, 117–18.
69. *PHA* 10:4661–63.
70. Ibid., 4663.
71. Ibid., 4662.
72. Cray, *General of the Army*, 252.
73. *PHA* 10:4663–64.
74. Bergamini, *Japan's Imperial Conspiracy*, 882.
75. Prange, *December 7, 1941*, 247–48.
76. Lash, *Roosevelt and Churchill*, 486.
77. Prange, *December 7, 1941*, 247; Lombard, *While They Fought*, 10.
78. *PHA* 10:4736–38.
79. *PHA* 4:1762–63; 9:4229–30.
80. Costello, *Days of Infamy*, 207, 399.
81. *PHA* 10:4670.
82. *PHA* 3:1430.
83. Ibid., 1176.
84. Costello, *Days of Infamy*, 207, 399.
85. *PHA* 11:5543–44.
86. Ibid., 5544.
87. Ibid., 5545.
88. *PHA* 32:857.
89. *PHA* 19:3536–37; 11:5247–48, 5482–83.

90. *PHA* 11:5248; 19:3537.
91. *PHA* 11:5248–49, 5252, 5265.
92. Ibid., 5556–59.
93. *PHA* 29:2402.
94. *PHA* 11:5483, 5265.
95. *PHA* 2:926.
96. *PHA* 33:826.
97. *PHA* 3:1114, 1184.
98. *PHA* 11:5193–94; 3:1110.
99. *PHA* 11:5232.
100. Ibid.
101. *PHA* 5:2291.
102. Layton, *And I Was There*, 295, 332; According to Layton (555), originals of Stahlman's letters are in Kimmel Papers, University of Wyoming, Laramie; Beach, *Scapegoats*, 90, 91, 168, 204.
103. Stahlman letter to Kemp Tolley, November 26, 1973, copy in my files.
104. *PHA* 6:2846.
105. Toland, *Infamy*, 1st ed., 301.
106. Hoehling, *Week Before Pearl Harbour*, 112–13.
107. Morton, *Fall of the Philippines*, 73.
108. Hoehling, *Week Before Pearl Harbour*, 112–13. See also C. Lee, *They Call It Pacific*, 32; Bartsch, *December 8, 1941*, 128.
109. *PHA* 12:245.
110. Ibid., 248.
111. *PHA* 29:2385; 36:84.
112. *PHA* 3:1532.
113. *PHA* 8:3910; 36:84; Hoehling, *Week Before Pearl Harbour*, 128.
114. *PHA* 36:25–26.
115. *PHA* 4:1766–68; 8:3393ff.; 36:25.
116. Prados, *Combined Fleet Decoded*, 166.
117. McCollum, Oral History, 413.
118. Ibid., 411.
119. Ibid., 412.
120. Stafford, *Roosevelt and Churchill*, 113; Bridgeman, "Saturday December 6, 1941," 167.
121. Hoehling, *Week Before Pearl Harbour*, 165.
122. Pogue, *Marshall: Ordeal and Hope*, 228.
123. *PHA* 9:4549.

124. *PHA*. 14:1411; Toland, *Infamy*, 1st ed., 320; Barnes, "Historian Investigates," 15.
125. *PHA* 9:4573.
126. *PHA* 3:1115; 34:30.
127. *PHA* 14:1410.
128. *PHA* 2:929; 14:1391.
129. *PHA* 29:2198.
130. *PHA* 33:822; 3:1108.
131. *PHA* 29:2312, 2346–47; 9:4518.
132. *PHA* 39:95; 2:813, 934; 3:1213, 29:2403–4; Gannon, *Pearl Harbor Betrayed*, 233; Pogue, *Marshall: Ordeal and Hope*, 230.
133. *PHA* 3:1213.
134. Prange, *Pearl Harbor*, 224–25.
135. *PHA* 3:1523–24.
136. *PHA* 18:3321.
137. Ibid.
138. Le Vien and Lord, *Winston Churchill*, 123; Churchill, *Grand Alliance*, 606–8.
139. Costello, *Days of Infamy*, 124.
140. Harriman, *Special Envoy*, 112.
141. Eleanor Roosevelt, *This I Remember*, 233.
142. McLaughlin, "Mrs. Roosevelt," 41.
143. Sherwood, *Roosevelt and Hopkins*, 428.
144. Ibid., 431.
145. Mowrer, *Triumph and Turmoil*, 324, 327.
146. Stinnett, *Day of Deceit*, 203.
147. Vandenberg, *Private Papers*, 1–2, 16.
148. Mintz, *Revisionism and Pearl Harbor*, 17.
149. *PHA* 19:3506; 20:4471; 35:677, 684–85, 687.
150. Clubb, *20th Century China*, 151, 231.
151. Van Mook, *Netherlands Indies and Japan*, 107.

AFTERWORD: HISTORY AND THE UNTHINKABLE

1. Jaspers, *Goal of History*, 149.
2. Feis, "War at Pearl Harbor," 378–79. Also Prange, *Pearl Harbor*, 42; Gannon, *Pearl Harbor Betrayed*, 323.
3. C. Beard and M. Beard, *Rise of American Civilization*, 1:604–5;

Hofstadter, Miller, and Aaron, *United States*, 319–30; Ross, *Annexation of Mexico*, 28, 32; Williams, *History of American Wars*, 145–55.

4. Williams, *History of American Wars*, 155; Takaki, *Different Mirror*, 175.

5. Brooks, *Abraham Lincoln*, 242–57; Hofstadter, Miller, and Aaron, *United States*, 319–30; C. Beard and M. Beard, *Rise of American Civilization*, 2:63–65; Williams, *History of American Wars*, 198–211; B. Wood and Edmonds, *Civil War*, 11–16; Hofstadter, *American Political Tradition*, 120ff.; Sandburg, *Abraham Lincoln*, 188–93.

6. Williams, *History of American Wars*, 320–21; Millis, *Martial Spirit*, 82, 89, 93–146.

7. Clyde, *Far East*, 278.

8. Hofstadter, *American Political Tradition*, 155.

9. Ibid., 450.

10. Prange, *At Dawn We Slept*, 313.

11. Willoughby and Chamberlain, *MacArthur*, 27.

12. Langer and Gleason, *Undeclared War*, 43.

13. Morton, *Fall of the Philippines*, 67.

14. Collier, *Road to Pearl Harbor*, 213.

15. Bartsch, *December 8, 1941*, before 1, 193; MacArthur, *Reminiscences*, 113; Rovere and Schlesinger, *MacArthur Controversy*, 44.

16. Bartsch, *December 8, 1941*, 241.

17. Perkins, "President Faces War," 115.

18. Bartsch, *December 8, 1941*, 55–56, 410ff.

19. Pogue, *Marshall: Ordeal and Hope*, 222; Morton, *Fall of the Philippines*, 35ff.

20. Beck, *MacArthur and Wainwright*, 5–6, 21, 24.

21. Ibid., 24.

22. Ibid.

23. Ibid., 63.

24. Ibid., 61.

25. Rovere and Schlesinger, *MacArthur Controversy*, 58–59; C. Lee, *They Call It Pacific*, 240.

26. Beck, *MacArthur and Wainwright*, 89.

27. Ibid., 90.

28. Whitney, *MacArthur*, 27ff.

29. *PHA* 3:1510.

30. Ibid., 1512.

31. Ibid., 1533.

32. Ibid., 1444; Wohlstetter, *Pearl Harbor*, 92, 168–69.

33. *PHA* 2:877.

34. Ibid.

REFERENCES

Abaya, Hernando. *Betrayal in the Philippines*. New York: Wyn, 1946.

Abbazia, Frank. *Mr. Roosevelt's Navy: The Private War of the U.S. Atlantic Fleet, 1939-1942*. Annapolis, MD: Naval Institute Press, 1975.

Adamthwaite, Anthony. *The Making of the Second World War*. London: Allen and Unwin, 1977.

Agawa, Hiroyuki. *The Reluctant Admiral: Yamamoto and the Imperial Navy*. Tokyo: Kodansha, 1979.

Albright, Harry. *Pearl Harbor: Japan's Fatal Blunder; The True Story behind Japan's Attack on December 7, 1941*. New York: Hippocrene, 1988.

Aldrich, Richard. *Intelligence and the War Against Japan: Britain, America and the Politics of Secret Service*. Cambridge: Cambridge University Press, 2000.

Alsop, Stewart, and Thomas Braden. *Sub Rosa: The OSS and American Espionage*. New York: Harvest, 1964.

Amery, Leo. *The Unforgiving Years*. London: Hutchinson, 1955.

Anderson, Irvine. *The Standard-Vacuum Oil Company and United States East Asian Policy, 1933-1941*. Princeton, NJ: Princeton University Press, 1975.

Andrew, Christopher. *For the President's Eyes Only: Secret Intelligence and the American Presidency from Washington to Bush*. New York: HarperCollins, 1995.

Andrew, Christopher, and Oleg Gordievsky. *KGB: The Inside Story of Its Foreign Operations from Lenin to Gorbachev*. New York: HarperCollins, 1990.

Anesaki, Masaharu. *Art, Life and Nature in Japan*. Rutland, VT: Tuttle, 1973.

Arnold, Henry. *Global Mission*. New York: Harper, 1949.

Asahi Shimbun. *The Pacific Rivals: A Japanese View of Japanese-American Relations*. New York: Weatherhill/Asahi, 1972.

Aster, Sidney. "Guilty Men." In *Paths to War: New Essays on the Origins of the Second World War*, edited by Robert Boyce and Esmonde Robertson. New York: St. Martin's, 1989.

Badsey, Stephen. *Pearl Harbor*. New York: Mallard, 1971.

Baker, Kevin. "FDR: Not Guilty," *American Heritage*, July 2001.

Baldwin, Hanson. *Battles Lost and Won: Great Campaigns of World War II*. New York: Harper and Row, 1966.

Barnes, Harry. "A Historian Investigates a Tough Question." *Chicago Tribune*, December 7, 1966.

Bartlett, Bruce. *Cover-Up: The Politics of Pearl Harbor, 1941-1946*. New Rochelle, NY: Arlington House, 1978.

Bartsch, William. *December 8, 1941: MacArthur's Pearl Harbor*. College Station: Texas A&M University Press, 2003.

_____. *Doomed at the Start: American Pursuit Pilots in the Philippines, 1941-1942*. College Station: Texas A&M University Press, 1992.

Baudot, Maurice, Henri Bernard, Hendrik Brugmans, Michael Foot, and Hans-Adolf Jabobsen, eds. *The Historical Encyclopedia of World War II*. New York: Facts on File, 1980.

Beach, Edward. *Scapegoats: A Defense of Kimmel and Short at Pearl Harbor*. Annapolis, MD: Naval Institute Press, 1995.

Beard, Charles. *President Roosevelt and the Coming of the War, 1941: A Study in Appearances and Realities*. New Haven: Yale University Press, 1948.

Beard, Charles, and Mary Beard. *The Rise of American Civilization*. New York: Macmillan, 1935.

Beasley, W. G. *The Modern History of Japan*. New York: Praeger, 1973.

Beatty, Frank. "Another Version of What Started War with Japan." *U.S. News and World Report*, May 28, 1954.

_____. "The Background of the Secret Report." *National Review*, December 23, 1966.

Beck, John. *MacArthur and Wainwright: Sacrifice of the Philippines*. Albuquerque: University of New Mexico Press, 1974.

Ben-Zvi, Abraham. *The Illusion of Deterrence: The Roosevelt Presidency and the Origins of the Pacific War*. Boulder: Westview, 1987.

Bergamini, David. *Japan's Imperial Conspiracy*. New York: Pocket, 1972.

Berle, Adolf. *Navigating the Rapids*. New York: Harcourt Brace Jovanovich, 1973.

Bernstein, Marvin, and Francis Loewenheim. "Aid to Russia." In *American Civil-Military Decisions*, edited by Harold Stein. Birmingham: University of Alabama Press, 1963.

Bland, Larry, ed. *The Papers of George Catlett Marshall*. Vol. 2. Baltimore: Johns Hopkins University Press, 1986.

Blum, John. *Roosevelt and Morgenthau*. Boston: Houghton Mifflin, 1972.

_____. *Years of Urgency*. Boston: Houghton Mifflin, 1965.

Bohlen, Charles. *The Transformation of American Foreign Policy*. New York: Norton, 1969.

Borquist, Daryl. "Advance Warning? The Red Cross Connection" *Naval History*, May/June 1999.

Brandenburg, Erich. "Otto Bismarck." In *Encyclopaedia Britannica*. Vol. 3. Chicago: Encyclopaedia Britannica, 1952.

Brereton, Lewis. *The Brereton Diaries*. New York: Morrow, 1946.

Bridgeman, Jon. "Saturday, December 6, 1941." In *Pearl Harbor Revisited*, edited by Robert Love. New York: St Martin's, 1995.

Brinkley, David. *Washington Goes to War*. New York: Knopf, 1988.

Brooks, Noah. *Abraham Lincoln*. New York: Putnam, 1988.

Brown, Anthony. *C: The Secret Life of Sir Stewart Graham Menzies, Spymaster to Winston Churchill*. New York: Macmillan, 1987.

_____. *The Last Hero: Wild Bill Donovan; The Biography and Political Experience of Major General William J. Donovan . . . .* New York: Times Books, 1982.

Browne, Courtney. *Tojo: The Last Banzai*. New York: Paperback Library, 1968.

Browne, Waldo, and Nathan Dole. *The New America and the Far East*. Boston: Jones, 1907.

Brownlow, Donald. *The Accused: The Ordeal of Rear Admiral Husband Edward Kimmel, U.S.N.* New York: Vantage, 1968.

Bryant, Arthur. *The Turn of the Tide: A History of the War Years Based on the Diaries of Field-Marshal Lord Alanbrooke, Chief of the Imperial General Staff.* Garden City, NY: Doubleday, 1957.

Buell, Thomas. *Master of Sea Power: A Biography of Fleet Admiral Ernest J. King.* Boston: Little, Brown, 1980.

Burns, James. *Roosevelt: The Lion and the Fox*. New York: Harvest, 1956.

_____. *Roosevelt: The Soldier of Freedom*. New York: Harcourt Brace Jovanovich, 1970.

Burtness, Paul, and Warren Ober, eds. *The Puzzle of Pearl Harbor*. Evanston, IL: Row, Peterson, 1962.

Butow, Robert. *The John Doe Associates: Backdoor Diplomacy for Peace, 1941.* Stanford, CA: Stanford University Press, 1974.

_____. *Tojo and the Coming of the War*. Stanford, CA: Stanford University Press, 1969.

Byas, Hugh. *Government by Assassination*. New York: Knopf, 1942.

Byrnes, James. *Speaking Frankly*. New York: Harper, 1947.

Carney, Robert. "A Well-Kept Secret." *Shipmate*, June 1983.

Casey, William. *The Secret War Against Hitler*. Washington, DC: Regnery Gateway, 1988.

Chamberlain, Basil. *Japanese Things: Being Notes on Various Subjects Connected with Japan, for the Use of Travelers and Others*. Rutland, VT: Tuttle, 1971.

Chang, Iris. *The Rape of Nanking: The Forgotten Holocaust of World War II*. New York: Basic Books, 1997.

Churchill, Winston. *Great Contemporaries*. Chicago: University of Chicago Press, 1933.

_____. *The Gathering Storm*. Boston: Houghton Mifflin, 1948.

_____. *The Grand Alliance*. Boston: Houghton Mifflin, 1951.

Clark, Ronald. *The Man Who Broke Purple: The Life of the World's Greatest Cryptologist, Colonel William F. Friedman*. London: Weidenfeld and Nicolson, 1977.

Clarke, Thurston. *Pearl Harbor Ghosts: A Journey to Hawaii, Then and Now*. New York: Morrow, 1991.

Clausen, Henry, and Bruce Lee. *Pearl Harbor: Final Judgement*. New York: Crown, 1992.

Clubb, Edmund. *20th Century China*. New York: Columbia University Press, 1964.

Clyde, Paul. *The Far East: A History of the Impact of the West on Eastern Asia.* New York: Prentice-Hall, 1962.

Cohen, Stan. *East Wind Rain: A Pictorial History of the Pearl Harbor Attack.* Rev. ed. Missoula, MT: Pictorial Histories, 1991.

Coleman, Joseph. "Losing Was Never So Glorious" *Newark (NJ) Star-Ledger,* March 23, 2004.

Collier, Richard. *The Road to Pearl Harbor–1941.* New York: Atheneum Books, 1981.

Colville, John. *The Fringes of Power: Downing Street Diaries, 1939–1955.* London: Hodder and Stoughton, 1985.

Congressional Record. 85th Cong., 2nd sess., 1958, Vol. 104, p. 8148.

Conn, Stetson, Rose Engleman, and Byron Fairchild. *Guarding the United States and Its Outposts.* Washington, DC: Department of the Army, 1964.

Conn, Stetson, and Byron Fairchild. *The Framework of Hemispheric Defense.* Washington, DC: Department of the Army, 1959.

Connally, Tom. *My Name is Tom Connally.* New York: Crowell, 1954.

Conorton, John. "The Role of Radio Intelligence in the American-Japanese Naval War." In RG 38, box 46, RIP 87Z. National Archives, College Park, MD.

Corson, William. *The Armies of Ignorance: The Rise of the American Intelligence Empire.* New York: Dial, 1977.

Costello, John. *Days of Infamy: MacArthur, Roosevelt, Churchill, the Shocking Truth Revealed.* New York: Pocket Books, 1994.

_____. *The Pacific War.* New York: Rawson, Wade, 1981.

Cray, Ed. *General of the Army: George C. Marshall, Soldier and Statesman.* New York: Touchstone, 1991.

Crowley, James. *Japan's Quest for Autonomy: National Security and Foreign Policy, 1930-1938.* Princeton, NJ: Princeton University Press, 1966.

Dallek, Robert, ed. *The Roosevelt Diplomacy and World War II.* New York: Holt, Rinehart and Winston, 1970.

Davis, Kenneth. *FDR: The War President.* New York: Random House, 2000.

Dawson, Raymond. *The Decision to Aid Russia.* Chapel Hill: University of North Carolina Press, 1959.

Deakin, F., and Richard Storry. *The Case of Richard Sorge.* New York: Harper and Row, 1966.

Department of State. *Papers Relating to the Foreign Relations of the United States, Japan 1931–1941.* Washington, DC: Government Printing Office, 1943.

Dies, Martin. "Assassination and Its Aftermath, Part II." *American Opinion,* April 1964.

Divine, Robert. *The Illusion of Neutrality.* Chicago: University of Chicago Press, 1962.

_____. *The Reluctant Belligerent: American Entry into World War II.* New York: Knopf, 1979.

Dolan, Ronald, ed. *Philippines: A Country Study.* Washington, DC: Department of the Army, 1993.

Dorwart, Jeffery. *Conflict of Duty: The U.S. Navy's Intelligence Dilemma, 1919-1945.* Annapolis, MD: Naval Institute Press, 1983.

_____. "The Roosevelt-Astor Espionage Ring." *New York History*, 1961, no. 3: 307–22.

Douglas, Gregory. *The Gestapo Chief: The 1948 Interrogation of Heinrich Müller; From Secret U.S. Intelligence Files*. Vol. 1. San Jose: Bender, 1995.

Douglas, W. *The Creation of a National Air Force*. Vol. 2. Toronto: University of Toronto Press, 1986.

Doyle, William. *Inside the Oval Office: The White House Tapes from FDR to Clinton*. New York: Kodansha, 1999.

Dunmore, Spencer. *In Great Waters: The Epic Story of the Battle of the Atlantic, 1939–45*. Toronto: McClelland and Stewart, 1999.

Durant, Will. *Our Oriental Heritage*. New York: Simon and Schuster, 1954.

Dürckheim, Karlfried. *The Japanese Cult of Tranquility*. York Beach, ME: Weiser, 1991.

Dyer, George. *The Amphibians Came to Conquer: The Story of Admiral Richmond Kelly Turner*. Washington, DC: Department of the Navy, 1969.

Dziuban, Stanley. *Military Relations between the United States and Canada*. Washington, DC: Department of the Army, 1958.

Eden, Anthony. *Facing the Dictators: The Memoirs of Anthony Eden, Earl of Avon*. Boston: Houghton Mifflin, 1962.

Edmonds, Walter. *They Fought with What They Had: The Story of the Army Air Forces in the Southwest Pacific, 1941–1942*. Washington, DC: Center for Air Force History, 1992.

Erfurth, Waldemar. *Surprise*. Harrisburg, PA: Military Service, 1943.

Esthus, Raymond. *From Enmity to Alliance: U.S.-Australian Relations, 1931–1941*. Seattle: University of Washington Press, 1964.

Fairchild, Bryan. "Decision to Land United States Forces in Iceland, 1941." In *Command Decisions*, edited by Kent Greenfield. Washington, DC: United States Army, 2000.

Falk, Stanley. *Seventy Days to Singapore*. New York: Putnam, 1975.

Farago, Ladislas. *Burn After Reading: The Espionage History of World War II*. New York: Walker, 1961.

_____. *The Broken Seal: The Story of Operation Magic and the Pearl Harbor Disaster*. New York: Random House, 1967.

Farley, James. *Jim Farley's Story: The Roosevelt Years*. New York: Whittlesey House, 1948.

Fehrenbach, T. *F.D.R.'s Undeclared War, 1939–1941*. New York: McKay, 1967.

Feiling, Keith. *The Life of Neville Chamberlain*. London: Macmillan, 1946.

Feis, Herbert. *Churchill, Roosevelt, Stalin: The War They Waged and the Peace They Sought*. Princeton, NJ: Princeton University Press, 1957.

_____. *The Road to Pearl Harbor*. New York: Atheneum Books, 1962.

_____. "War Came at Pearl Harbor." In *The American Past: Conflicting Interpretations of the Great Issues*, edited by Sidney Fine and Gerald Brown. Vol. 2. New York: Macmillan, 1961.

FitzGibbon, Constantine. *Secret Intelligence in the Twentieth Century*. Briarcliff Manor, NY: Stein and Day, 1976.

Fleming, Thomas. *The New Dealer's War: FDR and the War within World War II*. New York: Basic Books, 2001.

Freidel, Frank. *Franklin D. Roosevelt: A Rendezvous with Destiny*. Boston: Little, Brown, 1990.

Friedrich, Carl. *The Pathology of Politics: Violence, Betrayal, Corruption, Secrecy, and Propaganda*. New York: Harper and Row, 1972.

Furer, Julius. *Administration of the Navy Department in World War II*. Washington, DC: Government Printing Office, 1959.

Gannon, Michael. *Pearl Harbor Betrayed: The True Story of a Man and a Nation under Attack*. New York: Henry Holt, 2001.

Garlinski, Jozef. *The Enigma War*. New York: Scribner, 1979.

Gellman, Irwin. *Secret Affairs: Franklin Roosevelt, Cordell Hull, and Sumner Welles*. 2nd ed. New York: Enigma, 2002.

Gentry, Curt. *J. Edgar Hoover: The Man and the Secrets*. New York: Norton, 1991.

Gilbert, Martin. *Winston S. Churchill*. Boston: Houghton Mifflin, 1983.

Goldstein, Donald, and Katherine Dillon, eds. *The Pearl Harbor Papers: Inside the Japanese Plans*. Washington, DC: Brassey's, 1993.

Goodwin, Doris. *No Ordinary Time: Franklin and Eleanor Roosevelt; The Home Front in World War II*. New York: Touchstone, 1995.

Gray, Edwyn. *Operation Pacific: The Royal Navy's War against Japan, 1941–1945*. Annapolis, MD: Naval Institute Press, 1990.

Greaves, Percy. "The Pearl Harbor Investigations." In *Perpetual War for Perpetual Peace: A Critical Examination of the Foreign Policy of Franklin Delano Roosevelt and Its Aftermath*, edited by Harry Barnes. New York: Greenwood, 1969.

Grenfell, Russell. *Main Fleet to Singapore*. New York: Macmillan, 1952.

Grew, Joseph. *Ten Years in Japan: A Contemporary Record Drawn from the Diaries and Private and Official Papers of Joseph C. Grew*. New York: Simon and Schuster, 1944.

Gutman, Roy. *Witness to Genocide: The 1993 Pulitzer Prize–Winning Dispatches on the "Ethnic Cleansing" of Bosnia*. New York: Macmillan, 1993.

Gwyer, J. *Grand Strategy*. Vol. 3, pt. 1. London: Her Majesty's Stationery Office, 1964.

Haight, John. *American Aid to France, 1938-1940*. New York: Atheneum Books, 1970.

―――. "Franklin D. Roosevelt and a Naval Quarantine of Japan." *Pacific Historical Review* 40 (May 1971): 203–26.

Halifax, Lord. *See* Wood, Edward.

Harootunian, H. D. *Toward Restoration: The Growth of Political Consciousness in Tokugawa Japan*. Berkeley: University of California Press, 1970.

Harriman, Averell. *Special Envoy to Churchill and Stalin, 1941–1946*. New York: Random House, 1975.

Harvey, John, ed. *The War Diaries of Oliver Harvey, 1941–1945*. London: Collins, 1978.

Haslach, Robert. *Nishi no Kaze, Hare* [West wind, clear]. Weesp, Holland: Van Kampen, 1985.

Hasluck, Paul. *The Government and the People*. Canberra: Australian War Memorial, 1952.

Heardon, Patrick. *Roosevelt Confronts Hitler: America's Entry into World War II*. Dekalb: Northern Illinois University Press. 1987.

Hearn, Lafcadio. *Japan: An Attempt at Interpretation*. Rutland, VT: Tuttle, 1953.

Heinrichs, Waldo. *Threshold of War: Franklin D. Roosevelt and American Entry into World War II*. New York: Oxford University Press, 1988.

Hersey, John. *Men in Bataan*. New York: Knopf, 1943.

Herzstein, Robert. *Roosevelt and Hitler: Prelude to War*. New York: Paragon, 1989.

Hewitt, Kent. Hewitt File. Naval Academy Library, Annapolis, MD.

Hinsley, Francis. *British Intelligence in the Second World War*. Vol. 1. New York: Cambridge University Press, 1979.

Hoehling, A. *The Week before Pearl Harbour*. London: Hale, 1964.

Hofstadter, Richard. *The American Political Tradition and the Men Who Made It*. New York: Vintage, 1958.

Hofstadter, Richard, William Miller, and Daniel Aaron. *The United States*. Englewood Cliffs, NJ: Prentice Hall, 1967.

Hornbeck, Stanley. *The United States and the Far East: Certain Fundamentals of Policy*. Boston: World Peace Foundation, 1942.

Horne, Alistair. *To Lose a Battle: France 1940*. Boston: Little, Brown, 1969.

Hough, Richard. *Mountbatten*. New York: Random House, 1981.

Hull, Cordell. *The Memoirs of Cordell Hull*. Vol. 2. New York: Macmillan, 1948.

Hunt, Frazier. *The Untold Story of Douglas MacArthur*. New York: Devin-Adair, 1954.

Hurt, John. "A Version of the Japanese Problem in the Signal Intelligence Service." SRH 252. National Archives, College Park, MD.

Ickes, Harold. *The Lowering Clouds*. New York: Simon and Schuster, 1954.

Ienaga, Saburo. *The Pacific War*. New York: Pantheon, 1978.

Ike, Nobutake. *Japan's Decision for War: Records of the 1941 Policy Conferences*. Stanford, CA: Stanford University Press, 1967.

Iriye, Akira. *Across the Pacific: An Inner History of American-East Asian Relations*. New York: Harcourt, Brace and World, 1967.

Irving, David. *Hitler's War*. New York: Avon, 1990.

James, Robert, ed. *Winston S. Churchill: His Complete Speeches*. Vol. 6. New York: Chelsea, 1974.

Jansen, Marius. *Japan and Its World: Two Centuries of Change*. Princeton, NJ: Princeton University Press, 1980.

Jaspers, Karl. *The Origin and Goal of History*. New Haven: Yale University Press, 1953.

Joint Committee on the Investigation of the Pearl Harbor Attack. *Pearl Harbor Attack*. Washington, DC: Government Printing Office, 1946.

Kahn, David. "Codebreaking in World Wars I and II." In *The Missing Dimension: Governments and Intelligence Communities in the Twentieth Century*, edited by Christopher Andrew and David Dilks. Urbana: University of Illinois Press, 1984.

Kase, Toshikazu. *Journey to the Missouri*. New Haven: Yale University Press, 1950.

Kennedy, David. *Freedom from Fear*. New York: Oxford University Press, 1999.

Kennedy, Ludovic. *Pursuit: The Chase and Sinking of the Bismarck.* New York: Viking, 1974.

Kenney, George. *The MacArthur I Know.* New York: Duell, Sloan and Pearce, 1951.

Kershaw, Ian. *Hitler: Nemesis.* New York: Norton, 2000.

Ketchum, Carlton. *The Recollections of Colonel Retread, USAAF 1942–1945.* Pittsburgh: Hart, 1976.

Kido, Koichi. *The Diary of Marquis Kido, 1931–45.* Frederick, MD: University Publications of America, 1984.

Kimball, Warren. *Forged in War: Roosevelt, Churchill, and the Second World War.* New York: Morrow, 1998.

Kimmel, Husband. *Admiral Kimmel's Story.* Chicago: Regnery, 1955.

_____. Papers. University of Wyoming Library, Laramie.

King, Ernest, and Walter Whitehill. *Fleet Admiral King: A Naval Record.* New York: Norton, 1952.

Kinsella, William. *Leadership in Isolation: FDR and the Origins of the Second World War.* Boston: Hall, 1978.

Kittredge, Tracy. "U.S. British Naval Cooperation 1940–45." Operational Archives. Washington Navy Yard, DC.

Klingaman, William. *1941: Our Lives in a World on the Edge.* New York: Harper and Row, 1989.

Komatsu, Keiichiro. *Origins of the Pacific War and the Importance of "Magic."* New York: St. Martin's, 1999.

Krock, Arthur. "Philippines as a Fortress." *New York Times,* November 19, 1941.

LaFeber, Walter. *The Clash: A History of U.S.-Japan Relations.* New York: Norton, 1997.

Lamont-Brown, Raymond. *Kamikaze: Japan's Suicide Samurai.* London: Cassel, 1999.

Landis, Kenneth, and Rex Gunn. *Deceit at Pearl Harbor.* N.p.: 1st Books, 2001.

Langer, William. *Our Vichy Gamble.* New York: Norton, 1966.

Langer, William, and S. Everett Gleason. *The Challenge to Isolation, 1937–1940.* New York: Harper, 1952.

_____. *The Undeclared War, 1940–1941.* New York: Harper, 1953.

Lash, Joseph. *Roosevelt and Churchill, 1939–1941: The Partnership That Saved the West.* New York: Norton, 1976.

Layton, Edwin. *And I Was There: Pearl Harbor and Midway – Breaking the Secrets.* New York: Morrow, 1985.

Lazareff, Pierre. *Deadline: The Behind-the-Scenes Story of the Last Decade in France.* New York: Random House, 1942.

Leahy, William. *I Was There.* New York: Whittlesey, 1950.

Lee, Clark. *They Call It Pacific: An Eye-Witness Story of Our War against Japan from Bataan to the Solomons.* New York: Viking, 1943.

Lee, Raymond. *London Observer* (aka *The London Journal of General Raymond E. Lee*). London: Hutchinson, 1972.

Leigh, Michael. *Mobilizing Consent: Public Opinion and American Foreign Policy, 1937–1947.* Westport, CT: Greenwood, 1976.

Leighton, Richard, and Robert Coakley. *Global Logistics and Strategy.* Washington, DC: Department of the Army, 1955.

Leonard, Jonathan. *Early Japan.* New York: Time-Life, 1968.

Leutze, James. *A Different Kind of Victory: A Biography of Admiral Thomas C. Hart.* Annapolis, MD: Naval Institute Press, 1981.

_____. *Bargaining for Supremacy: Anglo-American Naval Collaboration, 1937–1941.* Chapel Hill: University of North Carolina Press, 1977.

Le Vien, Jack, and John Lord. *Winston Churchill: The Valiant Years.* New York: Geis, 1962.

Lewin, Ronald. *The American Magic: Codes, Ciphers, and the Defeat of Japan.* New York: Farrar, Straus and Giroux, 1982.

_____. *The Other Ultra,* London: Hutchinson, 1982.

Loewenheim, Francis, Harold Langley, and Manfred Jonas. *Roosevelt and Churchill: Their Secret Wartime Correspondence.* New York: Saturday Review Press, 1975.

Lombard, Helen. *While They Fought: Behind the Scenes in Washington, 1941–1946.* New York: Scribner, 1947.

Long, Breckinridge. *The War Diary of Breckinridge Long: Selections from the Years 1939–1944.* Lincoln: University of Nebraska Press, 1966.

Lowe, Peter. *Great Britain and the Origins of the Pacific War: A Study of British Policy in East Asia, 1937–1941.* Oxford: Clarendon, 1977.

_____. "Great Britain's Assessment of Japan before the Outbreak of the Pacific War." In *Knowing One's Enemies: Intelligence Assessment before the Two World Wars,* edited by Ernest May. Princeton, NJ: Princeton University Press, 1984.

MacArthur, Douglas. *Reminiscences.* New York: McGraw-Hill, 1964.

Macleod, Iain. *Neville Chamberlain.* New York: Atheneum Books, 1962.

Marder, Arthur. *Old Friends, New Enemies: The Royal Navy and the Imperial Japanese Navy.* Oxford: Clarendon, 1981.

Marks, Frederick. *Wind Over Sand: The Diplomacy of Franklin Roosevelt.* Athens: University of Georgia Press, 1988.

Martinez, Oscar. *Troublesome Border.* Tucson: University of Arizona Press, 1988.

Matloff, Maurice, and Edwin Snell. *Strategic Planning for Coalition Warfare: 1941–1942.* Washington, DC: Department of the Army, 1953.

McCollum, Arthur. Oral History. Naval Academy Library, Annapolis, MD.

McCurry, Dan. "Newsman Claims Secretary of State Shared Decoded Japanese Attack Plans before Pearl Harbor." *Stars and Stripes,* December 8, 1983.

McJimsey, George. *Harry Hopkins: Ally of the Poor and Defender of Democracy.* Cambridge, MA: Harvard University Press, 1981.

McLaughlin, Kathleen. "Mrs. Roosevelt Wants 'Just a Little Job.'" *New York Times Magazine,* October 8, 1944.

Meissner, Hans-Otto. *The Man with Three Faces.* New York: Rinehart, 1955.

Melosi, Martin. *The Shadow of Pearl Harbor: Political Controversy over the Surprise Attack, 1941–1946.* College Station: Texas A&M University Press, 1977.

Miller, Edward. *War Plan Orange: The U.S. Strategy to Defeat Japan, 1897–1945.* Annapolis, MD: Naval Institute Press, 1991.

Millis, Walter. *The Martial Spirit.* Boston: Houghton Mifflin, 1931.

_____. *This Is Pearl! The United States and Japan, 1941.* New York: Morrow, 1947.

Mintz, Frank. *Revisionism and the Origins of Pearl Harbor.* Lanham, MD: University Press of America, 1985.

Montagu, Ewen. *Beyond Top Secret Ultra.* New York: Coward, McCann and Geoghegan, 1978.

Moore, Frederick. *With Japan's Leaders: An Intimate Record of Fourteen Years as Counsellor to the Japanese Government, Ending December 7, 1941.* New York: Scribner, 1942.

Moore, Joseph. Foreword to *December 8, 1941: MacArthur's Pearl Harbor*, by William Bartsch. College Station: Texas A&M University Press, 2003.

Morgenthau, Henry. *Morgenthau Diary.* Vol. 1. Washington, DC: Government Printing Office, 1965.

_____. Morgenthau Diary. Franklin D. Roosevelt Library, Hyde Park, NY.

Morison, Samuel. *The Battle of the Atlantic.* Boston: Little, Brown, 1947.

_____. *The Rising Sun in the Pacific.* Boston: Little, Brown, 1948.

_____. *The Two-Ocean War: A Short History of the United States Navy in the Second World War.* Boston: Little, Brown, 1963.

Morris, Ivan. *The Nobility of Failure: Tragic Heroes in the History of Japan.* New York: Holt, Rinehart and Winston, 1975.

_____. *The World of the Shining Prince: Court Life in Ancient Japan.* Harmondsworth, UK: Penguin Books, 1979.

Morton, Louis. "Germany First." In *Command Decisions*, edited by Kent Greenfield. Washington, DC: Department of the Army, 2000.

_____. "Japan's Decision for War." In *Command Decisions*, edited by Kent Greenfield. Washington, DC: Department of the Army, 2000.

_____. *The Fall of the Philippines.* Washington, DC: Department of the Army, 1953.

Mosely, Leonard. *Hirohito, Emperor of Japan.* Englewood Cliffs, NJ: Prentice-Hall, 1966.

_____. *Marshall: Hero for Our Times.* New York: Hearst, 1982.

_____. *On Borrowed Time: How World War II Began.* New York: Random House, 1969.

Mowrer, Edgar. *Triumph and Turmoil: A Personal History of Our Time.* New York: Weybright and Talley, 1968.

Muggah, Mary. *The MacArthur Story.* Chippewa Falls, WI: Chippewa Falls Book Agency, 1945.

Murphy, Robert. *Diplomat among Warriors.* Garden City, NY: Doubleday, 1964.

Nelson, Donald. *The Arsenal of Democracy: The Story of American War Production.* New York: Harcourt, Brace, 1946.

Neu, Charles. *The Troubled Encounter: The United States and Japan.* Malabar, FL: Krieger, 1981.

Neumann, William. *The Genesis of Pearl Harbor.* Philadelphia: Pacifist Research Bureau, 1945.

Norman, Herbert. *Japan's Emergence as a Modern State: Political and Economic Problems of the Meiji Period.* New York: Institute of Pacific Relations, 1946.

_____. "The Genyosha." In *Imperial Japan, 1800–1945,* edited by Jon Livingston, Joe Moore, and Felicia Oldfather. New York: Pantheon, 1973.

Offner, Arnold. *American Appeasement: United States Foreign Policy and Germany, 1933–1938.* Cambridge, MA: Harvard University Press, 1969.

Orchard, John. "The Japanese Dilemma." In *Empire in the East,* edited by Joseph Barnes. Garden City, NY: Doubleday, Doran, 1934.

Parker, Frederick. *Pearl Harbor Revisited: United States Navy Communications Intelligence, 1924–1941.* Fort Meade, MD: National Security Agency, 1994.

Pelz, Stephen. *Race to Pearl Harbor.* Cambridge: Harvard University Press, 1974.

Perkins, Frances. "The President Faces War." In *Air Raid: Pearl Harbor!* edited by Paul Stillwell. Annapolis, MD: Naval Institute Press, 1981.

_____. *The Roosevelt I Knew.* New York: Viking, 1946.

Persico, Joseph. *Roosevelt's Secret War: FDR and World War II Espionage.* New York: Random House, 2001.

Piper, Michael. "Aide Says FDR Knew Attack on Pearl Harbor Was Coming." *Spotlight,* February 27, 1984.

Pogue, Forrest. *George C. Marshall: Ordeal and Hope.* New York: Viking, 1966.

Popov, Dusko. *Spy/Counter-Spy: The Autobiography of Dusko Popov.* New York: Grosset and Dunlap, 1974.

Potter, John. *Yamamoto: The Man Who Menaced America.* New York: Paperback Library, 1967.

Prados, John. *Combined Fleet Decoded: The Secret History of American Intelligence and the Japanese Navy in World War II.* New York: Random House, 1995.

Prange, Gordon. *At Dawn We Slept: The Untold Story of Pearl Harbor.* New York: Penguin Books, 1982.

_____. *December 7, 1941: The Day the Japanese Attacked Pearl Harbor.* New York: McGraw-Hill, 1988.

_____. *Pearl Harbor: The Verdict of History.* New York: McGraw-Hill, 1986.

_____. *Target Tokyo: The Story of the Sorge Spy Ring.* New York: McGraw-Hill, 1984.

Preble, George. *The Opening of Japan: A Diary of Discovery in the Far East, 1853–1856.* Norman: University of Oklahoma Press, 1962.

Quezon, Manuel. *The Good Fight.* New York: Appleton Century, 1946.

Quinlan, Robert. "The United States Fleet." In *American Civil-Military Decisions,* edited by Harold Stein. Birmingham: University of Alabama Press, 1963.

Rauch, Basil. *Roosevelt: From Munich to Pearl Harbor; A Study in the Creation of a Foreign Policy.* New York: Barnes and Noble, 1967.

Reischauer, Edwin. *Japan.* 3rd ed. New York: Knopf, 1981.

Reitman, Valerie. "Japan Broke U.S. Code before Pearl Harbor, Researcher Finds." *Los Angeles Times,* December 7, 2001.

Reynolds, David. *The Creation of the Anglo-American Alliance, 1937–41: A Study in Competitive Co-operation*. Chapel Hill: University of North Carolina Press, 1982.

Richardson, James. *On the Treadmill to Pearl Harbor: The Memoirs of Admiral James O. Richardson as Told to George C. Dyer*. Washington, DC: Department of the Navy, 1973.

Riebling, Mark. *Wedge: The Secret War between the FBI and CIA*. New York: Knopf, 1994.

Roberts, Stephen. *The House That Hitler Built*. 2nd ed. New York: Harpers, 1938.

Robertson, John, and John McCarthy. *Australian War Strategy 1939–1945*. Saint Lucia, Australia: University of Queensland Press, 1985.

Rollins, Alfred. *Roosevelt and Howe*. New York: Knopf, 1962.

Roosevelt, Eleanor. *This I Remember*. New York: Harper, 1949.

Roosevelt, Elliott. *As He Saw It*. New York: Duell, Sloan and Pearce, 1946.

Roscoe, Theodore. *United States Destroyer Operations in World War II*. Annapolis, MD: Naval Institute Press, 1953.

Rosenman, Samuel. *Working with Roosevelt*. New York: Harper, 1952.

Ross, John. *The Annexation of Mexico: From the Aztecs to the IMF; One Reporter's Journey Through History*. Monroe, ME: Common Courage, 1998.

Rovere, Richard, and Arthur Schlesinger. *The MacArthur Controversy and American Foreign Policy*. 2nd ed. New York: Farrar, Straus and Giroux, 1965.

Rusbridger, James, and Eric Nave. *Betrayal at Pearl Harbor: How Churchill Lured Roosevelt into World War II*. New York: Summit, 1991.

Russell, E. F. *The Knights of Bushido: The Shocking History of Japanese War Atrocities*. New York: Dutton, 1958.

Russell, Henry. *Pearl Harbor Story*. Macon, GA: Mercer University Press, 2001.

Ryusaku, Tsunada, William de Bary, and Donald Keene, eds. *Sources of Japanese Tradition*. Vol. 2. New York: Columbia University Press, 1964.

Sanborn, Frederic. *Design for War: A Study of Secret Power Politics, 1937–1941*. New York: Devin-Adair, 1951.

Sandburg, Carl. *Abraham Lincoln*. Vol. 3. New York: Scribner, 1940.

Sansom, George. *Japan: A Short Cultural History*. Stanford, CA: Stanford University Press, 1978.

Sato, Hiroaki. *Legends of the Samurai*. Woodstock, NY: Overlook, 1995.

Schroeder, Paul. *The Axis Alliance in Japanese-American Relations, 1941*. Ithaca: Cornell University Press, 1958.

Schuler, Frank, and Robin Moore. *The Pearl Harbor Cover-Up*. New York: Pinnacle, 1976.

Sherwood, Robert. *Roosevelt and Hopkins: An Intimate History*. New York: Harper, 1948.

———. *The White House Papers of Harry L. Hopkins*. 2 vols. London: Eyre and Spottiswoode, 1948–49.

Shiroyama, Saburo. *War Criminal: The Life and Death of Hirota Koki*. Tokyo: Kodansha, 1977.

Simpson, Mitchell. *Admiral Harold R. Stark: Architect of Victory, 1939–1945.* Columbia: University of South Carolina Press, 1989.

Singer, Kurt. *Mirror, Sword and Jewel.* New York: Braziller, 1973.

Slessor, John. *The Central Blue: Autobiography.* New York: Praeger, 1957.

Smith, Bradley. *The Shadow Warriors: O.S.S. and the Origins of the C.I.A.* New York: Basic Books, 1983.

Smith, Michael. *The Emperor's Codes: The Breaking of Japan's Secret Ciphers.* New York: Penguin Books, 2002.

Smith, Myron. *Pearl Harbor, 1941.* New York: Greenwood, 1991.

Smith, Richard. *Thomas E. Dewey and His Times.* New York: Simon and Schuster, 1982.

Spector, Ronald. *Listening to the Enemy: Key Documents on the Role of Communications Intelligence in the War with Japan.* Wilmington, DE: Scholarly Resources, 1988.

Stacey, Charles. *Arms, Men and Governments: The War Policies of Canada, 1939–1945.* Ottawa, ON: Ministry of National Defence, 1970.

Stafford, David. *Roosevelt and Churchill: Men of Secrets.* Woodstock, NY: Overlook, 2000.

Stevenson, William. *A Man Called Intrepid: The Secret War.* New York: Harcourt Brace Jovanovich, 1976.

Stimson, Henry. Diaries. Yale University Library, New Haven, CT.

Stimson, Henry, and McGeorge Bundy. *On Active Service in Peace and War.* New York: Harper, 1948.

Stinnett, Robert. *Day of Deceit: The Truth About FDR and Pearl Harbor.* New York: Free Press, 2000.

Stonehouse, David. "Pearl Harbor Conspiracy Theories Called Bunk." *Calgary (AB) Herald,* May 27, 2001.

Storry, Richard. *A History of Modern Japan.* Rev. ed. Baltimore: Penguin Books, 1968.

_____. *The Double Patriots: A Study of Japanese Nationalism.* Boston: Houghton Mifflin, 1957.

Takaki, Ronald. *A Different Mirror: A History of Multicultural America.* Boston: Little, Brown, 1993.

Theobald, Robert. *The Final Secret of Pearl Harbor: The Washington Contribution to the Japanese Attack.* New York: Devin-Adair, 1954.

Thompson, Laurance. *1940.* New York: Morrow, 1946.

Thompson, Robert. *A Time for War: Franklin Delano Roosevelt and the Path to Pearl Harbor.* New York: Prentice-Hall, 1991.

Thorne, Christopher. *The Approach of War, 1938–1939.* London: Macmillan, 1967.

Thorpe, Elliott. *East Wind, Rain: The Intimate Account of an Intelligence Officer in the Pacific, 1939–49.* Boston: Gambit, 1969.

Toland, John. *Infamy: Pearl Harbor and Its Aftermath.* Garden City, NY: Doubleday, 1982.

_____. *Infamy: Pearl Harbor and Its Aftermath.* 2nd ed. New York: Berkley, 1983.

_____. *The Rising Sun: The Decline and Fall of the Japanese Empire, 1936–1945.* New York: Random House, 1970.

_____. Papers. Franklin D. Roosevelt Library, Hyde Park, NY.

Tolischus, Otto. *Tokyo Record*. New York: Reynal and Hitchcock, 1943.

Tolley, Kemp. *Cruise of the Lanikai: Incitement to War*. Annapolis, MD: Naval Institute Press, 1973.

Trewartha, Glenn. *Japan: A Physical, Cultural and Regional Geography*. Madison: University of Wisconsin Press, 1945.

Tully, Grace. *F.D.R., My Boss*. New York: Scribner, 1949.

United States Strategic Bombing Survey. *The Campaigns of the Pacific War*. New York: Greenwood, 1969.

Utley, Jonathan. *Going to War with Japan*. Knoxville: University of Tennessee Press, 1985.

U.S. Congress. Joint Congressional Committee on the Investigation of the Pearl Harbor Attack. *Pearl Harbor Attack*. Washington, DC: Government Printing Office, 1946.

Vandenberg, Arthur. *The Private Papers of Senator Vandenberg*. Boston: Houghton Mifflin, 1952.

Van Der Rhoer, Edward. *Deadly Magic: A Personal Account of Communications Intelligence in World War II in the Pacific*. New York: Scribner, 1978.

Van Mook, Hubertus. *The Netherlands Indies and Japan: Their Relations, 1940–1941*. London: Allen and Unwin, 1944.

Victor, George. *Hitler: The Pathology of Evil*. Washington, DC: Brassey's, 1998.

Wainwright, Jonathan. *General Wainwright's Story*. Garden City, NY: Doubleday, 1946.

Watson, Mark. *Chief of Staff: Prewar Plans and Preparations*. Washington, DC: Department of the Army, 1950.

Weintraub, Stanley. *Long Day's Journey into War: December 7, 1941*. New York: Dutton, 1991.

Wellborn, Charles. "The Fog of War" In *Air Raid: Pearl Harbor!* edited by Paul Stillwell. Annapolis, MD: Naval Institute Press, 1981.

Welles, Sumner. *The Time for Decision*. New York: Harper, 1944.

West, Nigel. *A Thread of Deceit: Espionage Myths of World War II*. New York: Random House, 1985.

Wheeler, Gerald. *Prelude to Pearl Harbor: The United States Navy and the Far East, 1921–1931*. Columbia: University of Missouri Press, 1963.

Whitcomb, Edgar. *Escape from Corregidor*. Chicago: Regnery, 1958.

Whitehead, Don. *The FBI Story: A Report to the People*. New York: Random House, 1956.

Whitney, Courtney. *MacArthur: His Rendezvous with History*. New York: Knopf, 1956.

Wilford, Timothy. *Pearl Harbor Redefined: USN Radio Intelligence in 1941*. Lanham, MD: University Press of America, 2001.

Willey, Mark. *Pearl Harbor: Mother of All Conspiracies*. Philadelphia: Xlibris, 2001.

Williams, Harry. *The History of American Wars from 1745 to 1918*. New York: Knopf, 1981.

Willoughby, Charles, and John Chamberlain. *MacArthur, 1941–1951*. New York: McGraw-Hill, 1954.

Wilson, Charles. *Churchill: The Struggle for Survival, 1940–1965*. Boston: Houghton Mifflin, 1966.

Wilson, Theodore. *The First Summit: Roosevelt and Churchill at Placentia Bay, 1941*. Rev. ed. Lawrence: University Press of Kansas, 1991.

Winslow, Walter. *The Fleet the Gods Forgot: The U.S. Asiatic Fleet in World War II*. Annapolis, MD: Naval Institute Press, 1982.

Wohlstetter, Roberta. *Pearl Harbor: Warning and Decision*. Stanford, CA: Stanford University Press, 1962.

Wood, Birbeck, and J. Edmonds. *A History of the Civil War in the United States, 1861–5*. New York: Putnam, 1905.

Wood, Edward. *Fullness of Days*. New York: Dodd, Mead, 1957.

Wray, Harry. "Japanese-American Relations and Perceptions." In *Pearl Harbor Reexamined: Prologue to the Pacific War*, edited by Hilary Conroy and Harry Wray. Honolulu: University of Hawaii Press, 1990.

Wyman, David. *Paper Walls: America and the Refugee Crisis, 1938–1941*. 2nd ed. New York: Pantheon, 1985.

Young, Howard. "Racial Attitudes and the U.S. Navy's Unpreparedness for War with Japan." In *New Aspects of Naval History: Selected Papers Presented at the Fourth Naval History Symposium*, edited by History Department of Naval Academy. Baltimore: Nautical and Aviation, 1985.

INDEX

ABC-1 (American-British Conversations #1), 171–175
Admiral Scheer, 182
Akhmerov, Ishkak, x–xi
America First Committee, 2. *See also* noninterventionist movement
anti-Semitism. *See* Jews
Arita Hachiro, 132
Army Pearl Harbor Board, 14, 33
  information withheld from, 29, 61–63, 65–66, 67
  report suppressed before 1944 election, 54–57
  warnings/decoded messages and, 70, 72, 73, 75, 84
Arnold, Gen. Henry, 21, 89, 139, 196, 198
Astor, Vincent, 30
Atlantic Conference, 209–215
Auchinleck, Gen. Claude, 266
Axis Pact, 154, 219

Baecher, Capt. John, 64–65
Baldwin, Stanley, 137, 140
Barkley, Alben, 63
Beatty, Capt. Frank, 17–18, 270, 282, 283
Bedell Smith, Gen. Walter, 75, 98, 268
Bellinger, Adm. Patrick, 86, 87, 88
Bender, George, 50
Berle, Adolf, 276
Biddle, Francis, 240
Biffle, Leslie, 50
Bismarck, 181–182

Bismarck, Otto von, ix
Bissell, Gen. John, 69, 78
Bloch, Adm. Claude, 82, 89, 268
Bode, Capt. Howard, 267, 268–269
bomb-plot messages, 38–41, 45, 74–79, 267–268
Bonin Islands, 120
Bratton, Col. Rufus, 32, 34
  evidence suppression and, 68, 74–75
  warnings/decoded messages and, 39, 268–269, 275–276, 278, 279, 285
Brereton, Gen. Lewis, 21, 196–197, 198, 283
Briggs, Warrant Officer Ralph, 73
Bristol, Adm. Arthur, 176–177
Brooke-Popham, Marshal Robert, 4
Brown, Cdr. Cedric, 73
Bryden, Gen. William, 111
Buass, Lt. Marion, 272
Bullitt, William, 179–186
Burwell, Col. H. S., 96

Canada, 147–148, 167
Cannon, Clarence, 13
Carter, Jimmy, 31, 60
Casey, Richard, 243
Casey, William, 43, 256
Cavendish-Bentinck, Victor, 42–43, 256
Chamberlain, Neville, 133–134, 140–141, 144
Chang Hseuh-liang, 130
Chang Tso-lin, 130

345

Cherry Blossom Society, 128–129
Chiang Kai-shek, 131, 132, 202, 218,
    243–245, 249–251, 291
China
    pre–World War II Japan and, 115–
        121, 128–132, 218
    U.S. and, 114, 131–132
    U.S. and Japan's negotiations
        about, 229–249
Choshu-Satsuma rebellion, 119
Churchill, Winston S., 8, 20, 43–44,
        140, 177, 187, 263
    Atlantic Conference and, 209–215
    Chiang Kai-Shek and, 250–251
    German-Russian war and, 204,
        207–208
    Hitler and, 134, 261
    reaction to Pearl Harbor attack, 289
    speeches after fall of France, 149–
        150
    "thin diet" cable to FDR, 255–256
    works to draw U.S. into war, 146–
        147, 169, 265–267
Civil War, 295
Clark, Bayard, 300–301
Clarke, Col. Carter, 54–55, 78
Clausen, Maj. Henry, 56–57, 60, 74–75
    "explosive pouch" and, 67–69,
        310n36
Clear, Maj. Warren, 35, 73
Clinton, William, 16
Club, the, 30
code breaking, 31–33, 54–55, 69–74.
    See also specific messages
Colclough, Adm. Oswald, 63, 65
Committee to Defend America First, 2.
    See also noninterventionist
    movement
Communism, in China, 132
congressional investigation, 54,
        59–60
    information withheld from, viii, 29,
        63–65, 67
    warnings/decoded messages and,
        31, 71–72, 75, 79, 101–102
Connally, Tom, 7
convoys, U.S. aid to British and,
        175–178
Cooper, Duff, 143
Coordinator of Information (COI), 31
Costello, John, 46, 255

Cramer, JAG Myron, 56, 67
Czechoslovakia, 138–144

Daladier, Edouard, 140, 142–143, 148
Danckwerts, Adm. Victor, 173
Deane, Col. John, 285
de Gaulle, Charles, 151
deterrence, versus provocation, 186
Dewey, Thomas, 54–55
Dies, Martin, 47–48, 50
Dillon, Capt. John, 283
diplomatic codes. *See* code breaking;
    specific messages
Dixon, Lt. H. C., 73
Donovan, William, 31, 33, 254, 257
Drought, Father James, 220
Duncombe, Col. Harmon, 63–64
Dutch East Indies, 37, 49, 158, 168,
    191, 192, 266, 291

earthquakes, Japanese character and,
    115–117, 127
Eden, Anthony, 141, 166, 250
embargoes, on Japan, 137–139, 154–
    157, 187–216
Embick, Gen. Stanley, 25
Emmons, Gen. Delos, 167
Ethiopia, 136–137

FBI, 65. *See also* Hoover, J. Edgar
Feis, Herbert, 169, 294
Fellers, Gen. Bonner, 78
Ferguson, Homer, 79
Fillmore, Millard, 114
Flying Fortress (B-17) bombers, 152,
    196–197
Forrestal, Adm. James, 57–59
Fort Sumter, 295
France
    British raid on, to distract
        Germany, 208
    falls to Germany, 146, 148–149,
        163
    reactions to fascist countries'
        moves in late 1930s, 134, 136–
        137, 139–140
    U. S. military aid to, 139, 145
Friedman, William, 77

Gatch, Adm. Thomas, 57–58
Genyosha, 128

Germany
    aggressive moves of, 12, 137–150,
        163, 203–209
    knowledge of Japan's plans to
        attack, 35
    myths in, after World War I, 5
    pre-World War II Japan and, 122,
        124
    U.S. attempts to provoke, 179–186
    urges Japan to invade Siberia, 201
Gerow, Gen. Leonard, 21, 97, 287
    Japan's negotiations with U.S. and,
        243
    Philippines and, 299
    on Short's reconnaissance orders,
        88–89
    warnings/decoded messages and,
        39, 268
Ghormley, Adm. Robert, 167, 170
Gillette, Guy, 36
Gillette, Thomas, 36
Glover, Cato, 280, 281
Great Britain. *See also* Churchill,
        Winston S.
    German codes broken by, 288
    Japanese coded messages
        intercepted by, 43, 45, 255–256
    location of Japanese fleet and, 270
    misjudgment of Japan's strength,
        4–5
    pre-World War II Japan and, 131
    reactions to fascist countries'
        moves in late 1930s, 136–137,
        140–145
    secret U.S.-British alliance and, 2,
        3, 6–7, 165–177
    U.S. military aid to, 139, 145–153
Green, Gen. Joseph, 197, 198
Greenland, 167, 175
Greer, 183
Grew, Joseph, 35, 175, 201, 208, 263
    embargoes on Japan and, 11, 188
    Japan's negotiations with U.S. and,
        215, 229–230
Grunert, Gen. George, 193–194
Haan Kilsoo, 36, 257
Hagood, Gen. Johnson, 24–25
Haleakala radar unit, 110–111
Halifax, Lord. *See* Wood, Edward
Hamilton, Maxwell, 36
Hara Yoshimichi, 227–228, 238

Harness, Forest, 54
Harriman, Averell, 289
Harrison, Landreth, 252
Harrison, Maj. Eugene, 280, 285
Hart, Adm. Thomas, 22, 104, 292, 296–
        297
    secret investigation of, 53–54
    secret U.S.-British alliance and, 168
    three-small-vessels order and, 269–
        272
    warnings/decoded messages and,
        70, 189, 264–265
Harvey, Oliver, 255
Herron, Gen. Charles, 110
Hewitt, Adm. Kent, 58–60, 77–78
Higashikuni Naruhiko, 223, 228–229,
        232, 234
Hirohito, emperor of Japan, 223–228,
        232, 235, 277
Hitler, Adolf, 6, 133, 141–143, 260–261
Holocaust denial, 261, 293
Hood, 181
Hoover, Herbert, 24–25
Hoover, J. Edgar, 35–36, 50–51, 263
Hopkins, Harry, 169, 290
    Soviet Union and, x–xi, 211–213
    warnings/decoded messages and,
        276–278
Hornbeck, Stanley, 36–37, 253
Hosner, Lt. Ellsworth, 47, 270
Hull, Cordell, 159–160, 180, 263
    on stalling negotiations while
        arming for war with Japan,
        15
    embargoes on Japan and, 187, 188
    German-Russian war and, 205
    Japan's negotiations with U.S. and,
        220–224, 228–230, 235–236,
        242–249, 252–253, 263
    Nomura's note to, 11
    Spanish Civil War and, 137
    statement after Pearl Harbor attack,
        7
    warnings/decoded messages and,
        36–37, 77, 276
Hurd, Charles, 241
Hu Shih, 243–245, 249, 277

Iceland, 167, 174–175
Ickes, Harold, 111, 163, 189–190
    urges FDR to war, 145, 261

Indochina, embargoes on Japan and, 190–191
Ingersoll, Adm. Royal, 73, 166–167, 185, 272–273, 278, 280
    intelligence sources, public and private, 30–31
Isabel, 270–273
Ishiwara Kanji, Gen., 132
isolationists. *See* noninterventionist movement
Italy, 136–137, 208

Jackson, Robert, 151
Japan, 3, 7, 9, 15, 113–114
    attacks on Philippines, 22–28
    China and, 115–121, 128–132, 218
    expansionist policy of, 217–218
    FDR's reaction to invasion of China, 137–139
    fleet sails for Pearl Harbor, 249
    indications from, of war intentions, 10–11
    Meiji Restoration and samurai's power, 119–120, 125–132
    military preparedness of, 3–4
    natural disasters and character of Japanese people, 115–117
    naval strategy and, 33–34
    plans to attack known, 34–37
    radio silence of task force and, 37–38
    responses to Western colonialism, 114–115, 118–120
    Soviet Union and, 119–126, 218, 242
    U.S. embargoes on, 137–139, 154–157, 187–216
    U.S. lists steps likely to provoke, 187–188
    U.S. negotiations with, 192, 193, 214, 219-254
Jews
    anti-Semitism and, 2, 6
    Holocaust denial and, 261, 293
    Nazi persecution of, 143, 150, 260–261
Joint Congressional Committee. *See* congressional investigation
Jones, Jesse, 176

kamikaze (divine wind), 117, 129

Kaya Okinori, 234
Kearny, 184
Keefe, Frank, 71, 278
Keenan, Joseph, 50
Kerr, Philip, (Lord Lothian),146
Ketchum, Col. Carlton, 50
Kido Koichi, 227, 231
Kimmel, Adm. Husband, 99–103, 175
    attempt to restore reputation of, in 2000, 16
    barred from active defense measures, 86–87
    charges against, 81
    congressional investigation and, 54
    court martial requested by, 53
    evidence suppression and, 67
    information withheld from, 14, 103–112, 267–269
    in Naval Court board report, 57–59
    November 27 war warning sent to, 99
    questioned by Knox about warning, 17–18
    reconnaissance orders and lack of air defense, 87–94, 99–103
    replaces Richardson, 162, 164
    Roberts Commission and, 19, 22, 28
    rumors about, 6, 13, 14–15
    wants Naval Court report made public, 58–59
    warnings/decoded messages and, 32, 49, 69–70, 81–86, 99, 260, 265, 282–284, 289, 294, 296–303
King, Adm. Ernest, 19–20, 175, 176
    evidence suppression and, 62, 63, 67
    Naval Court report and, 57–58
King, Mackenzie, 146
Kirk, Capt. Alan, 39, 106, 268–269
Knox, Frank, 4, 7, 17–18, 159–160
    Hart investigation and, 53–54
    location of Japanese fleet and, 273–274
    on Philippines, 297
    Roberts Commission and, 19
    secret U.S.-British alliance and, 170, 173, 176
    urges FDR to war, 145, 261

urges strengthening of Pearl Harbor
defenses, 34
warnings/decoded messages and,
39, 278, 280, 281
Kokuryukai, 128
Konoe Fumimaro, 201, 208, 215, 216,
222–226, 229–233
Korea, 119, 120, 126, 219
Kramer, Cdr. Alwin, 39–40, 72, 73, 74,
275–276, 278
Krick, Capt. Harold, 76, 278–281
Kristallnacht, 143
Krock, Arthur, 241–242
Kroner, Col. Hayes, 215–216
Kublai Khan, 117
Kurusu Saburo, 11, 235–236, 243, 247–
248
Kwantung Army, 130–132

Lanikai, 271
Layton, Adm. Edwin, 106, 108, 272
League of Nations, 122, 136–137
League of the Divine Wind, 126
Leahy, Adm. William, 158, 205
Lee, Gen. Raymond, 167
Leib, Joseph, 50
Liberator (B-24) bombers, 152
Lincoln, Abraham, 152–153, 295
Lindbergh, Charles A., 2
Lindsay, Ronald, 166
Lloyd George, David, 134
Long, Breckinridge, 177, 242
Lothian, Lord. *See* Philip Kerr
Loudon, Alexander, 243, 283
Lurline, 48–49

MacArthur, Gen. Douglas
arming of Philippines and, 195,
198–199
FDR and, 162
ordered not to initiate hostilities, 104
reputation after attacks on
Philippines, 22–23
secret U.S.-British alliance and,
175
on U.S. defense of Philippines, 25–
26
warnings of attacks and, 21, 108,
260, 296–299
Mackie, Thomas, 73
Maine, 295–296

makoto (sincerity of spirit), 126–127
Manchukuo, 130–131
Manchuria, 124, 128, 130–132, 219
Marshall, Gen. George
activities of December 6 and 7,
263–264
aid to Great Britain and, 152, 153
in Army Board report, 56
evidence suppression and, 54–55,
62, 108–110
expectations about damage in Pearl
Harbor attack, 4
Hawaii's lack of air defense and, 86
Japan's negotiations with U.S. and,
237, 252
on maneuvering to be attacked,
254–255, 256, 258–260
order to leave fleet in Hawaii and,
155
Philippines and, 194, 195–196,
198, 298–299
Roberts Commission and, 19
sabotage danger and, 95
secret briefing of reporters, 240–
242
secret U.S.-British alliance and,
173, 175
warnings/decoded messages and,
18, 39, 48, 66, 70, 75–78, 98–
99, 105, 278–279, 281–282,
284–289
withholds information from
Congress, viii
Martin, Gen. Frederick, 87, 88
Matsuoka Yosuke, 201, 208, 221–223,
233
McCollum, Adm. Arthur, 32, 158–159
evidence suppression and, 63, 67,
106–107, 108
recommends using Pearl Harbor
fleet as lure, 294
warnings/decoded messages and,
267–269, 278, 284–285
McCrea, Cdr. John, 282
McCullough, Capt. Richard, 47
McKinley, William, 152–153, 295–296
McNarney, Gen. Joseph, 62, 187–188
Meiji Restoration, 119–120, 125–132
messages #901 and #902. *See* pilot
message
Mexican War, 113–114, 294–295

Miles, Gen. Sherman, 29, 41, 216, 300–
    301
  concerned about attack, 34, 41
  embargoes on Japan and, 192
  evidence suppression and, 28, 61–
    63, 79, 108
  sabotage danger and, 96
  warnings/decoded messages and,
    268–269, 276, 278, 285–287
Modoc, 182
Molotov, Vyacheslav, 212, 214
Monroe Doctrine, 180–181
Morgenthau, Henry, 146, 163, 191,
    256–257, 261
Mowrer, Edgar, 47, 49, 254, 290
Munich Pact, 141–143
Murfin, Adm. Orin, 57
Mussolini, Benito, 136–137

Nagano Osami, Adm., 224–225, 227–
    228, 231, 234
Nagumo Chuichi, Adm., 37
"national security," as justification for
    evidence suppression, 66
Naval Court of Inquiry on Pearl Harbor,
    13, 14
  information withheld from, 29, 67
  report suppressed before 1944
    election, 57–59
  warnings/decoded messages and,
    70, 72, 73
Naval Security Group, 41–41
Neutrality Act of 1935, 135
New Deal, 135
Newfoundland, 167
Niblack, 181
Nicolson, Harold, 150
Nomura Kichisaburo, Adm., 11, 15,
    274–275
  embargoes on Japan and, 190, 191,
    203
  Japan's negotiations with U.S. and,
    214, 220–223, 235–238, 242–
    243, 247–248, 264
  Japan and Soviet Union and, 216
  on U.S. relations with Soviet
    Union, 209
  noninterventionist movement, 2,
    9, 134–135, 137–138, 145, 152,
    178, 290, 305n3
Noyes, Adm. Leigh

evidence suppression and, 53, 62
  warnings/decoded messages and,
    70, 72–74, 107, 268–269, 278,
    285

Ogg, Seaman Robert, 47, 50, 270
Oikawa Koshiro, 34, 227, 230, 231
Okawa Shumei, 131–132
ONI (Office of Naval Intelligence), 45–
    46, 64–65, 105–106, 158–159
Osmun, Gen. Russell, 62–63
Oumansky, Constantin, 205

Panay, 123, 159, 185
Patterson, Robert, 55, 63–64
Payne, Lt. John, 271
Pearl Harbor
  attacks on, contrasted to Philippine
    attacks, 21–22
  effect on undeclared war and,
    179
  FDR's speeches about, 7–10, 12
  fleet ordered to remain at, 154–
    164, 186
  Japan's war games about, 225
  lack of air defense and, 86–92
  public reactions to attacks on, 1–6,
    12–15
Percival, Gen. Arthur, 4
Perkins, Frances, 195, 273, 298
Perry, Commodore Matthew, 114–115,
    117, 118, 122–123
Petain, Henri, 149
Philippines. *See also* MacArthur, Gen.
    Douglas
  Japan's attack and, 20–28, 119
  1941 arming of, 193–199, 229,
    241–242
Philips, Adm. Tom, 298
pilot message (#901), 17–18, 274–283
  delay of delivery, 275, 283–289
Poland, 144–145
Polk, James, 113, 152–153, 294–295
Popov, Dusan (Tricycle), 35–37
Port Arthur, Japan's surprise attack on,
    121
Pound, Adm. Dudley, 182
Pownall, Gen. Henry, 4
Pre-Pearl Harbor Japanese Naval
Prinz Eugen, 181–182
private intelligence sources, 30–31

Purnell, Capt. William, 168, 283
Pu Yi, 130–131

Quezon, Manuel, 25–27, 193

racism, 3–5, 122–123
radio direction-finding, 46
radio silence, of Japanese task force,
    37–38
Rainbow-5, 172–174
Ranneft, Capt. Johan, 37, 45–47, 270,
    283
Reagan, Ronald, 152
Redman, Capt. Joseph, 268
Reuben James, 185
"revisionists," viii
Reynaud, Paul, 148–149
Rice, Eunice, 74, 311n43
Richardson, Adm. James, 93–94, 154–
    164, 168, 294
Roberts, Owen, 19, 28, 29. *See also*
    Roberts Commission
Roberts Commission, 13, 29
    evidence suppression and, 63
    limited scope of, 19–20, 27–28
Robin Moor, 183
Rochefort, Cdr. Joseph, 43
Room, the, 30, 31
Roosevelt, Eleanor, 135, 189, 289–290
Roosevelt, Elliott, 188–189
Roosevelt, Franklin D.
    activities before attack, 263–264,
        274
    address to Filipinos, 27
    aid to Great Britain and France
        and, 139, 145–153
    army and navy reports, before 1944
        election, 56
    Atlantic Conference and, 209–215
    deterrence versus provocation in
        Pacific, 185–186
    embargoes on Japan and, 137–139,
        154–157, 187–216
    emphasizes war in Europe over
        Pacific, 144–145
    grasp of Hitler's intentions, 133–
        136, 143–145
    hatred and suspicions of, 1–2, 6–7
    intelligence services and, 30–31
    Japan's negotiations with U.S. and,
        192, 193, 214, 219–254

Japan policy determined by need to
        aid Great Britain, 154–164
    location of Japanese fleet and, 270,
        273–274
    as Machiavellian, vii, x–xi, 291–
        293
    maneuvering to have Japan attack,
        254–261
    message to Hirohito, 277
    Panay incident and, 123, 159
    reactions of to challenges, 162–163
    reaction to fascist countries' moves
        in late 1930s, 136–139
    reaction to Japan's invasion of
        China, 137–139
    reaction to Pearl Harbor attack, 290
    sabotage danger and, 95
    Short and Kimmel's court martial
        request and, 53
    speeches about attacks, 7–10, 12
    three-small-vessel order of, 264,
        269–273
    warnings/decoded messages and, 3,
        39, 49–50, 75–76, 276–278,
        281–282, 285
Roosevelt, Sara, 135
Roosevelt, Theodore, 123, 296
Russell, Gen. Henry, 65, 83
Russia. *See* Soviet Union

sabotage, Short's defense orders and,
    94–99
Sadtler, Col. Otis, 68, 70, 77, 268–269
Safford, Cdr. Laurence, 32, 53, 54, 62,
    69–74, 267–269
Saigo Takamori, 126
Sakurakai. *See* Cherry Blossom Society
Salinas, 185
samurai, 119–120, 125–132
Satsuma. *See* Choshu-Satsuma rebellion
Sayre, Francis, 27
Schofield, Adm. Frank, 33
Schuirmann, Adm. Roscoe, 256
Schulz, Lt. Lester, 276, 277
Sevareid, Eric, 36
Seymour, Murton, 256
Sherwood, Robert, 135, 139, 169, 171
Shimabara rebellions, 115
Short, Gen. Walter
    in Army Board report, 54–57,
        59

attempt to restore reputation of, in 2000, 16
barred from active defense measures, 86–87
charges against, 81
court martial requested by, 53
defense orders and sabotage, 94–99, 103
information withheld from, 14, 32, 49, 70, 82–86, 103–112, 104, 260, 267–269, 294, 296–303
questioned by Knox about warning, 17–18
reconnaissance orders and lack of air defense, 87–94
Roberts Commission and, 19, 22, 28
rumors about, 6, 13, 14–15
Singapore, surrender of, 8
Smith, Cdr. Oscar, 63
Smith, Don, 51
Sonnett, John, 59, 67–68, 71–74
Soong, T.V., 243–244
Sorge, Richard, 36
Soviet Union, 121, 123–124, 131
Germany invades, 150, 221
Hopkins and, x–xi
Japan and, 199–216, 218, 242
warnings from, 36
Spalding, Gen. Isaac, 78
Spanish Civil War, 137
Stahlman, James, 282
Stalin, Joseph, 207–208, 211–212
Standley, Adm. William, 19
Stark, Adm. Harold
activities of December 6 and 7, 263–264
aid to Great Britain and, 151
on arming the Philippines, 194–195
British air defense and, 89
embargoes on Japan and, 189, 192, 203
evidence suppression and, 108–112
on FDR, 261
German-Russian war and, 205
Japan's negotiations with U.S. and, 237, 243, 252
Japan and Soviet Union and, 207
on maneuvering to be attacked, 254–255, 256, 258–260

order to leave fleet in Hawaii and, 155–164
on Philippines, 298
Roberts Commission and, 19
secret U.S.-British alliance and, 168, 170–175, 178
three-small-vessels order and, 269
warnings/decoded messages and, 18, 39, 70, 75–76, 82, 93, 101, 102, 104, 279–282, 284
State Department, warnings destruction and, 66
Stephenson, William, 171
Stimson, Henry, 133, 257
aid to Great Britain and, 152, 153
arming of Philippines and, 194, 195, 199
in Army Board report and, 54–57, 59
German-Russian war and, 205
Japan's negotiations with U.S. and, 240, 244–245, 249, 252, 254–255
on maneuvering to be attacked, vii, 257–258, 260
Roberts Commission and, 19
sabotage danger and, 95, 96
secret U.S.-British alliance and, 170, 173
urged to strengthen Pearl Harbor defenses, 34
urges FDR to war, 145, 261
warnings/decoded messages and, 39, 48, 77, 104–105, 281
Strong, Gen. George, 167
Sudetenland, 141–143
Sugiyama Hajime, 222, 224–228, 231
suicide, revered in Japan, 117, 126–129
Sutherland, Gen. Richard, 195, 283
Suzuki Sugeru, 44

Taiwan, 120
Tansill, Charles, 78
ter Poorten, Gen. Hein, 37, 49
Thomsen, Hans, 47
Thorpe, Gen. Elliot, 37, 48, 49
three-small-vessels order, of FDR, 264, 269–273
Tirpitz, 182
Togo Shigenori, 11, 234, 236, 240, 243, 274–275

Tojo Hideki, Gen., 219, 224, 228, 230–238
Tokugawa peace, 114–115
Toland, John, 46–47, 223
Tolley, Lt. Kemp, 271, 272
Tovey, Adm. John, 181
Toyoda Teijiro, 192, 202, 230
Truman, Harry, 13, 63–65
tsunami wave, 116–117
Turner, Adm. Richmond, 34, 161
    arming of Philippines and, 193
    Japan and Soviet Union and, 216
    on steps likely to provoke Japan, 187–188
    warnings/decoded messages and, 39, 100–102, 106, 269, 278
Tutuila, 159, 185
typhoons, Japanese character and, 116–117

United States. *See also* Roosevelt, Franklin D.
    attempts to provoke Germany to declare war, 179–186
    Japan and, prior to World War II, 114–115, 117, 121–124, 131, 154–164, 219–254
    per-World War II expansion of, 113–114
    secret alliance with Great Britain, 165–177
    undeclared war and, 177–179

Vandenberg, Arthur, 290
Vinson, Carl, 19

volcanic eruptions, and Japanese character, 115–117

Wainwright, Jonathan, 196
Wakasugi Kaname, 238
Walsh, Bishop James, 220
Ward, Col. Orlando, 98
Watson, Gen. Edwin, 49–50
Weeks, Adm. Robert, 72
Weijerman, Col. F. G., 48
Wellborn, Capt. Charles, 104
Welles, Sumner, 8, 159–160, 190, 251
    Atlantic Conference and, 213, 214
    German-Russian war and, 204, 206
Wheeler, Burton, 177
Whitney, Gen. Courtney, 299
Wilkinson, Adm. Theodore
    location of Japanese fleet and, 270
    warnings/decoded messages and, 29, 40, 42, 43, 267–269, 278, 284–285
Willoughby, Gen. Charles, 40, 297
Wilson, Woodrow, 134, 135–136
Winant, John, 204, 289
winds execute message, 69–74, 310nn40–41, 311n46
Wood, Edward (Lord Halifax), 170, 243, 251, 253, 255, 263

Yamamoto Isoroku, Adm., 34–35, 219–220, 225
Yoshida Shoin, 127

ABOUT THE AUTHOR

A retired psychologist, George Victor, PhD, was educated at Columbia, Harvard, and New York Universities. He is the author of three books and many articles in psychology and history. His first book in history was *Hitler: The Pathology of Evil*.